# EUREKA!
## GRADE 3-5 SCIENCE ACTIVITIES AND STORIES

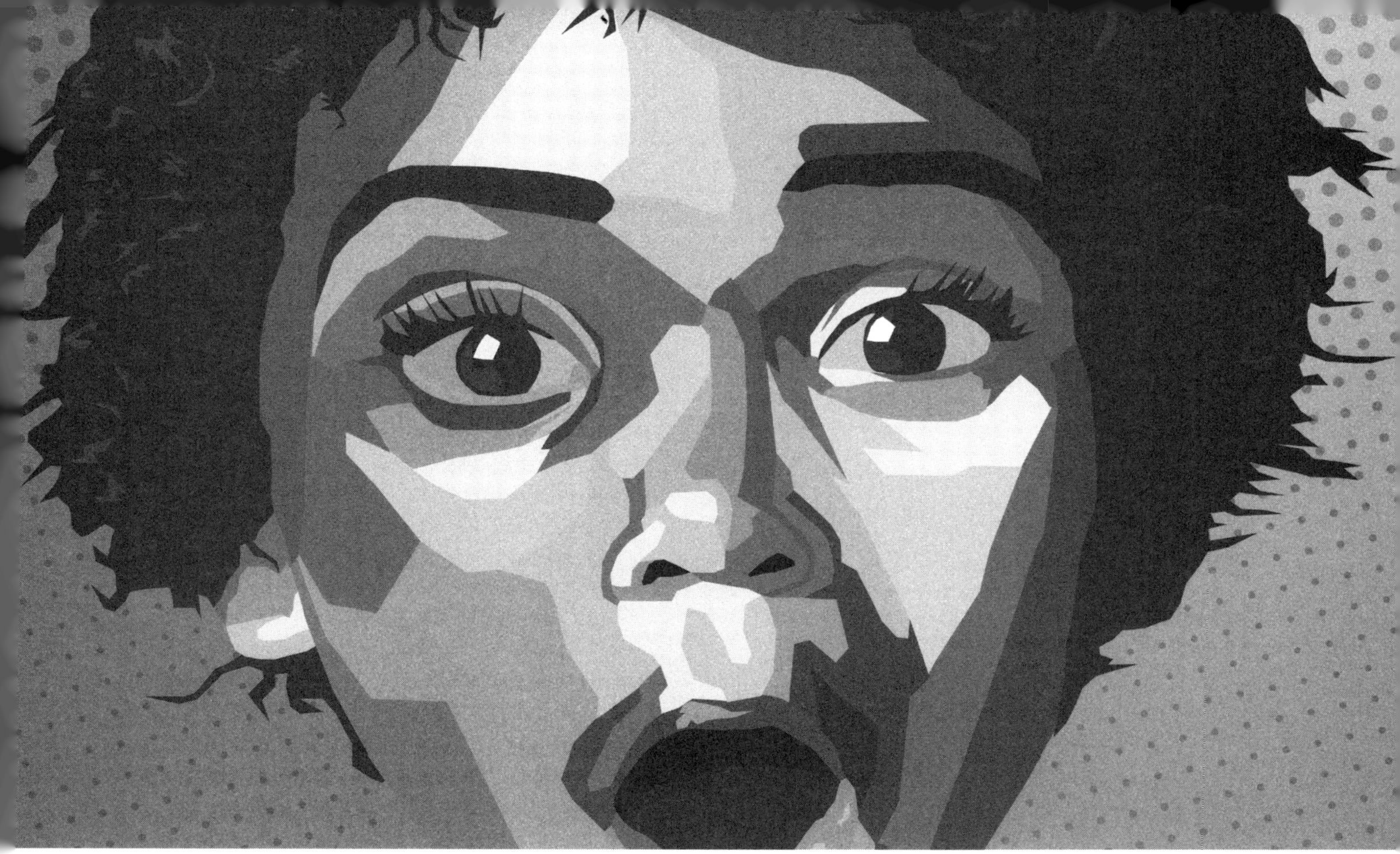

# EUREKA!

## GRADE 3–5 SCIENCE ACTIVITIES AND STORIES

**DONNA FARLAND-SMITH**
**JULIE THOMAS**

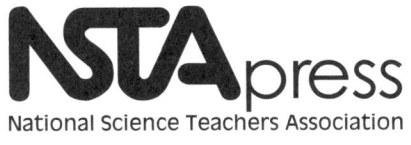

NSTApress
National Science Teachers Association
Arlington, Virginia

National Science Teachers Association

Claire Reinburg, Director
Rachel Ledbetter, Managing Editor
Deborah Siegel, Associate Editor
Amanda Van Beuren, Associate Editor
Donna Yudkin, Book Acquisitions Manager

**ART AND DESIGN**
Will Thomas Jr., Director
Joe Butera, Senior Graphic Designer, cover and interior design

**PRINTING AND PRODUCTION**
Catherine Lorrain, Director

**NATIONAL SCIENCE TEACHERS ASSOCIATION**
David L. Evans, Executive Director
David Beacom, Publisher

1840 Wilson Blvd., Arlington, VA 22201
www.nsta.org/store
For customer service inquiries, please call 800-277-5300.

Copyright © 2017 by the National Science Teachers Association.
All rights reserved. Printed in the United States of America.
20 19 18 17    4 3 2 1

NSTA is committed to publishing material that promotes the best in inquiry-based science education. However, conditions of actual use may vary, and the safety procedures and practices described in this book are intended to serve only as a guide. Additional precautionary measures may be required. NSTA and the authors do not warrant or represent that the procedures and practices in this book meet any safety code or standard of federal, state, or local regulations. NSTA and the authors disclaim any liability for personal injury or damage to property arising out of or relating to the use of this book, including any of the recommendations, instructions, or materials contained therein.

**PERMISSIONS**
Book purchasers may photocopy, print, or e-mail up to five copies of an NSTA book chapter for personal use only; this does not include display or promotional use. Elementary, middle, and high school teachers may reproduce forms, sample documents, and single NSTA book chapters needed for classroom or noncommercial, professional-development use only. E-book buyers may download files to multiple personal devices but are prohibited from posting the files to third-party servers or websites, or from passing files to non-buyers. For additional permission to photocopy or use material electronically from this NSTA Press book, please contact the Copyright Clearance Center (CCC) (www.copyright.com; 978-750-8400). Please access www.nsta.org/permissions for further information about NSTA's rights and permissions policies.

**Cataloging-in-Publication Data**

Names: Farland-Smith, Donna, author. | Thomas, Julie, 1947- author.
Title: Eureka! grades 3-5 science activities and stories / Donna Farland-Smith, Julie Thomas.
Description: Arlington, VA : National Science Teachers Association, [2017] | Includes bibliographical references and index.
Identifiers: LCCN 2017021228 | ISBN 9781681402574 (print)
Subjects: LCSH: Science--Study and teaching (Elementary)--Activity programs--United States.
Classification: LCC LB1585.3 .F37 2017 | DDC 372.35/044--dc23 LC record available at https://lccn.loc.gov/2017021228

e-ISBN: 9781681402581

# CONTENTS

FOREWORD ........................................................................................................... ix
DEDICATION ........................................................................................................ xvii
ACKNOWLEDGMENTS ........................................................................................ xvii
ABOUT THE AUTHORS ....................................................................................... xvii

## 1 INTRODUCTION: WHAT WE DID IN THIS BOOK AND WHY ... 1

## 2 ASKING QUESTIONS AND DEFINING PROBLEMS ... 9

Recommended Science Teaching Strategy: Designating Makerspaces ........................................... 9

### Scientists and Engineers Are THINKERS—Learning About Philo Farnsworth ............... 11
*The Boy Who Invented TV: The Story of Philo Farnsworth* by Kathleen Krull

### Scientists and Engineers Are INSPIRED—Learning About Thomas Edison ................... 22
*Young Thomas Edison* by Michael Dooling

### Scientists and Engineers Are DILIGENT—Learning About George Washington Carver ........ 35
*A Picture Book of George Washington Carver* by David A. Adler

## 3 DEVELOPING AND USING MODELS ... 47

Recommended Science Teaching Strategy: Graphic Organizers as Models ....................................... 47

### Scientists and Engineers Are IMAGINATIVE—Learning About Annie Jump Cannon ........... 49
*Annie Jump Cannon, Astronomer* by Carole Gerber

### Scientists and Engineers Are VISIONARY—Learning About George Washington Ferris Jr. ..... 60
*Mr. Ferris and His Wheel* by Kathryn Gibbs Davis

### Scientists and Engineers Are PATIENT—Learning About Gregor Mendel ........................ 69
*Gregor Mendel: The Friar Who Grew Peas* by Cheryl Bardoe

# CONTENTS

## 4   PLANNING AND CARRYING OUT INVESTIGATIONS    81

Recommended Science Teaching Strategy: Effective Questioning ................................................. 81

### Scientists and Engineers Are OBSERVANT—Learning About Jane Goodall ..................... 83
*The Watcher: Jane Goodall's Life With the Chimps* by Jeanette Winter

### Scientists and Engineers Are PUZZLERS—Learning About Charles Darwin ..................... 93
*Darwin: With Glimpses Into His Private Journal and Letters* by Alice B. McGinty

### Scientists and Engineers Are INTUITIVE—Learning About Barnum Brown ..................... 104
*Barnum's Bones: How Barnum Brown Discovered the Most Famous Dinosaur in the World* by Tracey Fern

## 5   ANALYZING AND INTERPRETING DATA    119

Recommended Science Teaching Strategy: Integration of Science and Mathematics ............... 119

### Scientists and Engineers Are DEDICATED—Learning About Wilson Bentley ..................... 121
*Snowflake Bentley* by Jacqueline Briggs Martin

### Scientists and Engineers Are DREAMERS—Learning About Luke Howard ..................... 131
*The Man Who Named the Clouds* by Julie Hannah and Joan Holub

### Scientists and Engineers Are CURIOUS—Learning About John James Audubon ............. 141
*The Boy Who Drew Birds: A Story of John James Audubon* by Jacqueline Davies

## 6   USING MATHEMATICS AND COMPUTATIONAL THINKING    157

Recommended Science Teaching Strategy: Probeware and Digital Media ............................... 157

### Scientists and Engineers Are INNOVATIVE—Learning About Ada Byron Lovelace ........... 159
*Ada Byron Lovelace and the Thinking Machine* by Laurie Wallmark

### Scientists and Engineers Are COURAGEOUS—Learning About Galileo Galilei ................ 173
*Starry Messenger* by Peter Sís

### Scientists and Engineers Are CONFIDENT—Learning About Jacques Cousteau ............. 182
*Manfish: A Story of Jacques Cousteau* by Jennifer Berne

# CONTENTS

## 7 CONSTRUCTING EXPLANATIONS (SCIENCE) AND DESIGNING SOLUTIONS (ENGINEERING) — 193

Recommended Science Teaching Strategy: KLEW Charts ............................................. 193

### Scientists and Engineers Are CLEVER—Learning About Elijah McCoy .............. 195
*The Real McCoy: The Life of an African-American Inventor* by Wendy Towle

### Scientists and Engineers Are PERSISTENT—Learning About John Roebling .............. 208
*The Brooklyn Bridge: The Story of the World's Most Famous Bridge and the Remarkable Family That Built It* by Elizabeth Mann

### Scientists and Engineers Are INVENTIVE—Learning About William Kamkwamba .............. 218
*The Boy Who Harnessed the Wind* by William Kamkwamba and Bryan Mealer

## 8 ENGAGING IN ARGUMENT FROM EVIDENCE — 235

Recommended Science Teaching Strategy: Science Talk ............................................. 235

### Scientists and Engineers Are RISK TAKERS—Learning About Nikola Tesla .............. 237
*Electrical Wizard: How Nikola Tesla Lit Up the World* by Elizabeth Rusch

### Scientists and Engineers Are FEARLESS—Learning About Sylvia Earle .............. 249
*Life in the Ocean: The Story of Oceanographer Sylvia Earle* by Claire A. Nivola

### Scientists and Engineers Are CREATIVE—Learning About Waterhouse Hawkins .............. 260
*The Dinosaurs of Waterhouse Hawkins* by Barbara Kerley

## 9 OBTAINING, EVALUATING, AND COMMUNICATING INFORMATION — 273

Recommended Science Teaching Strategy: Citizen Science ............................................. 273

### Scientists and Engineers Are PERSUASIVE—Learning About Rachel Carson .............. 276
*Rachel Carson and Her Book That Changed the World* by Laurie Lawlor

### Scientists and Engineers Are PASSIONATE—Learning About Wangari Maathai .............. 286
*Seeds of Change: Wangari's Gift to the World* by Jen Cullerton Johnson

### Scientists and Engineers Are INQUISITIVE—Learning About Carl Sagan .............. 296
*Star Stuff: Carl Sagan and the Mysteries of the Cosmos* by Stephanie Roth Sisson

# CONTENTS

## 10 BEYOND *EUREKA!* TEACHING HOW SCIENTISTS AND ENGINEERS WORK — 309

Recommended Science Teaching Strategy: Concept Mapping .................................................. 310

### Scientists and Engineers Use MODIFICATION ........................................................................ 311
*Papa's Mechanical Fish* by Candace Fleming

### Scientists and Engineers Use IDEA DEVELOPMENT ............................................................. 321
*What Do You Do With an Idea?* by Kobi Yamada

### Scientists and Engineers Use DESIGN PROCESS .................................................................. 327
*Rosie Revere, Engineer* by Andrea Beaty

## LESSON GUIDELINES — 335

**Appendix A:** Overview of Featured Books .................................................................................. 339

**Appendix B:** Timeline of Featured Scientists and Engineers ................................................... 342

**Appendix C:** Lesson Connections to the *NGSS* and the Nature of Science, Grades 3–5 ..... 343

**Appendix D:** Glossary of Character Traits .................................................................................. 350

**Appendix E:** Recommended Science Teaching Strategies ....................................................... 351

Index ................................................................................................................................................ 363

# FOREWORD

Kevin D. Finson

Elementary teachers know the challenges of balancing literacy instruction with high-stakes testing and content area instruction. One way to do this is by incorporating literature relating to the content area into the lessons of that content area. In the case of science, the use of trade books to integrate literacy into science instruction is commonly used as a means of maximizing students' understanding of specific content-related concepts. Some educators, however, have expressed concern that not all books containing science information meet a suitable standard for both science and literature content. Perhaps more troublesome, some studies have demonstrated that science literature books can actually create or increase misconceptions about the content they include (Trundle, Troland, and Pritchard 2008). Should these concerns derail elementary teachers' selection and use of science trade books in their classrooms? Certainly, the answer is *no*. However, these concerns do heighten the need for teachers to have a clear understanding of the quality of science trade book content that appropriately conveys the desired information and concepts. Included with such considerations is the need to make trade book selections with very clear and purposeful rationales, having a definite sense for how a book's content can be used to address specific science messages to students while at the same time providing support for high-quality literacy instruction.

A perusal of many science trade books might quickly reveal that the science content targeted in them can range from concepts (such as lightning, magnets, or volcanoes) to gizmos (such as science equipment and devices) to history (such as science during a specific era) or to other aspects of the discipline. One aspect of science that is sometimes difficult to tease out of trade books is the nature and work of scientists. What are scientists like? What do they do? How do they do it? Who can be a scientist? These are among the questions that arise when a teacher wishes to find a trade book that focuses on scientists. A trade book whose primary focus is on gizmos might mention scientists in passing but is likely going to do a poor job of addressing the actual nature of scientists. In short, it might be difficult for teachers to find high-quality science trade books that focus on the nature and work of scientists. The authors of this book have undertaken the task of helping elementary teachers with this problem. They have carefully identified key elements about the nature and work of scientists that should be considered in trade book selection and then developed and followed a process for assessing trade books to derive a set of books that could best meet the need.

Among those key features about the nature and work of scientists that are included in the authors' selection process are (1) personal stories about scientists' lives (who scientists are), (2) portrayal of science as a human endeavor (what inspires scientists' work), (3) features of the processes scientists use (what we know as the science process skills describing how scientists do what they do), and (4) illustrations of scientists (how they are depicted) within the

# FOREWORD

books. For many elementary teachers, locating personal stories (who scientists are) is likely to be the easiest of these three things to accomplish. Finding the science processes (how scientists do their work) within the pages of these same books might be a little more difficult but still relatively easy. However, finding trade books that clearly identify science as a human endeavor is more difficult but certainly possible in trade books (Segun 1988; Tapscott 2009). Let's look briefly at aspects of these last three elements the authors dealt with in this book.

## Science Process Skills

How do scientists actually do science? Shortly after the launching of the satellite *Sputnik* by the Soviet Union on October 4, 1957, this became a key question for American education to answer. It was important because leaders in our nation realized we needed to do a better job of helping future citizens not only understand science but also how to actually do science. Congress provided millions of dollars in funding to various agencies and universities to develop science curricula that could help teachers accomplish this task. The three major elementary curriculum projects that emerged were Elementary Science Study (ESS), Science Curriculum Improvement Study (SCIS), and Science: A Process Approach (SAPA) (Shymansky 1989). Each of these curricula had at its heart the most significant science concepts and science process skills. The process skills were derived from observations and interviews with actual practicing scientists to assess the procedures they followed when doing their work (i.e., process skills). Hence, one of the aspects of the nature of scientists is the process skills scientists choose to use and how they employ them.

The set of science process skills derived varies depending on the source one reads, but all sets include essentially the same process skills. These skills can be categorized as either basic process skills or integrated process skills. The basic science process skills are the foundational skills upon which all other skills are based. The integrated science process skills are those that can be seen as integrated combinations of two or more of the basic science process skills. Although educators often view the basic science process skills as being taught only at the elementary level, many of them need to be revisited during later grades and at higher levels of sophistication. The essentials about the science process skills are described below.

## Basic Science Process Skills

### Observing
*Observing* is using the senses (or extensions of them) to gather information about an object or event. An example is watching and describing an ice cube as it melts.

### Inferring
*Inferring* is making a conclusion or interpretation based on observations, whether observed by oneself or others, using reasoning to explain data or information. An example is concluding that the lid of a container filled with water was pushed off the container by the expansion of water as it turned to ice.

### Measuring
*Measuring* is using both standard and nonstandard measures or estimates to describe dimensions of objects or events in quantitative ways. An example is using a metric ruler to measure the length and width of an ice cube in centimeters.

### Communicating
*Communicating* is sharing or transferring ideas through spoken, written, graphic, or pictoral form. An example is using graphs to show the

relationship of an ice cube's melting to time exposed to the air.

## Using Numbers
*Using numbers* is applying mathematical rules and/or formulas to calculate quantities or determine relationships. An example is calculating the average time for an ice cube to melt in 25 ml of room-temperature water.

## Manipulating Materials
*Manipulating materials* is handling or treating materials and equipment skillfully and effectively. An example is pouring a liquid from a graduated cylinder into another container when making ice.

## Classifying
*Classifying* is grouping, ordering, or arranging objects, events, or information into groups or categories based on their properties or the criteria specified in some method or system. An example is placing ice crystals in groups based on their shape.

## Predicting
*Predicting* is stating an outcome for a future event or condition one expects to exist based on a pattern of evidence derived from observations and measurements. An example is stating that an ice cube will melt within a specified amount of time.

## Developing Vocabulary
*Developing vocabulary* is using and understanding terminology, specific and unique to uses of words in a discipline, in ways that have meaning. An example is applying working definitions of science concepts in verbal discussions, such as *melting* or *heat exchange* for an ice cube.

# Integrated Science Process Skills
## Questioning
*Questioning* is using questions to focus inquiry or to determine prior knowledge and establish purposes or expectations for an investigation. An example is formulating a question about how an ice cube wrapped in newspaper will melt.

## Identifying and Controlling Variables
*Identifying and controlling variables* is identifying and describing the factors that are thought to be constant or changing under differing conditions that can affect the outcome of an experiment, keeping all of them constant except for the one being investigated. An example is identifying the factors that might affect the melting of an ice cube and keeping all of them the same except for the amount of light that shines on the ice cube.

## Defining Operationally
*Defining operationally* is stating how to measure a variable or stating what a phenomenon is according to the actions or operations to be performed on it. An example is stating that an ice cube has "melted" when there is no solid material left in the cup where the ice cube was kept.

## Recording Data
*Recording data* is setting down data in writing or some other permanent form (e.g., taking notes, making lists, and entering in data tables) in an organized manner to facilitate analysis to determine whether patterns or relationships exist in the data. An example is recording data about the mass of the ice remaining in an ice cube compared with the time it has been in a cup on the table.

## Formulating Models
*Formulating a model* is creating a mental or physical model or representation of a process, object, or

# FOREWORD

event. An example is making a three-dimensional model of the molecules in an ice cube.

### Hypothesizing

*Hypothesizing* is stating or constructing a statement that is tentative and testable about what is thought to be the expected outcome of the interaction of two or more variables. An example is stating that if one ice cube is placed in water and another is left in an open container, the one in the water will melt more quickly.

### Experimenting

*Experimenting* is conducting procedural steps to test a hypothesis, including asking appropriate questions, stating the hypothesis, identifying and controlling variables, operationally defining variables, designing a "fair test," and interpreting and then communicating the results. An example is investigating whether hot water or cold water freezes more quickly in a freezer.

### Making Decisions

*Making decisions* is drawing conclusions based on the results of experiments or collections of data, including identifying alternatives and choosing a course of action from among them based on the judgment for the selection with justifiable reasons. An example is identifying alternative ways to store ice cubes to avoid causing some of them to melt within a specific amount of time.

## Science as a Human Endeavor

Science as a human endeavor is a significant component of both the American Association for the Advancement of Science (AAAS) *Benchmarks for Science Literacy* (Project 2061) (*AAAS Benchmarks*; 1993), the *National Science Education Standards* (*NSES*; NRC 1996), and *A Framework for K–12 Science Education: Practices, Crosscutting Concepts, and Core Ideas* (*Framework*; NRC 2012), which delineated how science as a human endeavor is evidenced by the following: (1) being people engaged in science and technology for a long time, (2) those who have contributed throughout history to the knowledge base have been both men and women and of various ethnicities—some of whom make careers in the sciences, and (3) science is an ongoing endeavor that does not end. It would seem logical that educators interested in teaching science would therefore look for ways to help students see science as a human endeavor.

A very human aspect of doing science is engaging in scientific inquiry (Akerson and Hanuscin 2005). Scientific inquiry consists of posing questions and then conducting investigations in attempts to find evidence-based answers to them. This is central to the scientific enterprise and necessitates the appropriate development of scientific habits of mind and thinking. Seeing science as a human endeavor helps students develop an image of science going beyond familiar bodies of knowledge, helps them perceive science as something they can engage in successfully, and becomes something to them that is clearly a human endeavor. Abd-El-Khalick, Bell, and Lederman (1998) and Lederman (2007) emphasized that science as a human enterprise is practiced within the context of the culture in which it is situated. Hence, how science and scientists are portrayed in trade books can help contextualize students' views and understanding about science as a human endeavor.

## Illustrations of Scientists

Good picture books include colorful images students will want to look at and be able to refer to over and again (House and Rule 2005; Verhallen and Bus 2011; Xiung 2009). Analysis of images differentiates between photographs and other types of illustrations and considers their attributes, qualities, and appropriateness for use with targeted student age groups. The differentiation between photographs and illustrations is an important consideration because students' preferences—and subsequent attentiveness to the images in a book—help them comprehend the content being presented (Fang 1996; Glenberg and Langston 1992).

Included in the extant research regarding the impact of illustrations and images on elementary students were examinations of image attributes of color (bold and bright versus muted and pastels), realistic versus conventionalized presentation, sharp versus rounded lines, line drawings versus drawn images, and drawings or paintings versus photographs. Rationales for considering the importance of such elements encompass improvement of reader comprehension and development of specific language. The overall design of visual features and illustrations typically guides the reader in comprehending and linking elements of stories (Andrews, Scharff, and Moses 2002; Wolfenbarger and Sipe 2007). Appropriate and well-done illustrations help children develop a language of science (beyond simple vocabulary) extending to the language of inquiry: observation, logically derived hypothesizing, question posing, and examination of evidence (Pappas 2006). So, it is important to select trade books that have appropriately designed illustrations of scientists that are constructed in ways students prefer. Students' preferences include such qualities as:

- being realistic and life-like (Rudisill 1952), with life-like realism being more important than color when those aspects are considered separately (King 1967);

- photographs, particularly in color, over drawings and paintings (Rudisill 1952; Simcock and DeLoache 2006);

- being simplified and less complex (French 1952), although they accept more complexity increases with each grade level; and

- being more realistically colored over those either using no color or including colors too bold and not seen in the "real" things represented in the images (Rudisill 1952; Welling 1931). Younger children prefer bright primary colors, while older children tend to prefer softer colors (Andrews, Scharff, and Moses 2002; Stewig 1972). Freeman and Freeman (1933) noted that preschool-age children favored bolder and more life-like colors.

Illustrations in nonfiction picture books play an integral role in how the reader understands the content. They "serve a special comprehension function in that these [visual] elements help readers link information-containing portions of the text" (Donovan and Smolkin 2002, p. 510). Thus, illustrations are an essential component in not only understanding science content but also aiding students' understanding of science as a human endeavor or something they themselves could engage in.

Illustrations can go a long way in influencing students not only with respect to understanding where scientists work and what they do but also with regard to instilling interest and later engagement in actual career choices (Archer et al. 2010; Shope 2006). Children are very likely to formulate much of their perceptions about scientists from what they see in the illustrations in books. This factor can have a number of implications teachers may not readily consider. For example, the perceptions students hold about scientists may relate to their attitudes toward science and scientists (Finson 2003; Fung 2002). Finson (2003) found that students having more negative attitudes toward science tended to have more stereotypical perceptions of scientists, which in turn led to

# FOREWORD

a reduced desire to pursue science as a vocation later in life.

Another component influencing student interest and choice is self-efficacy. O'Brien, Kopala, and Martinez-Pons (1999) linked self-efficacy (with respect to a given field) to the probability of an individual choosing a career in that field. Individuals who perceive themselves as being successful or potentially successful engaging in science are those who will have higher science self-efficacy. From this finding, one could reasonably conclude that individuals holding negative perceptions of science or scientists may be less interested in science and less likely to select science courses or pursue science as a career.

The specifics with respect to the *NSES* (NRC 1996) are as follows:

**Standard Statement 1:** "The long-term and ongoing practice of science and technology is done by many people" (NRC 1996, p. 141).

- The practice of science must include students' practice and learning. The content of a trade book must be both age- and developmentally appropriate for its intended audience so readers can cognitively connect with what is presented. An example of a book that meets these criteria is *Gregor Mendel: The Friar Who Grew Peas* by Cheryl Bardoe (2006), which tells how Mendel had paired different species of plants to see what offspring (hybrids) would result and then would count the numbers of specific traits that exhibited themselves in each hybrid to determine whether a mathematical pattern would emerge.

- The storytelling aspect of the book is more likely to reflect science as a human endeavor than are presentations of sets of facts. As an example, in *Rachel Carson: Preserving a Sense of Wonder,* Locker and Bruchac (2004) wrote about Carson hearing stories of robin deaths linked to pesticides, leading her to write a story in which the songbirds of the world had disappeared. Carson followed that up with *Silent Spring* in which she explained how every strand within the web of life is connected to the other strands and how the collapse of one endangers all the others.

**Standard Statement 2:** "Both men and women have made significant contributions to science and technology throughout history" (NRC 1996, p. 141).

- A trade book should include images of both males and females inasmuch as this is historically appropriate. In addition, the images of persons included within a trade book should be as nonstereotypical as possible (Farland 2006a; Farland 2006b).

**Standard Statement 3:** "By its nature, science will never be finished. Although much has been learned through inquiry about phenomena, objects, and events, there remains ever more to be discovered and learned" (NRC 1996, p. 141).

- Two things need consideration: (1) accuracy of the science information (Rice and Snipes 1997) and (2) attributes of the processes of science as delineated by the *NSES* and National Science Teachers Association documents on scientific literacy (Showalter et al. 1974). An example of a trade book that meets the requisites for accuracy of science information is Dan Yaccarino's (2009) *The Fantastic Undersea Life of Jacques Cousteau,* in which he describes how Cousteau conducted life inventories of sea flora and fauna in books and documentaries and how that inventory information changed over decades of study.

**Standard Statement 4:** "Many men and women choose science as a vocation and devote their lives to studying it. Many also derive great pleasure from doing so" (NRC 1996, p. 141).

- The story presented in a trade book should illustrate the roles of people engaging in the scientific enterprise. A good example is Jacqueline Briggs Martin's (1998) *Snowflake Bentley,* in which she describes how a farmer became interested in and persisted in photographing snowflakes over many years until he was able to publish a book about them at the age of 66—and even then he continued his work about them.

## Conclusion

In writing this book, the authors have been diligent and deliberate in selecting the science trade books that serve as the anchors for each of the chapters. Through careful examination of each of those books, the authors identified the science process skills that were attendant to the work of the person at the focus of each book and then matched those process skills to suggested activities that clearly lead children in their learning of how to apply those essential skills for investigations in science.

Elementary teachers who read and use this book will benefit from the extensive work already completed by the authors. Teachers can be confident that the trade books used as the focus within the chapters are high quality and meet well-established standards for both literacy and science with respect to the nature of scientists. Making use of this book will help teachers save precious time, will help them make science more personable to their students, and will guide them in how to connect the science process skills central to excellent science activities they can select to accompany literature that truly engages students.

### References

Abd-El-Khalick, F., R. L. Bell, and N. G. Lederman. 1998. The nature of science and instructional practice: Making the unnatural natural. *Science Education* 82: 417–436.

Akerson, V. L., and D. L. Hanuscin. 2007. Teaching nature of science through inquiry: Results of a 3-year professional development program. *Journal of Research in Science Teaching* 44 (5): 653–680.

American Association for the Advancement of Science (AAAS). 1993. *Benchmarks for science literacy: Project 2061.* New York: Oxford University Press.

Andrews, J., L. Scharff, and L. Moses. 2002. The influence of illustrations in children's storybooks. *Reading Psychology* 23 (4): 3223–3339.

Archer, L., J. Dewitt, J. Osborne, J. Dillon, B. Willis, and B. Wong. 2010. Construction of science through the lens of identity. *Science Education* 94 (4): 617–639.

Bardoe, C. 2006. *Gregor Mendel: The friar who grew peas.* New York: Harry N. Abrams.

Briggs Martin, J. 1998. *Snowflake Bentley.* New York: Houghton Mifflin.

Donovan, C. A., and L. B. Smolkin. 2002. Considering genre, content, and visual features in the selection of trade books for science instruction. *The Reading Teacher* 55: 502–520.

Fang, Z. 1996. Illustrations, text, and the child reader: What are pictures in children's storybooks for? *Reading Horizons* 37 (2): 130–142.

Farland, D. 2003. "The effect of historical non-fiction trade books on students' perceptions of scientists." PhD diss., University of Massachusetts: Lowell.

Farland, D. 2006a. The effect of historical, nonfiction trade books on elementary students' perceptions of scientists. *Journal of Elementary Science Education* 18 (2): 31–48.

# FOREWORD

Farland, D. 2006b. Trade books and the human endeavor of science. *Science and Children* 44: 35–37.

Finson, K. D. 2003. Applicability of the DAST-C to the images of scientists drawn by students of different racial groups. *Journal of Elementary Science Education* 15 (1): 15–26.

Freeman, L., and R. S. Freeman. 1933. Selecting books for the nursery child. *Childhood Education* 10: 68–72.

French, J. E. 1952. Children's preference for pictures of varied complexity of pictorial pattern. *Elementary School Journal* 53: 90–95.

Fung, Y. 2002. A comparative study of primary and secondary school students' images of scientists. *Research in Science and Technological Education* 20 (2): 199–213.

Glenberg, A. M., and W. E. Langston. 1992. Comprehension of illustrated text: Pictures help to build mental models. *Journal of Memory and Language* 31: 129–151.

House, C. A., and A. C. Rule. 2005. Preschoolers' ideas of what makes a picture book illustration beautiful. *Early Childhood Education Journal* 32 (5): 283–290.

King, E. M. 1967. Critical appraisal of research on children's reading interests, preferences, and habits. *Canadian Educational Research Digest* 7: 312–326.

Lederman, N. G. 2007. Nature of science: Past, present, and future. In *Handbook of research on science education*, ed. S. K. Abel and N. G. Lederman, 831–877. New York: Routledge.

Locker, T., and J. Bruchac. 2004. *Rachel Carson: Preserving a sense of wonder.* Golden, CO: Fulcrum Publishing.

National Research Council (NRC). 1996. *National Science Education Standards.* Washington, DC: National Academies Press.

National Research Council (NRC). 2012. *A framework for K–12 science education: Practices, crosscutting concepts, and core ideas.* Washington, DC: National Academies Press.

O'Brien, V., M. Kopala, and M. Matrinez-Pons. 1999. Mathematics self-efficacy, ethnic identity, gender, and career interests related to mathematics and science. *Journal of Educational Research* 92: 231–235.

Pappas, C. C. 2006. The information books genre: Its role in integrated science literacy research and practice. *Reading Research Quarterly* 41: 226–250.

Rice, D. C., and C. Snipes. 1997. Children's tradebooks: Do they affect the development of science concepts? Paper presented at the annual meeting of the National Association for Research in Science Teaching, St. Louis, MO.

Rudisill, M. 1952. Children's preferences for color versus other qualities in illustrations. *The Elementary School Journal* 52 (8): 444–451.

Segun, M. 1988. The importance of illustrations in children's books. In *Illustrating for Children,* ed. M. Segun, 25–27. Ibadan: CLAN.

Shope III, R. E. 2006. The Ed3U science model: Teaching science for conceptual change. Retrieved from *http://theaste.org/publications/proceedings/2006proceedings/shope.html.*

Showalter, V., D. Cox, P. Holobinko, B. Thomson, and M. Orledo. 1974. *What is unified science education? (Part 5) Program objectives and scientific literacy, Prism II.* Arlington, VA: National Science Teachers Association.

Shymansky, J. A. 1989. What research says about ESS, SCIS, and SAPPA. *Science and Children,* 26 (7): 33–35.

Simcock, G., and J. DeLoache. 2006. Get the picture? The effects of iconicity on toddlers' reenactment from picture books. *Developmental Psychology* 42: 1352–1357.

Stewig, J. W. 1972. Children's preference in picture book illustration. *Educational Leadership* 30 (3): 273–277.

Tapscott, D. 2009. *Grown up digital. How the net generation is changing your world.* New York: McGraw-Hill.

Trundle, K., T. Troland, and T. Pritchard. 2008. Representations of the moon in children's literature: An analysis of written and visual text. *Journal of Elementary Science Education* 20 (1): 17–28.

Verhallen, M. J. A. J., and A. G. Bus. 2011. Young second language learners' visual attention to illustrations in storybooks. *Journal of Early Childhood Literacy* 11 (4): 480–500.

Welling, J. B. 1931. Illustrated books for the four- to eight-year-old. *Childhood Education* 8: 132–138.

Wolfenbarger, C. D., and L. R. Sipe. 2007. A unique visual and literary art form: Recent research on picturebooks. *Language Arts* 84 (3): 273–280.

Xiung, Y. 2009. Levels of meaning and children: An exploratory study of picture books' illustrations. *Library and Information Science Research* 31: 240–246.

Yaccarino, D. 2009. *The fantastic undersea life of Jacques Cousteau.* New York: Knopf.

# Dedication

This book is dedicated to the best science teacher I know, who teaches at Eastford Elementary School in Connecticut.
—Donna Farland-Smith

This book is dedicated to my most supportive husband, who has helped me brainstorm, craft, and edit these ideas and lessons from the very beginning.
—Julie Thomas

# Acknowledgments

We would like to thank NSTA Press for the opportunity to publish this work. Special thanks to Amanda Van Beuren for her editorial expertise.

We're especially grateful to the many teachers at Alton Darby Elementary, Ridgewood Elementary, and Darby Creek Elementary in the Hilliard City School District (Columbus, Ohio) and to Alexandria Walenz at Roper Elementary in the Lincoln Public School District (Lincoln, Nebraska) for their willingness to participate in the development of many of these lessons. Thank you also to their administrators—Herb Higginbotham, Tara Grove, and Cindy Teske—for their support. Thanks to the amazing Andrew Queler for sharing photographs of his unique sawfish nostrums for use in this book. And thanks to Susie Scott, whose passion for teaching science is unmatched!

# About the Authors

**Donna Farland-Smith** has over a decade of experience in the classroom and previously taught science in all grades K–12. She currently serves as an associate professor of science education in The School of Teaching and Learning at The Ohio State University-Mansfield. Her areas of expertise include teacher education, students' perceptions of science and scientists, and encouraging girls to explore science and engineering fields. Along with several book chapters and many articles about science education, Farland-Smith has written and published four books that inspire children to understand and appreciate scientists and their work: *Jungle Jane* (Authentic Perceptions Press, 2002), *It Takes Two: The Story of the Watson and Crick Team* (Authentic Perceptions Press, 2002), and *The Simple Truth About Scientists* (Authentic Perceptions Press, 2002). Farland-Smith received a BA in elementary education, a BA in natural science, an MA in science education, and an EdD in mathematics and science education from the University of Massachusetts-Lowell. In 2017, she published the book *Many Hands, One Vision: 20 Principles That Built a Children's Museum and Revitalized a Downtown Community* (CreateSpace), which tells about her experience in founding The Little Buckeye Children's Museum in Mansfield, Ohio.

**Julie Thomas** is an experienced elementary classroom teacher and elementary gifted-program coordinator. Now a research professor of science education in the College of Education and Human Sciences at the University of Nebraska-Lincoln, Thomas

## ABOUT THE AUTHORS

focuses her efforts on elementary science—for teachers and their students. She has led both state-funded and federally funded projects and has published research about children's science learning and teacher professional development. Thomas's accomplishments include collaborative efforts such as No Duck Left Behind, a partnership with waterfowl biologists to promote wetland education efforts; and Engineering Is Everywhere (E2), a partnership with a materials engineer to develop a time-efficient model for STEM career education. Throughout her teaching career, Thomas has been active in professional associations such as the School Science and Mathematics Association, for which she is a past executive director; the National Science Teachers Association, for which she has authored articles in the journal *Science and Children* and has served on the Awards Committee and Nominations Committee; and the Council for Elementary Children International, for which she is a past president.

# 1

# Introduction
## WHAT WE DID IN THIS BOOK AND WHY

We are so grateful you are reading this book right now, and as experienced classroom educators, our goal is to make your teaching easier and more meaningful for your students. As former teachers, we have a deep and long-standing passion for teaching science and an unwavering respect for your efforts to meet new demands associated with the teaching profession. Today's classrooms are multifaceted; we know that what you do is challenging and that you have many choices for the resources you select in your classroom. We also realize that you choose to spend a great deal of your personal time and money to maximize learning options for your students. So we designed the lessons in this book around trade books you can borrow from your school library to enable you to manage the hands-on activities on a modest budget.

## The Book's Title

The book's title is inspired by a familiar, centuries-old expression: "Eureka, I've found it!" This saying comes from a legend about Archimedes, one of the very first scientists (and the founder of modern-day physics). As the story goes, Heiro, the king of Syracuse in that day, was skeptical about the goldsmith who had made his new crown, suspecting that instead of using pure gold, the goldsmith had mixed in some silver. King Heiro sought someone who could prove whether the crown was made of pure gold, and he summoned Archimedes, the greatest mathematical thinker of the time. Archimedes mulled over the problem night and day—and then one day, the answer came to him as he was stepping into his bath. He was so excited about solving the problem that he forgot he wasn't wearing clothes and, wearing nothing but his birthday suit, ran up and down the street yelling, "Eureka! Eureka! I have found it! I have found it!"

You might be wondering, "How did the bathtub help Archimedes answer his question?" Well, as Archimedes stepped into the bathtub, he noticed that his body caused the water to rise and some of it to flow over the sides of the tub. He connected this experience to the problem with the king's crown. Archimedes expected that the specific weights of gold and silver would be different, which would allow him to easily discern how much water a gold crown should displace and thus show whether King Heiro's crown was made of pure gold.

*Teacher's note:* The children's book *Mr. Archimedes' Bath* (1980) provides a whimsical rendition of this story, with some detail about how Archimedes might have measured the displaced bathtub water. You are likely to find this book in your school library. We caution you to read this story yourself before sharing

# INTRODUCTION

it with your students because some teachers have expressed concern about the "naked man" illustrations (which are cartoon-like views of Archimedes' backside).We have found that children do understand the author–illustrator's intended humor.

We were inspired to use the word *eureka* because we expect many people to be familiar with that old expression and the storied connection it has to the character and work of a scientist. There are many wonderful stories about scientists and engineers and their work, and we incorporate 27 of them in the activities of this book. We believe these biographical stories will expand students' knowledge and understanding of who scientists are, what scientists do, and why science is important—and will inspire children to see themselves as budding scientists. We hope, too, that the activities will help children recognize their own character traits and encourage them to think about their potential as future scientists.

## Chapters and Lessons

We created 27 lessons linking nonfiction historical trade books and science content that uniquely enable you to model scientific thinking by linking stories of scientists with your elementary (grade 3–5) science lessons. Our bold new idea is that biographies of scientists can allow you to highlight the human dimension of scientists and engineers while you encourage science learning. We think these stories will broaden students' perceptions of scientists and engineers as real people and add explicit and implicit opportunities for them to consider science and engineering careers.

We like to think of this book as a way to invite scientists and engineers into your classroom without the hassle of finding and scheduling guest speakers. Each chapter of this book presents three lessons based on a children's literature biography of a scientist. Each lesson is organized according to its *Next Generation Science Standards* (*NGSS*; NGSS Lead States 2013) support, a recommended science teaching strategy, the learning-cycle format, and the character trait of the scientist or engineer that contributed to his or her success. Appendix A (p. 339) lists all of these biographies with their publication information, and Appendix B (p. 342) places these scientists and engineers into a timeline. Each lesson includes a sample rubric to evaluate your students' understanding of practices and concepts associated with these lessons.

## Next Generation Science Standards

Each book chapter supports the science and engineering practices outlined in the *NGSS* (NGSS Lead States 2013) for grades 3–5. The *NGSS* connections provide the most universal organizational structure; however, we expect that teachers will approach these lessons from the standpoint of a variety of state standards and expectations. Within the *NGSS* connections, we focused on the *NGSS* language but linked the activities to grades 3–5 as a group rather than to the specific grade-band end points in the *Framework* (NRC 2012).

The real innovation of the *NGSS* is its integrated, three-dimensional performance expectations (NRC 2012): disciplinary core ideas (DCIs), science and engineering practices, and crosscutting concepts (ideas and practices that cut across the science disciplines). To help you and your students recognize science as a human endeavor, we encourage applying a fourth dimension of performance expectations: the nature of science. In each lesson, we suggest a variety of options, and we encourage you to choose components of all four dimensions as you hone each lesson to fit your own classroom needs.

Thus, we structured the lessons in *Eureka!* to include four elements—the three dimensions of high-quality science (DCIs, science and engineering practices, and crosscutting concepts), as well as their connections with the nature of science, as outlined by the *Framework* (NRC 2012). First, each chapter is organized according to one of the eight science and engineering practices. Three scientist and engineer biographies in each chapter help students recognize these practices, and the lessons related to these biographies will guide students' active experiences in these practices. Next, each biography and its associated lesson are connected to the crosscutting concepts and the science and engineering practices in the DCIs. Teachers' decisions about how to implement each lesson may vary, and these *NGSS* references will help to guide teachers in lesson selection and implementation. Appendix C (p. 343) lists the *NGSS* connections by chapter and by scientist or engineer.

## Character Traits

Each featured scientist and engineer is introduced with a character trait. These capture the unique human qualities of the scientists and introduce the human assets of scientists' dispositions. It is important to mention that every individual has such traits, and the focus here is on helping students understand that scientists and engineers are people and express personal, human traits that enable them to be successful.

Character traits will be a familiar focus for your students from their previous learning involving review of fictional literature and development of insight into the specific events in a story (e.g., "Why was Goldilocks asleep in the mother bear's bed when the bears returned home?"). Character traits include a person's behaviors, thoughts, and beliefs related to universal principles, moralities, and integrity and their commitment to live by those principles. Positive character traits can engender personal and societal benefits and encourage other people to believe in you—and have been integral to the successful endeavors of the historic men and women of science and engineering depicted in the biographies in this book.

Scientists' and engineers' character traits also describe their dispositions toward science and engineering. Binns, Koehler, and Bloom (2015) became interested in the universal nature of the character traits and dispositions of scientists (DOS) because these guide our perception of scientists and their work. Through their study of popular films about scientists, they identified nine such dispositions: passion, excitement, pragmatic, collaborative, intuitive, inquisitive, creative, risk-taking, and persistent. In this book, we followed on the work of Binns, Koehler, and Bloom (2015) to identify the character traits of the 24 scientists and engineers introduced through the biographies. (See Appendix D, Glossary of Character Traits [p. 350].) We believe explicitly teaching a human character trait along with learning the stories of scientists and engineers will help to humanize children's conception of scientists and engineers and the nature of their work. As we suggest later in this chapter, this improved awareness of the nature of scientists' and engineers' work may be integral to inspiring the next generation of science, technology, engineering, and mathematics (STEM) workers.

## Recommended Science Teaching Strategies

In each chapter, we recommend a science teaching strategy that relates to each of the science and engineering practices. These include our own stories of tried and true experiences in the science classroom—often lessons learned by the teacher!

As an example, Donna remembers the fall she grabbed her fading sunflowers out of the ground (roots and all) and took them to school to teach students about making observations. She directed her students to observe the sunflowers, draw a picture of them, and write five observations about

# INTRODUCTION

them in sentence format. Donna thought she had given her third graders a simple, straightforward task but was disappointed to read their simplistic notes: "The stalks are green," "the plants are tall," and the "flowers are beautiful." In this teacher lesson moment, Donna learned how to teach her students to observe like scientists.

Although observation can be interpreted as a simple process skill, its value should not be underestimated. Scientists often begin their work with long-term observations to help them form their research questions—but one does not need to be a professional scientist to observe. Observing people, places, and things is a natural inclination for the youngest of people—and yet is one of the most misunderstood and underused of the process skills. The broader application of the term *observation* includes the use of all of the senses as a means of understanding the world in which we live (Bell 2007). Observations are subject to interpretation, and it is important to teach children to focus on the facts and not their opinions.

What Donna learned was that children need explicit instructions about how to observe like a scientist observes. She began teaching them this by asking students to make observations about her as a teacher. As soon as one child suggested something such as "You're pretty," Donna began to question the list of observations and focus on the evidence (or lack thereof). As Donna questioned students, "Am I as pretty as Jennifer Aniston?," the class began to giggle. Now she could help the class focus on factual observations. She pointed to the list of statements and asked which were true: "How about the fact that the teacher is wearing glasses or a green sweater?" Students nodded their heads, "Yes, those are facts." Well, let's talk through how those are different.

The trouble with teaching observation is that humans observe 100 times a day, every day, and have done so since the moment we were born. Because of this, we automatically assume that children already know how to do it. However, it's true that they may understand how to observe, but not in the sense of observation as a foundational skill for science. And it is an ever-important foundational tool in the early years. In teaching it specifically, Donna and the students learned so much more (including how to write a complete thought in a sentence), and it became a benchmark lesson Donna could refer to when observing anything else that year. Donna learned that her students needed to be taught how to make and record observations. And the students learned how to be more specific in their observations.

For the rest of the year, all Donna had to say was "Think about the sunflowers," and the students would carefully prune their observations to remove opinions and generalities. Observations quickly made it into Donna's yearly repertoire of teaching. Asking children to search for observations and illustrate them became opportunities for them to think like scientists. It no longer mattered whether Donna brought in soil, old bones, or sunflowers each year. What mattered was giving her students many opportunities to observe and sharpen their skills. That's how this became a benchmark lesson Donna could refer to throughout the year: "Remember the sunflowers?" continued to guide detailed, factual observations sans opinion. Asking students to observe, illustrate, and think like scientists and engineers allowed lessons about observations to be much more than simple observation exercises.

The science teaching strategies we recommend in these chapters not only introduce commonly held standards for science teaching practices but also tie the science lessons to our personal experiences as science teachers. These strategies are fully described in each chapter and briefly outlined in Appendix E (p. 351).

## Learning-Cycle Format

Each science lesson was developed in the 5E learning-cycle format, as described in Settlage and Southerland (2007) and based on the original learning cycle designed by Robert Karplus (1964). Although there are many variations on the process commonly referred to as the *learning cycle*, it remains a model for hands-on, inductive science teaching that helps students use the experiences the teacher provides in the classroom to build on personal understanding. The structure of the learning cycle is important because each part represents an important process in learning. We include it here because we both have extensive experience with following this lesson structure, and we expect it to support the types of lessons we have developed. The purpose of each stage is as follows:

- **Engage:** To awaken student interest or prior knowledge and to lead students into the topic of the lesson and connect it with their previous experiences.
- **Explore:** To provide a shared experience to guide students' investigation of concrete materials and recording of their work.
- **Explain:** To provide (1) an opportunity for students to express differing experiences and refine and deepen their understanding of the central science concepts (via inferences and predictions) and (2) an opportunity for teachers to identify the focus of the science lesson and introduce scientific vocabulary.
- **Extend:** To help students take their new knowledge and apply it to another situation.
- **Evaluate:** To assess what students have learned and inform them about how well they understand the lesson at hand.

Importantly, this evaluative step of the learning cycle is a bit different in that it can happen (formally and informally) at several points throughout the lesson, although most teachers make sure to include an assessment at the end of the lesson.

## Safety Considerations for Hands-On Activities

With hands-on, process-based, and inquiry-based classroom and laboratory activities, the teaching and learning of science and STEM today can be both effective and exciting. The challenge to securing this success needs to be met by addressing potential safety issues as appropriate relative to engineering controls (ventilation, eye-wash station, and so on), administrative procedures and safety operating procedures, and use of appropriate personal protective equipment (indirectly vented chemical splash goggles or safety glasses meeting ANSI/ISEA Z87.1 D3 standard, chemical-resistant and nonlatex aprons and gloves, and so on). Teachers can make it safer for students and themselves by adopting, implementing, and enforcing legal safety standards and better professional safety practices in the science classroom and laboratory. Before undertaking any science or STEM activity or investigation, a hazard analysis, risk assessment, and review of safety actions need to be done to ensure a safer teaching and learning experience. Also remember that personal protective equipment should be worn during the setup, hands-on, and takedown segments of the activity.

Always provide safety training and demonstrate proper use of hand tools, lab equipment, personal protective equipment, and so forth before having students undertake any hands-on activities. Also

# INTRODUCTION

provide follow-up safety reminders before each activity.

Throughout this book, safety precautions are provided for classroom and laboratory activities and should be adopted and enforced to provide for a safer teaching and learning experience. Teachers should also review and follow local policies and protocols used within their school district and school (e.g., chemical hygiene plan, Board of Education safety policies).

Additional applicable standard operating procedures can be found in the National Science Teachers Association's "Safety in the Science Classroom, Laboratory, or Field Sites" position paper (*www.nsta.org/docs/SafetyInTheScienceClassroomLabAndField.pdf*). Students should be required to review the document or one similar to it under the direction of the teacher. Both the student and the parent or guardian should then sign the document, acknowledging procedures that must be followed for a safer working and learning experience in the laboratory.

The Council of State Science Supervisors (CSSS) provides information about classroom science safety, including a safety checklist for science classrooms. See the CSSS website at *www.csss-science.org/safety.shtml* to access this information and for links to other science safety-related resources.

*Disclaimer:* The safety precautions of each activity are based in part on use of the recommended materials and instructions, legal safety standards, and better professional practices. Selection of alternative materials or procedures for these activities may jeopardize the level of safety and therefore is at the user's own risk.

## The Backstory

Our experiences have taught us about the importance of children understanding scientists' work as a human endeavor. Several other researchers have examined how children view scientists and determined that students hold stereotypical views of scientists as white males, occasionally as monsters, who primarily work indoors (Barman 1997; Finson 2003; Finson, Beaver, and Cramond 1995; Losh, Wilke, and Pop 2008). We, too, have each conducted a number of studies using the Draw-a-Scientist Test (DAST) or a modified DAST (mDAST). We have also developed new prompts and scoring rubrics for the DAST (Farland-Smith 2012) and a new instrument, the Draw-an-Engineer Test (Thomas et al. 2016).

Donna Farland's (2003, 2006) research examined the influence that reading historical, nonfiction trade books has on children's images of scientists. The finding was that in Full Option Science System (FOSS) unit instruction, when teachers read biographies to their students, the students more fully recognized the science processes they were applying in their lessons. The Farland (2003, 2006) study involved students ($N = 156$) in 13 classrooms, each with one teacher. Six classrooms/teachers ($n = 72$ students) were randomly assigned to supplement their third-grade FOSS instruction by reading one scientist biography each week for six weeks (FOSS + Biography [FB] group). Seven classrooms/teachers ($n = 84$ students) followed the usual FOSS lesson procedures (FOSS-Only [FO] group).

To evaluate the difference between the FO and FB classes, Farland reviewed scientist drawings completed by all students before the unit of instruction and another set of drawings from a readministered test after the unit instruction. Farland found that, compared with the FO students, the FB students demonstrated a broader perception of who does science, where science is done, and what activities scientists do.

Julie Thomas and her graduate students (Hulings, Thomas, and Orona 2013; Thomas 2012) used the DAST to learn what influenced rural fifth graders' (310 boys and 385 girls) thinking about

FIGURE 1.1

Examples of Fifth Graders' Drawings of Scientists, Showing Influences on Their Perceptions of Scientists

| Motion Picture Influence | Television Influence | School Influence |
|---|---|---|
| (A) | (B) | (C) |

These examples of fifth graders' drawings of scientists suggest that these students have confused perceptions of who scientists are and what work they do. Example A shows how these perceptions are shaped by motion pictures, which, designed to entertain, promote sensationalized images of scientists rather than realistic ones. Example B suggests that television advertisements promote limited ideas about the creative experimental goals of a scientist. From example C, we realize that school science activities—though interactive and fun—can limit children's thinking about the purpose and value of scientists' work.

science and STEM careers. They found that boys and girls had similarly traditional ideas about where scientists work; however, boys' drawings of scientists were Einstein-like or did not resemble a normal human, and girls' drawings of scientists were more likely to include females and groups of scientists working together. This analysis helped to determine some ways that public media and school science lessons limited these rural students' ideas about the work of scientists (see Figure 1.1) and led to the reasoning that an improved awareness of scientists' work may well motivate and inspire students' thinking about potential careers. Such explicit connections may be a necessary component to the National Science Foundation's (2008) mission to broaden STEM participation among diverse populations by providing "for the discovery and nurturing of talent wherever it may be found" (p. iii).

## How to Use This Book

Each chapter includes three literature-based lessons that support the *NGSS* and introduce complementary, skill-building, inquiry investigations to highlight the science processes and the human nature of scientists' endeavors. You may decide to teach one lesson from each chapter or all three—it's up to you. The appendixes can guide you in your choices.

For example, Appendix A (p. 339) might inspire you to teach one of these science lessons because your students learned about one of the featured scientists or engineers in another class (e.g., John

# 1 INTRODUCTION

James Audubon). Or you might decide to teach a lesson on patience, and it fits in with your science curriculum. Or you may need to find creative ways to meet the standards and you are looking for an appropriate lesson (say, on friction).

Our goal is that these will be the lessons you cannot wait to teach every year with a new group of students. In addition to teaching science content and supporting the NGSS, *Eureka! Grade 3–5 Science Activities and Stories* is unique in that it brings science to life through learning the personal traits of well-known scientists and engineers as they are portrayed in biographical trade books.

## References

Allen, P. 1980. *Mr. Archimedes' bath.* New York: HarperCollins.

Barman, C. R. 1997. Students' views of scientists and science: Results from a national study. *Science and Children* 35 (1): 18–24.

Bell, R. L. 2007. *Teaching the nature of science through process skills: Activities for grades 3–8.* Boston: Allyn and Bacon.

Binns, I. C., C. M. Koehler, and M. A. Bloom. 2015. Dispositions of scientists in mainstream film: The extraordinary person called a scientist. In *Application of visual data in K–16 science classrooms*, ed. K. Finson and J. Pederson, 153–166. Charlotte, NC: Information Age Publishing.

Farland, D. 2003. "The effect of historical non-fiction trade books on students' perceptions of scientists." PhD diss., University of Massachusetts: Lowell.

Farland, D. 2006. Trade books and the human endeavor of science. *Science and Children* 44 (3): 35–37.

Farland-Smith, D. 2012. Development and field test of the modified draw-a-scientist test and the draw-a-scientist rubric. *School Science and Mathematics* 112 (2): 109–116.

Finson, K. D. 2003. Applicability of the DAST-C to the images of scientists drawn by students of different racial groups. *Journal of Elementary Science Education* 15 (1): 15–26.

Finson, K. D., J. B. Beaver, and B. L. Cramond. 1995. Development and field test of a checklist for the draw-a-scientist test. *School Science and Mathematics* 95 (4): 195–205.

Hulings, M., J. Thomas, and C. Orona. 2013. Influences on 5th grade students' images of scientists and career aspirations. Paper presented at the Association for Science Teacher Educators (ASTE) Annual Conference, Charleston, SC.

Karplus, R. 1964. The science curriculum improvement study. *Journal of Research in Science Teaching* 2: 293–303.

Losh, S. C., R. Wilke, and M. Pop. 2008. Some methodological issues with "Draw a Scientist Tests" among young children. *International Journal of Science Education* 30 (6): 773–792.

National Research Council (NRC). 2012. *A framework for K–12 science education: Practices, crosscutting concepts, and core ideas.* Washington, DC: National Academies Press.

National Science Foundation (NSF). 2008. *Broadening participation at the National Science Foundation: A framework for action.* Washington, DC: NSF.

NGSS Lead States. 2013. *Next Generation Science Standards: For states, by states.* Washington, DC: National Academies Press. www.nextgenscience.org/next-generation-science-standards.

Settlage, J., and S. Southerland. 2007. *Teaching science to every child.* New York: Routledge.

Thomas, J. 2012. The "take away" in elementary science: Kids say the darndest things! Keynote presentation at the Council for Elementary Science International (CESI) Breakfast at the NSTA Regional Conference, Phoenix, AZ.

Thomas, J., N. M. Colston, T. Ley, B. DeVore-Wedding, L. R. Hawley, J. Utley, and T. Ivey. 2016. Fundamental research: Developing a rubric to assess children's drawings of an engineer at work. In *Proceedings of the 2016 ASEE Annual Conference and Exposition.* Washington, DC: American Society for Engineering Education.

# Asking Questions and Defining Problems

The practices of asking questions and defining problems are integral to both science and engineering. This chapter focuses on three scientists—Philo Farnsworth, Thomas Edison, and George Washington Carver—all of whom asked questions to define problems in their work in science and engineering. Through asking questions and rethinking problems, Farnsworth invented television, Edison created multiple uses for electricity, and Carver developed peanut butter to expand farming opportunities. It is easy to see why the words *thinker*, *inspired*, and *diligent* might be used to describe the character traits of these three individuals.

The *Next Generation Science Standards* (*NGSS*) state that science usually begins with asking questions, whereas engineering usually begins with defining problems to solve (NGSS Lead States 2013). Although instances of the reverse may occur, lessons that begin by asking questions provide a frame for thinking about the similarities and differences between these two disciplines in the classroom. Children are naturally curious, but in our experience, the school setting tends to disconnect them from their natural inclination to ask a variety of questions. To help students hold on to their curiosity, we have learned to model explicit and implicit questioning. Along with questions to gauge their understanding of content, we ask questions that promote students' thinking about what scientists do such as, "What do you know about the work of scientists and engineers?" "What activities have you heard or seen scientists or engineers doing?" and "How did you know they were scientists or engineers?"

## Recommended Science Teaching Strategy: Designating Makerspaces

The maker movement focuses on student creativity and engineering and is revolutionizing education (Martinez and Stager 2013a; Martinez and Stager 2013b). This movement promotes the creation of designated "makerspaces" within schools, in which students can explore and experiment with both science and engineering simultaneously. The *NGSS* stress increased incorporation of two engineering components: building and design.

The steps of the design process will be discussed as a teaching strategy later in this book (see Chapter 10, p. 309); this chapter focuses on the importance of questions. As teachers of the next generation of makers, we need to understand both what lesson models will help us incorporate the principles of the maker movement in our classrooms and how the *NGSS* practice of "asking questions (for science) and defining problems (for engineering)" (NGSS Lead States 2013) relates to

# 2  ASKING QUESTIONS AND DEFINING PROBLEMS

this movement. Regardless of whether a scientific investigation begins with a problem or with an observation, young scientists and engineers will ask questions. Although students may need guidance during their first few experiences in the makerspace, encouraging them to ask questions will help them begin to explore attributes and possibilities of the maker materials. For example, you might guide students' observations of the properties of various types of cardboard (e.g., thickness, strength, and weight) and their choice of tools (e.g., scissors, paper cutter, and scoring tools) but leave them to solve the problem of cutting the cardboard and have a follow-up discussion about which tools worked best for each cardboard type.

The maker approach requires teachers to become comfortable with clutter and chaos (not always welcome in traditional classrooms, yet vital for tinkering and maker-based learning models). However, the critical factor is teachers' comfort with and ability to allow time for asking questions, defining problems, and finding answers. As science educators transition to teaching content that relates to procedural knowledge, incorporating these design ideas into a science classroom can be challenging, but not impossible!

Some ways to integrate maker thinking into your science classroom or school building that will also facilitate authentic arts learning within an integrated science, technology, engineering, art, and mathematics (STEAM) education model include the following:

1. Think of the students as explorers and designers and position yourself as someone with an agile mind-set who responds to their thinking.

2. Incorporate different stations in the classroom that allow students to tinker and explore. Provide appropriate construction materials for exploration and representation.

3. Use the *NGSS* science and engineering practices to guide the structure of the stations.

4. Require students to provide evidence of how they used *NGSS* practices in the makerspace.

Follow the tenets of the maker movement by combining multiple ways of thinking across content areas, emphasizing creativity and uniqueness, and providing mini–maker faires as a culminating outlet for students to share and present their work. (For more information, see the website *Nation of Makers* [The White House 2015]). Graves (2015) provides many ideas for building and supporting makerspaces in the classroom. Keep in mind that makerspaces can but need not include machines (such as sewing machines) and computer technologies.

When Donna was teaching, she found much guidance in the art of questioning from Wynne Harlen, who reminds us that when students ask questions, they indicate what they want to know and when they want to know it (Harlen 2001). Questions help generate students' interest in science and mathematics if they are allowed to investigate and satisfy their curiosity. Although the culture of classrooms has changed much over time, questioning is one thing that will never go out of style.

In this chapter, we introduce three very different lessons to connect students' questions about scientists to their biographies. The first lesson suggests ways to incorporate a mini-makerspace into your classroom. In the second lesson, students follow exploratory questions through four different stations. The third lesson is a model of how a teacher might introduce an overarching question and guide students through a series of activities.

# SCIENTISTS AND ENGINEERS ARE THINKERS

## Learning About **Philo Farnsworth**

Thinker (n.): a person who reflects on or ponders

### Lesson: Thinking and Tinkering
**Description**

In this lesson, students will create a new invention or a replica of an invention from recyclables or everyday materials and discuss how their invention might contribute to society.

### Objectives

Students will consider how the character trait *thinker* helped Philo Farnsworth invent television and engage in the design cycle process to create a new invention.

- As students begin this lesson, they will recall an invention of their choice.
- As a class, students will discuss how inventions improve our lives.
- Students will hear the story *The Boy Who Invented TV: The Story of Philo Farnsworth* by Kathleen Krull and discuss how it relates to the word *thinker*.
- Students will make a replica television from household materials and explain how this invention has benefited society and been modified over time.
- To conclude the lesson, students will demonstrate understanding of how questions and problems become part of the design process and how inventions have affected society.

### Learning Outcomes

Students will (1) make a science notebook entry to explain what it means to be a thinker and why being a thinker is an important trait for scientists and engineers and (2) gather feedback from their peers on the design and function of their creative invention.

# Connections to the *NGSS* and the Nature of Science, Grades 3–5

## Disciplinary Core Ideas

**ETS1.A: DEFINING AND DELIMITING ENGINEERING PROBLEMS**

- <u>Possible solutions to a problem are limited by available materials and resources (constraints). The success of a designed solution is determined by considering the desired features of a solution (criteria).</u> Different proposals for solutions can be compared on the basis of how well each one meets the specified criteria for success or how well each takes the constraints into account.

**ETS1.B: DEVELOPING POSSIBLE SOLUTIONS**

- At whatever stage, communicating with peers about proposed solutions is an important part of the design process, and shared ideas can lead to improved designs.

## Science and Engineering Practices

***Asking Questions and Defining Problems:*** A practice of science is to ask and refine questions that lead to descriptions and explanations of how the natural and designed world works and which can be empirically tested. Asking questions and defining problems in grades 3–5 builds from grades K–2 experiences and progresses to specifying qualitative relationships.

- Use prior knowledge to describe problems that can be solved.
- Define a simple design problem that can be solved through the development of an object, tool, process, or system and includes several criteria for success and constraints on materials, time, or cost.

***Constructing Explanations and Designing Solutions:*** The products of science are explanations and the products of engineering are solutions. Constructing explanations and designing solutions in 3–5 builds on K–2 experiences and progresses to the use of evidence in constructing explanations that specify variables that describe and predict phenomena and in designing multiple solutions to design problems.

- Use evidence (e.g., measurements, observations, patterns) to construct or support an explanation or design a solution to a problem.

## Crosscutting Concept

***Patterns:*** Observed patterns in nature guide organization and classification and prompt questions about relationships and causes underlying them.

- Patterns can be used as evidence to support an explanation.

SCIENTISTS AND ENGINEERS ARE **THINKERS**—PHILO FARNSWORTH

### Nature of Science Connections
**SCIENTIFIC INVESTIGATIONS USE A VARIETY OF METHODS**

- Science methods are determined by questions.
- Science investigations use a variety of methods, tools, and techniques.

**SCIENTIFIC KNOWLEDGE IS OPEN TO REVISION IN LIGHT OF NEW EVIDENCE**

- Science explanations can change based on new evidence.

**SCIENCE IS A HUMAN ENDEAVOR**

- Men and women from all cultures and backgrounds choose careers as scientists and engineers.
- Most scientists and engineers work in teams.
- Science affects everyday life.
- Creativity and imagination are important to science.

*Source:* NGSS Lead States 2013.
*Note:* When an activity supports only part of a standard, underlining indicates the relevant part.

## Overview

In this lesson, students will learn how Philo Farnsworth invented television and shared his invention to meet societal needs and then students will create a new invention of their own. Through the featured book, students learn that men and women from all backgrounds choose careers as scientists. The character trait *thinker* references Farnsworth's meticulous and creative attempts to use light to create something new. In this lesson, students focus on prototyping, testing, and improving their inventions.

## Materials

You will need one copy of the featured book, *The Boy Who Invented TV: The Story of Philo Farnsworth* by Kathleen Krull (ISBN 978-0375845611). Provide students with a variety of construction materials, including an assortment of cardboard and posterboard scraps, toilet paper and paper towel cardboard tubes, tape, construction

# 2
ASKING QUESTIONS AND DEFINING PROBLEMS

paper, string, brad fasteners, recycled materials (e.g., plastic bottles), paint, markers, paper clips, pencils, and paint.

## Safety Notes
(1) Personal protective equipment should be worn during the setup, hands-on, and takedown segments of the activity. (2) Use caution when working with sharps (scissors, wires, and so on). They can cut or puncture skin. (3) Use caution when working with tools; use only as instructed by teacher. Misuse can cause serious injury. (4) Use caution when working with or around glue guns. They get hot and can burn skin. (5) Wash hands with soap and water upon completing this activity.

## Setting the Context
### Engage
Invite students to brainstorm a list of inventions and then discuss how these inventions help us. Encourage them to think about the problem each invention solved, and tease out their ideas about how the inventors thought of their solutions. Then, invite students to practice tinkering and thinking to invent something that would make their lives easier, safer, or more fun. To begin, engage them in a conversation about how Philo Farnsworth tinkered with machine parts to help imagine how to make it easier to wash clothes or how he might make a television (which essentially is a radio with moving pictures). Students will create an invention of their choice using household or recyclable materials in a mini–makerspace in the classroom. This classroom makerspace can include any safe materials you can gather. We have indicated some simple craft items in the materials list, but you might also include electric components (e.g., magnets, wires, bells, or bulbs) to extend students' knowledge of electric circuitry and invite students to bring additional materials from home.

We encourage you to be open to the idea that anything a child sees as a potential design material is allowable, provided it is safe to use. This "anything-is-a-material" attitude encourages two things: (1) that teachers let go of controlling supplies and (2) that students invest more creativity and ingenuity in the making process. (Manage safety precautions by controlling the tools and how students use materials. For example, you could act as the hot-glue-gun operator or the cutter of heavy cardboard.) Activities in makerspaces can be very different from routine classroom lessons. In makerspaces, teachers organize processes and materials to help structure students' freewheeling problem solving and guide students toward

SCIENTISTS AND ENGINEERS ARE **THINKERS**—PHILO FARNSWORTH

**Philo Farnsworth**

a finished product that meets the lesson goals and objectives.

## Guided Reading

Ask students whether they have ever wondered how the television was invented. Inform students that they will be learning about inventions and the work of a scientist who was an especially good thinker by reading *The Boy Who Invented TV: The Story of Philo Farnsworth*. Introduce the book by asking, "What do you notice about the person on the front cover? What seems to be happening on the front cover?"

Read the story aloud. Encourage students to notice and think about the challenges Philo Farnsworth faced as a teenage scientist. Consider setting the context of the story by asking students to think about farm life in the early 1900s. Electricity was rare, as were phones and indoor bathrooms. There were no refrigerators or cars, no radio, and no television. The following questions may be used to guide

**EUREKA!** GRADE 3–5 **SCIENCE ACTIVITIES AND STORIES**   15

# 2
**ASKING QUESTIONS AND DEFINING PROBLEMS**

students' attention to detail as you read. (Page numbers reference unnumbered book pages, beginning with the title page as page 1.)

1. **Pages 4–6:** It seems that Philo Farnsworth began asking questions as soon as he learned to talk, but he didn't like school very much as a young boy. Why did Farnsworth like to skip school? *Farnsworth was the oldest child and had many chores (e.g., feeding the pigs, fetching firewood). At school, bullies teased him about his unusual name. He preferred to practice reading with his grandmother's Sears, Roebuck and Company catalog because it had toys and machines that used an invisible power called electricity.*

2. **Pages 12–13:** Farnsworth's family moved to Idaho when he was 11 years old. What two things pleased him about his new home in Idaho? *Farnsworth's new home had electricity. He found old* Popular Science *magazines in the attic and read about magnetism, electricity, and radios. With any spare change he got, he bought more magazines. He first saw the word* television *in these magazines.*

3. **Pages 14–15:** Soon, Farnsworth became the family's engineer. How did he become the family engineer? *Farnsworth watched the repairman fix their electric generator and "bombarded him with questions." Soon, Farnsworth taught himself how to fix the generator.*

4. **Pages 14–15:** Washing clothes was Farnsworth's least favorite chore. How did he modify the washing machine to make his life easier? *Farnsworth was a tinkerer—always messing around with wires, tools, and old or broken motors—which helped him invent gadgets to make his life easier (e.g., lights in the barn). To modify the washing machine, he attached a motor and pulley to the churning lever so it churned on its own, giving him more time to read.*

5. **Pages 18–19:** Farnsworth continued to wonder about the idea of making a television from the first day he read

## SCIENTISTS AND ENGINEERS ARE **THINKERS**—PHILO FARNSWORTH

about it in a science magazine. One day, while plowing a potato field, he had an inspiration. How did plowing a field inspire Farnsworth's idea about how to make a television? *Farnsworth was plowing in parallel rows and had time for thinking. The parallel furrows gave him the idea of breaking pictures down into parallel images of light; if the lines were seen quickly enough, people's eyes would be tricked into seeing pictures rather than lines.*

6. **Pages 20–31:** When Farnsworth reached high school, his chemistry teacher noticed that he "devoured books the way other students ate popcorn." Farnsworth hoped he had finally found someone who could understand the diagrams for his television idea, but his teacher understood only enough to encourage him to go to college. How did Farnsworth finally realize his invention of television? *Farnsworth was forced to quit college and return home to support his family after his father died. Here, he met his future wife, Pem Gardner, who encouraged him to pursue his television dream. He found investors for his invention who helped him build a laboratory, where he learned to make tube elements. At age 22, his television invention was announced in a newspaper article that identified him as a young genius for inventing a "revolutionary light machine."*

## Making Sense
### Explore

First, decide whether students are to work in groups or in pairs. Then, have students decide whether they will create a new invention to solve a problem or create a replica of an existing invention that solved a problem. Next, figure out a timeline for this project; this may range from a few days to a few weeks, depending on how much time you want to allow children to engage in the design process. The design process itself will be similar, but it would be better if students could focus their invention on a problem that needs a solution. Figure 2.1 shows an example of a classroom-developed engineering design process chart.

Next, help students develop a design cycle—a process of repeated

### Figure 2.1
**Example of an Engineering Design Process Chart Created in the Classroom**

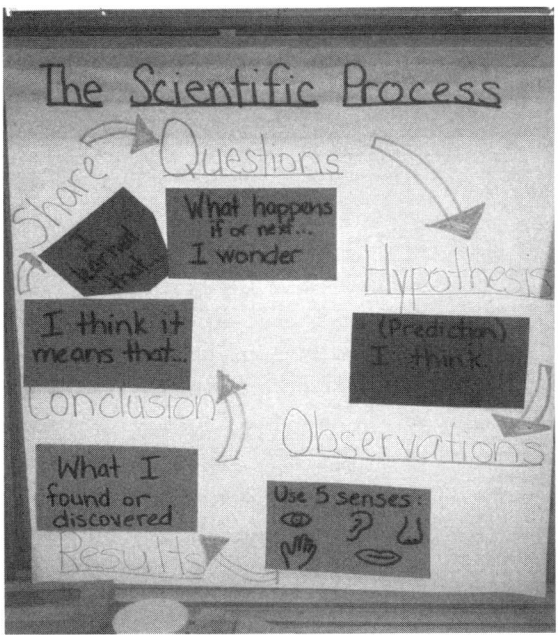

steps involving asking questions, inventing, testing, improving, and retesting. Ask students whether they are aware of the design cycle. If not, have them work in groups to generate a pictorial representation of the steps by which invention takes place. This can easily be done using sticky notes on a page in their science notebooks. When students are in groups, encourage them to answer this question: "What are the steps to creating something new?" Most students will benefit if you limit the number of steps to three or five. If students are struggling, have the whole class create a list of words that describe the invention process.

Prompt students to wonder whether a scientist or engineer makes an invention perfectly the very first time. Ask, "How do they know when it is perfect? What evidence do they have?" This will help students realize that revision is a natural part of the process. Your students will likely produce varying answers as they begin to think about the design process because there is no perfect model. The most important point here is the value of testing and revising.

## Explain

Once students have an idea of the steps in the design cycle, they will be ready to choose something to invent. Give each student a sticky note and then ask them to think about an invention they would like to see or one they have previously thought of. Provide ample time for each student to record an idea. Allow all ideas; for example, if a student suggests a machine to translate dog barks into English words. Place students in groups of four or five as they finish. Then, instruct students to share their ideas with their group members, and then select one of the ideas to work on. Prompt students to keep track of the problems they encounter as they work so they will be able to explain the critical decisions or improvements they made along the way. (The maker movement encourages students to actually tinker with objects and ideas until they build something unique—just as scientists and engineers do. These experiences allow students to improve their thinking skills and connect in-school learning to real-world applications.)

## Extend

Share other books with students that will help them recognize some of the inventions around them. *Steven Caney's Invention Book* (Caney 1985) will help students become familiar with common inventions in their everyday lives, from toothpaste to chocolate chip cookies. The book demonstrates ways to help get students into "an inventing frame of mind" and invites students to look at everyday objects in new ways. *Mistakes That Worked* (Jones 1994) will help students realize that many inventions were accidental or unintentional. Examples again include common everyday objects (e.g., donut holes, Frisbees, and leotards). To conclude the lesson, encourage students to choose inventions that interest them. Invite students to make an entry in their science notebooks to respond to the following prompts: "Draw and name

## Figure 2.2
### Examples of Student Inventions

(A)

(B)

(A) A student created a "storytelling" box that would allow her to produce her own stories (the child writes a story and pulls it through the television set). (B) A student developed a prototype for an oven with a large viewing window (so you can watch your food cook).

your chosen invention. How did questions and problems help the scientist or engineer think of this invention? How did this invention influence society?"

## Evaluate

Summative evaluation of this lesson will include assessment of students' understanding of (1) the character trait of being a thinker and (2) the design and function of their creative invention. See Figure 2.2 for examples of student inventions.

**CHARACTER TRAIT**

Encourage students to answer the following questions:

1. If Philo Farnsworth had not invented the television when he did, do you think someone else would have? *This question asks students to reflect on both the invention and the inventor, and there is no wrong or right answer.*

2. How would your life be different if the television had not been invented until 100 years later? *Although Farnsworth got the idea of television from an article in a science magazine, it was by being a thinker that led him to be the first person to figure out how to convert electric current into points of light. The point here is to review Farnsworth's invention of the television and his other engineering inventions through the lens of one character trait of scientists—that of being a thinker. It took a thinker to make this invention a reality and a necessity in just about everyone's home in a short period of time.*

# 2
## ASKING QUESTIONS AND DEFINING PROBLEMS

3. Recall a time when you were a thinker, and answer this question in your science notebook: "Why is being a thinker an important attribute for scientists to have, and how was Philo Farnsworth a thinker?" *Thinkers ask questions and wonder about possible solutions while others remain stuck in a seemingly impossible problem. As a thinker, Farnsworth came upon the main concept for his television invention while he was plowing rows in the field; his unusual solution was to create parallel lines of light using electricity instead of using a machine with moving parts inside.*

**CONTENT**

Students should be able to provide evidence as to what they created and how it would make their lives easier. Students might include illustrations and explanations in their science notebooks. You might provide formative feedback to your students throughout the lesson by encouraging them to be mindful of their own thinking skills throughout the invention design process and not to be discouraged through the test and retest sequences. At a specified time, prompt students to gather feedback from their peers on the design and function of their creative invention. Think about pairing students with one another to assess one another's experience with their makerspace inventions. Table 2.1 is a simple self-assessment rubric to help students provide feedback for one another. Table 2.2 is rubric you may use to assess your students' ability to ask questions as the practice describes. To plan a more extensive assessment of students' maker products, see Martinez and Stager (2013a).

### Table 2.1
### Method of Student Self-Assessment in the Thinking and Tinkering Lesson

| Question | Yes | No | Maybe/Unsure |
| --- | --- | --- | --- |
| Did I follow the design process? | | | |
| Does my invention perform a function? | | | |
| Does my invention solve a problem? | | | |
| Can my invention be improved? | | | |

Table 2.2

## Rubric for Assessing Students in the Thinking and Tinkering Lesson

| Content or Skill | Not Yet | Beginning | Developing | Secure |
|---|---|---|---|---|
| **Design Cycle** | Student did not participate in the discussion of the design cycle. | Student did not link his or her reasoning back to a design cycle. | Student linked his or her reasoning back to a design cycle. | Student linked his or her reasoning back to the evidence observed in class and correctly identified parts of the design cycle that are relevant. Student may recognize more than one cycle in the design process. |
| **Inventions** | Student did not create an invention. | Student's invention is still at the imagination level. | Student's invention is moving from imagination to evidence-based realities. | Student's invention was born from evidence-based realities and is a new item or replica that solves a problem. |
| **Asking Questions** | Student did not ask questions. | Student did not ask new evidence-based questions from the Explore phase. | Student asked new evidence-based questions from the Explore phase. | Student asked new evidence-based questions from the Explore phase and student has an idea about how to begin to answer these questions. |

## ASKING QUESTIONS AND DEFINING PROBLEMS

# SCIENTISTS AND ENGINEERS ARE
# INSPIRED

### Learning About **Thomas Edison**

Inspired (adj.): very good or clever; having a particular cause or influence

### Lesson: Edison's Three Questions
#### Description

In this lesson, students will ask Thomas Edison's three questions at four learning stations that are focused on different forms of energy (light, sound, heat, and electrical).

### Objectives

Students will consider how the character trait of *being inspired* helped Edison create uses for electricity and gain experience with forms of energy. Edison's three questions will shape students' observations with each investigation.

- At the beginning of the lesson, students will observe a demonstration of the relationship between temperature and energy.

- Students will hear the story *Young Thomas Edison* by Michael Dooling and discuss how the word *inspired* describes this scientist's character.

- Students will explore four different activity stations to infer the relationships among the energy forms from their observations across the stations.

- As a class, students will discuss how the activities at each station demonstrate a different form of energy. To conclude the lesson, students will (1) create an additional exploration of one of the aforementioned energy forms (sound, heat, light, electrical) following the model of Edison's three questions or (2) read *The Inventor's Secret: What Thomas Edison Told Henry Ford* to learn how scientists and engineers move beyond their mistakes as inventors.

SCIENTISTS AND ENGINEERS ARE **INSPIRED**—THOMAS EDISON

### Learning Outcomes

Students will (1) discuss what it means to be inspired and why being inspired is an important attribute for scientists and engineers and (2) explain how each of these activities demonstrates a form of energy or capacity for doing work.

## Connections to the *NGSS* and the Nature of Science, Grades 3–5

### Disciplinary Core Ideas

**PS3.A: DEFINITIONS OF ENERGY**

- Energy can be moved from place to place by moving objects or through sound, light, or electric currents.

**PS3.B: CONSERVATION OF ENERGY AND ENERGY TRANSFER**

- Energy is present whenever there are moving objects, sound, light, or heat. When objects collide, energy can be transferred from one object to another, thereby changing their motion. In such collisions, some energy is typically also transferred to the surrounding air; as a result, the air gets heated and sound is produced.
- Light also transfers energy from place to place.
- Energy can also be transferred from place to place by electric currents, which can then be used locally to produce motion, sound, heat, or light. The currents may have been produced to begin with by transforming the energy of motion into electrical energy.

**PS4.A: WAVE PROPERTIES**

- <u>Waves, which are regular patterns of motion, can be made in water by disturbing the surface.</u> When waves move across the surface of deep water, the water goes up and down in place; there is no net motion in the direction of the wave except when the water meets a beach. (Note: This grade band endpoint was moved from K–2.)

### Science and Engineering Practice

*Asking Questions and Defining Problems:* A practice of science is to ask and refine questions that lead to descriptions and explanations of how the natural and designed world works and which can be empirically tested. Asking questions and defining problems in grades 3–5 builds from grades K–2 experiences and progresses to specifying qualitative relationships.

- Ask questions that can be investigated and predict reasonable outcomes based on patterns such as cause and effect relationships.
- Use prior knowledge to describe problems that can be solved.

## Crosscutting Concepts

*Energy and Matter:* Tracking energy and matter flows, into, out of, and within systems helps one understand their system's behavior.

- Energy can be transferred in various ways and between objects.

*Cause and Effect:* Events have causes, sometimes simple, sometimes multifaceted. Deciphering causal relationships, and the mechanisms by which they are mediated, is a major activity of science and engineering.

- Cause and effect relationships are routinely identified, tested, and used to explain change.

## Nature of Science Connections
### SCIENTIFIC INVESTIGATIONS USE A VARIETY OF METHODS

- Science methods are determined by questions.
- Science investigations use a variety of methods, tools, and techniques.

### SCIENCE IS A WAY OF KNOWING

- Science is both a body of knowledge and processes that add new knowledge.
- Science is a way of knowing that is used by many people.

### SCIENCE IS A HUMAN ENDEAVOR

- Men and women from all cultures and backgrounds choose careers as scientists and engineers.
- Science affects everyday life.
- Creativity and imagination are important to science.

*Source:* NGSS Lead States 2013.

*Note:* When an activity supports only part of a standard, underlining indicates the relevant part.

# SCIENTISTS AND ENGINEERS ARE **INSPIRED**—THOMAS EDISON

**Thomas Edison**

## Overview

In this lesson, students consider the four ways energy can be transferred from place to place: sound, light, heat, and electric current. Thomas Edison shared his electrical inventions with others, which profoundly changed how people lived. Through reading the featured book, students learn that men and women from all backgrounds choose careers as scientists. The character trait of being inspired references Edison's urge to imagine new inventions. Students share ideas about whether scientists are inventors or inventors are scientists.

## Materials

You will need a copy of the book *Young Thomas Edison* by Michael Dooling (ISBN 978-0823418688). Each student will need his or her science notebook and a copy of the Edison's Three Questions Worksheet (provided later). For the activity

# 2 ASKING QUESTIONS AND DEFINING PROBLEMS

stations, you will need a set of Station Activity Cards (provided later) and the following materials:

- **Station 1:** A tuning fork, a transparent cup filled halfway with room-temperature water, indirectly vented chemical splash goggles, and nonlatex aprons

- **Station 2:** A laser light (pointer), a transparent cup filled with room-temperature water, 1 tsp of milk, indirectly vented chemical splash goggles, and nonlatex aprons

- **Station 3:** A spoon, a transparent cup filled with warm water, a metal spoon, indirectly vented chemical splash goggles, and nonlatex aprons

- **Station 4:** A battery, a lightbulb, two wires, and safety glasses or goggles

## Safety Notes

(1) Personal protective equipment should be worn during the setup, hands-on, and takedown segments of the activity. (2) Use caution when working with sharps (scissors, wires, and so on). They can cut or puncture skin. (3) Immediately wipe up spilled water—it creates a slip-and-fall hazard. (4) Use caution when working with lightbulbs—they can get hot and burn skin. They are also fragile and can cut skin if broken. (5) Use caution when working with a laser pointer—never point in eyes. Laser light can damage eyes! Also be careful of laser light reflecting off other objects. (6) Wash hands with soap and water upon completing this activity. *Teachers:* **Some states prohibit the use of laser pointers in schools. Check with the State Department of Education for regulations.**

## Setting the Context
### Engage

This part of the lesson introduces the "Edison Three" (the three questions Thomas Edison's mother encouraged him to ask: "What is this?" "Why does it happen?" and "How does it happen?"). Encourage students to answer these questions as well as they can so they focus on their observations and begin to hypothesize about what they observe. Correct answers are not important at this stage; rather, students' responses will tell you about their prior experiences with and knowledge of heat energy.

Begin the lesson with the following demonstration. Fill one transparent cup with warm water and another with cold water. Do not tell students which is which. Invite students to the front of the room to observe as you add two drops of red food coloring to the warm water and two drops of blue food coloring to the cold water.

# SCIENTISTS AND ENGINEERS ARE INSPIRED—THOMAS EDISON

## Figure 2.3

### Engage Phase Demonstration to Observe the Flow of Energy in Hot and Cold Water

The red water (*left*) is warm and the blue water (*right*) is cool. Help students visualize this heat energy principle by letting them know you purposely used red coloring in the cup of warm water (i.e., think red-hot, like an electric stove burner or fire ember).

Students will observe that the red color disperses more rapidly in the warm water than the blue color does in the cold water (see Figure 2.3). Temperature is a measure of the amount of energy in a substance, which affects the amount of movement by the particles making up the substance. Thus, particles move more quickly at higher temperatures than at lower temperatures. In the demonstration, the particles in the food coloring come to the same temperature as the water they are dropped in, so those dropped in the warm water move more quickly than those in the cold water.

## Guided Reading

Inform students that they will be learning about inventions and the work of an inspired scientist by reading *Young Thomas Edison*. Introduce the book by asking "What do you notice about the person on the front cover?" and "What does it look like is happening on the front cover?" Read the story aloud. Encourage students to notice and think about the challenges Thomas Edison faced as a scientist. The following questions may be used to guide students' attention to detail as you read. (Page numbers reference unnumbered book pages, beginning with the title page as page 1.)

1. **Page 4:** When Thomas Edison was a young boy, he set up a chemistry lab in his family home. He would mix a little of this and a little of that, sometimes following experiments in his chemistry book. What three questions did Edison's mother always encourage him to ask? *Edison's mother encouraged him to ask the questions "What is this?" "Why does it happen?" and "How does it happen?"*

2. **Pages 6–9:** Thomas Edison was not a good student in elementary school. Why do you think Edison did not do well in school? *The author suggests two possibilities. One is that a bout of scarlet fever had left Edison hard of hearing, so he didn't ask many questions at school (although he asked many at home). Another is that Edison was a daydreamer in school and was always in trouble for one reason or another. Edison's mother believed this was because he was a genius and school was not challenging enough for him; when he*

## 2 ASKING QUESTIONS AND DEFINING PROBLEMS

*was made to sit in the corner for misbehaving one day, she withdrew him from school and taught him at home.*

3. **Pages 10–17:** At age 12, Thomas Edison decided to look for a job. How did he earn money as a teenager? *Edison became a paperboy on the train. He could sell papers in the morning and evening and read books in the library in between. Eventually, he was able to set up a laboratory in a baggage car on the train.*

4. **Pages 24–29:** Once Thomas Edison had decided to become an inventor, he continued to set up laboratories as he moved across the country. Why do you think people nicknamed him "The Wizard"? *Edison earned this nickname when he began to patent strange and wonderful inventions (e.g., the carbon transmitter, the phonograph, and the lightbulb). By the age of 84, Edison had patented 1,093 inventions.*

### Figure 2.4
### Example of a Student Science Notebook Entry

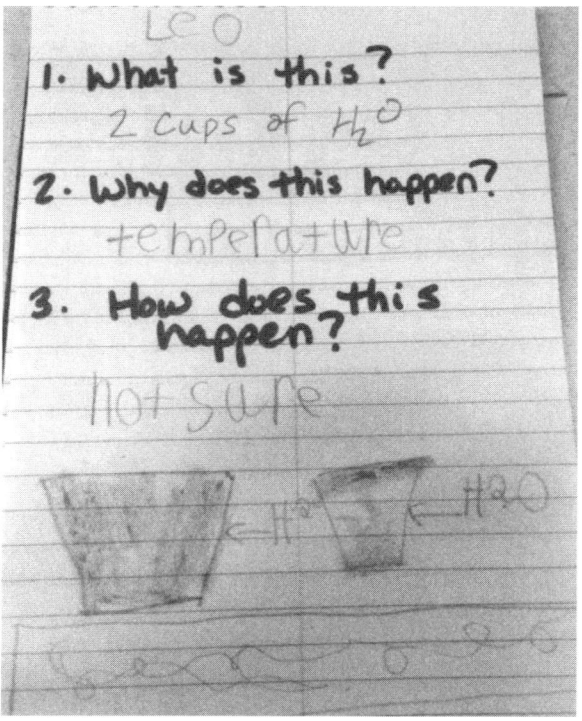

Science notebook entries for this activity might include an illustration of the two cups, with pictures and labels, as well as thoughtful responses to Edison's three questions.

Invite students to record their observations in their science notebooks, focusing on Edison's three questions. Key things to look for in their science notebook entries are (1) whether the student answered all three questions and (2) whether there is a diagram. Figure 2.4 shows an example of a student science notebook entry.

Encourage students to create a picture with words. By drawing lines to show what the words mean, students are creating a model. Use this opportunity to discuss how important models are to science and how scientists might use models in their work.

SCIENTISTS AND ENGINEERS ARE **INSPIRED**—THOMAS EDISON

## Making Sense
### Explore
In the Explore phase, students have opportunities to focus on answering Edison's three questions at each of four stations at which different forms of energy are demonstrated (sound, light, heat, and electrical). Students will perform the activity as a group at each station and then individually complete the Edison's Three Questions Worksheet (Figure 2.5, p. 30). Print the Activity Station Cards (Figure 2.6, p. 31) and laminate them if possible. Place one card at each station with the corresponding station materials (see "Materials," p. 25) for students to read when their group arrives at that station. The teacher should circulate among the stations to answer students' questions. The time allotted for each station should be based on the total class time available, less a 10-minute introduction and a 10-minute closure for the lesson.

**Station 1:** Set up a tuning fork and a transparent cup filled halfway with room-temperature water and a tuning fork. Students should tap the tuning fork on a book (or their forearm) and then dip it in the water.

**Station 2:** Set up a transparent cup of room-temperature water to which 1 tsp of milk has been added and provide a laser light (e.g., a laser pointer). Students should shine the light through the liquid in the cup.

**Station 3:** Set up a cup of warm water and two metal teaspoons that are at room temperature. Students should feel one spoon before and after placing it in the water. The other spoon should be kept at room temperature and serves as the control.

**Station 4:** Depending on the number of students in each group, provide three or four sets of materials, each containing a lightbulb, a battery, and two wires. Students should try to make the bulb light up.

### Explain
For each station, students should be able to provide evidence of what they saw and why it happened. (See the worksheet, Figure 2.5, p. 30.) Students might complete the station activities over several days. The following guides will help to prompt students' thinking about their observations.

**Station 1:** Students will see ripples in the water when they dip the activated tuning fork into the cup of water. They will observe sound energy being transferred from place to place in the form of vibration that causes waves in the cup of water.

**Station 2:** Two observations by students are possible: (1) that the light beam does not bend (refract) when the laser is pointed straight down into the water and (2) that the

# 2 ASKING QUESTIONS AND DEFINING PROBLEMS

Figure 2.5

Name: _____

# EDISON'S THREE QUESTIONS WORKSHEET

Figure 2.5 is available for download in larger formats at *www.nsta.org/eureka*.

### Station 1

1. What is it?

2. Why does this happen?

3. How does this happen?

What form of energy are we observing?

### Station 2

1. What is it?

2. Why does this happen?

3. How does this happen?

What form of energy are we observing?

### Station 3

1. What is it?

2. Why does this happen?

3. How does this happen?

What form of energy are we observing?

### Station 4

1. What is it?

2. Why does this happen?

3. How does this happen?

What form of energy are we observing?

SCIENTISTS AND ENGINEERS ARE **INSPIRED**—THOMAS EDISON

## Figure 2.6
## Activity Station Cards

Figure 2.6 is available for download in larger formats at *www.nsta.org/eureka*.

### Station 1

You have tuning forks of various sizes and several clear cups of room-temperature water. Tap the tuning fork on your forearm or a book and then touch it to the rim of the cup; what do you observe? Tap the tuning fork again and touch it to the surface of the water; what do you observe? Work with your group to explore and answer Edison's three questions. As a group, try to answer the question "What form of energy are we observing?" Record the answers on your Edison's Three Questions Worksheet.

### Station 2

You have laser pointers and several clear cups of room-temperature water. Shine the light through the water at an angle. What do you notice? Shine the light across the water at an even angle. What do you notice? As a group, try to answer question "What form of energy are we observing?" Record the answers on your Edison's Three Questions Worksheet.

### Station 3

You have two spoons and a cup of warm water. Feel both spoons at room temperature and discuss your observations with your group. Leave one spoon on the table and place one in the warm water. After five minutes, feel the part of the spoon that was in the water. What do you notice? Place that spoon back in the water. After ten minutes, feel the part of the spoon that was in the water. What do you notice? As a group, try to answer the question "What form of energy are we observing?" Record the answers on your Edison's Three Questions Worksheet.

### Station 4

You have two wires, a lightbulb, and a battery. Try to make the lightbulb light. What do you notice? As a group, try to answer the question "What form of energy are we observing?" Record the answers on your Edison's Three Questions Worksheet.

light beam refracts when the laser is shone through the water from one side of the cup and out the other. *The milk allows students to see the light beam more clearly.* Light travels at different speeds in different media (e.g., water versus air).

In (1), the light slows down when it hits the water surface because water is denser than air; however, because all of the light particles across the beam hit at the same time, they all slow at once and the beam does not refract. In (2), the beam refracts when it travels from the water to the air on the other side of the cup, where it gains speed (see Figure 2.7). The side of the cup is not directly parallel to the beam, so all the particles in the light beam do not enter the air at the same time, which causes it to bend. Note that part of the light is reflected when it hits the surface of the water, so the beam appears dimmer when it exits the cup.

Refraction can also be seen by putting a pencil in the cup of water; when viewed from the side, the pencil will appear to break in half at the surface of the water.

## Figure 2.7

### Light Beam Experiment

Part of the light beam is reflected when a laser light is aimed at an upward angle into the side of a cup of water (with a little milk added to help make the beam visible). The beam is refracted as it exits the water and continues on (evident here by the dot of red light on the opposite side of the cup).

**Station 3:** Students will feel that the metal spoon is warmer after being in the warm water and so observe that heat travels. They can confirm the heat energy transferred from the water by comparing the temperature of the spoon that went into the water with the one that did not (the control at room temperature).

**Station 4:** Students will connect the battery and bulb to observe light. The increase in the temperature of the bulb (from the excited bulb filament) indicates that electrical energy is converted to both light energy and heat energy as it moves around the circuit.

## Extend

To conclude the lesson, invite students to create an additional exploration of one of the energy forms studied in this lesson. Have them follow a simplified scientific method, such as (1) ask a question, (2) make a hypothesis, (3) design an experiment to answer the question, and (4) discuss what was learned. This is one of several accepted scientific methods. Don't worry too much about the sequence because the process is more important here. The main point is to ask a question and come up with a simplified series of steps to find an answer to a particular question, and some students might begin with a question, whereas others might begin with an observation or a hypothesis. Think of this as a miniature science fair. Students love to do science experiments at home, and this extension encourages them to explore one of the forms of energy they experimented with in class.

As a reading extension, you could also share the book *The Inventor's Secret: What Thomas Edison Told Henry Ford* (Slade 2015; ISBN 978-1580896672). In that story, Thomas Edison shares the secret of an inventor's success with a young Henry Ford. Ford dreamed of creating a motorized car, but his engine designs were a flop. He was frustrated, and he wondered how Thomas Edison had earned so many patents. They met one day, and Thomas Edison shared his secret. This true story is touching and motivational!

## Evaluate

Summative evaluation of this lesson will include assessment of students' understanding of (1) the character trait of being inspired and (2) how each of the four station activities demonstrates a form of energy or capacity for doing work.

### CHARACTER TRAIT

Encourage students to answer the following questions:

1. If Thomas Edison hadn't invented the electric lightbulb, the phonograph, or the motion picture, do you think someone else would have? How was it possible for Edison to invent so many items? Is there some relationship among these inventions? *Although others might eventually have thought of all these ways to use electricity, it is unusual that they were all developed by the same person. Thomas Edison was inspired, and he thought of these things before anyone else did. The point here is to review Edison's lightbulb and other electrical engineering inventions through the lens of one character trait of scientists—that of being inspired.*

2. Why is being inspired an important character trait for scientists to have? How was Thomas Edison inspired? *Inspired people are clever and dedicated to thinking of innovative ideas. Thomas Edison was first inspired by his mother's encouragement to ask questions, read, and dream about his next experiment. Although he sold newspapers on the train, he usually carried a book about his next experimental idea in his pocket. He even set up a laboratory at the back of the railway station so he could experiment in his off hours.*

## 2 ASKING QUESTIONS AND DEFINING PROBLEMS

3. Choose a partner and tell each other about a time you were inspired.

**CONTENT**

Students should be able to describe what happens when each of the four forms of energy is transferred from place to place and how each station demonstrated a type of energy. You might create a rubric like the one in Table 2.3 to assist you in evaluating their verbal and written work. Scientific accuracy for the four stations includes the following:

**Station 1:** Understanding that sound energy is a vibration that caused the movement of water in the cup.

**Station 2:** Understanding that light energy was reflected when it hit the surface of the water and refracted (bent) when it passed from water (denser matter) to air (less dense matter).

**Station 3:** Understanding that heat energy traveled from the warm water to the metal spoon.

**Station 4:** Understanding that metal (the wires) conducted electricity, which caused the bulb to light. Some students may also know or learn that these activities introduce the properties and behaviors of kinetic energy.

It is important for students to develop some understanding that each station introduced a form of energy: sound, light, heat, or electrical. The takeaway is that there are several forms of energy. Look for evidence in their science journal writing of a new awareness that energy can be present in different forms.

Table 2.3

### Method of Evaluating Students' Verbal and Written Work in the Edison's Three Questions Activity

| Station | Communicated observations orally with minimal scientific accuracy | Communicated observations either orally or in writing with scientific accuracy | Communicated observations both orally and in writing with scientific accuracy |
| --- | --- | --- | --- |
| Station 1: Sound energy | | | |
| Station 2: Light energy | | | |
| Station 3: Heat energy | | | |
| Station 4: Electrical energy | | | |

# SCIENTISTS AND ENGINEERS ARE DILIGENT

## Learning About **George Washington Carver**

Diligent (adj.): applying a constant effort to accomplish something; attentive and persistent in doing something

### Lesson: How Are Fruits and Vegetables Different?

**Description**

In this lesson, students will become familiar with six plant parts as they explore the differences between fruits and vegetables.

## Objectives

Students will think about how the character trait of *diligence* helped George Washington Carver develop peanut butter and many other substances and understand how the different parts or structures of plants help them grow, survive, behave, and reproduce.

- Before beginning the lesson, students will describe the difference between a fruit and a vegetable and will observe the anatomy of a lima bean.

- Students will hear the story *A Picture Book of George Washington Carver* by David A. Adler and discuss how it relates to being diligent.

- Students will categorize fruits and vegetables while learning the six edible parts of a plant.

- To conclude the lesson, students will dissect a variety of fruits and think about how various seed adaptations might be an advantage to a plant.

# 2 ASKING QUESTIONS AND DEFINING PROBLEMS

## Learning Outcomes

Students will (1) make a science notebook entry to explain what it means to be diligent and why being diligent is an important trait for scientists and engineers and (2) create a sorting activity to build a model of the edible parts or structures of plants and describe the supportive function of these plant parts to the overall plant.

## Connections to the *NGSS* and the Nature of Science, Grades 3–5

### Disciplinary Core Idea
#### LS1.A: STRUCTURE AND FUNCTION

- Plants and animals have both internal and external structures that serve various functions in growth, survival, behavior, and reproduction.

### Science and Engineering Practices

***Asking Questions and Defining Problems:*** A practice of science is to ask and refine questions that lead to descriptions and explanations of how the natural and designed world works and which can be empirically tested. Asking questions and defining problems in grades 3–5 builds from grades K–2 experiences and progresses to specifying qualitative relationships.

- Ask questions that can be investigated and predict reasonable outcomes based on patterns such as cause and effect relationships.

***Developing and Using Models:*** A practice of both science and engineering is to use and construct models as helpful tools for representing ideas and explanations. These tools include diagrams, drawings, physical replicas, mathematical representations, analogies, and computer simulations. Modeling in 3–5 builds on K–2 experiences and progresses to building and revising simple models and using models to represent events and design solutions.

- Develop a model using an analogy, example, or abstract representation to describe a scientific principle or design solution.

### Crosscutting Concept

***Structure and Function:*** The way an object is shaped or structured determines many of its properties and functions.

- Different materials have different substructures, which can sometimes be observed.
- Substructures have shapes and parts that serve functions.

SCIENTISTS AND ENGINEERS ARE **DILIGENT**—GEORGE WASHINGTON CARVER

**Nature of Science Connections**

**SCIENCE MODELS, LAWS, MECHANISMS, AND THEORIES EXPLAIN NATURAL PHENOMENA**

- Science theories are based on a body of evidence and many tests.
- Science explanations describe the mechanisms for natural events.

**SCIENCE IS A WAY OF KNOWING**

- Science is both a body of knowledge and processes that add new knowledge.
- Science is a way of knowing that is used by many people.

**SCIENCE IS A HUMAN ENDEAVOR**

- Men and women from all cultures and backgrounds choose careers as scientists and engineers.
- Science affects everyday life.

*Source*: NGSS Lead States 2013.

## Overview

In this lesson, students learn the difference between a fruit and a vegetable while studying the anatomy of a lima bean. Through the featured book, students learn that men and women from all backgrounds choose careers as scientists. The character trait of being diligent references George Washington Carver's consistent and creative attempts to use peanuts to develop new products. Students share ideas about the struggles they notice Carver faced as an African American.

## Materials

You will need one copy of the book *A Picture Book of George Washington Carver* by David A. Adler (ISBN 978-0823416332); 6 to 12 fresh fruits and vegetables, including a tomato, that represent the six possible plant parts; and dried, large lima beans (at least one per student). For best results, soak the lima beans in water overnight to improve the ability to split the seed open and view the embryo. Provide each student group with an Edible Plant Parts Diagram, an Umbrella Template, and a Raindrops Template. (Templates are provided later.) You will also need one hand lens and paper towels for each group of four or five students and a nonlatex apron for each student.

# 2 ASKING QUESTIONS AND DEFINING PROBLEMS

## Safety Notes
(1) Personal protective equipment should be worn during the setup, hands-on, and takedown segments of the activity. (2) Immediately wipe up spilled water—it creates a slip-and-fall hazard. (3) Remember to never eat any food used in lab activities! (4) Wash hands with soap and water upon completing this activity.

## Setting the Context
### Engage
Hold up or pass around a fresh tomato for the class to observe. Ask students whether it is a fruit or a vegetable. Then, ask them whether they know the difference between a fruit and a vegetable. Record their answers on paper or on the board so you can return to these ideas at the close of the lesson. *We purposely introduced this lesson with a tomato because students will likely say it is a vegetable (and this is certainly what it is commonly called); however, a tomato is a fruit because fruits have seeds and a tomato has seeds.* Explain to the students that they will revisit these ideas later in the lesson.

### Guided Reading
Introduce the book *A Picture Book of George Washington Carver* by asking "What appears to be happening on the front cover?" Read the story aloud. Encourage students to notice and think about the additional challenges George Washington Carver faced as an African American scientist. The following questions may be used to guide students' attention to detail as you read. (Page numbers reference unnumbered book pages, beginning with the title page as page 1.)

1. **Pages 6–11:** George Washington Carver was raised not by his mother and father but by two families who saw to his early learning. How did he get interested in plants as a young boy? *Carver's owners did not make him work as hard as other slaves, so he had time to learn about flowers in the nearby woods. When he went to the African American school, he learned about medicinal plants and herbs from his "Aunt" Mariah.*

2. **Pages 4–5 and 10–11:** As a slave born sometime near the end of the Civil War, George Washington Carver experienced considerable prejudice. What prejudicial tragedies marked his young life? *Night raiders separated him from his mother when he was an infant. Later, he witnessed a mob of masked white men hang and burn a black prisoner they had pulled out of jail. This memory haunted Carver for the rest of his life.*

3. **Pages 14–17:** George Washington Carver graduated from high school and wanted to go to college. Why did he have trouble getting into college? *He was*

*accepted at Highland University; however, when he arrived, he was told he could not attend the school because he was black. He later was accepted at Iowa State College, where he studied agriculture. He was that school's first African American student and went on to become its first African American teacher.*

4. **Pages 18–22:** When he moved to Alabama, George Washington Carver devoted his life to improving the lives of Southerners, especially African Americans. When cotton production began to fail, he discovered the benefits of growing peanuts and sweet potatoes and developed 300 peanut products and more than 100 sweet-potato products. Why did Carver not accept money for these ideas? *Carver believed in the goodness of all people and that successful African American people should become models who could transform others' racial prejudices.*

5. **Pages 26–29:** George Washington Carver won many awards for his research. The featured book says he is known for saying, "Know science and science shall set you free, because science is truth." How was asking questions important to his work? *From the time he was a young boy, Carver wanted to learn, even when his only book was a spelling book he had memorized. His persistent questions about plants encouraged him to keep trying to find a way to go to school. His questions about how to improve the lives of Southern cotton farmers led to his notable discoveries that are still influential today.*

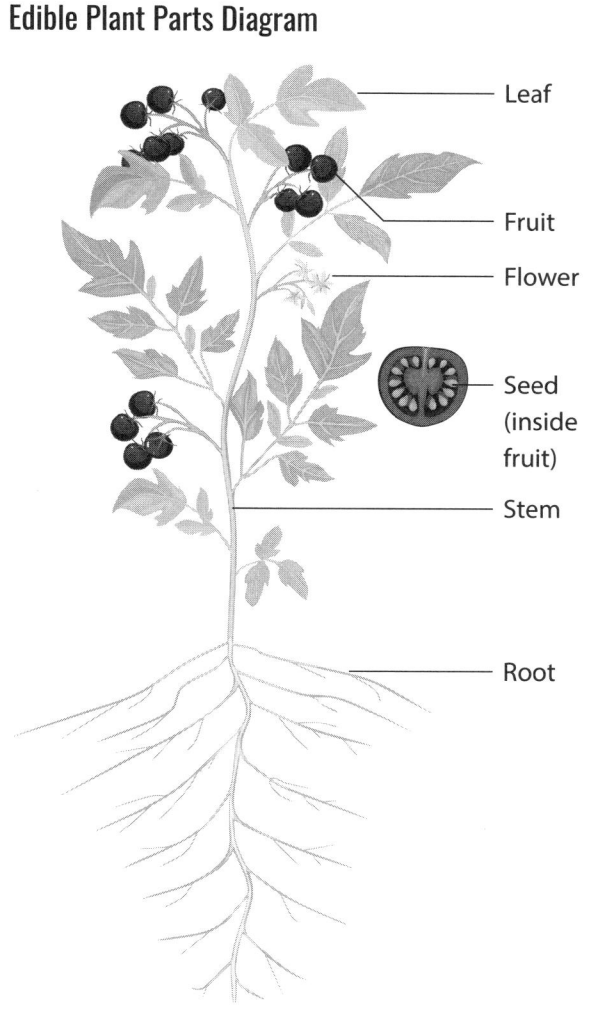

Figure 2.8

**Edible Plant Parts Diagram**

# 2 ASKING QUESTIONS AND DEFINING PROBLEMS

**George Washington Carver**

## Making Sense
### Explore

Lay out a collection of fresh vegetables and give each student group a copy of the Edible Plant Parts Diagram (Figure 2.8, p. 39). Project the Edible Plant Parts Diagram or sketch a similar diagram on the board. Ask students to think about the parts of the plant that we eat. For example, ask, "When we eat lettuce, what part of the plant are we actually eating?" *We are eating the leaves.* Ask students, "Why do plants have leaves? What is their purpose for a plant?" *The purpose of leaves is to gather energy from sunlight. The leaf uses the energy it collects to make food for the plant through the process of photosynthesis.*

Label the leaf on the displayed Edible Plant Parts Diagram. Ask students to think of other leaves that we eat. *They may suggest cabbage.* Ask them how leaves help plants to survive. *If plants did not have leaves, they would not be able to collect the sun's energy and thus would be unable to produce food through photosynthesis.* **Continue**

SCIENTISTS AND ENGINEERS ARE **DILIGENT**—GEORGE WASHINGTON CARVER

Figure 2.9

**Umbrella Template**

Figure 2.9 is available for download in a larger format at *www.nsta.org/eureka*.

by helping students think about the important roles that the other parts of the plant have in supporting plant functions of growth, survival, behavior, and reproduction.

When the displayed plant diagram is complete, write or project the following statement on the board: "All vegetables are plants, but not all plants are vegetables." Ask students whether that statement is true, and encourage them to provide evidence to support or refute it. Invite them to work in groups of four to five to decide whether they can support the statement. Give each group an Umbrella Template (Figure 2.9) and a set of raindrops (Raindrop Template, Figure 2.10, p. 42). Write "edible plant

# 2 ASKING QUESTIONS AND DEFINING PROBLEMS

### Figure 2.10
### Raindrops Template

Figure 2.10 is available for download in a larger format at *www.nsta.org/eureka*.

### Figure 2.11
### Example of a Completed Umbrella

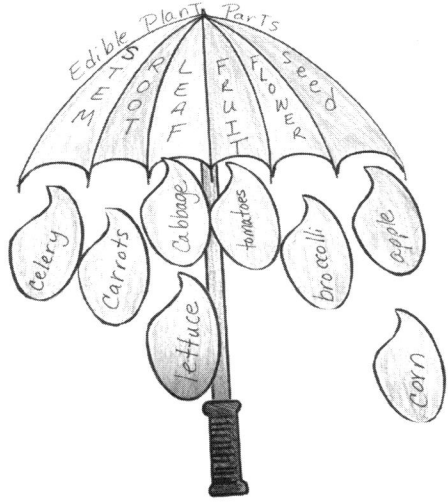

parts" at the top of the displayed edible plant parts diagram and ask students to work cooperatively in their groups to show how this phrase might be used as an umbrella term for the six edible parts of a plant.

Student groups should write the six plant parts on their umbrella handout. Then, as they discuss the evidence and decide on their agreement (or not) with the statement on the board, beneath each labeled section of their umbrella, the groups should put a raindrop labeled with an example plant whose labeled part we eat. (Figure 2.11 shows an example of a completed umbrella.) Allow students enough time to place all of their raindrops.

### Explain

Refer again to the plant diagram showing the six edible parts of plants. Invite students to share their ideas about the truth of the statement you placed on the board earlier. Explain that scientists classify vegetables differently than we (nonscientists) often do. For example, according to the scientific classification, vegetables do not contain seeds. Invite students to think about why seeds are an important part of the plant. Student responses should include something about reproduction, such as that another plant cannot be produced without the genetic material (ovaries). Tell students you will now give each of them a part of a plant and they are to determine what plant part it is.

Provide students in each group with lima beans (previously soaked overnight), a hand lens, and paper towels. Lima beans are inexpensive and readily available, so it is desirable to provide each student with his or her own lima bean; however, if you have a limited quantity of beans, one bean per group will suffice. Task students with identifying the name of this plant

SCIENTISTS AND ENGINEERS ARE **DILIGENT**—GEORGE WASHINGTON CARVER

part and, going around the room, keep asking, "How do you know?" In addition, ask questions along the way, such as "Is it a leaf?" to encourage students to use a process of elimination until they determine that a lima bean is a seed.

Once students come to this determination, ask them what evidence they found that the lima bean is a seed. They can check their hypothesis by looking for a tiny plant growing inside. They should notice an almost translucent layer covering the lima bean. Ask students whether they know what that is and what purpose it serves. It is the seed coat that protects the seed until it is ready to germinate. Then, have students carefully remove the seed coat, break apart the two halves of the lima bean, and use their hand lenses to observe the tiny embryo (i.e., the rudimentary leaves and root of a lima bean, as shown in Figure 2.12).

Figure 2.12

Lima Bean Plant Embryo in a Lima Bean Seed

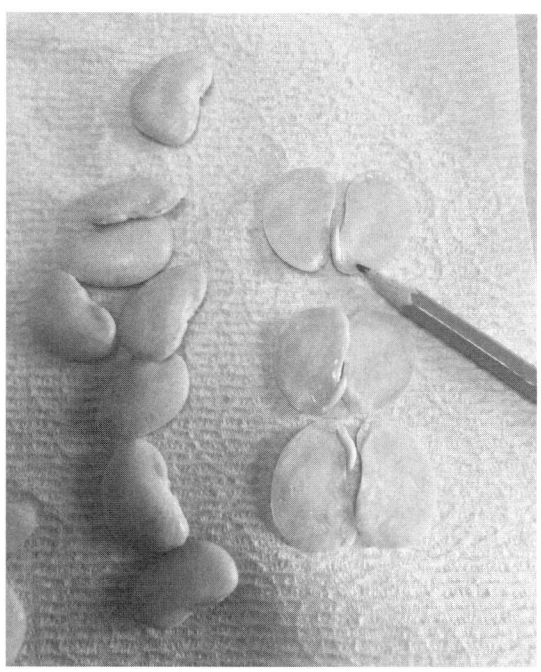

Revisit the question in the "Engage" section (p. 38) asking whether a tomato is a fruit or a vegetable. According to scientists, fruits are the seed-bearing part of a plant, so all fruits have seeds; therefore, tomatoes—which have seeds—are fruits, as are cucumbers, squash, green beans, and pumpkins, even though nonscientists refer to them as vegetables. For most fruits, the seeds are inside, but for some fruits, such as strawberries, they are on the outside. Vegetables, as classified by scientists, are the other edible parts of a plant and are usually grouped according to which plant part is eaten—for example, the leaves (lettuce), stem (celery), roots (carrot), and flowers (broccoli).

## Extend

Encourage students to bring in a fruit to class to dissect (or open) to view the seeds. *To ensure having a wide variety of fruits to encourage students' thinking, you might want to bring in some yourself to augment the students' collection.* Ask, "How are these seeds similar or different?" "Do all fruits have the same number of seeds?" and "How might a seed's characteristics and structures work to the advantage of a plant?" *Help students to think how fruits protect the seeds until they germinate and grow into new plants.* Ask, "Do all plants produce the same number of fruits?" *Help students think about the number of apples on one tree versus the number of tomatoes on one plant. This question and conversation will help students hypothesize about why some plants need to produce more fruit (and thus more seeds).*

# 2  ASKING QUESTIONS AND DEFINING PROBLEMS

### Evaluate

Summative evaluation of this lesson will include assessment of students' understanding of why being diligent is an important character trait for scientists and engineers and how various edible plant parts support plant functions such as growth, survival, and reproduction.

**CHARACTER TRAIT**

Encourage students to answer the following questions:

1. If George Washington Carver had not developed uses for sweet potatoes or peanuts, do you think someone else would have? *Although others might have eventually thought of these ideas, George Washington Carver was diligent and did not rest until his persistent questioning produced results. The point here is to review George Washington Carver's agricultural discoveries through the lens of one scientist's character trait—that of being diligent.*

2. Why is being diligent an important attribute for scientists to have, and how was George Washington Carver diligent? *Diligent people are hardworking, persistent people who keep working until they find answers. In George Washington Carver's case, he overcame considerable personal tragedies as an African American by studying hard and working hard to improve the lives of Southerners, especially other African Americans.*

3. Choose a partner and tell each other about a time you were diligent or someone you know was diligent. *As an example, students may identify Barack Obama as someone who is diligent because he became our first African American president.*

4. Why is being diligent an important trait for scientists and engineers? Record your answer in your science notebook.

**CONTENT**

You might formatively assess students' increasing understanding of the structure and function of plant parts as students assemble their umbrella models. To summatively assess students' understanding of the structure and function of plant parts, invite students to list the six different edible plant parts in their science notebooks and write a descriptive sentence explaining how each plant part helps the plant grow, survive, or reproduce. Consider having students work in groups and use a notebook chart such as the one in Table 2.4. Table 2.5 provides a rubric for assessing students' models of edible plant parts and their understanding of how those parts support the overall plant.

## Table 2.4

**Chart for Student Science Notebooks to Communicate Concept Understanding**

| Edible Plant Part | Example | How the Plant Part Supports Plant Functions |
|---|---|---|
| Leaf | Lettuce in salad | Leaves collect energy from the sunlight. |
| Stem | | |
| Root | | |
| Flower | | |
| Fruit | | |
| Seed | | |

## Table 2.5

**Rubric for Assessing Student Understanding of How Fruits and Vegetables Are Different**

| Content | Not Yet | Beginning | Developing | Secure |
|---|---|---|---|---|
| Fruit or Vegetable Classification | Student did not participate. | Student linked one or two raindrops to the appropriate umbrella panel. | Student linked three to five raindrops to the appropriate umbrella panel. | Student linked all six raindrops to the appropriate umbrella panel and verbally explain why he or she placed each raindrop under its panel. |
| Edible Plant Part Notebook Chart | Student did not complete chart. | Student provided examples and sentences for one to two edible plant parts. | Student provided examples and sentences for three to five edible plant parts. | Student provided examples and sentences for all six edible plant parts. |

## ASKING QUESTIONS AND DEFINING PROBLEMS

### References

Adler, D. A. 2000. *A picture book of George Washington Carver.* New York: Holiday House.

Caney, S. 1985. *Steven Caney's invention book.* New York: Workman Publishing.

Dooling, M. 2014. *Young Thomas Edison.* New York: Holiday House.

Graves, C. 2015. *Starting a school makerspace from scratch.* Edutopia. *www.edutopia.org/blog/starting-school-makerspace-from-scratch-colleen-graves.*

Harlen, W. 2001. *Primary science: Taking the plunge.* 2nd ed. Portsmouth, NH: Heinemann.

Jones, C. 1994. *Mistakes that worked.* New York: Random House.

Krull, K. 2009. *The boy who invented TV: The story of Philo Farnsworth.* New York: Alfred A. Knopf.

Martinez, S. L., and G. S. Stager. 2013a. *Elements of a good maker project.* We Are Teachers. *www.weareteachers.com/blogs/post/2015/04/03/8-elements-of-a-good-maker-project.*

Martinez, S. L., and G. S. Stager. 2013b. *Making matters! How the maker movement is transforming education.* We Are Teachers. *www.weareteachers.com/blogs/post/2015/04/03/how-the-maker-movement-is-transforming-education.*

NGSS Lead States. 2013. *Next Generation Science Standards: For states, by states.* Washington, DC: National Academies Press. *www.nextgenscience.org/next-generation-science-standards.*

The White House. 2015. *Nation of makers. www.whitehouse.gov/nation-of-makers.*

### Additional Resource

Slade, S. 2015. *The inventor's secret: What Thomas Edison told Henry Ford.* Watertown, MA: Charlesbridge.

# 3

# Developing and Using Models

The practice of developing and using models is very important in science and engineering. This chapter focuses on three scientists who developed and used models for their work—Annie Jump Cannon, who developed a star classification system; George Washington Ferris Jr., who designed the Ferris wheel; and Gregor Mendel, who used the Punnett square to find patterns in inherited traits. Cannon's and Mendel's work improved our understanding of the natural world, and Ferris introduced a new opportunity for public entertainment. The words *imaginative, visionary,* and *patient* well describe the character traits of these scientists and engineers.

Science seeks to understand the way nature works. The *Next Generation Science Standards* (*NGSS*) say that science models include diagrams, physical replicas, mathematical representations, analogies, and computer simulations (NGSS Lead States 2013) in investigating that understanding. The goal of engineering is to develop solutions to problems, so engineering models test possible solutions to a problem and help to explain a system or understand where and under what conditions flaws might develop. Engineering models can also be used to visualize and refine a design, communicate a design's features to others, and explain a new prototype's design performance.

Models can often be the source of misconceptions (see Posner, Strike, Hewson, and Gertzog 1982), especially if students do not also have a direct experience with the "real thing." Models do not correspond exactly to the real world; rather, they provide a visual representation that explains a phenomenon or how something works. They have limitations, and students need opportunities to experience models to realize them. Students in grades 3–5 can learn to identify limitations of models by building and revising simple models and using a variety of models to represent phenomena and design solutions.

## Recommended Science Teaching Strategy: Graphic Organizers as Models

We like to teach students about the limitations of models sometime in the fall (or before winter break) because it's something we will reference throughout the rest of the year. All you need is a store-bought plastic model of any part of the human body. If your school lacks models, borrow one from a doctor or nurse for a short time. We have used models of a tongue, skin, and an ear, and they all worked equally well for teaching students about the limitations of models.

We begin by holding up a body-part model in front of the class and ask students to tell us what

# 3 DEVELOPING AND USING MODELS

it is. When they identify it, we probe for evidence as to why they have identified it as that body part. After students have had time to observe the model, we pass out mirrors and ask students to observe their corresponding body part. Then, we discuss the idea that a model is a representation, and we suggest that not everything about a model is exactly like the thing it represents. Next, we ask the students to provide several of their own observations about what is the same and what is different about the model and the real thing it represents. The point of this lesson is to encourage students, when they encounter a model, to ask themselves, "How is this model like the real thing, and how is it different?"

The first lesson in this chapter includes a foldable model. Foldables are a type of graphic organizer that students manipulate (Zike 2004). They are made primarily of paper and do not require any additional materials. Because using models can become expensive, we like to incorporate foldables throughout the year to reinforce models of all types. In the second lesson, students build a three-dimensional (3-D) model of a Ferris wheel. There is evidence that 3-D models assist students' visualization and cognitive processing of the lesson concepts in diverse science classrooms. For example, Bradley and Farland-Smith (2010) discuss the use of 3-D models to help science students who have a variety of learning disabilities and learning styles. In the third lesson, students build a model to show the random manner in which physical characteristics are passed down from one generation to the next and how siblings and their parents might or might not look alike.

# SCIENTISTS AND ENGINEERS ARE
# IMAGINATIVE

## Learning About **Annie Jump Cannon**

Imaginative (adj.): creative or having the ability to think of unique ideas

### Lesson: Starlight—Light From the Sun
### Description

In this lesson, students will learn about how scientist Annie Jump Cannon observed variations in the brightness of stars and explored behaviors of light from the Sun.

### Objectives

Students will consider how the character trait of *being imaginative* helped Annie Jump Cannon develop a classification system for stars and explore the nature of reflected light.

- Before starting the lesson, students will make a two-dimensional (2-D) foldable model of their place in the solar system.

- As a class, students will make a model to show the position of Earth and the solar system within the Milky Way galaxy.

- Students will hear the story *Annie Jump Cannon, Astronomer* by Carole Gerber and discuss how it relates to the word *imaginative*.

- Students will explore the behaviors and benefits of luminous and reflected light.

- To conclude the lesson, students will engage in a light-tag activity to further explore the behavior of reflected light.

# 3 DEVELOPING AND USING MODELS

### Learning Outcomes

Students will (1) make a science notebook entry to explain what it means to be imaginative and why being imaginative is an important trait for scientists and engineers and (2) demonstrate their understanding of the behavior and benefits of reflected light.

## Connections to the *NGSS* and the Nature of Science, Grades 3–5

### Disciplinary Core Ideas

#### ESS1.A: THE UNIVERSE AND ITS STARS

- The sun is a star that appears larger and brighter than other stars because it is closer. Stars range greatly in their distance from Earth.

#### PS3.B: CONSERVATION OF ENERGY AND ENERGY TRANSFER

- Energy is present whenever there are moving objects, sound, light, or heat. When objects collide, energy can be transferred from one object to another, thereby changing their motion. In such collisions, some energy is typically also transferred to the surrounding air; as a result, the air gets heated and sound is produced.

- Light also transfers energy from place to place.

#### PS4.B: ELECTROMAGNETIC RADIATION

- An object can be seen when light reflected from its surface enters the eyes.

### Science and Engineering Practices

***Asking Questions and Defining Problems:*** A practice of science is to ask and refine questions that lead to descriptions and explanations of how the natural and designed world works and which can be empirically tested. Asking questions and defining problems in grades 3–5 builds from grades K–2 experiences and progresses to specifying qualitative relationships.

- Ask questions that can be investigated and predict reasonable outcomes based on patterns such as cause and effect relationships.

- Define a simple design problem that can be solved through the development of an object, tool, process, or system and includes several criteria for success and constraints on materials, time, or cost.

***Developing and Using Models:*** A practice of both science and engineering is to use and construct models as helpful tools for representing ideas and explanations. These tools include diagrams, drawings, physical replicas, mathematical representations, analogies, and computer simulations. Modeling in 3–5 builds on K–2 experiences and progresses to building and revising simple models and using models to represent events and design solutions.

- Develop and/or use models to describe and/or predict phenomena.
- Use a model to test cause and effect relationships or interactions concerning the functioning of a natural or designed system.

## Crosscutting Concepts

***Patterns:*** Observed patterns in nature guide organization and classification and prompt questions about relationships and causes underlying them.

- Similarities and differences in patterns can be used to sort, classify, communicate and analyze simple rates of change for natural phenomena and designed products.
- Patterns can be used as evidence to support an explanation.

***Scale, Proportion, and Quantity:*** In considering phenomena, it is critical to recognize what is relevant at different size, time, and energy scales, and to recognize proportional relationships between different quantities as scales change.

- Natural objects and/or observable phenomena exist from the very small to the immensely large or from very short to very long time periods.
- Standard units are used to measure and describe physical quantities such as weight, time, temperature, and volume.

## Nature of Science Connections

**SCIENTIFIC INVESTIGATIONS USE A VARIETY OF METHODS**

- Science methods are determined by questions.
- Science investigations use a variety of methods, tools, and techniques.

**SCIENCE KNOWLEDGE IS BASED ON EMPIRICAL EVIDENCE**

- Science findings are based on recognizing patterns.
- Science uses tools and technologies to make accurate measurements and observations.

**SCIENCE IS A WAY OF KNOWING**

- Science is both a body of knowledge and processes that add new knowledge.

**SCIENCE IS A HUMAN ENDEAVOR**

- Men and women from all cultures and backgrounds choose careers as scientists and engineers.
- Most scientists and engineers work in teams.
- Creativity and imagination are important to science.

# 3 DEVELOPING AND USING MODELS

**SCIENCE ADDRESSES QUESTIONS ABOUT THE NATURAL AND MATERIAL WORLD**

- Science findings are limited to questions that can be answered with empirical evidence.

*Source:* NGSS Lead States 2013.

## Overview

In this lesson, students learn how Annie Jump Cannon invented a model for classifying stars based on the stars' temperatures and shared her classification system with others in her science community. This challenged the way people thought about female astronomers. Through the featured book, students learn that men and women from all backgrounds choose careers as scientists and engineers. The character trait *imaginative* references Cannon's meticulous and creative attempts to organize the starlight behaviors she observed. Students also share ideas about women being scientists. In the hands-on exploration, students explore the nature of reflected light.

## Materials

You will need supply of 9 in. × 14 in. or 8.5 in. × 11 in. colored paper in seven colors, enough for one color set for each student; and one copy of the featured book, *Annie Jump Cannon, Astronomer,* by Carole Gerber (ISBN 978-1589809116). Each group of students will need one rock, a cup of water, a piece of aluminum foil, a piece of white paper, and a small plastic bag. Each student will need a set of colored papers prepared ahead by the teacher, a glue stick, his or her science notebook, a flashlight, safety glasses or goggles, and a small acrylic mirror (e.g., 3 in. × 5 in.). *Note:* Acrylic mirrors minimize the safety risks of glass mirrors. Sheets of mirrored acrylic are available online and in most building supply stores and can be cut to any size.

## Safety Notes

(1) Personal protective equipment should be worn during the setup, hands-on, and takedown segments of the activity. (2) Immediately wipe up spilled water—it creates a slip-and-fall hazard. (3) Wash hands with soap and water upon completing this activity.

# SCIENTISTS AND ENGINEERS ARE **IMAGINATIVE**—ANNIE JUMP CANNON

## Setting the Context
### Engage

Ask students whether they have ever wondered how humans fit in the universe; that is, where we are relative to galaxies, the universe, and the solar system. Ask, "Which is larger, a galaxy, the universe, or a solar system?" Help students build a model of the universe so they appreciate how they actually fit into the big picture.

### Figure 3.1

**Example of a Student's Stacked-Paper Model of the Universe**

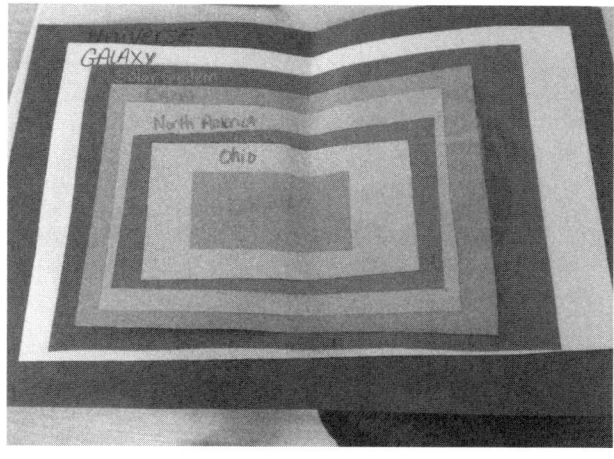

This model helps students conceptualize the relative sizes of the various parts of the universe and their location within it. See Zike 2004 for more information.

1. Before class, prepare the colored paper sets for students, planning for all students to create their stacks in the same color sequence. Leave the sheets of the first color of paper whole. For each subsequent color, cut the sheet to be 1 in. shorter and 1 in. narrower than for the previous color.

2. Provide each student with one set of precut colored paper and a glue stick. Have students stack the seven paper sheets by descending size (see Figure 3.1) and glue them in place.

3. Help students label their models. First, have them label the bottommost paper "Universe" (the outermost location in the universe model) and the topmost paper "Home" (the innermost location in the universe model). *Students might instead use the city name and/or street addresses for the innermost label.* Involve students in a conversation about which colors in this model represent the Milky Way galaxy, the solar system, Earth, North America, the United States, and their state. Prompt students with questions about relative size; for example, ask, "If the universe is the biggest, what fits inside it?" It is sometimes easier to begin with the home city and expand outward. You might use the book *My Place in Space* by Robin and Sally Hirst to help your students think about the smaller and larger components of this model.

4. Prompt students to connect their models to the classification of the stars by asking, "Where would the stars be found?" and "How might scientists find out the temperature of a star?" Guide the discussion to the idea that collecting data about space is challenging because stars are far away.

# 3 DEVELOPING AND USING MODELS

## Guided Reading

Inform students that by reading *Annie Jump Cannon, Astronomer,* they will be learning about how stars are classified and about the work of Annie Jump Cannon, a scientist who was especially imaginative. Introduce the book by asking, "Can you describe the person on the front cover? What seems to be happening on the front cover?" Read the story aloud. Encourage students to notice and think about the challenges Cannon faced as a female astronomer. The questions below may be used to guide students' attention to detail as you read. (Page numbers reference unnumbered book pages, beginning with the title page as page 1.)

1. **Pages 3–5:** When she was young, Annie Jump Cannon enjoyed stargazing with her mother. How did Cannon and her mother know what stars they were looking at? *Cannon and her mother climbed onto the roof of their house and matched their view of the night sky to her mother's school star charts. This was how Cannon learned the names of the visible constellations.*

2. **Pages 6–10:** Cannon enrolled in a nearby boys' school after they began admitting girls and graduated at the top of her class. How did Cannon happen to then enroll in Wellesley College? *Annie's father had toured Wellesley on a business trip and was impressed that Wellesley, a women's college, offered the same courses as all-male universities.*

3. **Pages 12–15:** Cannon loved attending Wellesley College, especially the laboratory experiments in her science classes. What challenges did she encounter as a student? *During her sophomore year, Cannon had scarlet fever and developed an ear infection that left her partially deaf. Despite that, she graduated with her class.*

4. **Pages 16–18:** After her mother died, Cannon remembered how much she had enjoyed studying the stars with her mother, so she returned to Wellesley to study astronomy. How did Cannon's astronomy studies set the course for her career? *While at Wellesley, Cannon arranged a way to use the telescope at the Harvard College Observatory.*

5. **Pages 19–21:** The director of Harvard College Observatory hired Cannon to help photograph and classify all the stars in the sky; however, Cannon soon learned that she would not actually be photographing stars. How did astronomers take photographs of the stars? Why did Cannon not photograph stars? *Astronomers used a special system to photograph the stars. They attached prisms to telescopes that separated the light from each star into different wavelengths, similarly to how raindrops separate sunlight into a rainbow. Cannon did not take photographs of the stars because only the male astronomers were allowed to. Women could only be assistants who worked as "human*

## SCIENTISTS AND ENGINEERS ARE **IMAGINATIVE**—ANNIE JUMP CANNON

**Annie Jump Cannon**

computers" to examine the photographic plates (spectrographs) to analyze the type of light from each star. Women were paid one-fourth the amount that men were paid.

6. **Pages 24–28:** Cannon had sharp eyes and a good memory and soon became the fastest computer—she could classify three stars per minute. How did she identify a problem with the classification system? *The computers used magnifying glasses to examine the spectrographs. They used the dark lines on the spectrographs to determine what the star was made of and how hot it was and then ranked the stars (named according to letters of the alphabet) on the basis of their spectral characteristics. Cannon noticed, for example, that the O stars (the brightest) were the hottest and the A stars were the third hottest. So, she developed a shorter, more accurate star classification system that organized the classes of stars from hottest to coolest—O, B, A, F, G, K, M. Her system is still used today and is remembered by the mnemonic "Oh Be A Fine Guy/Girl, Kiss Me."*

**EUREKA!** GRADE 3–5 **SCIENCE ACTIVITIES AND STORIES**

# 3 DEVELOPING AND USING MODELS

7. **Pages 26–29:** Introduce a discussion of the importance of Cannon's model for classifying stars in ranked order from hottest to coolest by asking the following questions. How did Cannon become known as "the census taker of the stars"? Why is this system needed, and why is it important to science? How does this science activity of re-creating Cannon's classification system on a model help you think about Cannon's imaginative model for classifying the stars? *This is a complex model, and students are expected to understand only that she saw patterns in both the spectra and the temperatures of stars and that she reorganized the alphabetical lettering system (OBAFGKM) to classify stars from hottest (O) to coolest (M).*

## Making Sense
### Explore

Begin by holding a discussion about rainbows to help students recall their knowledge of refraction—the bending and separating of light into a spectrum of colors. Although refraction is not the lesson focus, this discussion will help students connect the lesson to Annie Jump Cannon's interest in and research about stars. Initiate the discussion by asking, "When do we see rainbows?" "What are the colors of the rainbow?" and "What causes rainbows?" *Rainbows appear when rain and sunlight interact in a specific manner. When sunlight passes through water droplets, the droplets act like prisms and refract (bend) the various wavelengths of light that make up white light, which we then see as a spectrum of colors—red, orange, yellow, green, blue, indigo, and violet (ROYGBIV). Cannon worked with images collected through telescopes equipped with prisms and recognized that the different classes of stars emitted light composed of particular wavelengths, which could be distinguished by their refraction through the prisms.*

Extend the discussion to students' experience of light from the Sun and other stars. Ask, "What do we know about the light that comes from the Sun, which is one of the largest stars in our galaxy?" Encourage students to share personal experiences and observations of the nature of light from the Sun (e.g., what sunlight feels like on their skin, that sunlight passes through clouds and windows, and that blocking sunlight produces shadows). Then, inform students that they will conduct an exploration of how the Sun's light behaves when it strikes various objects. *This exploration focuses on reflection, the bouncing of light rays off an object, which allows us to see the object. It is organized in two parts and will work best in a darkened classroom with the lights off and the shades drawn.* The steps of the exploration are as follows:

1. Organize students into table groups and provide each group with a rock, a cup of water, a piece of aluminum foil, a piece of white paper, and a small plastic bag. Each student will need a flashlight. Invite students to examine each item and predict what will happen when they shine a flashlight on it. Encourage students to think of the flashlight as the Sun. Guide their thinking

by asking, "What will happen to the light when it hits this object?" "Where will the light go?" and "Will the light rays pass through, be blocked, or be reflected?" Have students record their predictions in their science notebooks; encourage them to create a chart so they can record both their predictions and their test results. Then, allow some time for students to use their flashlights to test their predictions. *Students should find that the opaque objects (rock and paper) will block some light and cast a shadow; the shiny object (aluminum foil) will reflect or redirect some of the light; and the clear objects (water and plastic bag) will allow most or all of the light to pass through. Note that all the objects actually reflect some light, although this will not be obvious to your students. This fine point may become clear in the "Extend" and "Explain" sections that follow.*

2. Have students work in pairs. Provide each pair with a flashlight and a small acrylic mirror. Begin with the guiding question, "What happens when the Sun's light reflects off a mirror?" Prompt students to think of their flashlight as the Sun, and invite them to work together to observe what happens when they shine their flashlight on the mirror. They should easily observe a reflected light beam if they lay the flashlight on the table and shine it into a mirror held perpendicular to the table so that some of the light spills onto the table. Once they recognize the line of reflected light, ask, "How can you change the line of reflected light?" Challenge students to record their data by creating three diagrams in their science notebooks. Each diagram should include an arrow to show the direction of the reflected (outgoing) light. *Students may need to adjust the angle of the mirror and the distance between the flashlight and the mirror. Once students have completed their three diagrams, ask, "What pattern do you see?" Students should be able to explain that light reflecting from the mirrors travels in a straight line and that the angle of reflection changes when the position of the mirror changes.*

## Explain

Encourage students to summarize their understanding of the different ways the Sun's light (modeled by the flashlight) behaved when it struck opaque, shiny, and clear objects and the relationship between the angle of the mirror and the line of reflection. *Note: There is a rule for mirror reflections—that the angle of the incidence equals the angle of the reflection—but this is not the point in this lesson. Rather, this lesson introduces the concept of a definite line of light that reflects from the mirror.*

## Extend

Organize a light-tag activity. Darken the classroom (turn the lights off and draw the shades) and seat students in two facing rows. Each pair of facing rows is a group. Give a flashlight to a student seated at the end of a row and give small acrylic mirrors to the other students. The goal is for the group members with mirrors to adjust

# 3 DEVELOPING AND USING MODELS

Figure 3.2

One Way to Organize Students in Rows for Light Tag

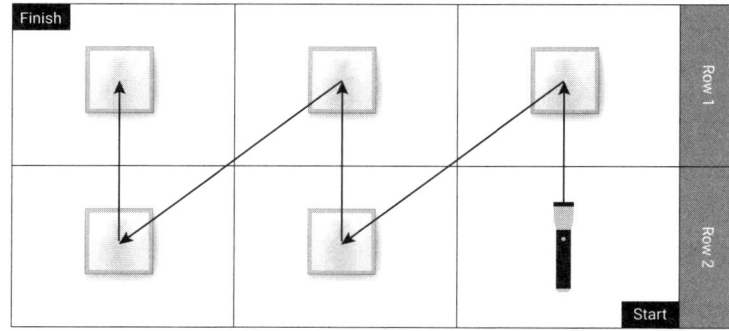

them so that the light from the flashlight reflects off each mirror in turn until the light reaches the last person in the group (see Figure 3.2). Then, ask each group to explain what they learned about how to position the mirrors.

## Evaluate

Summative evaluation of this lesson will include assessment of students' understanding of (1) what it means to be imaginative and how scientists and engineers might benefit from the character trait of being imaginative and (2) the behavior of light when it hits an object and the benefits of reflected light.

**CHARACTER TRAIT**

Encourage students to answer the following questions:

1. If Annie Jump Cannon had not designed the starlight classification system, do you think someone else would have? *Although others might eventually have thought of these ideas, Cannon was imaginative and saw a relationship between the heat of the stars and the light being emitted.*

2. Why is being imaginative an important attribute for scientists to have and how was Cannon imaginative? *Imaginative people are clever and often see things that others overlook. In Cannon's case, she perceived the relationship between a star's spectra and its temperature (i.e., she recognized that hotter stars are bluer and cooler stars are redder). From that, she developed a shorter, more accurate system for classifying stars than any astronomer before or since her time.*

3. Brainstorm with a partner about a time when you were (or wished you were) imaginative and/or to think of someone else you consider to be imaginative, such as a family member or neighbor.

**CONTENT**

You will want to assess students' understanding about how the Sun's light behaves when it strikes opaque, shiny, and clear objects and how light is reflected in a mirror. Table 3.1 is a rubric you might use to evaluate their science notebook entries.

Table 3.1

Rubric for Assessing Student Science Notebook Entries for Starlight—Light From the Sun

| Content | Not Yet | Beginning | Developing | Secure |
|---|---|---|---|---|
| **Opaque Objects** | Student did not include information about the rock and paper blocking some light and casting a shadow. | Student included some information about the rock and paper blocking some light and casting a shadow. | Student included much information about the rock and paper blocking some light and casting a shadow. | Student included much information about the rock and paper blocking some light and casting a shadow and a clear explanation for that phenomenon. |
| **Shiny Objects** | Student did not include information about the aluminum foil reflecting or redirecting some light. | Student included some information about the aluminum foil reflecting or redirecting some light. | Student included much information about the aluminum foil reflecting or redirecting some light. | Student included much information about the aluminum foil reflecting or redirecting some light and a clear explanation for that phenomenon. |
| **Clear Objects** | Student did not include information about the water and plastic bag allowing the light to pass through them. | Student included some information about the water and plastic bag allowing the light to pass through them. | Student included much information about the water and plastic bag allowing the light to pass through them. | Student included much information about the water and plastic bag allowing the light to pass through them and a clear explanation for that phenomenon. |
| **Mirror** | Student did not produce three diagrams with an arrow showing the direction of the reflected (outgoing) light. | Student produced three diagrams but they did not all have an arrow showing the direction of the reflected (outgoing) light. | Student produced three diagrams and all had an arrow showing the direction of the reflected (outgoing) light. | Has three diagrams that include an arrow to show the direction of the reflected (outgoing) light. Highlights the relationship between the angle of incidence and the angle of reflection. |

# 3 DEVELOPING AND USING MODELS

# SCIENTISTS AND ENGINEERS ARE
# VISIONARY

### Learning About **George Washington Ferris Jr.**

Visionary (adj.): having or marked by foresight and imagination

## Lesson: Round and Round We Go!
### Description

In this lesson, students will create a three-dimensional (3-D) model of a Ferris wheel and learn how the original Ferris wheel worked.

### Objectives

Students will consider how being visionary helped George Washington Ferris Jr. design the Ferris wheel as they discover how his invention works.

- Before beginning the lesson, students will describe the types of Ferris wheels they are familiar with.
- As a class, students will look at photographs of Ferris wheels and share personal experiences of riding on Ferris wheels.
- Students will hear the story *Mr. Ferris and His Wheel* by Kathryn Gibbs Davis and discuss how it relates to the word *visionary*.
- Students will make a model of a Ferris wheel and observe how a Ferris wheel works.
- To conclude the lesson, students will review the features of the Ferris wheel as an amusement park ride and propose an idea for a new, unique amusement park ride.

### Learning Outcomes

Students will (1) make a science notebook entry explaining what it means to be visionary and why being visionary is an important trait for scientists and engineers and (2) experience the merits and limitations of creating a model Ferris wheel.

# Connections to the NGSS and the Nature of Science, Grades 3–5

## Disciplinary Core Ideas

**ETS1.A: DEFINING AND DELIMITING ENGINEERING PROBLEMS**

- Possible solutions to a problem are limited by available materials and resources (constraints). The success of a designed solution is determined by considering the desired features of a solution (criteria). Different proposals for solutions can be compared on the basis of how well each one meets the specified criteria for success or how well each takes the constraints into account.

**ETS1.B: DEVELOPING POSSIBLE SOLUTIONS**

- At whatever stage, communicating with peers about proposed solutions is an important part of the design process, and shared ideas can lead to improved designs.
- Tests are often designed to identify failure points or difficulties, which suggest the elements of the design that need to be improved.

## Science and Engineering Practices

***Asking Questions and Defining Problems:*** A practice of science is to ask and refine questions that lead to descriptions and explanations of how the natural and designed world works and which can be empirically tested. Asking questions and defining problems in grades 3–5 builds from grades K–2 experiences and progresses to specifying qualitative relationships.

- Ask questions that can be investigated and predict reasonable outcomes based on patterns such as cause and effect relationships.
- Define a simple design problem that can be solved through the development of an object, tool, process, or system and includes several criteria for success and constraints on materials, time, or cost.

***Developing and Using Models:*** A practice of both science and engineering is to use and construct models as helpful tools for representing ideas and explanations. These tools include diagrams, drawings, physical replicas, mathematical representations, analogies, and computer simulations. Modeling in 3–5 builds on K–2 experiences and progresses to building and revising simple models and using models to represent events and design solutions.

- Identify limitations of models.
- Use a model to test cause and effect relationships or interactions concerning the functioning of a natural or designed system.

# 3 DEVELOPING AND USING MODELS

## Crosscutting Concepts

*Cause and Effect:* Events have causes, sometimes simple, sometimes multifaceted. Deciphering causal relationships, and the mechanisms by which they are mediated, is a major activity of science and engineering.

- Cause and effect relationships are routinely identified, tested, and used to explain change.

*Patterns:* Observed patterns in nature guide organization and classification and prompt questions about relationships and causes underlying them.

- Patterns can be used as evidence to support an explanation.

## Nature of Science Connections

### SCIENTIFIC INVESTIGATIONS USE A VARIETY OF METHODS

- Science methods are determined by questions.
- Science investigations use a variety of methods, tools, and techniques.

### SCIENTIFIC KNOWLEDGE IS BASED ON EMPIRICAL EVIDENCE

- Science findings are based on recognizing patterns.
- Science uses tools and technologies to make accurate measurements and observations.

### SCIENCE IS A WAY OF KNOWING

- Science is both a body of knowledge and processes that add new knowledge.
- Science is a way of knowing that is used by many people.

### SCIENCE IS A HUMAN ENDEAVOR

- Men and women from all cultures and backgrounds choose careers as scientists and engineers.
- Most scientists and engineers work in teams.
- Science affects everyday life.
- Creativity and imagination are important to science.

*Source:* NGSS Lead States 2013.

*Note:* When an activity supports only part of a standard, underlining indicates the relevant part.

SCIENTISTS AND ENGINEERS ARE **VISIONARY**—GEORGE WASHINGTON FERRIS JR.

## Overview

In this lesson, students learn how George Washington Ferris Jr. worked through many challenges to complete a Ferris wheel for the World's Fair in Chicago, 1893. Through the featured book, they learn that men and women from all backgrounds choose careers as scientists and engineers. The character trait of being *visionary* references the way that George Washington Ferris Jr. could "see" the "monster wheel" (as he called it) before it was actually built. Students share ideas about scientists and engineers and discuss how they approach problems differently.

## Materials

You will need one copy of the featured book, *Mr. Ferris and His Wheel* by Kathryn Gibbs Davis (ISBN 978-0547959221). Individual students will need their science notebooks and safety glasses or goggles. Provide a beginning set of materials to each group of two or three students, including craft sticks, pasta (e.g., long pieces, such as linguini, and a variety of other shapes), glue, string, paper clips, and cardboard pieces, such as tubes and corrugated boxes.

## Safety Notes

(1) Personal protective equipment should be worn during the setup, hands-on, and takedown segments of the activity. (2) Use caution when working with sharps (craft sticks, paper clips, and so on). They can cut or puncture skin. (3) Do not eat food used in lab activity. (4) Use caution when working with or near glue guns—they can get hot and cause serious skin burns. (5) Wash hands with soap and water upon completing this activity.

## Setting the Context
### Engage

Ask students whether they have ever been on a Ferris wheel. If so, what words can they use to describe how they felt? Have they ever wondered where the Ferris wheel came from? As students share stories, ask, "How do Ferris wheels work?" You might share images of different Ferris wheels. (A quick internet search will provide many images.) Then, have students in pairs work with one image of a Ferris wheel and record five observations about it in their science notebooks. Pairs can then discuss their observations with the entire class.

George Washington Ferris Jr. developed his Ferris wheel to create a new star attraction for the World's Fair in Chicago, 1893. Locate Chicago on a map for the class, and explain that the World's Fair has not always been held in Chicago and that its location changes. Invite students to research World's Fairs to find out why

# 3 DEVELOPING AND USING MODELS

a World's Fair might be important and whether they are still held. *They can start at the website World's Fairs at http://worldsfairs.com.*

## Guided Reading

Introduce the book by holding up the cover and asking, "What do you think this story is about?" Read the story aloud. The questions below may be used to guide students' attention to detail as you read. (Page numbers reference unnumbered book pages, beginning with the title page as page 1.)

1. **Pages 2–9:** This story tells of the excitement among American engineers in preparation for the Chicago World's Fair in 1893. What weighed on George Washington Ferris's mind as he developed his engineering construction idea for the World's Fair? *Ferris was an ambitious young engineer who could not allow the Eiffel Tower (the star attraction of the previous World's Fair) to overshadow America's World's Fair. He was confident in his idea of a structure that would dazzle and move people.*

2. **Pages 8–11:** The judges could not decide which attraction to pick. Why do you think the judges picked the "monster wheel" but did not give Ferris any money for materials? *The judges needed a star attraction but were very skeptical about Ferris's idea. They would not give him any money to build it because they decided that his wheel idea was far-fetched, even though Ferris was a steel expert and an engineer.*

3. **Pages 12–17:** The weather in Chicago became a challenge for the construction crew. How were the crews able to dig into the frozen ground? *The crews used dynamite and steam to help them dig the trenches that were needed to secure the wheel structure.* How did the high winds in Chicago affect the design of the wheel? *Workers had to place two steel towers in the ground and hang a 70-ton axle between them. This heavy, sturdy structure held the wheel steady in the strong Chicago winds.*

4. **Pages 18–29:** When opening day arrived, Ferris blew the whistle and began to lift and spin passengers for "twenty glorious airborne minutes." Was Ferris's "monster wheel" a success? *Yes. The wheel was safe, and everyone begged to go around again. Passengers rode on velvet seats in elegant cars that were the size of a living room. Once they reached the highest point on the wheel, they could see the entire city, Lake Michigan, and parts of neighboring states. At night, the wheel was lit by another new invention: electric lightbulbs.*

SCIENTISTS AND ENGINEERS ARE **VISIONARY**—GEORGE WASHINGTON FERRIS JR.

5. **Pages 30–35:** The first Ferris wheel has inspired many variations on it. How have Ferris wheels changed since then? How have they remained the same? *Ferris wheels are unlikely to have enclosed cars today. They are more likely to be open and much taller. Ferris wheels continue to be a featured ride in most amusement parks.*

**George Washington Ferris Jr.**

## Making Sense
### Explore

Invite teams of two or three students to use pasta to construct a model of a Ferris wheel. In this phase, they will explore the engineering design of a Ferris wheel as they develop knowledge of how it works. Refer to the illustrations of the Ferris wheel in the featured book (or to images from the internet) and ask, "How might you make a model of a Ferris wheel?" and "What parts and pieces must line up for the wheel to spin?" Students will explore these questions as they look at the

# 3 DEVELOPING AND USING MODELS

pictures and begin to plan out the designs for their models. In addition, Figure 3.3 shows examples of student Ferris wheel models.

1. Begin by having students review the building materials, decide which materials they plan to use, and sketch their engineering plan. They can use any of the building materials, but the goal is to end up with a Ferris wheel that turns. Encourage students to write and illustrate their observations and reasoning in their science notebooks.

2. Provide at least two class periods for construction. In our pilot test, some students asked to bring materials from home, and a few wanted to work at home as well. The teacher positioned herself at the "glue station" to manage safety concerns with the hot glue gun. *A few students brought glue guns—and parent permission slips—for their own use.*

3. Ask each group to share their Ferris wheel model. Students should point out any special features (strengths) and discuss the one thing that gave them the most trouble (challenges).

## Figure 3.3
### Examples of Students' Ferris Wheel Designs

(A)

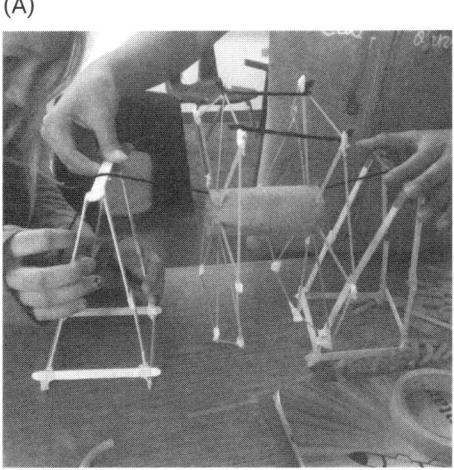

(B)

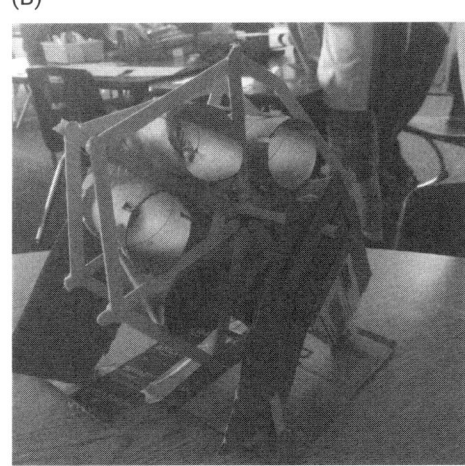

(A) Students used linguini and craft sticks for the structure and masking tape as an adhesive. A piece of yarn strung through the axle (a toilet paper tube) allowed the wheel to turn, but this Ferris wheel was unstable because of the weight of the wheel. (B) Students used craft sticks, corrugated cardboard, and cardboard tubes for the structure and a pencil as the axle.

## Explain

Encourage student groups to discuss how the Ferris wheel works. When students refer to the parts and functions, you might need to introduce and explain the science term *axis*. Ask each group to present their ideas of how the Ferris wheel works. *Look for consistency and similarity among the ideas from the various groups. Ferris wheels rotate on a central axis. Seats are attached to the outer rim of the wheel and always hang down. As the Ferris wheel spins, the seats rotate freely around the points at which they are connected to the wheel. Gears and motors help the Ferris wheel move upward while gravity pulls the wheel down.*

## Extend

Ferris was a visionary engineer who wanted to create something that would "dazzle and move" (see p. 6 of the featured book). Challenge students to create a variety of amusement rides and explain how they function. Ask, "What ideas do you have about a new ride?" "How would it be like other rides?" and "How would it be unique?" Have students build or draw a model of their ride idea. Encourage students to focus on the desired solution and criteria for success (e.g., for the design to account for particular constraints).

## Evaluate

Summative evaluation of this lesson will include assessment of students' understanding of (1) the character trait of being visionary and (2) the merits and limitations of creating a model Ferris wheel.

### CHARACTER TRAIT

Encourage students to answer the following questions:

1. George Washington Ferris Jr. was a visionary man who could imagine creative uses for steel. What struggles do you think someone who is a visionary might have? Why is being a visionary an important character trait for scientists and engineers to have? *Visionary people are thoughtful and often envision solutions and creations that others cannot. Ferris was able to bring to life the monster wheel he imagined—a large steel structure that would do more than just stand still, like the Eiffel Tower—despite the judges considering his proposed invention to be a far-fetched idea and so not providing any money to build it with. This first Ferris wheel inspired Walt Disney to build world-famous, year-round amusement parks.*

2. Working in pairs, discuss a time when you had a vision for a project or an idea. Then, record your ideas in your science notebooks and then share them with the larger group.

# 3 DEVELOPING AND USING MODELS

**CONTENT**

Encourage student table groups to share their successes and frustrations with creating a model Ferris wheel. What engineering practices did they follow? What frustrations did they have? Next, prompt students to create a T-chart such in their science notebooks to organize their observations about the merits and limitations of creating a model Ferris wheel. Table 3.2 is a sample T-chart students could use. A rubric such as the one in Table 3.3 can be used to assess students' understanding about developing a model.

Table 3.2

### Sample T-Chart for the Ferris Wheel Model Activity

| Model Successes | Model Challenges |
|---|---|
| • The model can complete one rotation.<br>• The axle allowed the Ferris wheel to turn.<br>• A working model was created. | • The weight of the wheel limited the number of rotations made consistently.<br>• The axle did not allow for continuous motion.<br>• The adhesive was not applied consistently and affected the working model's ability to turn properly. |

Table 3.3

### Rubric for Assessing Students on Developing and Using a Ferris Wheel Model

| Skill | Not Yet | Beginning | Developing | Secure |
|---|---|---|---|---|
| **Developing and Using a Ferris Wheel Model** | Student did not create a model. | Student created a model focused on a Ferris wheel and began to develop his or her ideas on a T-chart. | Student created a model focused on a Ferris wheel and provided one or two ideas to evaluate the merits and limitations of the model on a T-chart. | Student created a model focused on a Ferris wheel and provided three or four ideas to evaluate the merits and limitations of the model on a T-chart. |

# SCIENTISTS AND ENGINEERS ARE
# PATIENT

### Learning About **Gregor Mendel**

Patient (adj.): able to quietly and steadily wait or work toward something

## Lesson: Pass It Along

### Description

In this lesson, students will learn about commonly inherited human traits and create a model of inherited traits in a snow-people family to understand how offspring inherit characteristics from their parents.

### Objectives

Students will represent the idea that parents pass their traits on to their offspring.

- Before beginning the lesson, students explore the phenomenon of inherited human traits.
- Students will hear the story *Gregor Mendel: The Friar Who Grew Peas* by Cheryl Bardoe and will discuss how it relates to the word *patient*.
- In small groups, students will create a model of snow family generations to map inherited characteristics.
- To conclude the lesson, students will explore the ways that Mendel's laws influence current science efforts in crime laboratory investigation and crop production.

### Learning Outcomes

Students will (1) journal reasons about what it means to be patient and why being patient is an important trait for scientists and engineers and (2) make a visual representation of how parents pass traits on to their offspring.

# 3 DEVELOPING AND USING MODELS

# Connections to the *NGSS* and the Nature of Science, Grades 3–5

## Disciplinary Core Ideas

**LS3.A: INHERITANCE OF TRAITS**

- Many characteristics of organisms are inherited from their parents.

**LS3.B: VARIATION OF TRAITS**

- Different organisms vary in how they look and function because they have different inherited information.

## Science and Engineering Practices

***Asking Questions and Defining Problems:*** A practice of science is to ask and refine questions that lead to descriptions and explanations of how the natural and designed world works and which can be empirically tested. Asking questions and defining problems in grades 3–5 builds from grades K–2 experiences and progresses to specifying qualitative relationships.

- Ask questions about what would happen if a variable is changed.
- Ask questions that can be investigated and predict reasonable outcomes based on patterns such as cause and effect relationships.

***Developing and Using Models:*** A practice of both science and engineering is to use and construct models as helpful tools for representing ideas and explanations. These tools include diagrams, drawings, physical replicas, mathematical representations, analogies, and computer simulations. Modeling in 3–5 builds on K–2 experiences and progresses to building and revising simple models and using models to represent events and design solutions.

- Develop a model using an analogy, example, or abstract representation to describe a scientific principle or design solution.
- Develop and/or use models to describe and/or predict phenomena.

## Crosscutting Concept

***Patterns:*** Observed patterns in nature guide organization and classification and prompt questions about relationships and causes underlying them.

- Similarities and differences in patterns can be used to sort, classify, communicate and analyze simple rates of change for natural phenomena and designed products.
- Patterns of change can be used to make predictions.
- Patterns can be used as evidence to support an explanation.

## Nature of Science Connections

**SCIENTIFIC INVESTIGATIONS USE A VARIETY OF METHODS**

- Science methods are determined by questions.
- Science investigations use a variety of methods, tools, and techniques.

**SCIENTIFIC KNOWLEDGE IS BASED ON EMPIRICAL EVIDENCE**

- Science findings are based on recognizing patterns.
- Science uses tools and technologies to make accurate measurements and observations.

**SCIENCE IS A WAY OF KNOWING**

- Science is both a body of knowledge and processes that add new knowledge.
- Science is a way of knowing that is used by many people.

**SCIENCE IS A HUMAN ENDEAVOR**

- Men and women from all cultures and backgrounds choose careers as scientists and engineers.
- Science affects everyday life.
- Creativity and imagination are important to science.

**SCIENCE ADDRESSES QUESTIONS ABOUT THE NATURAL AND MATERIAL WORLD**

- Science findings are limited to questions that can be answered with empirical evidence.

*Source:* NGSS Lead States 2013.

# 3 DEVELOPING AND USING MODELS

## Overview

In this lesson, students learn how Gregor Mendel worked patiently through many challenges to create a model for inheritance. Through the featured book, students learn that men and women from all backgrounds choose careers as scientists and engineers. The character trait of being patient references the manner in which Gregor Mendel worked on a model for many years. Students then share ideas about ways in which scientists must demonstrate patience.

## Materials

You will need one copy of the book *Gregor Mendel: The Friar Who Grew Peas* by Cheryl Bardoe (ISBN 978-0810954755). Each student will need his or her science notebook and a copy of the Snow Family Generations handout (provided later). Student pairs will need 6 plastic cups; 24 buttons (6 each of 4 colors); and crayons, colored pencils, or colored markers (to match the button colors).

## Safety Notes

(1) Personal protective equipment should be worn during the setup, hands-on, and takedown segments of the activity. (2) Wash hands with soap and water upon completing this activity.

## Setting the Context
### Engage

Have students work in pairs to conduct research on inherited human traits. A good source for this is the website of the Genetic Science Learning Center at the University of Utah (*http://learn.genetics.utah.edu/content/basics/observable*). Have students choose three inherited traits (we recommend choosing from tongue rolling, dimples, curly hair, and hairline shape) and then observe the frequency with which those inherited characteristics occur in students in the class. Invite students to record their findings using a yes/no tally for each trait and then describe in their science notebooks the pattern they see. Student pairs might then share their notes in table groups or with the class as a whole. *Although some traits are inherited and others are developed, most are determined by a combination of genes and environmental factors. This lesson focuses on the pattern of inheritance of traits that was discovered by Mendel.*

### Guided Reading

Students will learn about Gregor Mendel's discovery of the pattern in how parents pass on traits to their children. Introduce the book by holding up the cover and asking "What can we tell about this story from the cover?" *Encourage students to look for details in this illustration of Mendel.* Read the title of the featured book aloud and

SCIENTISTS AND ENGINEERS ARE **PATIENT**—GREGOR MENDEL

ask, "Do you know what a friar is?" *A friar is a member of a religious order of men who live together and do good work, such as preaching and caring for the sick. Students may have heard of Robin Hood's companion, Friar Tuck.* The questions below may be used to guide students' attention to detail as you read. (Page numbers reference unnumbered book pages, beginning with the title page as page 1.)

1. **Pages 1–3:** Gregor Mendel was the son of a hardworking farmer who hoped Mendel would follow in his footsteps. What early life experiences led Mendel to become a scholar instead of a farmer? *As a young boy, Mendel wondered about such things as why breeding two different kinds of sheep together produced thicker wool. He sought knowledge and answers to his questions. Mendel's parents paid for his schooling until his father was injured and no longer able to work. At age 16, Mendel began tutoring students to pay for his own schooling but he still often went hungry.*

2. **Pages 6–11:** Soon Mendel decided to become a friar. How did becoming a friar help to solve his problems? *As a friar, Mendel could study with other great thinkers—mathematicians, botanists, philosophers, and geologists—and do meaningful work in the community, such as preach sermons, care for the sick, and teach school. This balance of work and study suited him well. He learned how some of nature's miracles could be explained by universal laws, such as the law of gravity, which tells how and why apples always fall down toward Earth's surface.*

3. **Pages 12–15:** As he had hoped, Mendel became an excellent science teacher, but he also wanted to make his own discovery. What question motivated his continued science studies? *Mendel wanted to know whether there was a universal law for all plants and animals that explained how parents passed traits on to their children. He knew that scientists before him had paired different species of plants to see what traits their offspring would have. Mendel was interested in determining how often specific traits would occur in offspring over several generations.*

4. **Pages 16–21:** Mendel chose to use pea plants in his experiments. How did he choose which traits or characteristics to follow? *Mendel studied many individual pea plants to find clear, distinct traits he might track. He chose to follow color (yellow or green) and texture (smooth or wrinkled). He bred pairs of plants and recorded how often each trait appeared in the next generation. He followed careful procedures so he knew which plant had pollinated which.*

5. **Pages 22–27:** When Mendel saw that the hybrid children looked like only one of the parent peas, he wondered whether the lost traits were gone forever. What did Mendel realize when he studied the parent peas' grandchildren and great-grandchildren? *Mendel discovered a mathematical model that showed that each trait was made up of two parts that mix and match to create a pattern. When one trait disappeared in the first generation, it showed*

**EUREKA!** GRADE 3–5 **SCIENCE ACTIVITIES AND STORIES**

# 3 DEVELOPING AND USING MODELS

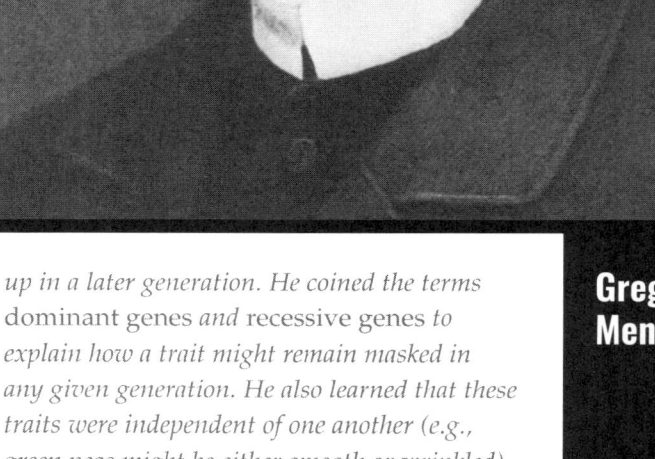

**Gregor Mendel**

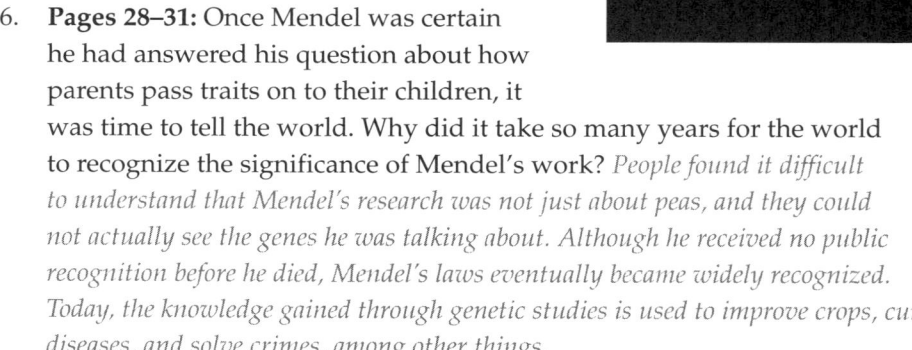

*up in a later generation. He coined the terms* dominant genes *and* recessive genes *to explain how a trait might remain masked in any given generation. He also learned that these traits were independent of one another (e.g., green peas might be either smooth or wrinkled).*

6. **Pages 28–31:** Once Mendel was certain he had answered his question about how parents pass traits on to their children, it was time to tell the world. Why did it take so many years for the world to recognize the significance of Mendel's work? *People found it difficult to understand that Mendel's research was not just about peas, and they could not actually see the genes he was talking about. Although he received no public recognition before he died, Mendel's laws eventually became widely recognized. Today, the knowledge gained through genetic studies is used to improve crops, cure diseases, and solve crimes, among other things.*

SCIENTISTS AND ENGINEERS ARE **PATIENT**—GREGOR MENDEL

## Making Sense
### Explore

Begin the exploration by explaining that everyone has specific traits, such as eye color and hair color, that are passed from parent to child. As a simulation of this, students will model how traits are passed down through generations of a snow-people family. Students will transfer the traits for each offspring by drawing a random set of buttons from a cup of buttons. *Have students close their eyes and mix the buttons with their hands each time before drawing some to yield a random, varied result.*

1. To begin, have students label six cups as follows: Snow Mother's father, Snow Mother's mother, Snow Father's father, Snow Father's mother, Snow Mother, and Snow Father.

2. Have students prepare four sets of six same-color buttons (e.g., six blue, six yellow, and so on) and then place one set in each grandparent cup. *These colored buttons represent the specific traits of each Snow grandparent.* Then, ask students to color in the traits (buttons) for each Snow grandparent on the Snow Family Generations handout (Figure 3.4, p. 76).

3. Invite students to close their eyes and draw three traits (buttons) from the cup of each of Snow Mother's parents and place them in the cup labeled *Snow Mother*. (There will be six traits in the Snow Mother cup.) These are the traits that Snow Mother inherited from her parents. Have students record Snow Mother's traits by coloring in her buttons on the handout.

4. Invite students to close their eyes and draw three traits from the cup of each of Snow Father's parents and place them in the cup labeled *Snow Father*. These are the traits that Snow Father inherited from his parents. Have students record Snow Father's traits by coloring in his buttons on the handout.

5. Snow Mother and Snow Father have four children. To determine the traits of Snow Child 1, have students close their eyes and take three buttons from Snow Father's cup and three from Snow Mother's cup. Then they should record Snow Child 1's traits by coloring in those buttons on the handout.

6. Students should return the buttons they took from Snow Mother's and Snow Father's cups. (To remember what came from where, they can refer to the Snow Mother and Snow Father cups they previously colored on their handouts.) Then, ask them to close their eyes and again take three buttons from Snow Mother's cup and three from Snow Father's cup to find the traits of Snow Child 2. Remind them to color their handout to record that Snow child's traits.

7. Have students repeat step 6 to determine the traits of the other two Snow children.

# 3 DEVELOPING AND USING MODELS

Figure 3.4

SNOW FAMILY GENERATIONS

## Explain

Plants and animals inherit traits from their parents. Some of these traits remain hidden in some generations and then become evident in later generations. By tracking traits through three Snow family generations, students see how each Snow child randomly inherited an assortment of traits. *Every organism follows a set of instructions (genes) that determine its traits. Heredity is the passage of these traits from one generation to the other. Traits can only be inherited from parents (and their parents)—not from aunts, uncles, or cousins.*

## Extend

Students might be interested in learning how Gregor Mendel's discovery of genetic traits laid the foundation for some wonders of modern science. Consider inviting a community expert to speak to your class about how Mendel's law guides investigations in crime laboratories or leads to improved crop production. A dog breeder might talk about how dogs are paired to achieve the features judges look for in the show ring. *Internet resources are available to support these extended studies, but they are rife with advertisements and are intended primarily for adults. Resources such as the book* Crime Scene Investigations *(Walker and Wood 1998) can help you involve students in solving crimes such as theft, dog-napping, vandalism, and water pollution; however, the cases in that book encourage evidence-based thinking but do not involve inherited genetic traits.*

## Evaluate

Summative evaluation of this lesson will include assessment of students' understanding of why being patient is an important character trait for scientists and engineers and of the random way in which traits from both parents are passed on to their children.

### CHARACTER TRAIT

Encourage students to answer the following question:

1. If Gregor Mendel had not been so patient, do you think people today would understand where our traits come from? Why is being patient an important character trait for scientists and engineers to have? *Although others might have discovered this universal law, Mendel was patient and so was able to think about the possibilities and conduct a labor-intensive study over a long period of time. Patient people are thoughtful and capable of hard work over a long period of time; they do not hurry their work. In Mendel's case, he persevered (even when he was poor and hungry) and found a way to conduct the research needed to answer his question. Still today, new discoveries in disease prevention, crime solutions, and crop production rely on Mendel's laws.*

# 3 DEVELOPING AND USING MODELS

Ask students to remember and think about a time they were patient. Record all of the classes's responses in some manner so you can encourage the entire class to share. This is a character trait for which students will recall examples very easily; for example, learning to tie shoes or waiting for a younger brother or sister. Invite students to record an explanation in their science notebooks of why being patient is an important trait for scientists and engineers.

**CONTENT**

Ask students to think about their experience with the Snow family generations by asking "Did all of the Snow children inherit the same traits?" and "How many Snow children inherited a trait from each Snow grandparent?" Children randomly inherit half of their traits from each parent, so siblings inherit different combinations of traits. Table 3.4 may assist you in assessing students' understanding of developing and using a genetics model.

Table 3.4

### Rubric for Assessing Students on Developing and Using a Genetics Model

| Skill | Not Yet | Beginning | Developing | Secure |
|---|---|---|---|---|
| **Developing and Using a Genetics Model** | Student did not create a model. | Student created a model for how parents relate genetically to their offspring using the Snow Family Generations handout but did not accurately complete the handout. | Student created a model of how parents relate genetically to their offspring using the Snow Family Generations handout and accurately completed the handout. | Student created a model of how parents relate genetically to their offspring using the Snow Family Generations handout, accurately completed the handout, and can verbally articulated how offspring inherit characteristics from their parents. |

## References

Bardoe, C. 2006. *Gregor Mendel: The friar who grew peas*. New York: Harry N. Abrams.

Bradley, J., and D. Farland-Smith. 2010. 3-D teaching models for all: A series of activities that allow students to "see" through touch. *The Science Teacher* 78 (3): 33–37.

Davis, K. G. 2014. *Mr. Ferris and his wheel*. Boston: Houghton Mifflin Harcourt.

Gerber, C. 2011. *Annie Jump Cannon, astronomer*. Gretna, LA: Pelican Publishing.

NGSS Lead States. 2013. *Next Generation Science Standards: For states, by states*. Washington, DC: National Academies Press. *www.nextgenscience.org/next-generation-science-standards*.

Posner, G. J., K. A. Strike, P. W. Hewson, and W. A. Gertzog. 1982. Accommodation of a scientific conception: Toward a theory of conceptual change. *Science Education* 66: 211–227.

Zike, D. 2004. *Big book of science: Elementary K–6*. Comfort, TX: Dinah-Might Adventures.

## Additional Resources

Annenberg Learner. 1997. Minds of our own. *www.learner.org/vod/vod_window.html?pid=76*. *A video containing a five-minute segment titled "It Might Take Ten Years" (beginning at 10:58) in which students expect they will be able to see an apple in a totally dark room.*

Genetic Science Learning Center at the University of Utah. Learn.genetics. Basic genetics. *http://learn.genetics.utah.edu/content/basics/observable*. *A website with a nice visual presentation of visible human characteristics (e.g., tongue rolling, handedness, and dimples) and explanation of genetic probabilities.*

Hirst, R., and S. Hirst. 1990. *My place in space*. New York: Orchard Books.

MacRobert, A. 2016. This week's night sky at a glance. Sky and Telescope Media. *www.skyandtelescope.com/observing/sky-at-a-glance*. *A weekly column that lists specific sky features to look for.*

National Aeronautics and Space Administration (NASA). 2016. The electromagnetic spectrum: What is it? *http://science.hq.nasa.gov/kids/imagers/ems/ems.html*. *A website with a good visual graphic that helps students better understand the electromagnetic spectrum in general and the wavelengths of light in particular.*

Walker, P., and E. Wood. 1998. *Crime scene investigations: Real-life science labs for grades 6–12*. San Francisco: Jossey-Bass.

World's Fair, Inc. 2015. World's fairs. *http://worldsfairs.com*. *A website on which students can learn why we have world's fairs and read reviews of recent fairs.*

# 4

# Planning and Carrying Out Investigations

Many scientists begin their work with observations before they actually conduct their experiments. In some instances, scientists spend many years gathering data and thinking about how to conduct experiments. That is the case for the three scientists in this chapter, whose long-term investigations with chimpanzees (Jane Goodall), the plants and animals of the Galapagos Islands (Charles Darwin), and the dinosaur *Tyrannosaurus rex* (Barnum Brown) changed the way people thought about the world. It is easy to understand how the words *observant, puzzler*, and *intuitive* best define these scientists' character traits and dispositions. We expect that in helping students to identify each of these traits, you will be helping to humanize the work and procedures of science while you teach science lessons.

## Recommended Science Teaching Strategy: Effective Questioning

Asking effective questions is critical to teaching science well. One suggestion is to use formative assessments to help you in this strategy. Formative assessments are integral to informed teaching and can significantly improve student learning (Keeley 2008). In this chapter, we describe a formative assessment procedure to bridge students' thinking and understanding to accepted scientific ideas.

As the *Next Generation Science Standards* (*NGSS*; NGSS Lead States 2013) say, the goal of science is to construct explanations for the way the natural world works. Scientists, then, ask and answer questions to improve our understanding of the natural world, whereas engineers figure out how things work and make new things to improve our quality of life. Whether students are engaged in scientific investigation or engineering design, it is critical that they plan a course of steps and measurements that will answer their questions. In time, students will naturally come to plan their investigations carefully, as they experience experimental error and see the effects of it on their work.

There is great value in highlighting the investigation process by telling students we are choosing the best way to find a solution, thus ensuring that the investigation will ultimately answer our question. Donna frequently reminds students that the best science and engineering investigations both answer the initial question and generate a new one. This awareness helps them to appreciate the continuous cycle of scientific processes, but we have learned that we need to formally teach and continually assess students' understanding of a fair test.

In early fall, when you have a day before beginning another unit (or sometime after teaching

# 4  PLANNING AND CARRYING OUT INVESTIGATIONS

students how to be safe in the science lab), think about implementing a meaningful, whole-class activity that helps students conceptualize ways to plan and carry out investigations. You might begin the school year with a memorable, shared experience to help your students visualize how scientists conduct a fair test. An activity such as Orange Float will give you a reference point for the remainder of the year.

For the Orange Float activity, all you need is two oranges (any size) and a bowl of water (a clear bowl is preferable). Simply ask students, "Do you think an orange will float or sink in water?" To answer this question scientifically, students need to plan a fair test. Here, we refer to the scientific processes and focus on the definition of a fair test, variables, hypotheses, and conclusions based on data. You may be amazed by the surprising simplicity and effectiveness of this experience. These class conversations, however, will help to elicit detailed questions, such as, "Do you mean with or without the peel?" Encourage the class to agree on floating the orange with its peel first, and prompt table groups of students to make their hypotheses about whether the orange will float or sink.

Once students have had a chance to finalize their hypotheses, ask, "Why did you choose sink or float? What experiences have you had that lead you to these predictions?" Some students will remember bobbing for apples and liken their expectation of the orange's behavior to that of the floating apples. Others might think the surface of the orange will help to keep it afloat and suggest that the skin of an orange resembles the surface of a basketball. Once you have exhausted students' predictions, ask table groups, "What do we need to do to set up a test to answer this question fairly?" Much discussion will take place and generally will result in definition of specific details and procedures. One important definition arises when students need to determine the meaning of *float*. Here, the teacher might prompt students' thinking by asking, "Does *float* mean *not on the bottom of the bowl* or *fully submerged*?" The actual definition, of course, is neither here nor there—just that the students need to define the term for their test.

Once students are satisfied with the plans, encourage student groups to conduct the test. *The orange will float. It will not touch the bottom of the bowl, and some of the orange will rest above the surface of the water. When you push the top of it, you can make it bob up and down to further illustrate its buoyancy. The scientific explanation here is not important to this demonstration because the focus is on the procedures of scientific investigations, but you might want students to know that the orange floats because the peel holds pockets of air.* Likely, one or more students will pose a new question, such as, "What will happen if we peel the orange? Will it float or sink?" *Once you remove the orange's "life jacket," the orange will sink to the bottom of the bowl. You might encourage students to wonder about other oranges, such as older oranges with thinner peels, or other fruits, such as smaller or larger fruits, stone fruits, or cantaloupes. Cantaloupes are interesting in that they have a large air cavity in the center, so a cantaloupe of any weight or size will float in water.*

A simple experiment such as this one with an orange and a bowl of water can help your students understand the importance of planning out investigations. It can also teach students about other concepts, such as density; however, the focus in this case is on the fair-test procedures scientists follow when they ask and answer questions.

# SCIENTISTS AND ENGINEERS ARE
# OBSERVANT

**Learning About Jane Goodall**

Observant (adj.): good at noticing things

## Lesson: Chirping Crickets
### Description

In this lesson, students observe crickets and discover how crickets move and communicate.

## Objectives

As they identify the body parts of a cricket and the functions of those parts, students will consider how the character trait of being *observant* helped Jane Goodall make careful observations.

- Students will hear the story *The Watcher: Jane Goodall's Life With the Chimps* by Jeanette Winter and discuss how Jane Goodall's behavior since young girlhood showed her to be observant.

- Students will observe crickets and will record both illustrations and narrative descriptions in their science journals.

- To conclude the lesson, students will revisit their questions from the activity about crickets and plan investigations to answer them.

## Learning Outcomes

Students will (1) make a science notebook entry to explain what it means to be observant and why being observant is an important trait for scientists and engineers and (2) illustrate and describe insect parts and functions.

**EUREKA!** GRADE 3–5 **SCIENCE ACTIVITIES AND STORIES**

## 4 PLANNING AND CARRYING OUT INVESTIGATIONS

# Connections to the NGSS and the Nature of Science, Grades 3–5
## Disciplinary Core Idea
### LS1.A: STRUCTURE AND FUNCTION

- Plants and animals have both internal and external structures that serve various functions in growth, survival, behavior, and reproduction.

## Science and Engineering Practices

***Asking Questions and Defining Problems:*** A practice of science is to ask and refine questions that lead to descriptions and explanations of how the natural and designed world works and which can be empirically tested. Asking questions and defining problems in grades 3–5 builds from grades K–2 experiences and progresses to specifying qualitative relationships.

- Ask questions that can be investigated and predict reasonable outcomes based on patterns such as cause and effect relationships.

***Planning and Carrying Out Investigations:*** Scientists and engineers plan and carry out investigations in the field or laboratory, working collaboratively as well as individually. Their investigations are systematic and require clarifying what counts as data and identifying variables or parameters. Planning and carrying out investigations to answer questions or test solutions to problems in 3–5 builds on K–2 experiences and progresses to include investigations that control variables and provide evidence to support explanations or design solutions.

- Make observations and/or measurements to produce data to serve as the basis for evidence for an explanation of a phenomenon or test a design solution.

## Crosscutting Concepts

***Patterns:*** Observed patterns in nature guide organization and classification and prompt questions about relationships and causes underlying them.

- Similarities and differences in patterns can be used to sort, classify, communicate and analyze simple rates of change for natural phenomena and designed products.

- Patterns of change can be used to make predictions. Patterns can be used as evidence to support an explanation.

***Structure and Function:*** The way an object is shaped or structured determines many of its properties and functions.

- Different materials have different substructures, which can sometimes be observed.

- Substructures have shapes and parts that serve functions.

SCIENTISTS AND ENGINEERS ARE **OBSERVANT**—JANE GOODALL

**Nature of Science Connections**

**SCIENTIFIC INVESTIGATIONS USE A VARIETY OF METHODS**

- Science methods are determined by questions.
- Science investigations use a variety of methods, tools, and techniques.

**SCIENCE IS A HUMAN ENDEAVOR**

- Men and women from all cultures and backgrounds choose careers as scientists and engineers.
- Most scientists and engineers work in teams.
- Science affects everyday life.
- Creativity and imagination are important to science.

**SCIENCE ADDRESSES QUESTIONS ABOUT THE NATURAL AND MATERIAL WORLD**

- Science findings are limited to questions that can be answered with empirical evidence.

*Source:* NGSS Lead States 2013.

## Overview

In this lesson, students observe crickets in the classroom to practice observation skills, similar to Jane Goodall's observation of chimpanzees in the wild. Students learn how one person who had a passion for animals made a significant, long-lasting improvement in how we view animal communications. Goodall shared her observations about chimpanzees with others in the science community and the world at large and improved people's understanding of how these animals live and communicate. Through the featured book, students learn that people from all backgrounds choose careers as scientists. The character trait of being observant refers to Jane Goodall's patient chimpanzee-watching, which led to carefully planned investigations. In the hands-on portion of this lesson, students experience what it is like to observe live, wild animals for a period of time.

# 4 PLANNING AND CARRYING OUT INVESTIGATIONS

## Materials

You will need one copy of the featured book, *The Watcher: Jane Goodall's Life With the Chimps* by Jeanette Winter (ISBN 978-0375867743), and a class set of about 20 live crickets. *Crickets will cost about $1.20 at your local pet store. Any size will do, but larger ones might be the easiest for students to observe. Crickets can be stored in one large container until it is time for the lesson. They like to eat small pieces of fruit, such as oranges or apples, or potatoes. Crickets are almost maintenance free, other than not doing well in extreme temperatures, particularly low ones.* You will need observation containers for each small group of students. *Crickets are lively and their behavior is erratic. The observation containers will keep the crickets on the tables or desks. We used baby food jars (Figure 4.1), but you might want to purchase purposefully made magnifying bug boxes (that have a magnification lens built into one side), which are widely available from science supply companies.*

## Safety Notes

(1) Personal protective equipment should be worn during the setup, hands-on, and takedown segments of the activity. (2) Use caution in working with glass jars—glass can shatter if dropped and cut or puncture skin. (3) Wash hands with soap and water upon completing this activity.

## Setting the Context
### Engage

Ask students, "Have you ever watched wild animals?" and "Where and why did (or would) you watch wild animals?" Ask them, "Have you heard of Jane Goodall?" If students have heard about her, ask them to share stories of what they already know about her. If they have not, hold up the book and ask students to guess what wild animals Goodall studied.

### Guided Reading

By reading *The Watcher: Jane Goodall's Life With the Chimps*, students will learn about animal behavior, insect anatomy, and the life work of a scientist who was especially observant. Introduce the book by

Figure 4.1
### Cricket Inside a Baby Food Jar

SCIENTISTS AND ENGINEERS ARE **OBSERVANT**—JANE GOODALL

Jane Goodall

asking "What does it look like is happening on the front cover?" Read the story aloud. Encourage students to notice and think about the challenges Jane Goodall may have faced as a woman who was alone in the jungle and observing chimpanzees. The questions below may be used to guide students' attention to detail as you read. (Page numbers reference unnumbered book pages, beginning with the title page as page 1.)

1. **Pages 2–4:** How was Jane Goodall acting like a scientist from a very young age? *On these pages, we read Goodall shout, "I know how an egg comes out!" and the author tells us that "the robin even built a nest in Jane's bookcase!"*

2. **Page 11:** The author states, "She set up camp, far from any human dwelling." How do you imagine Goodall might have felt being so far from home and alone? What words could you use to describe her, here on this page? *Student responses will vary, but the text gives no indication that Goodall was frightened by the new sounds (e.g., the laugh of a hyena). The author suggests only,*

# 4 PLANNING AND CARRYING OUT INVESTIGATIONS

*"She knew she was Home."*

3. **Page 20:** What quality did Goodall say scientists needed to do their work? And why? *On this page, Goodall notes, "You have to be patient if you want to learn about animals."*

4. **Pages 22–26:** How did Goodall observe differently than other scientists did before her? *Goodall slept near the chimps, named the chimps, and earned their trust. The author writes that "David Greybeard let Jane come close. She watched him shape a stick into a tool to dig for termites. Before this, nobody knew that wild animals made tools."*

### Figure 4.2
### Students Gathered Around a Cricket Jar

## Making Sense
### Explore

Invite students to sit in groups of four or five. Place one or two crickets on the table in the middle of each group for them to observe (Figure 4.2). Review the difference between observation and inference and/or between fact and opinion. You want students to record what they actually see, and this can require fairly focused observations. Using hand lenses or magnifying bug boxes will enable them to see and then record realistic detail. In our experience, students will rise to the occasion and provide thoughtful, detailed observations if they know you will be reviewing them or reading them aloud.

Ask students, "What did you find out?" and "What have you learned about crickets and their body parts that you did not know before?" Direct them to write (five sentences) and draw (with labels) their observations and reasoning in their science notebooks. You might provide copies of the Cricket Observation Worksheet (Figure 4.3). *Look for accurate illustrations of students' observations. Artistic skills are not necessarily important here, but it is important that students pay attention to and record detail. Move from group to group as students are working, and ask students questions about what they see and what they have drawn. Challenge them to be accurate. This is the perfect*

SCIENTISTS AND ENGINEERS ARE **OBSERVANT**—JANE GOODALL

Figure 4.3 _____

Entomologist: _____

# CRICKET OBSERVATION WORKSHEET

**My Cricket Observations**

Record your observations below in complete sentences.

1.

2.

3.

4.

5.

Draw your cricket below. Add words and arrows to parts of the drawing to make it a diagram instead of a picture.

**EUREKA!** GRADE 3-5 **SCIENCE ACTIVITIES AND STORIES**

*opportunity to introduce the concept of scientific diagrams versus artistic illustrations. Encourage students to think about how a diagram includes text and arrows or lines of notes. If this opportunity is taken now when students are young, they will not be surprised when they encounter diagrams on standardized assessments. Another strategy to try is to show the class an illustration and diagram and ask them to compare the two. This might seem like a trivial detail, but it helps them begin to think about the similarities and differences between science and art. Ask students to record the questions that arise (things they wonder about) as they observe.*

## Explain

Encourage students to summarize their own observations and questions that were prompted by this investigation. Introduce discussion about the anatomy of the crickets—for example, by asking whether they can easily find the head, abdomen, and thorax. If they can, encourage them to include these labels on their illustrations. Ask students whether they observed any clues about how to differentiate between the male and female crickets. *Females do not chirp. Males chirp to attract a mate. They make the chirping sound by rubbing their forewings together.* At this time, we share a diagram of a cricket with our students, such as the one on the website enchantedlearning.com (*www.enchantedlearning.com/paint/subjects/insects/orthoptera/Cricket.shtml*). Ask students, "How does this science activity help you think about Jane Goodall's observant nature?" and "When planning and carrying out her investigations, what do you think Goodall had to consider?"

## Extend

If time allows, revisit the book and find specific examples to compare what the class initially thought was happening on the cover and what the book informed them was happening. Also revisit students' questions about crickets and plan some investigations to answer those questions. You might also read the book *Chirping Crickets* by Melvin Berger (1998), which will address most of the questions generated from students' observations. *Chirping Crickets is part of the HarperCollins Let's Read and Find Out series of science books, which we like because they present accurate science information in a friendly, understandable way.* Any remaining questions can be investigated by searching for answers on the internet and/or by reading other books available in the school and public libraries.

## Evaluate

Summative evaluation of this lesson will include assessment of students' understanding of (1) the character trait of being observant and (2) the structure and function of a cricket's body parts. You will also evaluate their ability to generate evidence-based questions.

SCIENTISTS AND ENGINEERS ARE **OBSERVANT**—JANE GOODALL

**CHARACTER TRAIT**

Encourage students to answer the following questions:

1. What made Jane Goodall such an effective, observant scientist? *As one example from the featured book (p. 20), the author wrote, "Jane watched every day, all day—even huddled in the rain. She kept notes about it all. 'You have to be patient if you want to learn about animals,' she wrote."*

2. Why is being observant an important character trait for a scientist or engineer? *Careful observations allow scientists to collect accurate data. In Goodall's case, her carefully skilled observations helped her to earn the trust of the chimpanzees she studied—and thus to gather even more data. On page 25, the author wrote, "And because David Greybeard trusted Jane, now the other chimps let Jane come close, too."*

3. How was Jane Goodall observant? *On pages 18–22 of the book, the author describes Goodall's patient observation. Pages 26–27 describe how Goodall watched the chimps when they were happy, holding hands, laughing, and throwing tantrums.*

4. Working in pairs, discuss a time when you were observant. Record notes about it in your science journals and then share it with the class.

### Figure 4.4
**Student Science Notebook Entry**

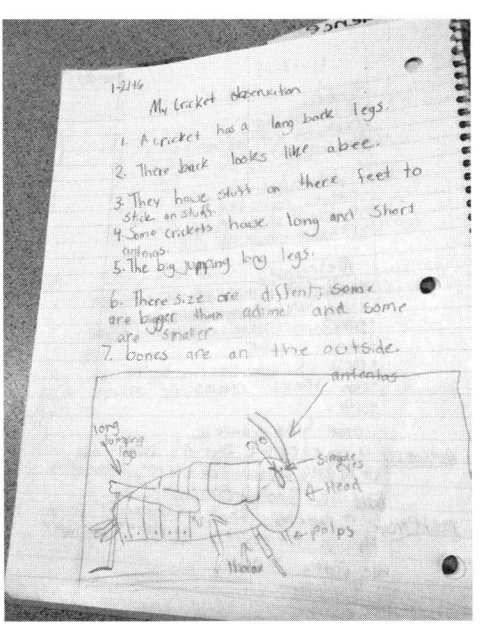

**CONTENT**

Students will have drawn a cricket diagram on a Cricket Observation Worksheet (Figure 4.3, p. 89) or in their science notebooks (Figure 4.4). You can evaluate these for the correctness of the anatomical parts and terms. Student observations about crickets can be evaluated by (1) punctuation (e.g., whether students wrote in complete sentences and began sentences with a capital letter), (2) accuracy (e.g., whether students recorded facts based on observation rather than opinions or inferences), and (3) content knowledge (i.e., whether students demonstrate understanding of cricket structures that support their growth, survival, behavior, and/or reproduction). You may want to assess students' work using a rubric such as the one in Table 4.1 (p. 92).

**EUREKA!** GRADE 3–5 **SCIENCE ACTIVITIES AND STORIES**

# 4 PLANNING AND CARRYING OUT INVESTIGATIONS

Table 4.1

Rubric for Assessing Students on the Cricket Observation Activity

| Content or Skill | Not Yet | Beginning | Developing | Secure |
|---|---|---|---|---|
| **Observation** | Student did not provide written observations. | Student did not link his or her reasoning to the evidence observed in class | Student linked his or her reasoning to the evidence observed in class. | Student linked his or her observation and reasoning back to the evidence observed in class and demonstrated understanding of cricket growth and structure. |
| **Drawing and Illustration** | Student did not provide a drawing or illustration. | Student provided a drawing but it is still at the imagination level. | Student provided a drawing that is moving from the imagination level to evidence-based reality. | Student provided a drawing that is moving from the imagination level to evidence-based reality and, included key words and lines or arrows. |
| **Questions** | Student did not provide new questions. | Student did not ask new evidence-based questions from the "Explore" phase. | Student asked new evidence-based questions from the "Explore" phase. | Student asked new evidence-based questions rom the "Explore" phase and has an idea about how to begin to conduct an experiment that would answer these questions. |

# SCIENTISTS AND ENGINEERS ARE
# PUZZLERS

## Learning About **Charles Darwin**

Puzzler (n.): a person who is occupied or amused by solving puzzles

### Lesson: Puzzling Potatoes
### Description

In this lesson, students will become familiar with how plant and animal adaptations influence survival and explore a bowl of potatoes to consider how differences among individual potatoes might provide advantages in survival and reproduction.

### Objectives

Students will consider how the character trait of being a puzzler helped Charles Darwin understand inheritance and variation of traits.

- Before beginning the lesson, students will engage in a camouflage simulation to prompt thinking about the advantages of species variation.

- Students will hear the story *Darwin: With Glimpses Into His Private Journal and Letters* by Alice B. McGinty and discuss how it teaches us that Darwin was a puzzler.

- Students will observe and discuss the observable traits of 20 different potato tubers.

- To conclude the lesson, students will explore mimicry (a variation on camouflage) as an example of how inherited traits can lead to natural selection.

# 4 PLANNING AND CARRYING OUT INVESTIGATIONS

## Learning Outcomes

Students will (1) make a science notebook entry to explain what a puzzler is and why being a puzzler is an important trait for scientists and engineers and (2) create a chart to highlight observed trait variations among individual potatoes and explain how these variations might ensure survival and reproduction.

## Connections to the *NGSS* and the Nature of Science, Grades 3–5
### Disciplinary Core Ideas
**LS3.B: VARIATION OF TRAITS**

- Different organisms vary in how they look and function because they have different inherited information.

**LS4.B: NATURAL SELECTION**

- Sometimes the differences in characteristics between individuals of the same species provide advantages in surviving, finding mates, and reproducing.

### Science and Engineering Practices

***Asking Questions and Defining Problems:*** A practice of science is to ask and refine questions that lead to descriptions and explanations of how the natural and designed world works and which can be empirically tested. Asking questions and defining problems in grades 3–5 builds from grades K–2 experiences and progresses to specifying qualitative relationships.

- Ask questions that can be investigated and predict reasonable outcomes based on patterns such as cause and effect relationships.

***Planning and Carrying Out Investigations:*** Scientists and engineers plan and carry out investigations in the field or laboratory, working collaboratively as well as individually. Their investigations are systematic and require clarifying what counts as data and identifying variables or parameters. Planning and carrying out investigations to answer questions or test solutions to problems in 3–5 builds on K–2 experiences and progresses to include investigations that control variables and provide evidence to support explanations or design solutions.Make observations and/or measurements to produce data to serve as the basis for evidence for an explanation of a phenomenon or test a design solution.

## Crosscutting Concepts

*Cause and Effect:* Events have causes, sometimes simple, sometimes multifaceted. Deciphering causal relationships, and the mechanisms by which they are mediated, is a major activity of science and engineering.

- Cause and effect relationships are routinely identified, tested, and used to explain change.
- Events that occur together with regularity might or might not be a cause and effect relationship.

*Patterns:* Observed patterns in nature guide organization and classification and prompt questions about relationships and causes underlying them.

- Patterns can be used as evidence to support an explanation.

## Nature of Science Connections

### SCIENTIFIC INVESTIGATIONS USE A VARIETY OF METHODS

- Science methods are determined by questions.
- Science investigations use a variety of methods, tools, and techniques.

### SCIENCE KNOWLEDGE IS BASED ON EMPIRICAL EVIDENCE

- Science findings are based on recognizing patterns.
- Science uses tools and technologies to make accurate measurements and observations.

### SCIENCE MODELS, LAWS, MECHANISMS, AND THEORIES EXPLAIN NATURAL PHENOMENA

- Science theories are based on a body of evidence and many tests.

### SCIENCE IS A WAY OF KNOWING

- Science is both a body of knowledge and processes that add new knowledge.
- Science is a way of knowing that is used by many people.

### SCIENTIFIC KNOWLEDGE ASSUMES AN ORDER AND CONSISTENCY IN NATURAL SYSTEMS

- Science assumes consistent patterns in natural systems.
- Basic laws of nature are the same everywhere in the universe.

# 4 PLANNING AND CARRYING OUT INVESTIGATIONS

**SCIENCE IS A HUMAN ENDEAVOR**

- Men and women from all cultures and backgrounds choose careers as scientists and engineers.
- Creativity and imagination are important to science.

*Source:* NGSS Lead States 2013.

## Overview

In this lesson, students will learn how a lifetime of studies in the natural world led Charles Darwin to understand how plants and animals inherit characteristics and how characteristics modify over time to enable survival. Darwin collected specimens from the time he was very young, traveled extensively in his studies, and worked to define a pattern that he came to call "survival of the fittest." The character trait of being a puzzler refers to Darwin's lifelong pleasure in figuring out this survival pattern. Students will observe similar and different characteristics of potatoes (similarly to how Darwin observed plants). In the lesson extension, students will engage in activities that model camouflage and mimicry in the natural world.

## Materials

You will need one copy of the featured book, *Darwin: With Glimpses Into His Private Journal and Letters*, by Alice McGinty (ISBN 978-0618995318). For the M&M Moth activity, you will need approximately 22 oz. of milk chocolate M&Ms, approximately 25 oz. of candy corn (we use the brand Brach's because the yellow and orange colors match the M&Ms so well), and a 12 in. × 9 in. × 1 in. container (such as a cake pan or resealable storage container). For the potato activity, you will need a bowl of 20 potatoes (any size) per class (5 per group); a hand lens for each student; and two or three rulers and a balance scale for each table group. For the extension activity, you will need one square of unsweetened baking chocolate, one square of semisweet baking chocolate, and two bowls lined with plastic wrap.

## Safety Notes

(1) Personal protective equipment should be worn during the setup, hands-on, and takedown segments of the activity. (2) Immediately wipe up spilled water—it creates a slip-and-fall hazard. (3) Wash hands with soap and water upon completing this activity. (4) Food used in lab activities is not to be eaten! This is to avoid risk of

SCIENTISTS AND ENGINEERS ARE **PUZZLERS**—CHARLES DARWIN

cross-contamination of food with hazardous chemicals in laboratories. *Accordingly, the M&M Moth and Chocolate Butterfly activities should be carried out only in a regular classroom, not in a laboratory.*

## Setting the Context
### Engage

Start by engaging students with an activity introducing them to camouflage. Prepare by mixing together the M&Ms and candy corn in your container, as shown in Figure 4.5. Mix them well so the orange and yellow M&Ms blend in as much as possible. *Safety reminder: Conduct this activity in a regular classroom, not in a laboratory environment, to avoid risk of cross-contamination of food with hazardous chemicals.* If students will be allowed to eat M&Ms and candy corn after the activity is complete, bring a separate supply of candies for that purpose.

Introduce students to your collection of "M&M moths" (modified from STAT 1996 and Lovering 2016). Walk around the room with the container of candy and invite each student to reach in to collect three M&M moths and then place them on their desks. *Remind students that for safety reasons, they should not eat these candies.* Once all students have collected their moths, call out each color of M&Ms and have students raise their hands to indicate whether they collected that color. Count the total for each color and record the data in a bar graph. Ask students, "Why were so few orange and yellow M&M moths chosen?" and "Why is this adaptation important to M&M moth survival?" *Students will want to say there were not many or were no orange and yellow M&Ms in the container when, in fact, they were there but hard to see. The yellow and orange M&Ms are actually camouflaged within their candy corn environment.*

Figure 4.5

M&M Moths Hiding Among the Candy Corn

A full-color version of this photograph is available at *www.nsta.org/eureka*.

Walk around with the tray one more time so the students can see how the orange and yellow M&Ms blend in. Camouflage— protective coloration—contributes to the survival of prey animals in a predator–prey relationship. The M&M moths vary in appearance and ability to survive because they have inherited different traits. The environment also affects what traits an organism acquires. You can carry this discussion as far as you like; some students may suggest that the surviving orange and yellow moths will produce offspring that, like themselves, are orange and yellow—the concept of survival of the fittest. In this activity, the pattern of change is very evident.

# 4 PLANNING AND CARRYING OUT INVESTIGATIONS

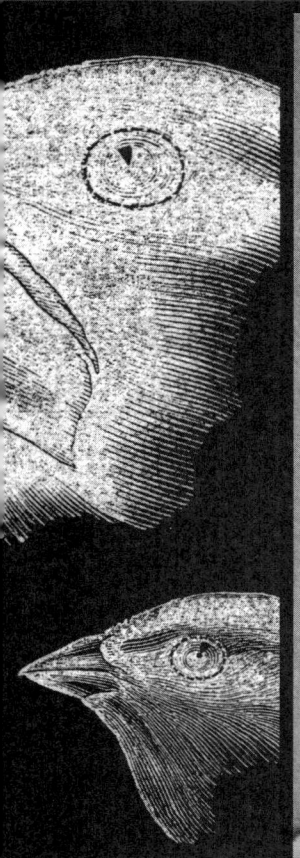

## Charles Darwin

### Guided Reading

Introduce the book *Darwin: With Glimpses Into His Private Journal and Letters* by asking, "What do you observe about the person on the front cover?" and "What does it look like is happening on the front cover?" Read the story aloud. Encourage students to notice and think about Charles Darwin's interests as a scientist. *This picture book includes many images of actual writings from Darwin's personal journals and letters. These add insight to the story of Darwin's troubled life as a scientist; however, the story stands alone without the notes, so you may leave them for a few students to read on their own, if you prefer.* The following questions may be used to guide students' attention to detail as you read. (Page numbers reference unnumbered book pages, beginning with the title page as page 1.)

1. **Pages 1–9:** Why did Darwin's father object to a trip to South America? How was Darwin able to persuade his father to approve of the trip? *From the time*

SCIENTISTS AND ENGINEERS ARE **PUZZLERS**—CHARLES DARWIN

*he was very young, Darwin liked to collect things. He preferred collecting things such as animals and rocks and doing experiments instead of focusing on his school studies. Darwin's father thought the trip to map the coast of South America was yet another of Darwin's useless undertakings, but Darwin succeeded in getting his uncle to write a letter back to his father.* **What might Darwin's Uncle Josiah's letter have said that convinced Darwin's father to let him go on the voyage?** *The text does not clearly state what Josiah's letter said, so use this open-ended question to encourage some insightful thinking by your students.*

2. **Pages 12–14:** How did Darwin's seasickness lead him to new discoveries? *Because of his tendency to become seasick, Darwin was even more anxious to get off the ship at every stop. These jaunts led to his extensive exploration of the islands, coastlines, mountains, and forests. He sent his notes and collections to Professor Henslow in England so he would be able to think about them more when he returned.*

3. **Pages 16–21:** Name three things that Darwin studied and/or collected during his stops along the voyage. *Darwin studied geology to learn about Earth's history (e.g., seashells on top of a mountain or rocks shifted by volcanoes), fossils, tortoises and lizards, and birds.*

4. **Page 21:** How did people know about Darwin by the time he returned home? *Professor Henslow had been sharing Darwin's letters and collections with other scientists—plants to botanists, fossils to paleontologists, and birds to an ornithologist.*

5. **Page 23:** What surprised Darwin about the species of birds he found on the Galapagos Islands? *Darwin thought he had collected a mixture of different bird species—finches, blackbirds, grosbeaks, and a wren. However, ornithologist John Gould pointed out to him the similarities in the structure of the birds' beaks, bodies, feathers, and tails, which showed that they were all related. All of the birds Darwin collected were finches.*

6. **Pages 34–36:** Darwin's ideas about how living things change over time met with some controversy. Why is it important for scientists' research to face examination by others? *These questions and exchanges drive the very essence of a body of science knowledge that changes over time as a result of new empirical evidence. Peer scientists, as well as members of the general public, probe scientists' work to better understand the findings and to ensure that the research processes are valid (e.g., that measurements and observations are accurate).*

# 4 PLANNING AND CARRYING OUT INVESTIGATIONS

## Making Sense
### Explore

Invite groups of four or five students to predict the number of ways that the potatoes will vary from one another and have them record this prediction in their science notebooks. Encourage them to make a dependable prediction by first carefully considering the coloration and other characteristics of the potatoes. Once students have recorded their predictions, direct them to continue to observe and gather around the five potatoes at their table. *Consider creating a list of students' ideas about variable characteristics that they can measure (e.g., number of eyes, length, circumference, and mass) to guide students' decisions about what to observe.* Point students to data-gathering tools, such as the hand lens, ruler, and balance scale they can use to measure mass. Then, guide their decision about what common attributes they will measure.

Encourage students to write and/or illustrate their observations and reasoning in their science notebooks, perhaps by placing their observations in a table such as Table 4.2. Students may use the characteristics given in the table or record whatever traits they choose. Ask, "What did you find out?" and "How does this relate to Charles Darwin's ideas?" *Some attributes of the potatoes will be similar, and some will be different. Although these potatoes are offspring of similar parents, some variations arise because of the growing conditions of this generation. For example, some will vary in size (dimension and mass), and some will vary in the number of eyes. Encourage students to recognize that small variations in the potatoes indicate micro-changes in the species. Here, the pattern of change is not as clear as it was in the M&M Moth activity.*

Table 4.2
Sample Notebook Chart for Potato Traits

| Potato | Dimensions | Mass | Number of Eyes | Other Variations |
|---|---|---|---|---|
| 1 | | | | |
| 2 | | | | |
| 3 | | | | |
| 4 | | | | |
| 5 | | | | |

## Explain

Ask students "How does this science activity help you to think about Charles Darwin's observations?" Encourage students to review and categorize the potato variations they have noted. In this way, they are developing ideas in the same manner as Darwin did about how and why things vary. If time allows, revisit the book and find specific examples of how Darwin developed ideas about how and why things vary.

## Extend

Invite students to participate in a Chocolate Butterfly activity (modified from STAT 1996 and Lovering 2016). This activity will encourage more thinking about camouflage and teach about a specific technique called mimicry, in which an organism changes in color or shape so it looks like another organism (usually one that tastes bad or is dangerous to predators). *Safety reminder: Conduct this activity in a regular classroom, not in a laboratory environment, to avoid risk of cross-contamination of food with hazardous chemicals.*

Prepare the chocolate butterflies before class. In one bowl lined with plastic wrap, put one square of unsweetened baking chocolate, and in another lined bowl, put one square of semisweet baking chocolate. Microwave the chocolate squares until melted (two to two and a half minutes). Spread the melted chocolate in a thin layer over the plastic wrap in each bowl, and then cool in the refrigerator until solidified. *The plastic wrap will help you remove the chocolate from the bowls after it has cooled.* Remove the solidified chocolate from each bowl and break into approximately 1-in. square pieces. Mix these semisweet and bitter chocolate "butterflies" together in one of the bowls, and dust them with powdered sugar to help disguise the difference in their color.

To start the activity, explain to students that they are pretending to be a predator of brown butterflies. Walk around the room with the bowl of chocolate butterflies and invite students to take one but to wait to eat their "prey" until everyone has one. Then, prompt the students to all eat their butterflies at the same time. Ask them, "Would anyone like to eat another chocolate butterfly?" and "Why or why not?" *Those who got a piece of unsweetened chocolate will not want a second taste.*

Next, show students images of a monarch butterfly and a viceroy butterfly. Explain that although these butterflies look much the same, the milkweed-feeding monarch butterfly actually tastes bad to predators. The viceroy butterfly has evolved to resemble the monarch butterfly so as to discourage predators. Ask students, "Which kind of chocolate represents the monarch butterfly, and which represents the viceroy butterfly?" This brief activity will encourage thinking about the four types of camouflage (concealing coloration, disruptive coloration, disguise, and mimicry). Encourage students to explore additional resources, such as those in "Additional Resources" section (p. 118).

# 4 PLANNING AND CARRYING OUT INVESTIGATIONS

### Evaluate

Summative evaluation of this lesson will include assessment of students' (1) understanding of the character trait of being a puzzler and (2) creation of a chart highlighting the differences among potato characteristics and giving an explanation about how these variations might ensure survival and reproduction.

**CHARACTER TRAIT**

Encourage students to answer the following questions:

1. How was Charles Darwin a puzzler? *Darwin collected and wondered about creatures and items in nature, such as bugs and shells, from the time he was very young. The book* Darwin *notes that Darwin much preferred exploring to studying (p. 2). As an adult, Darwin traveled the world to collect specimens. He collected everything he found and was interested in learning more about everything he saw. The book says Darwin could not stop thinking about the patterns of life he had seen in the Galapagos Islands and why species varied from one island to another (pp. 24–25).*

2. Why is being a puzzler an important trait for a scientist to have? *As a puzzler, Darwin enjoyed thinking deeply about his observations and specimens because he wanted to determine logical reasons for the pattern of species variations he noted worldwide.*

3. Working in pairs, discuss a time when you attempted to solve a problem and were a puzzler. Record notes about it in your science journals and then share it with the class.

**CONTENT**

Invite students to complete Table 4.3 as they work in their table groups and brainstorm ways the variations they observed might ensure survival and reproduction. Look for reasonable logic in the responses regarding contributions to survival and reproduction (e.g., more eyes might increase the root mass and thereby contribute to survival). You may use a rubric such as the one in Table 4.4 to assess student learning from the Puzzling Potatoes activity.

Table 4.3

Sample Notebook Chart for Potato Variations and Survival and Reproduction

| Observed Variation | How Variation Contributes to Survival | How Variation Contributes to Reproduction |
|---|---|---|
|  |  |  |
|  |  |  |
|  |  |  |

Table 4.4

Rubric for Assessing Students on the Puzzling Potatoes Activity

| Content or Skill | Not Yet | Beginning | Developing | Secure |
|---|---|---|---|---|
| Observation | Student did not record observations about the variations. | Student did not link his or her reasoning to the evidence observed. | Student linked his or her reasoning to the evidence observed and began to articulate how variations contribute to survival and reproduction. | Student linked his or her reasoning to the evidence observed and correctly identified how variations contribute to survival and reproduction. |
| Planning and Carrying Out Investigations | Student did not provide evidence of how the observed variations relate to the inherited variations. | Student provided some evidence of how the observed variations relate to the inherited variations. | Student provided complete evidence of how one observed variation relates to the inherited variations. | Student provided complete evidence of how two or more observed variations relate to the inherited variations. |

# 4 PLANNING AND CARRYING OUT INVESTIGATIONS

# SCIENTISTS AND ENGINEERS ARE
# INTUITIVE

### Learning About **Barnum Brown**

Intuitive (adj.): having the ability to know or understand things without any proof or evidence

## Lesson: Digging Up Dinosaurs

### Description

In this lesson, students assume the role of paleontologists as they assemble simulated dinosaur bones and think about how scientists determine logical explanations for fossils they find.

### Objectives

Students will consider how the character trait of being intuitive helped Barnum Brown identify bone fragments, assemble whole skeletons, and develop a broader understanding of dinosaur size and habitat.

- Before beginning the lesson, students will discuss how scientists hunt for dinosaur fossils, preserve fossils, and identify skeletal remains.

- As a class, students will discuss the word *paleontologist* in terms of where they have heard it before and what they think it means.

- Students will hear the story *Barnum's Bones: How Barnum Brown Discovered the Most Famous Dinosaur in the World* by Tracey Fern and discuss how it relates to the word *intuitive*.

- To conclude the lesson, students will assemble simulated dinosaur bones and decide whether the assembled dinosaur came from a plant eater or meat eater and whether it walked on two legs or four legs.

## Learning Outcomes

Students will (1) make a science notebook entry explaining what it means to be intuitive and why being intuitive is an important trait for scientists and engineers and (2) assemble a puzzle of dinosaur bones to demonstrate their understanding of fossils as evidence of animals that once roamed Earth.

## Connections to the *NGSS* and the Nature of Science, Grades 3–5
### Disciplinary Core Ideas
#### LS2.A: INTERDEPENDENT RELATIONSHIPS IN ECOSYSTEMS

- The food of almost any kind of animal can be traced back to plants. Organisms are related in food webs in which some animals eat plants for food and other animals eat the animals that eat plants. Some organisms, such as fungi and bacteria, break down dead organisms (both plants or plants parts and animals) and therefore operate as "decomposers." Decomposition eventually restores (recycles) some materials back to the soil. Organisms can survive only in environments in which their particular needs are met. A healthy ecosystem is one in which multiple species of different types are each able to meet their needs in a relatively stable web of life. Newly introduced species can damage the balance of an ecosystem.

#### LS4.A: EVIDENCE OF COMMON ANCESTRY AND DIVERSITY

- Some kinds of plants and animals that once lived on Earth are no longer found anywhere.
- Fossils provide evidence about the types of organisms that lived long ago and also about the nature of their environments.

## Science and Engineering Practices

***Asking Questions and Defining Problems:*** A practice of science is to ask and refine questions that lead to descriptions and explanations of how the natural and designed world works and which can be empirically tested. Asking questions and defining problems in grades 3–5 builds from grades K–2 experiences and progresses to specifying qualitative relationships.

- Identify scientific (testable) and non-scientific (non-testable) questions.
- Ask questions that can be investigated and predict reasonable outcomes based on patterns such as cause and effect relationships.

***Planning and Carrying Out Investigations:*** Scientists and engineers plan and carry out investigations in the field or laboratory, working collaboratively as well as individually. Their investigations are systematic and require clarifying what counts as data and identifying

# 4 PLANNING AND CARRYING OUT INVESTIGATIONS

variables or parameters. Planning and carrying out investigations to answer questions or test solutions to problems in 3–5 builds on K–2 experiences and progresses to include investigations that control variables and provide evidence to support explanations or design solutions.

- Make observations and/or measurements to produce data to serve as the basis for evidence for an explanation of a phenomenon or test a design solution.

***Analyzing and Interpreting Data:*** Scientific investigations produce data that must be analyzed in order to derive meaning. Because data patterns and trends are not always obvious, scientists use a range of tools—including tabulation, graphical interpretation, visualization, and statistical analysis—to identify the significant features and patterns in the data. Scientists identify sources of error in the investigations and calculate the degree of certainty in the results. Modern technology makes the collection of large data sets much easier, providing secondary sources for analysis. Analyzing data in 3–5 builds on K–2 experiences and progresses to introducing quantitative approaches to collecting data and conducting multiple trials of qualitative observations. When possible and feasible, digital tools should be used.

- Analyze and interpret data to make sense of phenomena, using logical reasoning, mathematics, and/or computation.
- Compare and contrast data collected by different groups in order to discuss similarities and differences in their findings.

## Crosscutting Concepts

***Patterns:*** Observed patterns in nature guide organization and classification and prompt questions about relationships and causes underlying them.

- Similarities and differences in patterns can be used to sort, classify, communicate and analyze simple rates of change for natural phenomena and designed products.
- Patterns can be used as evidence to support an explanation.

***Structure and Function:*** The way an object is shaped or structured determines many of its properties and functions.

- Different materials have different substructures, which can sometimes be observed.
- Substructures have shapes and parts that serve functions.

## Nature of Science Connections

**SCIENTIFIC INVESTIGATIONS USE A VARIETY OF METHODS**

- Science methods are determined by questions.
- Science investigations use a variety of methods, tools, and techniques.

**SCIENCE KNOWLEDGE IS BASED ON EMPIRICAL EVIDENCE**

- Science findings are based on recognizing patterns.
- Science uses tools and technologies to make accurate measurements and observations.

**SCIENTIFIC KNOWLEDGE IS OPEN TO REVISION IN LIGHT OF NEW EVIDENCE**

- Science explanations can change based on new evidence.

**SCIENCE IS A HUMAN ENDEAVOR**

- Men and women from all cultures and backgrounds choose careers as scientists and engineers.
- Most scientists and engineers work in teams.
- Science affects everyday life.
- Creativity and imagination are important to science.

**SCIENCE ADDRESSES QUESTIONS ABOUT THE NATURAL AND MATERIAL WORLD**

- Science findings are limited to questions that can be answered with empirical evidence.

Source: NGSS Lead States 2013.

Note: When an activity supports only part of a standard, underlining indicates the relevant part.

# 4 PLANNING AND CARRYING OUT INVESTIGATIONS

## Overview

In this lesson, students will learn how one person with a "nose for bones"—Barnum Brown—made tremendous discoveries in paleontology. Brown shared his fossil collection with others and educated people about many dinosaurs, especially his favorite "child," as he referred to it—*Tyrannosaurus rex*. Through the featured book, students learn that men and women from all backgrounds choose careers as scientists and engineers. The character trait of being intuitive refers to Brown's ability to sense and unearth a multitude of dinosaur bones and connect them to each other, to living plants, and to other archeological objects. In the hands-on portion of this lesson, students will experience the challenge of assembling dinosaur skeletons. In the lesson extension, students will have the opportunity to explore how paleontologists think about scientific evidence.

## Materials

You will need one copy of the book *Barnum's Bones: How Barnum Brown Discovered the Most Famous Dinosaur in the World* by Tracey Fern (ISBN 978-0374305161). For each student group, you will need a set of laminated paper dinosaur bones (template provided), a large envelope, a camera, a computer, and access to library books for research.

## Setting the Context
### Engage

Arrange students into four groups. Then invite students to share what they know about the work of paleontologists. *Paleontologists use fossils to study ancient plant and animal life, from dinosaurs to prehistoric plants, mammals, fish, insects, fungi, and even microbes. Fossils, such as dinosaur bones, provide evidence of what our planet was like long ago and how organisms have changed over time.* The following questions may be used to guide students' attention to detail as you read. (Page numbers reference unnumbered book pages, beginning with the title page as page 1.)

### Guided Reading

Through the book *Barnum's Bones: How Barnum Brown Discovered the Most Famous Dinosaur in the World*, students will learn how Barnum Brown planned and conducted his digs and how he was led by his intuition. Introduce the book by asking "What to you observe about the person on the front cover?" and "What does it look like is happening on the front cover?" Read the story aloud. Encourage

SCIENTISTS AND ENGINEERS ARE **INTUITIVE**—BARNUM BROWN

**Barnum Brown**

students to notice and think about the challenges Brown might have faced as a scientist digging for fossil bones.

1. **Page 1:** How did Barnum Brown come to have such an unusual name? *Brown was born in Carbondale, Kansas. His parents loved the circus, so they named their son after the famous American circus owner P. T. Barnum. The author explains, "They hoped Barnum's important sounding name would inspire him to do important, unusual things."*

2. **Page 5:** When was Barnum Brown first interested in fossils, and why? *Brown started his fossil collection as soon as he could follow behind his father's plow. When Brown was a young college student, a professor invited him to spend summers on fossil hunts in South Dakota and Wyoming. The author writes, "Each morning Barnum set out at sunrise. He hiked mountains, across creek beds, down precipices,*

# 4  PLANNING AND CARRYING OUT INVESTIGATIONS

*through streams, and around rattlesnake nests. Most folks would think this was torture. Barnum thought it was wonderful."*

3. **Pages 8–11:** Barnum Brown was described as having a good nose for bones. What do you think that means? *Soon after Brown began to work for My Dear Professor and the Museum of Natural History in New York City, he returned from an expedition to South America with four and a half tons of mammal fossils. My Dear Professor said about Brown that he must be able to smell fossils. But Brown had more than a good nose. He also read maps and geology books, chatted with local people, and studied the shape and color of rock layers. Although he seemed to sniff out bones, Brown's studies are what led him to search for bones in all the right places.*

4. **Page 20–24:** Barnum Brown had found fragments of the *T. rex*, but many pieces were still missing. Still, he wondered what it looked like, what it ate, and how it walked. What kinds of challenges would this present to a scientist trying to plan and conduct scientific investigations? *These missing pieces challenged Brown to continue searching, even though he sometimes spent weeks digging but finding nothing. The fragments he found helped him to hypothesize what the* T. rex *looked like and how it survived. Eventually, his passion (nose) led him to find an almost complete* T. rex, *including a perfect, four-foot-long skull. Only the leg bones were missing. However, using bones from his first* T. rex *find, he was able to piece together the entire dinosaur.*

5. **Page 29:** Why was Brown not satisfied with finding many, many bones on two Wyoming expeditions? *Brown dreamed of finding something new. Even though he collected more dinosaur bones than anyone in the world, the* T. rex *was still his "favorite child."*

## Making Sense
### Explore

Have students perform a "dinosaur dig" activity. Before class, use the templates in Figure 4.6 to prepare sets of dinosaur bones by cutting out the bones in each specimen set and laminating them. Package each set in an envelope. *Hint: Color code the laminated bones using adhesive color dots on the back to make it easier to sort them for storage after the activity.* Note: This activity is modified from ENSI 1999.

Begin by telling students that you have arranged an imaginary dig site for them where they will "discover" dinosaur bones and work in groups to determine how those bones should connect to each other. Invite them to sit on the floor in groups of four or five, and give each group an envelope of dinosaur bones. Instruct the students to begin by "digging up" three bones (i.e., removing them from the envelope). Allow students to discuss the arrangement of these bones for several minutes before asking them to dig up three more bones. Allow appropriate discussion time

### Figure 4.6
### Dinosaur Bone Sets

**Specimen A**

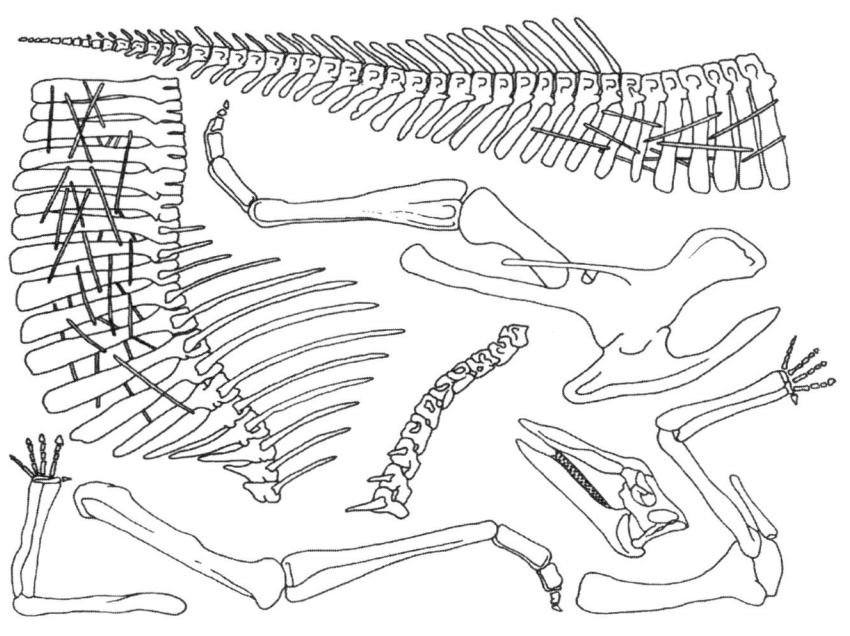

**Specimen B**

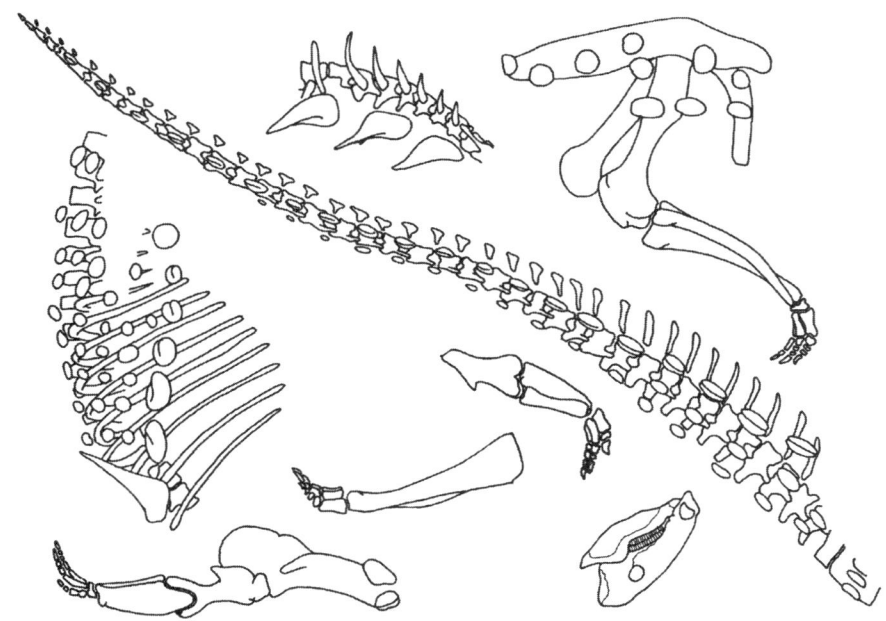

### Figure 4.6 (*cont.*)
### Dinosaur Bone Sets

**Specimen C**

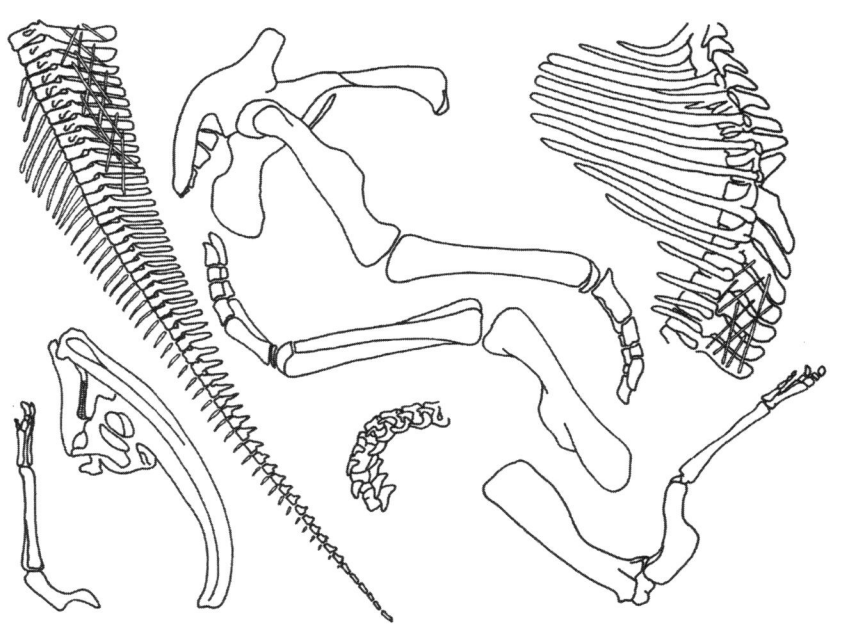

**Specimen D**

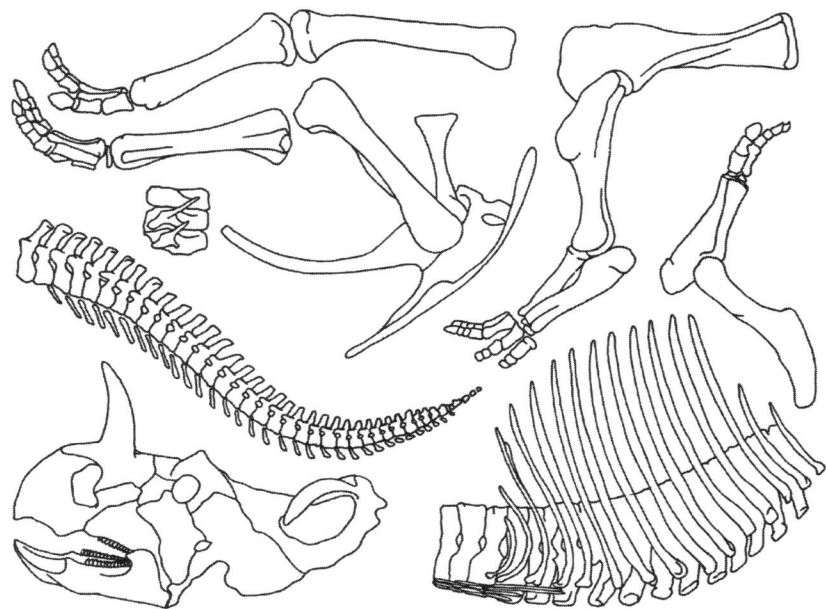

*Source:* Munsart 1993. Used with permission.

*Note:* Print each specimen set in full-page size. The four sets are available for download at *www.nsta.org/eureka*. Specimen A = *Ouranosaurusi;* specimen B = *Sauropelta;* specimen C = *Parasaurolophus;* specimen D = *Centrosaurus*.

SCIENTISTS AND ENGINEERS ARE **INTUITIVE**—BARNUM BROWN

Figure 4.7 _____

Paleontologist: _____

# DIGGING UP DINOSAURS WORKSHEET

Now that you have assembled your bones, answer the questions below.

1. What do you think your dinosaur ate? Why? What evidence do you have?

_____
_____
_____

2. Where do you think your dinosaur lived? Why? What evidence do you have?

_____
_____
_____

3. What type of climate did it live in? What evidence did you use to answer this question?

_____
_____
_____

4. Do you believe your dinosaur walked on two legs or four legs? Why? What evidence do you have?

_____
_____
_____

## Figure 4.8

### Example of a Student's Assembled Dinosaur Bones

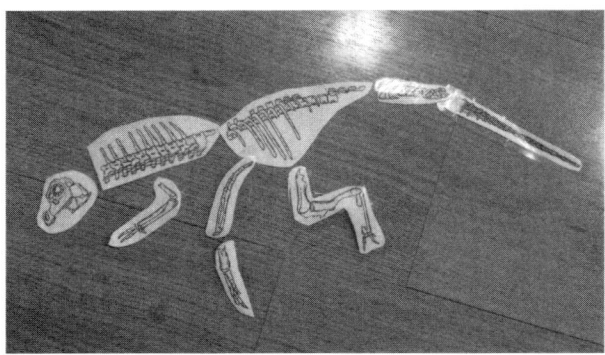

for students in the groups to offer their own hypotheses and debate one another's hypotheses. You may also provide students with the Digging Up Dinosaurs Worksheet (Figure 4.7, p. 113).

Continue this process until all of the bones are removed from the envelopes. Then, allow student groups to present their final hypothesis of how their bones should be assembled and explain their reasoning. Figure 4.8 shows an example of an assembled set of bones similar to those in Figure 4.6 (pp. 111–112).

To help students organize their thinking and do research to help them think about which dinosaur they have unearthed, ask questions such as "What did your dinosaur eat?" "Where did your dinosaur live?" "What type of climate did your dinosaur live in?" and "Did your dinosaur walk on two legs or four legs?" Encourage students to record these questions, their answers, and their reasoning in their science notebooks. Note that this process should not be about naming the "correct" dinosaur but rather about students focusing on scientific evidence and reasoning to help them prepare their conclusions. Finally, have students photograph their assembled bones for the next part of the lesson.

Next, have student groups compare their reconstructed dinosaur skeleton with dinosaur skeletons found in library books or through an internet search and hypothesize about what dinosaur most likely matches the one they reconstructed. Students may also refer to information they recorded in their science notebooks earlier to help them determine the most likely match. Ask them to agree on and record three pieces of evidence supporting the match (e.g., the ribs are similar). What's important here is that they use inductive reasoning in reviewing the evidence (skeletal components)—rather than name the correct dinosaur—because that is what paleontologists and all scientists do. It also might be interesting to provide students with images of the dinosaur species the activity templates represent (either reconstructed skeletons or living appearance inferred by professional paleontologists) to see whether they can select the bone set their group most likely reconstructed.

## Explain

Encourage students to conclude their dig and skeletal assembly by identifying the name of their dinosaur, possibly using the internet as a resource for information and ideas. Two websites we like are Dinosaurs for Kids (*www.kids-dinosaurs.com*)

and Dinosaur Fossils (*www.livescience.com/11266-dinosaur-fossils.html*). Encourage students to present findings based on evidence; this may require a class discussion about belief versus evidence. Students should present conclusions based on the evidence they gathered from the bones and their research. Have each group provide three pieces of evidence (gathered from their research) that their set of bones is from the dinosaur they name. Allow each group to present their photograph of assembled bones to the class along with their hypothesis about the actual name of the dinosaur. Students should also report to the class where they believe the dinosaur lived, what it ate, and whether it walked on two legs or four legs.

### Extend

To help your students think more deeply about how paleontologists work, introduce the story *Seven Blind Mice* (Young 1992). This short story tells of seven blind mice that discover a large strange "Something" in their pond. Each mouse sets out in turn to find out more about the Something, after which it returns to the group to describe the one thing it found out. By the end of the story, the mice realize they need to pool all the bits of information they have gathered. For example, one mouse thinks the Something is a snake, whereas another thinks it is a fan. From putting their bits together, the mice realize they "saw" an elephant (i.e., the snake was really the elephant's trunk and the fan was really the elephant's ear). The story ends with a mouse moral: "Knowing in part may make a fine tale, but wisdom comes from seeing the whole."

Ask your students, "How does this mouse moral describe the work of paleontologists?" *Paleontologists first gather data and then develop hypotheses and questions from the data. This scientific process is called deductive reasoning. Most scientists follow inductive reasoning, in which they first develop hypotheses and ask questions and then collect data. Students will recall how the blind mice first collected data and then deductively considered the data all together to reason that the Something was an elephant.*

We also highly recommend the book *How the Dinosaur Got to the Museum* by Jessie Hartland (2013). It is informative and describes the process of preserving dinosaur skeletons but is also very entertaining because it is written in delightful, repetitive verse, in much the same style as the children's rhyme *There Was an Old Lady Who Swallowed a Fly*.

### Evaluate

Summative evaluation of this lesson will include assessment of students' understanding of (1) how the character trait of being intuitive is a benefit to scientists and engineers and (2) how fossils provide evidence of animals that once lived on Earth.

# 4 PLANNING AND CARRYING OUT INVESTIGATIONS

**CHARACTER TRAIT**

Encourage students to answer the following questions:

1. If Barnum Brown had not discovered a complete skeleton of *T. rex*, do you think someone else would have? Why is being intuitive an important attribute for scientists and engineers to have? How was Barnum Brown intuitive?" *Although others might eventually have discovered the* T. rex, *Brown was intuitive, and his intuitive nature helped him to find the* T. rex *skeleton before anyone else did. The point here is to review Brown's science discoveries from the perspective of the character trait of being intuitive. Intuitive scientists are able to make connections where others do not find logical explanations (e.g., Brown connected what he read on maps and in geology books with how he found fossil remains in the field). Brown's reputation for being able to "smell fossils" is how others made sense of his intuitive nature.*

2. Working in pairs, discuss a time when you were intuitive. Record notes about it in your science journals and then share it with the class.

**CONTENT**

Evaluate students' explanations of how the physical characteristics of their dinosaur bone fragments (puzzle pieces) helped them to think about their dinosaur's environment, survival, and reproduction. In addition, evaluate how students used the information they recorded in their science notebooks to help them match their skeletal reconstructions to those they found in their internet and/or book research. Did students understand how these bone fragments provide evidence of dinosaurs' environments and demonstrate solid, inductive reasoning about the relationship between the bones and the environment?

You might create a rubric like the one in Table 4.5 to help you assess student learning from the Digging Up Dinosaurs activity.

Table 4.5

Rubric for Assessing Students on the Digging Up Dinosaurs Activity

| Content or Skill | Not Yet | Beginning | Developing | Secure |
|---|---|---|---|---|
| Evidence of Environmental Factors | Student did not discuss or document the relationship between the bones and the environment. | Student provided some discussion or documentation of the relationship between the bones and the environment. | Student showed some use of inductive reasoning, as evident in the discussion or documentation about the relationship between the bones and the environment. | Student showed strong use of inductive reasoning, as evident in the discussion or documentation about the relationship between the bones and the environment. |
| Evidence of Dinosaur Type | Student provided no evidence of dinosaur type. | Student provided one accurate piece of evidence. | Student provided two accurate pieces of evidence. | Student provided three accurate pieces of evidence provided. |
| Reasoning | Student provided no reasoning for how the group used evidence to form its conclusion. | Student provided limited reasoning for how the group used evidence to form its conclusion. | Student provided some reasoning for how the group used evidence to form its conclusion. | Student provided substantial reasoning for how the group used evidence to for its conclusion. |
| Team Cooperation | Student did not cooperate with the team in completing the task or the task was not completed. | Student showed little or no cooperation with the team in completing the task. | Student showed some cooperation with the team in completing the task. | Student fully cooperated with the team in completing the task. |

## References

Evolution and the Nature of Science Institute (ENSI). 1999. Indiana University Bloomington. *The great fossil find*. www.indiana.edu/~ensiweb/lessons/gr.fs.fd.html.

Fern, T. 2012. *Barnum's bones: How Barnum Brown discovered the most famous dinosaur in the world*. New York: Margaret Ferguson Books.

Keeley, P. 2008. *Science formative assessment*. Thousand Oaks, CA: Corwin Press.

Lovering, E. 1996. *Camouflage lesson plan*. Adapted from a DNA, dinosaurs, and Darwin workshop by J. Wood, J. Meneray, and C. Wood, presented at the Science Teachers Association of Texas Conference for the Advancement of Science Teaching, Austin, TX.

McGinty, A. B. 2009. *Darwin: With glimpses into his private journal and letters*. Boston: Houghton Mifflin.

Munsart, C. A. 1993. *Investigating science with dinosaurs*. Englewood, CO: Teacher Ideas Press.

NGSS Lead States. 2013. *Next Generation Science Standards: For states, by states*. Washington, DC: National Academies Press. www.nextgenscience.org/next-generation-science-standards.

Science Teachers Association of Texas (STAT). 1996. DNA, dinosaurs, and Darwin. Workshop presented by J. Wood, J. Meneray, and C. Wood at the Conference for the Advancement of Science Teaching, Austin, TX.

Winter, J. 2011. *The watcher: Jane Goodall's life with the chimps*. New York: Random House.

Young, E. 1992. *Seven blind mice*. New York: Philomel Books.

## Additional Resources

Berger, M. 1998. *Chirping crickets*. New York: HarperCollins.

Nature Watch. 2013. Viceroy. *www.natureblog.org/viceroy*.

EnchantedLearning.com. 2016. Cricket. *www.enchantedlearning.com/paint/subjects/insects/orthoptera/Cricket.shtml*. Schematic with scientific names of cricket body parts.

Hartland, J. 2013. *How the dinosaur got to the museum*. Maplewood, NJ: Blue Apple Books.

Kids-Dinosaurs.com. 2016. *www.kids-dinosaurs.com*.

Live Science. 2016. *Image gallery: Dinosaur fossils*. www.livescience.com/11266-dinosaur-fossils.html.

Ruth Patrick Science Education Center at the University of South Carolina Aiken. 2016. *Camouflage and mimicry*. http://rpsec.usca.edu/step/Lesson%20powerpoints/Camouflage%20and%20mimicry.ppt. Classroom-ready PowerPoint presentation that explains mimicry as an adaptation. It also provides an excellent example of mimicry wherein the nontoxic viceroy butterfly has adopted the coloration of the monarch butterfly, which is very unpleasant for its predators to eat.

# 5

# Analyzing and Interpreting Data

The practice of analyzing and interpreting data is central to science and engineering. This chapter focuses on three scientists whose efforts demonstrate the importance of data analysis and interpretation. The study of snow crystals (Wilson Bentley), the classification of clouds (Luke Howard), and the development of bird banding (John James Audubon) all required careful recording, review, and understanding of the data. It is easy to see how the character traits of being *dedicated,* being a *dreamer,* and being *curious* apply to these three individuals.

The *Next Generation Science Standards* (*NGSS*; NGSS Lead States 2013) describe the importance of analyzing and interpreting data as evidence to support one's conclusions. In science, quantifiable data and the concept of multiple trials are to be introduced in grades 3–5. In engineering, products and solutions are developed by analyzing a design as a prototype, collecting data about how it performs, and then revising the design. Also, the integration of science and mathematics is considered an optimal learning approach for analyzing and interpreting data.

## Recommended Science Teaching Strategy: Integration of Science and Mathematics

The *NGSS* emphasize the integration of the science, technology, engineering, and mathematics (STEM) subject areas in classroom lessons. Our years of research have shown us that it is not always best to teach subjects in isolation because their topics do not exist in isolation in the real world. Learning is more likely to occur in authentic learning environments that allow essential connections across content lines—the kind of problem solving found in integrated lessons (Bransford, Brown, and Cocking 2002). Now, science and mathematics professional organizations are again promoting integration of the two disciplines. A decline in student achievement has raised concern for continued national strength in an international business place. Science and mathematics are closely related systems of thought and are naturally correlated in the physical world. Science can provide students with concrete examples of abstract mathematical ideas that can improve learning of mathematics concepts (Thomas, Cooper, and Haukos 2004). Mathematics can enable students to achieve a deeper understanding of science concepts by providing

# 5 ANALYZING AND INTERPRETING DATA

ways to quantify and explain science relationships. Science activities illustrating mathematics concepts can provide relevancy and motivation for learning mathematics (Thomas, Cooper, and Ponticell 2000).

One of the best lessons Donna has found for teaching students about analyzing and interpreting data (and integrating mathematics and science) is a lesson on the properties of matter called "Product Testing" in the book *Chemistry Matters* (AIMS Education Foundation 2012), but this lesson can also be purchased individually. In it, students are prompted to answer a key question: "What is the best formula for Glubber?" Its activity pages guide students through a series of experiments involving three formulas of borax solution and white glue and five tests (print, imprint, bounce, stretch, and shape). It's a perfect lesson for introducing how scientists and engineers analyze and interpret data while focusing on both mathematics and science.

The product-testing lesson focuses on the creation of a new material and engages students in observing chemical changes and performing data-driven tests on the new products. This is one example of teaching an integrative lesson where mathematics and science learning opportunities complement one another within the same lesson. The rationale for the integration of mathematics and science comes from the idea that science and mathematics are interwoven in the real world and should be similarly treated as such in the classroom. Science encompasses questioning, hypothesizing, investigating, discovering, and communicating. Mathematics as a language provides scientists with clarity, objectivity, and understanding. In this approach, mathematics becomes more meaningful and more useful when it is applied to a particular context in which students are already learning, and the science also becomes more meaningful. In our experience, this learning is better retained by students because the content has meaning in and relevance to their lives.

# SCIENTISTS AND ENGINEERS ARE
# DEDICATED

## Learning About **Wilson Bentley**

Dedicated (adj.): devoted to an idea or purpose and willing to give a great deal of time and energy to it

### Lesson: Sizing Up Snowflakes
### Description

In this lesson, students learn how Wilson Bentley introduced the world to the hexagonal beauty of snowflakes and gave purpose to microphotography as a research technique.

### Objectives

Students will consider how the character trait of being dedicated helped Wilson Bentley observe the details of snowflakes and discover their mathematical (sixfold) symmetry.

- Before beginning the lesson, students will observe images of several snowflakes, including the largest recorded snow crystals.

- As a class, students will discuss how snowflakes demonstrate the occurrence of mathematics in nature.

- Students will hear the story *Snowflake Bentley* by Jacqueline Briggs Martin and discuss how it relates to the word *dedicated*.

- Depending on availability, students will either capture natural snowflakes or create artificial snowflakes and observe their mathematical symmetry.

- To conclude the lesson, students will investigate salt crystals under a microscope to learn more about crystal symmetry.

# 5 ANALYZING AND INTERPRETING DATA

## Learning Outcomes

Students will (1) make a science notebook entry to explain what it means to be dedicated and why being dedicated is an important trait for scientists and engineers and (2) analyze data to understand the symmetrical properties of snowflakes.

## Connections to the *NGSS* and the Nature of Science, Grades 3–5

### Disciplinary Core Idea
**PS1.A: STRUCTURE AND PROPERTIES OF MATTER**

- <u>Matter of any type can be subdivided into particles that are too small to see, but even then the matter still exists and can be detected by other means.</u> A model showing that gases are made from matter particles that are too small to see and are moving freely around in space can explain many observations, including the inflation and shape of a balloon and the effects of air on larger particles or objects.

- Measurements of a variety of properties can be used to identify materials. (Boundary: At this grade level, mass and weight are not distinguished, and no attempt is made to define the unseen particles or explain the atomic-scale mechanism of evaporation and condensation.)

### Science and Engineering Practices

*Asking Questions and Defining Problems:* A practice of science is to ask and refine questions that lead to descriptions and explanations of how the natural and designed world works and which can be empirically tested. Asking questions and defining problems in grades 3–5 builds from grades K–2 experiences and progresses to specifying qualitative relationships.

- Ask questions that can be investigated and predict reasonable outcomes based on patterns such as cause and effect relationships.

*Planning and Carrying Out Investigations:* Scientists and engineers plan and carry out investigations in the field or laboratory, working collaboratively as well as individually. Their investigations are systematic and require clarifying what counts as data and identifying variables or parameters. Planning and carrying out investigations to answer questions or test solutions to problems in 3–5 builds on K–2 experiences and progresses to include investigations that control variables and provide evidence to support explanations or design solutions.

- Make observations and/or measurements to produce data to serve as the basis for evidence for an explanation of a phenomenon or test a design solution.

***Analyzing and Interpreting Data:*** Scientific investigations produce data that must be analyzed in order to derive meaning. Because data patterns and trends are not always obvious, scientists use a range of tools—including tabulation, graphical interpretation, visualization, and statistical analysis—to identify the significant features and patterns in the data. Scientists identify sources of error in the investigations and calculate the degree of certainty in the results. Modern technology makes the collection of large data sets much easier, providing secondary sources for analysis. Analyzing data in 3–5 builds on K–2 experiences and progresses to introducing quantitative approaches to collecting data and conducting multiple trials of qualitative observations. When possible and feasible, digital tools should be used.

- Analyze and interpret data to make sense of phenomena, using logical reasoning, mathematics, and/or computation.
- Use data to evaluate and refine design solutions.

## Crosscutting Concepts

***Patterns:*** Observed patterns in nature guide organization and classification and prompt questions about relationships and causes underlying them.

- Similarities and differences in patterns can be used to sort, classify, communicate and analyze simple rates of change for natural phenomena and designed products.

***Scale, Proportion, and Quantity:*** In considering phenomena, it is critical to recognize what is relevant at different size, time, and energy scales, and to recognize proportional relationships between different quantities as scales change.

- Natural objects and/or observable phenomena exist from the very small to the immensely large or from very short to very long time periods.
- Standard units are used to measure and describe physical quantities such as weight, time, temperature, and volume.

***Structure and Function:*** The way an object is shaped or structured determines many of its properties and functions.

- Different materials have different substructures, which can sometimes be observed.
- Substructures have shapes and parts that serve functions.

## Nature of Science Connections
### SCIENTIFIC INVESTIGATIONS USE A VARIETY OF METHODS

- Science methods are determined by questions.
- Science investigations use a variety of methods, tools, and techniques.

# 5 ANALYZING AND INTERPRETING DATA

**SCIENCE KNOWLEDGE IS BASED ON EMPIRICAL EVIDENCE**

- Science findings are based on recognizing patterns.
- Science uses tools and technologies to make accurate measurements and observations.

**SCIENCE IS A WAY OF KNOWING**

- Science is both a body of knowledge and processes that add new knowledge.
- Science is a way of knowing that is used by many people.

**SCIENTIFIC KNOWLEDGE ASSUMES AN ORDER AND CONSISTENCY IN NATURAL SYSTEMS**

- Science assumes consistent patterns in natural systems.

**SCIENCE IS A HUMAN ENDEAVOR**

- Men and women from all cultures and backgrounds choose careers as scientists and engineers.
- Science affects everyday life.
- Creativity and imagination are important to science.

*Source:* NGSS Lead States 2013.

*Note:* When an activity supports only part of a standard, underlining indicates the relevant part.

## Overview

In this lesson, students learn how one person, Wilson Bentley, discovered and documented the fineness of snow crystals and the intricate details of snowflakes, work that is still important today. Through the featured book, students learn that men and women from all backgrounds choose careers as scientists and engineers. The character trait of being dedicated refers to Bentley's consistent determination to investigate snow crystals.

## Materials

You will need a computer and one copy of the featured book, *Snowflake Bentley* by Jacqueline Briggs Martin (ISBN 0-395861624). Each group will need a microscope and small amounts of salt and sugar, and each student will need his or her science notebook. If students will do the Observing Snow Crystals activity, you will need real falling snow, and each group will need black construction paper and a hand lens. For the

SCIENTISTS AND ENGINEERS ARE **DEDICATED**—WILSON BENTLEY

Preserving Snow Crystals activity, you will need liquid cyanoacrylate adhesive (not gel), microscope slides with cover slips, a small paintbrush, and black construction paper. For the Creating Snowflakes activity, you will need white construction paper and scissors.

## Safety Notes

(1) Personal protective equipment should be worn during the setup, hands-on, and takedown segments of the activity. (2) Use caution when working with cyanoacrylate adhesive—it bonds skin and eyes in seconds! Immediately wash off with soap and water. (3) Wash hands with soap and water upon completing this activity.

## Setting the Context

### Engage

Engage students before the lesson by asking "What do you know about snowflakes?" "What do snowflakes look like?" "How do snowflakes form?" and "Why do they disappear?" Display an image of the largest snowflake ever recorded—a "monster snow crystal"—on the website Snowcrystals.com (*www.snowcrystals.com*). Ask students to record five observations about that picture. Ask students "What do you observe about snowflakes?" and "What questions do you have?" Discuss students' observations and questions as a class.

### Guided Reading

Students will learn about the work of Wilson Bentley, whose life passion was observing and recording the vast variety of snowflakes. Introduce the book by showing students the cover and asking, "What does the front cover tell you about the story we are about to read?" Read the story aloud. Encourage students to notice and think about the challenges Bentley faced as simple farmer who was dedicated to exploring the nature of snowflakes. The following questions may be used to guide students' attention to detail as you read. (Page numbers reference unnumbered book pages, beginning with the title page as page 1.)

1. **Pages 8–11:** Wilson Bentley loved snow. As a youth, he began studying snowflakes under a microscope. What did he discover when he looked at snowflakes under the microscope? *Bentley learned that snowflakes have six branches and that no two are alike. He tried to draw them, but they melted before he could finish the drawing.*

2. **Pages 12–13:** Bentley read about a camera with its own microscope and wished he could have one. How did he convince his parents to buy him this new camera so he could photograph snowflakes before they melted? *The Wilsons loved their son and wanted him to be happy. Although his father thought*

# 5 ANALYZING AND INTERPRETING DATA

*"fussing with snow is foolishness," Wilson's parents spent their savings to buy him the microscope camera when he was 17 years old.*

3. **Pages 16–17:** Bentley's first snowflake photographs were a failure. Why did Bentley's first photographs fail? *Bentley had to figure out how to set the lens opening so it allowed just enough light to reach the negative.* What do you think inspired Bentley to try again? *Bentley was dedicated to learning and understanding all he could about snowflakes. He needed photographs to be able to study and compare the snow crystals because they melted too quickly to draw them.*

4. **Pages 18–27:** Although initially no one cared about Bentley's snowflake photographs, he persisted. How do you think this simple farmer became known as the snowflake man? *Bentley was so passionate about the thousands of snowflake images he captured over his lifetime that he shared them worldwide through speeches, publications, and neighborhood shows.* Why did Bentley continue to photograph snow until the day he died, even though he never grew rich from his book or his photographs? *Bentley loved snowflakes more than money. Even after he published his book, he was enthusiastic about continuing his photographic studies. As he said, "I can't afford to miss a single snowstorm. I never know when I will find some wonderful prize."*

## Making Sense
### Explore

Have students carry out one or more of the three activities described below. The Observing Snowflakes and Preserving Snowflakes activities require access to snow, so plan to teach this lesson during a snowy season to increase the likelihood of catching falling snowflakes. If it does not snow in your region or you cannot plan this lesson around your area's snowfall, have students manufacture their own snowflakes from paper (the Creating Snowflakes activity).

#### ACTIVITY: OBSERVING SNOW CRYSTALS

Take students outside when it is snowing and encourage them to catch snowflakes on a piece of black construction paper. The black paper will make the snowflakes more visible and so allow students to observe them more carefully. Ask them to use a hand lens and focus on the shape and mathematical symmetry of the snowflakes.

Have students journal their snow crystals by first drawing them and then writing five observations about them in their science notebooks. For their observations, tell students to focus on something true that they can observe through their senses (seeing, hearing, smelling, tasting, and feeling). You may want to prompt students' observations. For example, ask students whether they notice broken crystals; if they do, tell them to record such imperfections in their five observations. *As they become*

## SCIENTISTS AND ENGINEERS ARE **DEDICATED**—WILSON BENTLEY

**Wilson Bentley**

*heavier and journey down to Earth's surface, snowflakes may change many times, and they may collide with other crystals.* Ask students whether they notice parts of the snow crystal that appear to have melted. *As snowflakes travel through the different layers of Earth's atmosphere, the variation in temperature in the various layers can affect the shape of the snowflake.* Ask students to focus on lines of symmetry as they observe their snow crystals. *There are several ways snow crystals can be symmetrical. It is also possible for snow crystals to lose their symmetry by the time they reach Earth's surface; encourage students to record observations of irregular crystals as well.*

### ACTIVITY: PRESERVING SNOW CRYSTALS

Chill the microscope slides, cover slips, paintbrush, and cyanoacrylate adhesive before starting the activity. Take students outside when it is snowing and encourage them to catch a snowflake on their black paper. The black paper will make it possible for students to see the snow crystals clearly as they choose one. Once a student has chosen a snow crystal, quickly place a drop of adhesive on the slide. *For*

# 5 ANALYZING AND INTERPRETING DATA

*safety, only teachers should use the cyanoacrylate adhesive.* Then, use the paintbrush to lift the snow crystal onto the drop of adhesive. Quickly place the cover slip over the snow crystal and adhesive so you end up with a snow crystal trapped inside the adhesive. Leave the slides in a freezer for a few weeks so the adhesive completely hardens, after which it will be a perfect specimen to view under a microscope. Have students observe their snow crystals under a microscope, make drawings of them, and write five observations about them in their science notebooks.

### ACTIVITY: CREATING SNOWFLAKES

Your students may have prior experience using pieces of white paper to create snowflakes with random patterns. Hearing about Wilson Bentley's research will make students aware of the intricate, one-of-a-kind patterns of snowflakes. Teach the students how to make six-pointed, symmetrical snowflakes. (You can find step-by-step directions on the website Instructables.com [*www.instructables.com/id/How-to-Make-6-Pointed-Paper-Snowflakes*].) Invite students to put one of their snowflake cutouts in their science notebooks and make an entry that describes how they created it and how it is similar to actual snowflakes.

## Explain

Invite students to consider how their observation of snowflakes helped them understand the structure and properties of snow. Talk with students about Wilson Bentley's interest in the symmetry and uniqueness of snowflakes. Discuss how Bentley was awestruck by all things in nature but how his passionate interest in and research on snow crystals established him as the primary expert on snow crystals yet today. Bentley came to understand that snow crystals begin as a speck and, as water molecules attach to that speck, the six-branched crystal begins to grow. Many things determine the way these branches grow, including variation in temperature, wind, and moisture levels. Snowcrystals.com (*www.snowcrystals.com*) contains additional information about how snowflakes develop under different atmospheric conditions and how they can vary in their crystal shape. For example, snowflakes can be triangular, and not all arms of the snowflake are identical.

Instruct students to illustrate examples of snow crystals and write three to five observations about them in their science notebooks. Remind them to label the details of their examples. Talk with students about the radial symmetry of snow crystals and help them understand that the crystal shape is due to scientific factors (e.g., the weather conditions when and where the water molecules freeze). Scientists continue to study the science and mathematics of snowflakes by freezing water molecules under microscopes equipped with cameras, research that remains linked to the dedicated efforts of Wilson Bentley.

## Extend

Extend the lesson by having students look at and think about reflective properties of snow crystals. Begin by asking students "Why does a snowbank look white?" Remind them of some common sayings related to this phenomenon (such as "clear as glass" and "white as snow"), and ask them what those sayings mean. This will help students to recognize that the properties of snow crystals do not change when they accumulate into banks of snow and will prompt them to think about why we think of snow as white, when a snow crystal is actually clear. *Snow crystals are made of ice, and ice is clear, like glass. An individual snow crystal appears clear under a microscope, like a small piece of shaped glass. In a snowbank, light reflects off the surfaces of the countless snow crystals, making it appear white. A cloud looks white for the same reason, except that in clouds, the light reflects off small, clear water droplets.*

Encourage students to find a real portrait of Wilson Bentley on the Jericho Historical Society's official website of Snowflake Bentley (*http://snowflakebentley.com*). This will help students to conceptualize that the "snowflake man" was indeed a real person. If every student in the classroom has a laptop or iPad, have students view that website to find similarities and differences between its information and the text of the featured book, *Snowflake Bentley*, which was read aloud in class.

Another possible extension of the lesson would be to read the book *The Story of Snow: The Science of Winter's Wonder* by Mark Cassino and Jon Nelson (2009). That book contains excellent photographs of snow crystals and addresses three questions: (1) How do snow crystals form? (2) What shapes can snow crystals take? and (3) Are any two snow crystals alike?

## Evaluate

Summative evaluation of this lesson will include assessment of students' understanding of (1) the character trait of being dedicated and (2) the naturally occurring, symmetrical properties of snow crystals.

### CHARACTER TRAIT

Encourage students to answer the following questions:

1. In your science journal, write about what it means to be dedicated. *Because Wilson Bentley was dedicated, he gathered thousands of photographs to demonstrate the beauty of snowflakes, even when others thought his snowflake studies were foolish.*

2. Why is being dedicated an important disposition for scientists to have? How are scientists dedicated to their work? *Dedicated people are passionate and enthusiastic about their ideas, and they are not easily discouraged from pursuing their ideas. Wilson's snowflake photographs established him as a world authority on snowflakes, and his work is still important today.*

3. Think of a person who is dedicated and explain why you think so.

# 5 ANALYZING AND INTERPRETING DATA

**CONTENT**

Use a rubric such as the one in Table 5.1 to assess the science notebook entries students made during the Explore phase (p. 126). Invite students to make a final entry in their science notebooks that summarizes what they have learned about snowflakes and the technology that allows the human eye to see their intricate properties.

Table 5.1

## Rubric for Assessing Students on the Snow Crystals Activity

| Content | Not Yet | Beginning | Developing | Secure |
|---|---|---|---|---|
| **Snow Crystal Drawing** | Student provided no drawing. | Student drawing indicates student cannot link his or her reasoning to the evidence observed. | Student drawing indicates student can link his or her reasoning to the evidence observed. | Student provided an illustration (picture with words as labels) it indicates student can link his or her reasoning to the evidence observed. |
| **Observation** | Student provided no observations. | Student observations are still at the imagination level. | Student observations are moving from the imagination level to evidence-based reality, and student provides at least one observation that is evidence-based. | Two or more of the student observations are evidence-based and are accurate. |

# SCIENTISTS AND ENGINEERS ARE
# DREAMERS

## Learning About **Luke Howard**

Dreamer (n.): a person whose ideas and projects are regarded as impractical or not based in reality

### Lesson: Water Cycle in a Bag
#### Description

In this lesson, students observe clouds as water-cycle components and learn how clouds help scientists predict the weather.

### Objectives

Students will recognize and identify the components of the water cycle and analyze the role of clouds in condensation and precipitation. Students will discuss how the character trait of being a dreamer helped Luke Howard accomplish his life's work.

- Before beginning the lesson, students will observe and describe several types of clouds.

- Students will hear the story *The Man Who Named the Clouds* by Julie Hannah and Joan Holub and discuss how it relates to the word *dreamer*.

- As a class, students will create and observe a plastic-bag model of a water cycle to help them understand and describe the role of clouds in the water cycle.

- To conclude the lesson, students will create and observe a miniature water cycle and discuss how it relates to cloud formation.

## ANALYZING AND INTERPRETING DATA

### Learning Outcomes

Students will (1) make a science notebook entry to explain what a dreamer is and why being a dreamer is an important trait for scientists and engineer, (2) recognize and identify the components of the water cycle, and (3) analyze data to understand the role of clouds in condensation and precipitation.

## Connections to the *NGSS* and the Nature of Science, Grades 3–5
### Disciplinary Core Ideas
**ESS2.A: EARTH MATERIALS AND SYSTEMS**

- <u>Rainfall helps to shape the land and affects the types of living things found in a region.</u> Water, ice, wind, living organisms, and gravity break rocks, soils, and sediments into smaller particles and move them around.

**ESS2.C: THE ROLES OF WATER IN EARTH'S SURFACE PROCESSES**

- Nearly all of Earth's available water is in the ocean. <u>Most fresh water is in glaciers or underground; only a tiny fraction is in streams, lakes, wetlands, and the atmosphere.</u>

### Science and Engineering Practices

***Asking Questions and Defining Problems:*** A practice of science is to ask and refine questions that lead to descriptions and explanations of how the natural and designed world works and which can be empirically tested. Asking questions and defining problems in grades 3–5 builds from grades K–2 experiences and progresses to specifying qualitative relationships.

- Ask questions that can be investigated and predict reasonable outcomes based on patterns such as cause and effect relationships.

***Planning and Carrying Out Investigations:*** Scientists and engineers plan and carry out investigations in the field or laboratory, working collaboratively as well as individually. Their investigations are systematic and require clarifying what counts as data and identifying variables or parameters. Planning and carrying out investigations to answer questions or test solutions to problems in 3–5 builds on K–2 experiences and progresses to include investigations that control variables and provide evidence to support explanations or design solutions.

- Make observations and/or measurements to produce data to serve as the basis for evidence for an explanation of a phenomenon or test a design solution.

- Make predictions about what would happen if a variable changes.

***Analyzing and Interpreting Data:*** Scientific investigations produce data that must be analyzed in order to derive meaning. Because data patterns and trends are not always obvious, scientists use a range of tools—including tabulation, graphical interpretation, visualization, and statistical analysis—to identify the significant features and patterns in the data. Scientists identify sources of error in the investigations and calculate the degree of certainty in the results. Modern technology makes the collection of large data sets much easier, providing secondary sources for analysis. Analyzing data in 3–5 builds on K–2 experiences and progresses to introducing quantitative approaches to collecting data and conducting multiple trials of qualitative observations. When possible and feasible, digital tools should be used.

- Represent data in tables and/or various graphical displays (bar graphs, pictographs, and/or pie charts) to reveal patterns that indicate relationships.
- Analyze and interpret data to make sense of phenomena, using logical reasoning, mathematics, and/or computation.

## Crosscutting Concepts

***Patterns:*** Observed patterns in nature guide organization and classification and prompt questions about relationships and causes underlying them.

- Similarities and differences in patterns can be used to sort, classify, communicate and analyze simple rates of change for natural phenomena and designed products.
- Patterns of change can be used to make predictions.
- Patterns can be used as evidence to support an explanation.

***Scale, Proportion, and Quantity:*** In considering phenomena, it is critical to recognize what is relevant at different size, time, and energy scales, and to recognize proportional relationships between different quantities as scales change.

- Natural objects and/or observable phenomena exist from the very small to the immensely large or from very short to very long time periods.
- Standard units are used to measure and describe physical quantities such as weight, time, temperature, and volume.

***Systems and System Models:*** A system is an organized group of related objects or components; models can be used for understanding and predicting the behavior of systems.

- A system can be described in terms of its components and their interactions.
- A system is a group of related parts that make up a whole and can carry out functions its individual parts cannot.

# 5 ANALYZING AND INTERPRETING DATA

## Nature of Science Connections

**SCIENTIFIC INVESTIGATIONS USE A VARIETY OF METHODS**

- Science methods are determined by questions.
- Science investigations use a variety of methods, tools, and techniques.

**SCIENCE KNOWLEDGE IS BASED ON EMPIRICAL EVIDENCE**

- Science findings are based on recognizing patterns.

**SCIENTIFIC KNOWLEDGE IS OPEN TO REVISION IN LIGHT OF NEW EVIDENCE**

- Science explanations can change based on new evidence.

**SCIENCE MODELS, LAWS, MECHANISMS, AND THEORIES EXPLAIN NATURAL PHENOMENA**

- Science theories are based on a body of evidence and many tests.
- Science explanations describe the mechanisms for natural events.

**SCIENCE IS A WAY OF KNOWING**

- Science is both a body of knowledge and processes that add new knowledge.
- Science is a way of knowing that is used by many people.

**SCIENTIFIC KNOWLEDGE ASSUMES AN ORDER AND CONSISTENCY IN NATURAL SYSTEMS**

- Science assumes consistent patterns in natural systems.
- Basic laws of nature are the same everywhere in the universe.

**SCIENCE IS A HUMAN ENDEAVOR**

- Men and women from all cultures and backgrounds choose careers as scientists and engineers.
- Science affects everyday life.
- Creativity and imagination are important to science.

*Source:* NGSS Lead States 2013.

*Note:* When an activity supports only part of a standard, underlining indicates the relevant part.

SCIENTISTS AND ENGINEERS ARE **DREAMERS**—LUKE HOWARD

## Overview

In this lesson, students learn how Luke Howard used his observation skills as an amateur scientist and developed a way to categorize clouds that allowed scientists to discuss clouds efficiently. Through the featured book, students learn that men and women from all backgrounds choose careers as scientists. The character trait of being a dreamer references Luke Howard's ability to use his imagination in observing the similarities and differences among cloud formations. Students share ideas about how scientists are dreamers.

## Materials

You will need one copy of the book *The Man Who Named the Clouds* by Julie Hannah and Joan Holub (ISBN 978-0807549742). For the Water Cycle in a Bag activity, you will need a roll of masking tape. Each student will need one zip-top, quart-size, resealable plastic bag; a clear medicine cup showing incremental measurements for 3 tsp or 15 ml; his or her science notebook; indirectly vented chemical splash goggles; and a nonlatex apron. Each table group will need one or two permanent markers.

## Safety Notes

(1) Personal protective equipment should be worn during the setup, hands-on, and takedown segments of the activity. (2) Immediately wipe up spilled water—it creates a slip-and-fall hazard. (3) Wash hands with soap and water upon completing this activity.

## Setting the Context
### Engage

Ask students to go outside and gather some cloud observations over three to five days. *This may be done as a class or assigned as homework if science time is limited.* Have them record notes about and draw illustrations of clouds in their science notebooks. Invite students to share their cloud observations with one another in small table groups and then share notable findings with the whole class.

### Guided Reading

Introduce the featured book by showing students the cover and asking "What does the front cover tell you about the story we are about to read?" Read the story aloud. The following questions may be used to guide students' attention to detail as you read. (Page numbers reference unnumbered book pages, beginning with the title page as page 1.)

# 5 ANALYZING AND INTERPRETING DATA

1. **Pages 4–9:** Luke Howard noticed that not all clouds looked alike. When did Howard begin his serious study of clouds? *Howard began to keep a weather journal when he was 10 years old. At this time, many people kept weather journals, hoping to learn about what caused clouds, rain, and fog. They made up sayings such as "Mares' tails bring storms and gales."*

2. **Pages 12–13:** In this time period, the causes of weather were a mystery. What specific events in 1783 especially caused people to worry about appearances in the sky? *In 1783, wind blew volcanic ash into England from a volcano eruption in Iceland. It was so dark that the Sun was hardly visible during the day. Later that year, a meteor flashed across the sky and caused people to worry whether the world was coming to an end. These events prompted even more interest in atmospheric studies.*

3. **Pages 15–17:** Also in 1783, two scientist brothers reasoned that if clouds could float, a balloon filled with a cloud of smoke could float, too. What was the confused reasoning of these scientists about what made balloons float like clouds? *The brothers thought the black smoke caused the balloons to rise; however, it is heat that causes balloons to float. Hot air from the fire heats the air in the balloon, causing it to expand and become less dense than the air outside the balloon. This, in turn causes the balloon to rise and then float in the atmosphere.*

4. **Pages 22–31:** Luke Howard's father thought watching clouds was a waste of time, so he sent Howard away to learn to be a chemist. When Howard had found a good job, he returned to his hobby of weather study. How did Howard's science studies with the Askesian Society help him develop cloud names? *Howard decided that clouds should be given names so that weather scientists could discuss them using a universal classification system. His decision to assign Latin names to clouds turned out to be a good one. Although the number of cloud types has increased to 21, 5 of Howard's original cloud names are still on the list used by the World Meteorological Organization.*

## Making Sense
### Explore
Invite students to take pictures of clouds. Assemble these into one document and include examples of the three main cloud types (cumulus, cirrus, and stratus) if possible. Invite students to create a water-cycle bag to personally experience the function of clouds in the processes of the water cycle. *Note: There will be no observable clouds in this model.*

1. Have each student use a permanent marker to draw a landscape on a sandwich-size zip-top bag. Illustrations might include the Sun, some trees,

## SCIENTISTS AND ENGINEERS ARE **DREAMERS**—LUKE HOWARD

Luke Howard

a body of water (e.g., a river or a lake), varied landforms (i.e., some high and some low), and clouds. Students may also add arrows and water-cycle labels. Figure 5.1 (p. 138) is an example of a completed water-cycle bag showing drawings and labels.

2. Place a medicine cup filled with a measured quantity of water in the zip-top bag. The water cup simulates a body of water, such as a lake or a stream. The water will evaporate during the day and then condense and "rain" down the sides of the bag and accumulate on the bottom, simulating the formation of groundwater. The measurement marks on the side of the medicine cup will allow students to quantify the evaporation that occurs from one observation time to the next.

3. Direct students to seal the bag closed and tape it to a window. Now a little sunshine through it will produce a foggy mist on the inside. In their science

# 5 ANALYZING AND INTERPRETING DATA

notebooks, students should note the start date and starting measurement of water in the cup.

4. Encourage students to make observations for one week, both at the same time each day and at different times of day. Ensure that students record the indoor and outdoor temperatures, as well as the water level in the medicine cup. Invite students to compare the observations they made at the same time each day with those made at random times. For example, what patterns, differences, or similarities do they notice? Have students work with their data by organizing or grouping them into a graph or chart. As they work, students should be making sense of data by recognizing patterns and relationships.

Figure 5.1

**Example of a Water Cycle in a Bag**

## Explain
After about a week, ask students to explain the pattern they see. Look for opportunities that arise to introduce scientific terms that are used to describe the water cycle, such as evaporation, condensation, and precipitation. Students will notice condensation and precipitation at different times of day, depending on your area's climate and what differences there are between morning and afternoon air temperature. The water level in the cup should drop daily. Although they cannot see the evaporation happening, students can deduce that evaporation is occurring when they observe (1) the reduced amount of water in the cup and (2) the condensed waterdrops on the inside of the bag. Encourage students to record three to five observations about their miniature water cycles in their science journals every couple of days.

## Extend
Invite students to watch and write down notes about nightly weather predictions from two different weather stations (on local television or the internet) for five days. Make a chart to track the accuracy of the two weather reports for that time. Ask the following questions:

- What types of clouds were reported each day?
- On which day(s) did both stations forecast the weather correctly? On which day(s) did both forecast the weather incorrectly?
- On how many days was the forecast from weather station 1 correct? On how many days was the forecast from weather station 2 correct?
- Why might different weather teams make different weather predictions?

*Like all scientists, meteorologists make predictions based on the available data and likely consequences. This could include cloud formations, prevailing winds, and barometric pressure. Sometimes the data change—for example, the winds change or clouds do not build up as anticipated—and cause different weather than was predicted. Meteorologists use a variety of computer models to help them anticipate future weather based on current conditions; however, weather is a chaotic system in which a tiny change in conditions can have great consequences. Weather forecasts are only an approximation of what will occur.*

Share the book *It Looked Like Spilt Milk* (Shaw 1988; ISBN 978-0812460773) with your students. They will easily relate to the search for recognizable shapes in cloud formations. Invite students to paint or tear cloud shapes and name them for each other (see Figure 5.2). Torn white paper scraps also make nice cloud shapes.

### Figure 5.2
### Examples of Student-Created Cloud Formations

 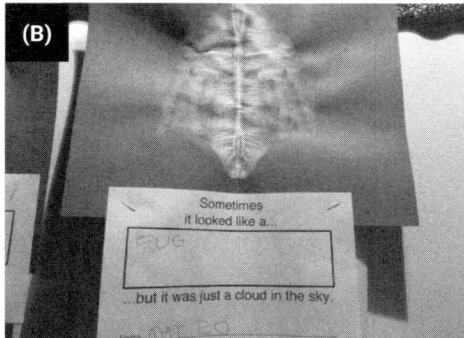

(A) After reading *It Looked Like Spilt Milk,* students explored with white paint on blue paper to make their own "cloud creations." (B) Students recorded what they thought their creations looked like.

## Evaluate
Summative evaluation of this lesson will include assessment of students' understanding of (1) the character trait of being a dreamer and (2) the role of clouds in condensation and precipitation.

# 5 ANALYZING AND INTERPRETING DATA

**CHARACTER TRAIT**

Encourage students to answer the following questions:

1. Why is being a dreamer an important trait for scientists and engineers? How was Luke Howard a dreamer? How did his daydreams about clouds help him to classify them? *Dreamers are persistent and often think of solutions while they are working on something else. In Howard's case, he worked as a chemist, and cloud studies were his hobby. Still, he kept his cloud observation notes and tried to answer questions about weather, and his notes helped him to see patterns in cloud formations and give them names.*

2. Working in pairs, discuss a time when you daydreamed about something you were trying to figure out. Record notes about it in your science journals and then share it with the class.

**CONTENT**

Review students' science notebook entries about the cloud formations they observed during the Engage phase (p. 135) as well as their entries about the changes they observed over time in their water-cycle bags during the Explore phase (p. 136). We have taught this water-cycle lesson many times and find that students really enjoy it. Once students begin to see a pattern, they will race into the classroom each morning to observe changes in their bag. As lessons go, this one is particularly dramatic and engenders considerable personal ownership! The rubric in Table 5.2 may be used for assessing students' observations in their science notebooks.

Table 5.2

**Rubric for Assessing Science Notebook Entries for the Water-Cycle-in-a-Bag Activity**

| Skill | Not Yet | Beginning | Developing | Secure |
|---|---|---|---|---|
| **Recording Data** | Student did not record any data. | Student recorded one data set. | Student recorded two data sets. | Student recorded more than two data sets. |
| **Analyzing Data** | Student did not analyze any data. | Student analyzed one data set. | Student analyzed two data sets. | Student analyzed more than two data sets. |
| **Interpreting Data** | Student did not interpret any data. | Student interpreted one data set. | Student interpreted two data sets. | Student interpreted more than two data sets. |
| **Conceptual Understanding of the Role of Clouds and Precipitation** | Student cannot articulate any connection between the role of clouds and condensation and precipitation. | Student can articulate an unclear connection between the role of clouds and condensation OR precipitation. | Student can articulate a clear connection between the role of clouds and condensation OR precipitation. | Student can articulate a clear connection between the role of clouds and condensation AND precipitation |

# SCIENTISTS AND ENGINEERS ARE CURIOUS

## Learning About John James Audubon

Curious (adj.): eager to learn or know; inquisitive

### Lesson: Sandhill Crane Migration

### Description

In this lesson, students will construct a puppet of a sandhill crane and "fly" it through its spring migration route as they learn why birds migrate and how they manage challenges along their migratory route.

### Objectives

Students will explain why birds migrate and how scientists continue to study the movement and behaviors of migratory birds.

- Before beginning the lesson, students will discuss bird migration and speculate why and how birds migrate.

- As a class, students will research lesser sandhill cranes and simulate their spring migration to experience these birds' long journeys and survival techniques.

- Students will hear the story *The Boy Who Drew Birds: A Story of John James Audubon* by Jacqueline Davies and discuss how it relates to the word *curious*.

- Students will become familiar with bird field guides and their use.

- To conclude this lesson, students might create a bird feeder so they can begin to observe and record nonmigratory and migratory birds in their own backyards.

# 5 ANALYZING AND INTERPRETING DATA

## Learning Outcomes

Students will make a science notebook entry to explain (1) what it means to be curious and why being curious is an important trait for scientists and engineers and (2) why birds migrate and how scientists continue to study the movement and behaviors of migratory birds.

## Connections to the NGSS and the Nature of Science, Grades 3–5

### Disciplinary Core Ideas

**LS1.B: GROWTH AND DEVELOPMENT OF ORGANISMS**

- Reproduction is essential to the continued existence of every kind of organism. Plants and animals have unique and diverse life cycles.

**LS3.A: INHERITANCE OF TRAITS**

- Many characteristics of organisms are inherited from their parents.

- Other characteristics result from individuals' interactions with the environment, which can range from diet to learning. Many characteristics involve both inheritance and environment.

**LS4.C: ADAPTATION**

- For any particular environment, some kinds of organisms survive well, some survive less well, and some cannot survive at all.

### Science and Engineering Practices

*Asking Questions and Defining Problems:* A practice of science is to ask and refine questions that lead to descriptions and explanations of how the natural and designed world works and which can be empirically tested. Asking questions and defining problems in grades 3–5 builds from grades K–2 experiences and progresses to specifying qualitative relationships.

- Ask questions about what would happen if a variable is changed.

- Identify scientific (testable) and non-scientific (non-testable) questions.

- Ask questions that can be investigated and predict reasonable outcomes based on patterns such as cause and effect relationships.

- Use prior knowledge to describe problems that can be solved.

- Define a simple design problem that can be solved through the development of an object, tool, process, or system and includes several criteria for success and constraints on materials, time, or cost.

***Planning and Carrying Out Investigations:*** Scientists and engineers plan and carry out investigations in the field or laboratory, working collaboratively as well as individually. Their investigations are systematic and require clarifying what counts as data and identifying variables or parameters. Planning and carrying out investigations to answer questions or test solutions to problems in 3–5 builds on K–2 experiences and progresses to include investigations that control variables and provide evidence to support explanations or design solutions.

- Evaluate appropriate methods and/or tools for collecting data.
- Make observations and/or measurements to produce data to serve as the basis for evidence for an explanation of a phenomenon or test a design solution.
- Make predictions about what would happen if a variable changes.

***Analyzing and Interpreting Data:*** Scientific investigations produce data that must be analyzed in order to derive meaning. Because data patterns and trends are not always obvious, scientists use a range of tools—including tabulation, graphical interpretation, visualization, and statistical analysis—to identify the significant features and patterns in the data. Scientists identify sources of error in the investigations and calculate the degree of certainty in the results. Modern technology makes the collection of large data sets much easier, providing secondary sources for analysis. Analyzing data in 3–5 builds on K–2 experiences and progresses to introducing quantitative approaches to collecting data and conducting multiple trials of qualitative observations. When possible and feasible, digital tools should be used.

- Analyze and interpret data to make sense of phenomena, using logical reasoning, mathematics, and/or computation.
- Analyze data to refine a problem statement or the design of a proposed object, tool, or process.

## Crosscutting Concept

***Patterns:*** Observed patterns in nature guide organization and classification and prompt questions about relationships and causes underlying them.

- Similarities and differences in patterns can be used to sort, classify, communicate and analyze simple rates of change for natural phenomena and designed products.
- Patterns of change can be used to make predictions.
- Patterns can be used as evidence to support an explanation.

# 5 ANALYZING AND INTERPRETING DATA

## Nature of Science Connections

**SCIENTIFIC INVESTIGATIONS USE A VARIETY OF METHODS**

- Science methods are determined by questions.
- Science investigations use a variety of methods, tools, and techniques.

**SCIENCE KNOWLEDGE IS BASED ON EMPIRICAL EVIDENCE**

- Science findings are based on recognizing patterns.
- Science uses tools and technologies to make accurate measurements and observations.

**SCIENTIFIC KNOWLEDGE IS OPEN TO REVISION IN LIGHT OF NEW EVIDENCE**

- Science explanations can change based on new evidence.

**SCIENCE IS A WAY OF KNOWING**

- Science is both a body of knowledge and processes that add new knowledge.
- Science is a way of knowing that is used by many people.

**SCIENTIFIC KNOWLEDGE ASSUMES AN ORDER AND CONSISTENCY IN NATURAL SYSTEMS**

- Science assumes consistent patterns in natural systems.
- Basic laws of nature are the same everywhere in the universe.

**SCIENCE IS A HUMAN ENDEAVOR**

- Men and women from all cultures and backgrounds choose careers as scientists and engineers.
- Science affects everyday life.
- Creativity and imagination are important to science.

**SCIENCE ADDRESSES QUESTIONS ABOUT THE NATURAL AND MATERIAL WORLD**

- Science findings are limited to questions that can be answered with empirical evidence.

*Source:* NGSS Lead States 2013.

*Note:* When an activity supports only part of a standard, underlining indicates the relevant part.

SCIENTISTS AND ENGINEERS ARE **CURIOUS**—JOHN JAMES AUDUBON

## Overview

In this lesson, students will learn about John James Audubon, the first person in North America to band a bird. His simple experiment proved that the small birds nesting near his home returned to the same nest each spring. Through the featured book, students learn that men and women from all backgrounds choose careers as scientists. The character trait of being curious references Audubon's strong desire to find out whether the same birds returned each spring and led to his inventive idea to place a marker on birds' legs so he could identify them uniquely. In the hands-on part of the lesson, students make a crane puppet to "fly" along a migratory route and build a bird feeder so they can document bird activity in their own yards.

## Materials

You will need one copy of the book *The Boy Who Drew Birds: A Story of John James Audubon* by Jacqueline Davies (ISBN 978-0618243433), a class map of the Western Hemisphere, and a sandhill crane migratory route chart, as well as safety glasses or goggles for each student. For the Sandhill Crane Puppet activity, each student will need a copy of the Sandhill Crane Puppet Template (provided in that section), and each group will need a roll of blue crepe paper, crayons, and scissors. For the Bird Feeder activity, you will need one empty 2-liter plastic bottle, a bag of birdseed, two wooden kitchen mixing spoons, a marker, a ruler, a sharp utility knife, a funnel, and a 1.5-in. screw-in hook.

## Safety Notes

(1) Personal protective equipment should be worn during the setup, hands-on, and takedown segments of the activity. (2) Use caution in working with sharps (scissors, knife, hook, and so on), which can cut or puncture skin or eyes. (3) Never eat any food used in lab activities. (4) Wash hands with soap and water upon completing this activity.

## Setting the Context
### Engage

Ask students to construct a migration model with classroom materials to illustrate their understanding. Typically, students have some knowledge that bird migration involves the birds flying to warmer regions for the colder seasons and then returning to cooler regions for the warmer seasons. Invite students to think about why birds migrate and how many miles they might travel during their migration. Ask, "How do birds know where and when they should migrate?" Students may visit the Bird Banding Laboratory website (*www.pwrc.usgs.gov/BBL/homepage/*

# 5 ANALYZING AND INTERPRETING DATA

*btypes.cfm*) to learn more about how bird banding is practiced today.

## Guided Reading

Inform students that they will be learning about bird migration and the work of a scientist who was especially curious by reading *The Boy Who Drew Birds: A Story of John James Audubon*. In 1803, John James Audubon became the first person in North America to mark birds, with that story featured in this book. A hundred years later, scientists began to use a numbered banding system to help track specific birds. *Banding* (or *ringing*, as it is called in Europe) allows scientists to know how far a bird has migrated, where it began and ended its migration, how long it has lived, and more. In the case of sandhill cranes, scientists also follow the birds' migratory behaviors by observing them from small airplanes. Refer to a classroom map of the Western Hemisphere to identify the migration route of the sandhill cranes from New Mexico and Texas to Siberia.

Introduce the book by asking "What do you observe about the person on the front cover?" and "What does it look like is happening on the front cover?" Read the story aloud. The following questions may be used to guide students' attention to detail as you read. (Page numbers reference unnumbered book pages, beginning with the title page as page 1.)

1. **Pages 2–7:** As a young boy, John James Audubon had learned to enjoy woodland walks with his father. He was happiest when he was watching birds. What bird behavior caused Audubon to wonder about bird migration? *It was early spring, and Audubon was walking in the woods. He passed by a limestone cave where he had watched a family of pewee flycatchers the summer before, and now he saw they had returned. He wondered whether these were the same pewees that had nested there the previous year, and where they had spent the winter.*

2. **Pages 8–11:** Audubon hurried home to think about his observations and questions. What kinds of things did he keep in his attic room, and why? *Audubon called his attic room his* musée *(which is French for* museum*). Here he kept his natural history books and his collections of nests, feathers, sketches, and stuffed birds.*

3. **Pages 12–13:** Audubon read all he could to try to answer his questions about bird migration. What did scientists of the day understand about where birds go in the winter? *The ancient Greek philosopher and scientist Aristotle had known that cranes migrated but reasoned that small birds hibernated underwater or in hollow logs. Most scientists in Audubon's time agreed with Aristotle, although one*

146　NATIONAL SCIENCE TEACHERS ASSOCIATION

## SCIENTISTS AND ENGINEERS ARE CURIOUS—JOHN JAMES AUDUBON

John James Audubon

claimed that birds traveled to the moon in the fall and returned to Earth in the spring.

4. **Pages 14–17:** Audubon was not satisfied with other scientists' explanations of bird migration, so he decided to do his own research. How did Audubon decide to answer his question about migration? *Audubon took his books and drawing materials to the cave, where he collected his own data. Those studies continued through the summer, during which two broods of eggs hatched.*

5. **Pages 18–19:** When fall weather began, Audubon knew the birds would soon leave. He devised a plan to band the baby birds in the same way medieval kings had marked their prized falcons. What problem did Audubon have with banding the birds, and how did he solve it? *At first, Audubon tried tying string around the baby bird's leg, but the bird pecked it off. Then, he tried woven silver thread, which is soft but strong, loosely tying it around one leg of each baby bird.*

# 5 ANALYZING AND INTERPRETING DATA

6. **Pages 20–25:** Over that winter, Audubon pondered his questions. As the weather warmed and the days grew longer, he watched for his pewee flycatchers to return to their cave. How did Audubon learn the answer to his question? *Sure enough, one spring day Audubon heard the pewee flycatchers and visited them as they flew in and out of the cave. But where were the grown babies? He searched the nearby meadows and listened for their call. There, he found a pair of nesting birds, one with a silver thread around its leg. Audubon did not find out where the birds had gone, but he did answer the question of whether they would return to the same home region in the spring.*

## Making Sense
### Explore

In this exploration, students will learn about the annual migration of lesser sandhill cranes. First, students will ask questions about and discuss possible reasons for why birds migrate, what makes the lesser sandhill cranes such a notable migrant, and why their stopover at the Platte River in central Nebraska is important. To conclude this phase, each student will prepare a sandhill crane puppet and "fly" it through the spring migration route from the winter resting areas to the summer nesting range.

Students might gather general information about migration and information specific to sandhill crane migration from books in your school library and from the internet. We suggest the books *How Do Birds Find Their Way?* by Roma Gans and *On the Wing: American Birds in Migration* by Carol Lerner. Students might also explore the Iain Nicolson Audubon Center at Rowe Sanctuary website (*rowe.audubon.org*) and relevant pages of the Nebraska Game and Parks Commission website (*http://outdoornebraska.gov/sandhillcrane*). These information sources are listed in the "Additional Resources" section (p. 156). An internet search will also bring up many beautiful images of sandhill cranes.

You might direct students to work in small research groups to answer the following questions:

- Why do birds migrate?

- How did sandhill cranes become such a well-known migratory bird?

- Why is the Platte River an important staging area along the lesser sandhill cranes' spring migration?

Encourage students to organize their research notes in their science notebooks.

## Explain

Students will first review and discuss their research notes as a class and then create puppets to simulate the sandhill crane spring migration.

### CLASS DISCUSSION

As students share their ideas about why birds migrate, show them the sandhill crane migration map (Figure 5.3) and point out the flyway arrows as well as the stopover and staging areas. Invite students to think about these map features and form some hypotheses about why cranes take these routes and choose these stopover areas. Encourage students to think about how the birds' needs vary from winter compared to summer (i.e., their needs for food, water, shelter, and space). Sandhill cranes and other migratory birds move from place to place to increase access to food. Migration helps to ensure a plentiful availability of food (grain, worms, bugs, and snails) for the large sandhill crane population, which numbers about 400,000. Like other migratory birds, sandhill cranes have different shelter needs during the summer compared to the winter. During nesting season, they prefer the shelter of the expansive grasslands in Canada and Siberia, where it is easier to protect nesting parents and their young.

To help students think about why these birds became such a well-known migratory bird, encourage them to notice the beauty and elegance of the sandhill crane, as shown in Figure 5.4 (A) on page 150. These are large wading birds with trumpet-like vocalizations that mate for life and share the rearing of their young (called *colts*), taking great care to teach them how to survive and how to recognize their migratory path. Fossil remains indicate that cranes—sandhill cranes and earlier close relatives such as the crowned crane—have successfully traveled this same migration path for many thousands and possibly millions of years. Therefore,

### Figure 5.3
### Sandhill Crane Migration Map

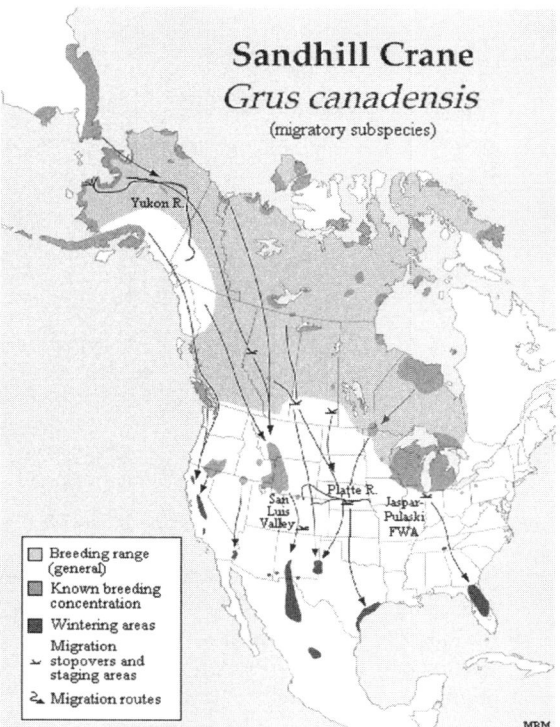

The lesser sandhill cranes winter in New Mexico and Texas and nest in Canada and Siberia.

*Source:* U.S. Geological Survey (accessed at *www.wildflorida.com*).

sandhill cranes are a highly successful wildlife population whose migration has helped them fulfill their needs for a very long time.

### Figure 5.4
### Sandhill Crane and the Platte River in Nebraska

(A) Flying sandhill crane. Sandhill cranes are well known for their beautiful gray coloring and crimson cap and for their energetic and graceful courting dance. (B) The great width of the Platte River and its many sandbars are important to lesser sandhill cranes, providing a feeding, roosting, and courtship environment that is relatively safe from predators.

*Sources:* (A) Public domain. U.S. Fish and Wildlife Service. (B) Public domain. Photo by Steven M. Condon, U.S. Geological Survey.

Finally, as you guide students' discussion about the Platte River as an important staging area along the sandhill cranes' spring migration path, share some images of the Platte River area with your students, such as Figure 5.4 (B), some of the images on the Iain Nicolson Audubon Center at Rowe Sanctuary website (*rowe. audubon.org*), and image results from an internet search for the term "Platte River." Encourage students to think about the birds' needs during their three- to four-week stopover at the Platte River during their 1,200-mile migratory route to their nesting grounds. This area provides two resources to help the cranes gain the strength they need to finish their journey north. First, nearby cornfields provide considerable food resources left behind by combines after the harvest. Second, the sandbars along this shallow length of the Platte River provide safe roosting spots during the night. If a predator such as a coyote should approach, its steps through the water would cause a wake that would alarm the sleeping birds.

**MIGRATION OF SANDHILL CRANE PUPPETS**

Students will prepare paper sandhill crane puppets and "fly" them through the stages of the sandhill crane migration from their winter resting areas to their summer nesting range.

1. Identify the area you want to become the sandhill crane's flyway, such as the lunchroom or gymnasium—any long, wide-open space. Decide which end will be the winter resting place and which will be the summer nesting place. Stretch a few lengths of blue crepe-paper streamers across the flyway about halfway between these two places to represent the Platte River. Leave spaces among the streamers to represent safe sandbars for the sandhill cranes' overnight staging areas.

2. In the classroom, invite students to color in the sandhill crane puppet outline (see Figure 5.5). Provide opportunities for students to view pictures of sandhill cranes while they work, either online through an internet search or websites already recommended here or in books from the school library.

3. Help students to identify where to fold the puppet in half so they will understand what to color before actually folding it and practicing flying. You might want to color and cut out a puppet in advance so you can demonstrate how the two-dimensional template will fold into a three-dimensional puppet. After students have cut and folded their puppets, have them experiment to find how to hold the puppet to get its wings to flap.

4. Take the students to the flyway you set up previously and introduce them to its important features. Have the students gather in the winter resting area, and let them know when the migration is to begin. Students may travel at different speeds, but they all must stop on a sandbar once they come to the river.

5. Next, have students act out the daytime feeding and nighttime resting behaviors of the sandhill cranes. You might signal the start of daytime and nighttime so students will know when to fly their puppet cranes around

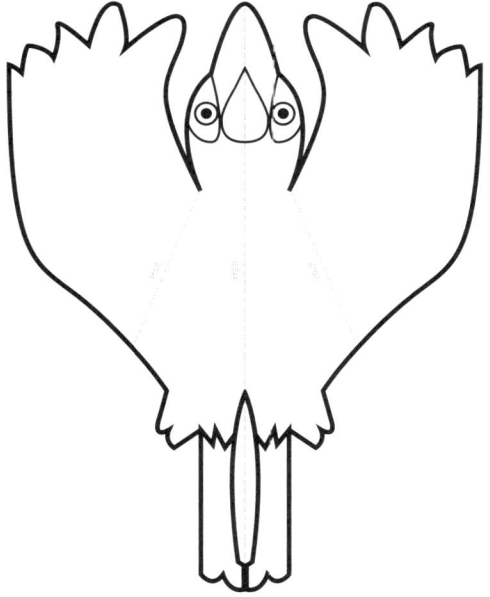

**Figure 5.5**

**Sandhill Crane Puppet Template**

Print the crane template in full-page size. A full-page downloadable version is available at *www.nsta.org/eureka*.

# 5  ANALYZING AND INTERPRETING DATA

looking for food and when to return to the sandbars to rest. We suggest having students fly out for food three times, representing the approximate number of weeks a sandhill crane spends at the sandbars. Students will enjoy acting out the gathering of food as they swoop down low, but these puppets will not hold up very well to eating like an actual sandhill crane!

6. Finally, have students fly their puppet cranes to their summer nesting area. Note that the sandhill cranes continue on this leg of their migration once they have eaten enough seeds, bugs, and roots to help them make the journey. They may also wait for a good tailwind to help increase their speed to 50 mph.

Encourage students to summarize their observations and any questions about sandhill crane migration that were prompted by this simulation. Ask, "Why do you think the sandhill cranes crowd into this short stretch of the Platte River?" *The Platte River has changed its depth and width over this time. Before humans came to the area, prairie fires and floods helped to keep the Platte River as a braided river with multiple channels and sandbars (i.e., fires exposed the sediment, which eroded and was moved into the river by floods and, when water levels receded, created the sandbars). It was once said to be a mile wide and an inch deep. Today, conservationists and sandhill crane lovers work to maintain this stretch of the river to satisfy the needs of the lesser sandhill crane.* The children's book *Have You Seen Mary?* by Jeff Kurrus (2012) tells a realistic story of a pair of sandhill cranes who get separated because of the crowded conditions along the Platte River during migration.

Introduce discussion of the work of conservationists to maintain a length of the Platte River to help sustain the sandhill cranes' annual migration. Ask, "How does crane puppet activity help you think about John James Audubon's migration experiment?" *Audubon wanted to know whether birds migrated. Here, scientists seek to understand the historic migration needs of sandhill cranes and conduct research to find ways to manage the river to suit the sandhill cranes' needs.* Prompt students to make an entry in their science notebooks to summarize their understanding of the sandhill crane migration, the role of the Platte River, and the work of conservationists.

Remind students that Audubon was an eager observer and note-taker. Encourage students to keep journals that describe the date, location, appearance, and behavior of the birds they see at the feeder. Soon, students will be ready for some bird identification tools. Every birder needs a field guide, and the *Young Birder's Guide to Birds of North America* by Bill Thompson III is excellent for students in grades 3–5. It includes identification basics, nice color plates, and sufficient details about what to look and listen for, as well as a catchy "Wow!" fact about each bird. The free Merlin Bird ID app (http://merlin.allaboutbirds.org) from the Cornell Lab of Ornithology is a bird identification tool that asks the user questions about a bird sighting to narrow the possibilities down and then provides a selection of photographs to review.

SCIENTISTS AND ENGINEERS ARE **CURIOUS**—JOHN JAMES AUDUBON

Each of those photographs can be clicked on to reveal a description; the app also provides a way to hear the bird's song—a nice identification tool all by itself!

## Extend

Help students build a bird feeder so they can begin to keep a record of nonmigratory and migratory birds in their own backyards (see Figure 5.6). First, wash out a soda bottle and remove the label. Have students use a ruler and a marker to put a mark 5 in. from the top of the bottle and another mark 5 in. from the bottom. Do the same thing on the opposite side. The teacher should then use a sharp utility knife to poke a hole through each of the four marks so there are two sets of openings opposite one another and at different levels. Push the handle of a wooden mixing spoon through the lower two openings; do the same for the two upper openings. Use a funnel to fill the bottle with birdseed. Screw a 1.5-in. hook into the cap of the bottle. The feeder is now ready to hang in a tree.

## Evaluate

Summative evaluation of this lesson will include assessment of students' understanding of (1) the character trait of being curious and (2) why birds migrate and the ways in which scientists continue to study the movement and behaviors of migratory birds.

**CHARACTER TRAIT**

Encourage students to answer the following questions:

1. How does John James Audubon's bird banding show that he was a curious person? Why is being curious an important disposition for scientists to have? *Audubon had a strong desire to*

### Figure 5.6
### Soda Bottle Bird Feeder

(A) Make perches by inserting wooden spoons through the two sets of openings on opposite sides of the soda bottle. (B) The finished bird feeder.

# 5 ANALYZING AND INTERPRETING DATA

*find out about the pewee flycatchers' behaviors, and that intense curiosity pushed him think of a method for answering his questions. This helped him to think of banding the birds before anyone else thought to do it. The point here is to review Audubon's bird banding from the perspective of one character trait—that of being curious. Whereas some people are satisfied with generally accepted explanations of scientific phenomena, curious people are innovative and devise ways to answer their questions. In Audubon's case, he did not accept Aristotle's explanation of how birds spent the winter. His discovery of the banding method inspired the development of bird banding as a system that is still used today to track and monitor bird migrations.*

2. Working in pairs, talk about a time when you were curious. Record notes about it in your science journals and then share it with the class.

**CONTENT**

To assess students' understanding of why birds migrate and the ways in which scientists continue to study the movement and behaviors of migratory birds, invite them to suggest ways to modify the crane puppet migration activity. Ask, "What variables might be added to the crane puppet migration to make it more realistic? How might these variables challenge scientists who study bird migration?" *Students might suggest variables such as including tokens to represent food for the cranes to collect when they feed during their stopover in the river so that cranes would need to gather sufficient food to survive, adding coyote predators so that slow or wounded cranes would not reach the nesting grounds, or having the river flood heavily so that there are few sandbars and thus fewer places for cranes to rest at night.*

As students generate realistic modifications to the puppet migration activity, encourage a class discussion about how and why scientists gather and record data on migratory birds. *Moving populations are certainly more difficult to monitor, but banding continues to be the primary means for monitoring traits and adaptations. Cameras also help to record ecosystem dynamics (environmental changes in one or both seasonal habitats). These data help to determine the health of a population and regulation of habitats for endangered species.*

You may use a rubric such as the one in Table 5.3 to assess students' understanding of sandhill crane migration and how scientists study cranes.

Table 5.3

**Rubric for Assessing Students' Science Notebook Entries for Crane Migration Variables**

| Content or Skill | Not Yet | Beginning | Developing | Secure |
| --- | --- | --- | --- | --- |
| Migration Variables | Student did not list any possible variables to crane migration. | Student listed at least one possible variable to crane migration. | Student listed at least two possible variables to crane migration. | Student listed more than two possible variables to crane migration. |
| Reasoning | Student did not explain how migration variables might challenge scientists. | Student explained how at least one migration variable might challenge scientists. | Student explained how at least two migration variables might challenge scientists. | Student explained how more than two migration variables might challenge scientists. |
| Migration Research | Student did not list any tools or methods for monitoring migratory birds. | Student listed one tool or method for monitoring migratory birds. | Student listed two tools or methods for monitoring migratory birds. | Student listed more than two tools or methods for monitoring migratory birds. |

# References

AIMS Education Foundation. 2003. Product testing. In *Chemistry matters*. Fresno, CA: AIMS Education Foundation. www.aimsedu.org.

Bransford, J. D., A. L. Brown, and R. R. Cocking, eds. 2002. *How people learn: Brain, mind, experience, and school*. Washington, DC: National Academies Press.

Cassino, M., and J. Nelson. 2009. *The story of snow: The science of winter's wonder*. San Francisco: Chronicle Books.

Davis, J. *The boy who drew birds: A story of John James Audubon*. Boston: Houghton Mifflin Harcourt.

Hannah, J., and J. Holub. 2006. *The man who named the clouds*. Park Ridge, IL: Albert Whitman and Company.

Instructables.com. 2016. DIY: How to make 6-pointed paper snowflakes. www.instructables.com/id/How-to-make-6-pointed-paper-snowflakes.

Martin, J. C. 1998. *Snowflake Bentley*. New York: Houghton Mifflin.

NGSS Lead States. 2013. *Next Generation Science Standards: For states, by states*. Washington, DC: National Academies Press. www.nextgenscience.org/next-generation-science-standards.

Shaw, C. G. 1988. *It looked like spilt milk*. New York: HarperCollins.

Thomas, J., S. Cooper, and D. Haukos. 2004. Skateboards or wildlife? Kids decide. *Science and Children* 41 (7): 20–24.

Thomas, J. A., S. D. Cooper, and J. A. Ponticell. 2000. Doing mathematics the science way: Staff development for integrated teaching and learning. In *Research on effective models for teacher education: Teacher education yearbook VIII*, ed. J. McIntyre and D. Byrd, 10–26. Thousand Oaks, CA: Corwin Press.

U.S. Geological Survey (USGS). 2005. https://pubs.usgs.gov.

WildFlorida.com. Sandhill crane migratory map. www.wildflorida.com/articles/images/sandhillcranemigrationrouteUSGSMap.jpg.

# 5 ANALYZING AND INTERPRETING DATA

## Additional Resources

Cornell Lab of Ornithology. 2016. Merlin bird ID app. *http://merlin.allaboutbirds.org. Available as a free download for iPhone/iOS and Android devices.*

Gans, R. 1996. *How do birds find their way?* New York: HarperCollins.

Jericho Historical Society. Snowflake Bentley: The official website of Snowflake Bentley (1865–1931). *http://snowflakebentley.com. This website provides a number of resources of interest to teachers and students alike.*

Kurrus, J. 2012. *Have you seen Mary?* Lincoln: University of Nebraska Press.

Lerner, C. 2001. *On the wing: American birds in migration.* New York: HarperCollins.

National Audubon Society. 2016. Iain Nicolson Audubon Center at Rowe Sanctuary. *rowe.audubon.org. Provides many photos of the Platte River and sandhill cranes. Also has a "Crane Cam" with a live video feed of cranes on the river during the spring migration stopover.*

Nebraska Game and Parks Commission. 2016. Sandhill crane migration. *http://outdoornebraska.gov/sandhillcrane.*

Thompson III, B. 2012. *Young birder's guide to birds of North America.* Boston: Houghton Mifflin.

U.S. Department of the Interior and U.S. Geological Survey. 2016. About bird banding. Bird Banding Laboratory. North American Bird Banding Program. *www.pwrc.usgs.gov/BBL/homepage/btypes.cfm. Provides some explanation about the types of bird bands and shows close-up photos of bird bands.*

# 6

# Using Mathematics and Computational Thinking

The practice of using mathematics and computational thinking is central to both science and engineering. This chapter will focus on three scientists who used mathematical and computational thinking in their work. The development of computer programming (Ada Byron Lovelace), an understanding of Earth's position in our solar system (Galileo Galilei), and the invention of a variety of underwater apparatuses (Jacques Cousteau) have improved the lives of many people. It is easy to see how the words *innovative, courageous,* and *confident* define the characters of these three scientists and engineers. We expect that in helping students to identify each of these traits, you will help humanize the work and procedures of science and engineering as you teach your science lessons.

## Recommended Science Teaching Strategy: Probeware and Digital Media

The *Next Generation of Science Standards* (*NGSS*; NGSS Lead States 2013) expect and anticipate that mathematics will be used to represent relationships and make predictions. Mathematics provides a tool to help us understand science, and therefore integration of these two subjects is a common occurrence in many grade 3–5 classrooms. Computers and other digital tools provide a useful mechanism for students to use mathematics and computational thinking. Students are expected to use laboratory tools connected to computers for observing, measuring, recording, and processing data. Having students create and use graphs or charts generated from simple algorithms can help them understand solutions to simple engineering problems.

In one example, we have students build and launch paper airplanes (see Teach Engineering 2016). Flight features are a common topic to get students of all ages involved in an engineering challenge in which collected data provide immediate feedback on the engineering design. In this experiment, students investigate how the design of a paper airplane affects the altitude, hang time, and distance of its flight. Students create planes in which different variables have been modified, make a prediction about which will fly the farthest, and then test them. Students become involved in test trials and a redesign of their planes.

We are impressed by a number of free tools that can be downloaded from the internet to help support integrated science and mathematics lessons. One of these is Desmos (*www.desmos.com*), a graphing tool to help you and your students draw graphs from data tables. (See the Extend phase of the "Innovative" lesson, p. 170.) Desmos allows the teacher to create work and make it

# 6 USING MATHEMATICS AND COMPUTATIONAL THINKING

available for individual students or entire classes. We have included a Desmos example in the lesson about Ada Byron Lovelace. Two other useful, free tools online are a graph-paper PDF generator from Incompetech.com (*http://incompetech.com/graphpaper/plain*) and an online stopwatch (*www.online-stopwatch.com/large-stopwatch*).

Electronic data probeware provides another way to facilitate and reinforce science connections to mathematics and computational thinking and to spark enthusiasm and understanding. Interactive, handheld data probes can collect meaningful data. When used with specified software, such sensors and probes help students create graphs and charts of their observations. Two widely used probeware devices from Vernier (*www.vernier.com*) are Go!Temp and Go!Motion. (Some teachers believe that probeware expedites the data collection and graphing processes, which makes these applications possible even when class time is short.)

Although these probes require a financial investment, students can work with them in groups, so a class set of six to eight probes should be sufficient. (They are available individually and in class sets.) The second and third lessons of this chapter use only one probe; if cost is an issue, your school can begin using data probes by purchasing one Go!Motion probe and downloading the free Logger Lite software used with it.

Go!Temp is used to collect data for temperature. Go!Motion is used to collect data for the position, velocity, and acceleration of moving objects. The probes connect to a computer directly or via a cable to a USB port, making it fast and easy to set up experiments and collect a wide range of real-time temperature and motion data. Logger Pro, Vernier's graphing program, is award-winning data collection and analysis software. Students can write their investigations using Logger Pro and export the data to word-processing or spreadsheet software.

Some challenges associated with electronic probeware technology include the initial expense, the requirement for teacher training, and the amount of time teachers need to explore and test out probes before classroom implementation. For these reasons, we did not include lessons in this book involving handheld data probes; however, we highly recommend that you try them. All probeware companies provide information on their websites (e.g., Pasco [*www.pasco.com*] or Einstein [*http://einsteinworld.com/home*]) demonstrating multiple ways to use probes to enhance student learning.

# SCIENTISTS AND ENGINEERS ARE
# INNOVATIVE

## Learning About **Ada Byron Lovelace**

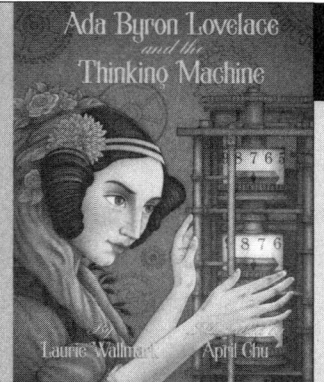

Innovative (adj.): introducing or using new ideas or methods or having new ideas about how something can be done

### Lesson: Airboat Race

### Description

In this lesson, students will use scientific methods to design, build, and test airboats for data collection.

### Objectives

Students will consider how the character trait of being innovative helped Ada Byron Lovelace use scientific methods to develop computer programming, design airboats, and collect data.

- As a class, students will explore how mathematical thinking relates to science trials.
- Students will hear the story *Ada Byron Lovelace and the Thinking Machine* by Laurie Wallmark and discuss how it relates to the word *innovative*.
- Students will make an airboat using index cards.
- To conclude the lesson, students will review the data collected and discuss how they might change the airboat design based on the data.

### Learning Outcomes

Students will (1) make a science notebook entry to explain what it means to be innovative and why being innovative is an important trait for scientists and engineers and (2) make an airboat, run trials to test the airboat design, record data from the trials, and then redesign the airboat based on the data.

# Connections to the *NGSS* and the Nature of Science, Grades 3–5

## Disciplinary Core Ideas

### PS2.A: FORCES AND MOTION

- The patterns of an object's motion in various situations can be observed and measured; when that past motion exhibits a regular pattern, future motion can be predicted from it. (Boundary: Technical terms, such as magnitude, velocity, momentum, and vector quantity, are not introduced at this level, but the concept that some quantities need both size and direction to be described is developed.)

### ETS1.A: DEFINING AND DELIMITING ENGINEERING PROBLEMS

- Possible solutions to a problem are limited by available materials and resources (constraints). The success of a designed solution is determined by considering the desired features of a solution (criteria). Different proposals for solutions can be compared on the basis of how well each one meets the specified criteria for success or how well each takes the constraints into account.

### ETS1.B: DEVELOPING POSSIBLE SOLUTIONS

- Research on a problem should be carried out before beginning to design a solution.
- Testing a solution involves investigating how well it performs under a range of likely conditions.

## Science and Engineering Practices

***Asking Questions and Defining Problems:*** A practice of science is to ask and refine questions that lead to descriptions and explanations of how the natural and designed world works and which can be empirically tested. Asking questions and defining problems in grades 3–5 builds from grades K–2 experiences and progresses to specifying qualitative relationships.

- Ask questions that can be investigated and predict reasonable outcomes based on patterns such as cause and effect relationships.

***Planning and Carrying Out Investigations:*** Scientists and engineers plan and carry out investigations in the field or laboratory, working collaboratively as well as individually. Their investigations are systematic and require clarifying what counts as data and identifying variables or parameters. Planning and carrying out investigations to answer questions or test solutions to problems in 3–5 builds on K–2 experiences and progresses to include investigations that control variables and provide evidence to support explanations or design solutions.

- Plan and conduct an investigation collaboratively to produce data to serve as the basis for evidence, using fair tests in which variables are controlled and the number of trials considered.

- Evaluate appropriate methods and/or tools for collecting data.
- Make observations and/or measurements to produce data to serve as the basis for evidence for an explanation of a phenomenon or test a design solution.
- Make predictions about what would happen if a variable changes.
- Test two different models of the same proposed object, tool, or process to determine which better meets criteria for success.

*Using Mathematics and Computational Thinking:* In both science and engineering, mathematics and computation are fundamental tools for representing physical variables and their relationships. They are used for a range of tasks such as constructing simulations; statistically analyzing data; and recognizing, expressing, and applying quantitative relationships. Mathematical and computational thinking at the 3–5 level builds on K–2 experiences and progresses to extending quantitative measurements to a variety of physical properties and using computation and mathematics to analyze data and compare alternative design solutions.

- Organize simple data sets to reveal patterns that suggest relationships.
- Describe, measure, estimate, and/or graph quantities such as area, volume, weight, and time to address scientific and engineering questions and problems.
- Create and/or use graphs and/or charts generated from simple algorithms to compare alternative solutions to an engineering problem.

*Constructing Explanations and Designing Solutions:* The products of science are explanations and the products of engineering are solutions. Constructing explanations and designing solutions in 3–5 builds on K–2 experiences and progresses to the use of evidence in constructing explanations that specify variables that describe and predict phenomena and in designing multiple solutions to design problems.

- Construct an explanation of observed relationships (e.g., the distribution of plants in the back yard).
- Use evidence (e.g., measurements, observations, patterns) to construct or support an explanation or design a solution to a problem.
- Generate and compare multiple solutions to a problem based on how well they meet the criteria and constraints of the design solution.

## 6 USING MATHEMATICS AND COMPUTATIONAL THINKING

### Crosscutting Concept

***Cause and Effect:*** Events have causes, sometimes simple, sometimes multifaceted. Deciphering causal relationships, and the mechanisms by which they are mediated, is a major activity of science and engineering.

- Cause and effect relationships are routinely identified, tested, and used to explain change.

### Nature of Science Connections

#### SCIENTIFIC INVESTIGATIONS USE A VARIETY OF METHODS

- Science methods are determined by questions.
- Science investigations use a variety of methods, tools, and techniques.

#### SCIENCE KNOWLEDGE IS BASED ON EMPIRICAL EVIDENCE

- Science findings are based on recognizing patterns.
- Science uses tools and technologies to make accurate measurements and observations.

#### SCIENCE IS A WAY OF KNOWING

- Science is both a body of knowledge and processes that add new knowledge.
- Science is a way of knowing that is used by many people.

#### SCIENTIFIC KNOWLEDGE ASSUMES AN ORDER AND CONSISTENCY IN NATURAL SYSTEMS

- Science assumes consistent patterns in natural systems.
- Basic laws of nature are the same everywhere in the universe.

#### SCIENCE IS A HUMAN ENDEAVOR

- Men and women from all cultures and backgrounds choose careers as scientists and engineers.
- Most scientists and engineers work in teams.
- Science affects everyday life.
- Creativity and imagination are important to science.

*Source:* NGSS Lead States 2013.

## SCIENTISTS AND ENGINEERS ARE **INNOVATIVE**—ADA BYRON LOVELACE

## Overview

In this lesson, students learn how one innovative person, Ada Byron Lovelace, used mathematical thinking to collect data. Lovelace used scientific methods to collect data from her experiments so she could analyze them. Through the featured book, students learn that men and women from all backgrounds choose careers as scientists and engineers. The character trait of being innovative refers to Lovelace's unique thinking and creative attempts to solve mathematical problems. The daughter of the famous romantic poet Lord Byron, Lovelace developed her creativity through science and mathematics and invented the first mechanical computer. She understood the machine better than anyone else and wrote the world's first computer program.

## Materials

You will need one copy of the featured book, *Ada Byron Lovelace and the Thinking Machine* by Laurie Wallmark (ISBN 978-1939547200). Each student will need four 5 in. × 8 in. index cards, a ruler, white school glue or clear cellophane tape, a sheet of graph paper, and safety glasses or goggles. Each group will need a stopwatch.

## Safety Notes

(1) Personal protective equipment should be worn during the setup, hands-on, and takedown segments of the activity. (2) Wash hands with soap and water upon completing this activity.

## Setting the Context
### Engage

Ada Byron Lovelace experimented with flying machines and sailboats. Ask students to raise their hands if they have been on a sailboat or an airplane. Record the data on the board. Ask students to come up with true statements based on the data you just collected. For example, students might say that twice as many students have been on a boat than have been on an airplane. The facts are not important; what is important is that you model collecting accurate data (counting hands) and developing true statements from the data collected. Ask students to imagine what a combination of an airplane and a boat might look like. If time allows, have students design and sketch their suggestions.

### Guided Reading

Inform students that they will learn about Ada Byron Lovelace, an inventor who was especially innovative, by reading *Ada Byron Lovelace and the Thinking Machine*. Introduce the book by asking "Think about the person on the front cover. What does it look like is happening on the front cover?" Read the story aloud. Encourage students to notice and think about the challenges Lovelace faced as a woman who enjoyed science and mathematics. The following questions may be used to guide students' attention to detail as you read. (Page numbers reference unnumbered book pages, beginning with the title page as page 1.)

1. **Pages 1–5:** Ada Byron Lovelace was lonely as a young girl. She only knew her father through his books, and her mother was often away on travels. How did Lovelace entertain herself as a young girl? *Lovelace kept journals and filled their pages with inventive ideas and equations.*

2. **Pages 6–15:** One of Lovelace's inventions was a flying machine. She expected its wings could make it fly—she just needed to calculate how the surface area and weight of the wings would respond to the wind and the machine's speed and angles of flight. In what creative way did Lovelace use a terrible storm one night to help her in inventing a flying machine? *One stormy night, Lovelace jumped up to close the window to keep the rain from coming in. She saw that the wind had caught the curtains, filling them like sails. She realized that sails are like wings! She could use the wind to help her experiment with her flying wings. She could learn how by adjusting the sails on her toy sailboat and seeing how that affected the boat's speed.*

3. **Pages 16–19:** Lovelace became very sick with the measles, so her mother came home from her travels to take care of her daughter. How did this illness affect Lovelace's life? *Lovelace's mother was a mathematician with a passion for geometry and was known as the "Princess of Parallelograms." Lovelace's mother quizzed her with mathematics problems to keep her mind sharp. Although the measles left Lovelace blind and paralyzed for a few weeks and it would be three years before she could put away her crutches, her mother continued to pose increasingly difficult mathematics problems, and Lovelace solved them all. Numbers kept her company and mattered to her more than ever.*

4. **Pages 20–23:** When Lovelace's mother realized her daughter's passion for numbers, she hired tutors to help her learn more mathematics. How did Lovelace come to meet Charles Babbage, the famous mathematician and inventor? *One of Lovelace's tutors, a well-known scientist and mathematician, invited her and her mother to a party to which scientists, mathematicians,*

SCIENTISTS AND ENGINEERS ARE **INNOVATIVE**—ADA BYRON LOVELACE

**Ada Byron Lovelace**

and inventors came to share their ideas with one another. Here, Lovelace met Babbage, who was impressed with her precision and understanding of mathematics.

5. **Pages 24–29:** Charles Babbage recognized Lovelace as a fellow mathematician and introduced her to his difference engine. How did Babbage and Lovelace become such good friends? *The difference engine was a revolutionary new calculator. Lovelace not only appreciated the machine, she understood it.*

6. **Pages 30–37:** Charles Babbage decided to share his idea of an analytical engine that would solve harder problems and even make decisions by itself. How did Lovelace respond when she learned of Babbage's plans to make an analytical engine? *Lovelace carried Babbage's laboratory notebooks home with her and studied the descriptions and pored over the diagrams. From this, she realized that the technical descriptions lacked instructions and that without instructions, the analytical engine would just be a pile of metal parts.* How did Lovelace become

**famous?** *She created an algorithm—a set of mathematical instructions—for the analytical engine. Once she had checked and rechecked her numbers to be sure there were no errors, Lovelace had completed what actually was the first computer program. Unfortunately, Babbage never finished building the analytical machine, so Lovelace never got to see her program run; however, the influence of her mathematical work continues. In creating that algorithm, Lovelace created a new profession—computer programming. Today there is a programming language that bears her name—Ada—and guides space satellites.*

## Making Sense
### Explore

In this lesson, students will apply their understanding of mathematical reasoning, fractional parts, and square area to create airboats—paper boats that will skim across the surface, powered by students blowing air on the sail. Before beginning the lesson, set up test tracks for students to test their airboats. If possible, set up more than one test track (e.g., by using tables in the cafeteria) to allow groups to conduct their trials simultaneously. An 8-ft. table would be ideal; mark the start and finish line using masking tape or something similar that can be removed after the lesson is finished. If you only have access to shorter tables, consider setting up tracks that require boats to sail around obstacles. Note that setting up test tracks on the floor will limit how many students can test their boats at the same time (Figure 6.1).

Organize students into groups of three or four, and inform them that each group will construct an airboat using two 5 in. × 8 in. index cards. Assist them in the following steps:

1. To prepare the airboat's base, have students use a ruler to measure and mark a line parallel with and 1 in. from a short edge of one card. Then, fold the card along that line, making a sharp crease. The folded flap will become the front of the airboat, as shown in Figure 6.2 (A).

2. To make the sail, have students measure and mark a line parallel with and 1 in. from a long edge of the other card. Then, fold the card along that line, making a sharp crease. Direct students to cut a notch in the center of the fold; you may want to demonstrate or assist them with this. The notch will allow the sail to curve when it is attached to the airboat base.

3. Tell students to determine the area of the sail. Explain that this includes only the part of the index card above the notched flap. You can limit your students to using their rulers to determine the area, but the graph paper might also be helpful (Figure 6.2 [B]). If using graph paper, students should trace the sail on the graph paper and then calculate the area of the card by

SCIENTISTS AND ENGINEERS ARE **INNOVATIVE**—ADA BYRON LOVELACE

Figure 6.1

Example of an Airboat Test Track

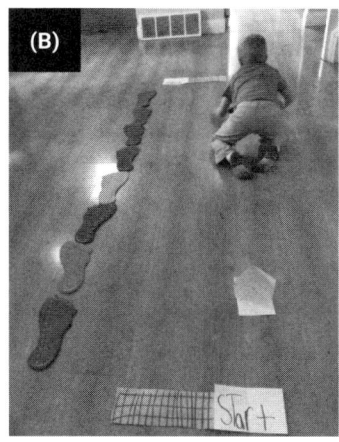

(A) Students race their airboats across a wooden floor. (B) Foot templates were used to outline the course. Paper labels marked the starting and ending lines.

counting the squares. We like to have students mark each square as they count. We also like to leave the problem of partial squares up to the students to resolve. Once students realize that not all graph paper squares will be a complete square, we ask them what to do about this. Any plan students devise will be fine, as long as all students follow the same procedure.

4. Finally, have students use glue or tape to attach the folded flap of the sail to the base of their airboats. Figure 6.2 (C) shows how the two index cards fit together.

Figure 6.2

Construction of an Airboat From Two Index Cards

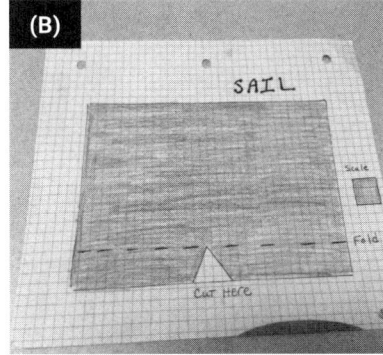
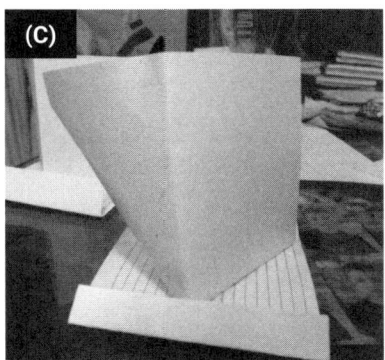

(A) The airboat base made from one of the index cards. The fold along the 5-in. side of the card forms a flap that becomes the front of the airboat. (B) Students can use graph paper to calculate the area of the sail. Notice the notch on the 8-in. side of the card to allow the sail to curve when attached to the airboat base. (C) Completed airboat.

When students have finished with construction, invite them to begin experimenting with moving their airboats by blowing on the sails. Tell them that they want to find out where to blow on the sail to get the most advantage of each breath. Our students continued to learn about how to blow on their sail throughout the trials. When you get to the discussion below about fair test rules, you might want to address the question of sail adjustments across the trials.

Tell students they will now test their airboat design by racing the airboats in four trials. Guide a discussion in which students agree on a set of rules for the trials to ensure that the tests are fair. For example, we learned that these boats may turn easily from the directional force of blown air, so we allowed students to touch their airboats to turn them around to face the finish line. This was the only reason students were allowed to touch their boats after a trial had begun. Explain to students that this first airboat, which they all made following the same design, is their test airboat (airboat A). After testing the design of the sail on airboat A, they will then make changes to improve the sail's design and use the new design on another airboat (airboat B).

Provide students with the Airboat Race Worksheet (Figure 6.3) to gather the necessary test data. In step 1 on the worksheet, students draw a picture of the sail on airboat A and record the square area of the sail. In step 2, students record the time it takes for them to move airboat A from the starting line to the finish line of the test track, find the total time (across all four trials), and then calculate the mean time for airboat A to complete the test track.

After they have recorded all data for airboat A on their worksheets, invite students to design a new sail for airboat B. Encourage them to think about important sail features, such as height and width, and how they think changing these features can maximize the potential of the sail. Allow time for students to construct and test their designs for airboat B. Ensure that they collect the data by completing worksheet steps 1 and 2 for airboat B.

Finally, have students complete step 3, in which they overlay a line graph in two colors (one color for airboat A and another for airboat B) so they can think about the relationship between the area of the sail and the time it took an airboat to travel the test track.

## Explain

Visit with students to talk about their experiences in engineering an airboat and comparing the design ideas mathematically. You might want to have them refer to their worksheets as they share data and conclusions. Check to see how they are thinking about the design features by asking "What enabled the boats to travel faster?" and "What other features would you like to try, and why?" *Your goal is to engage students in logical, mathematical reasoning that describes the airboat behavior or that predicts future behavior. For example, it would make sense that the greater the area of*

SCIENTISTS AND ENGINEERS ARE **INNOVATIVE**—ADA BYRON LOVELACE

Figure 6.3
Name: _____

# AIRBOAT RACE WORKSHEET

**Step 1.** Draw a picture of your airboat sail.

| Sail A | Sail B |
|---|---|
|  |  |
| Square area = | Square area = |

**Step 2.** Record your trial data for airboats A and B. Calculate your total time and mean time and include these data in the table below.

| Trial | Airboat A | Airboat B |
|---|---|---|
| Trial 1 |  |  |
| Trial 2 |  |  |
| Trial 3 |  |  |
| Trial 4 |  |  |
| **Total Time** |  |  |
| **Mean Time** |  |  |

**Step 3.** Record your trial times below. Use different colors to plot the line for each airboat.

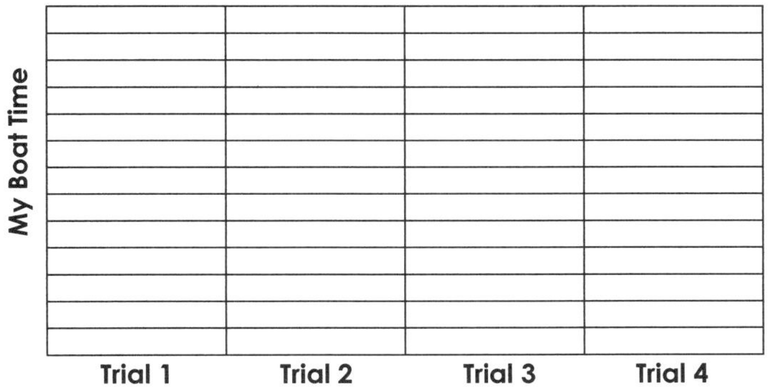

My Boat Time / Trial 1, Trial 2, Trial 3, Trial 4

What does this line graph tell you?

_____
_____
_____
_____
_____
_____

**EUREKA!** GRADE 3–5 **SCIENCE ACTIVITIES AND STORIES**

169

# 6 USING MATHEMATICS AND COMPUTATIONAL THINKING

*the sail, the faster the airboat will travel, given that a larger sail will capture more wind than a smaller sail.* Teams should have an opportunity to present their airboats and have these discussions after the trials for airboat A and again after the testing of airboat B.

## Extend

To extend the learning from this lesson, introduce students to an activity created using the Desmos tool (*www.desmos.com*). Figure 6.4 shows a graphic analysis of the airboat activity generated in Desmos, demonstrating one way Desmos can be applied as an evaluation exercise for your students. The graph represents the times of four trials for two boats. The teacher-created question asks students to reflect on the events that might have caused the graphed results. The teacher provides students with the lesson code, which students use to log into Desmos, type in their ideas, and then click on "Submit to Class." The teacher decides whether students can see others' responses after they have submitted their own answer. Allowing students to see each other's responses is beneficial; when the question is kept open-ended, as in this example, the opportunities for expanding students' thinking are amazing.

Another extension activity could be to organize an Ada Lovelace Day in your school to highlight and celebrate the achievements of women in science, technology, engineering, and mathematics (STEM). Think about inviting local community members, such as female physicians, veterinarians, engineers, or perhaps research faculty from your local university. You may be surprised to find out how many professionals are interested in encouraging women to follow careers in STEM fields. Visit the Ada Lovelace Day website (*http://findingada.com*) to see how Ada Lovelace Day is celebrated in the United Kingdom.

## Evaluate

Summative evaluation of this lesson includes assessment of students' understanding of (1) the character trait of being innovative and (2) the relationship between the design and performance of students' airboats.

### CHARACTER TRAIT

Encourage students to answer the following questions:

1. Why is being innovative an important character trait for scientists and engineers to have? How was Ada Byron Lovelace innovative? *Innovative thinking allows scientists and engineers to generate new ideas from ordinary experiences. For example, Lovelace watched the wind catch the curtains in her room one stormy evening, and this experience sparked her innovative thinking about the power of wings. Lovelace was a skilled mathematician, but she was also thoughtful about how she applied her knowledge. This allowed her to have new ideas about how things might be done and helped her invent computer programming.*

SCIENTISTS AND ENGINEERS ARE **INNOVATIVE**—ADA BYRON LOVELACE

Figure 6.4

**Desmos Screen Capture**

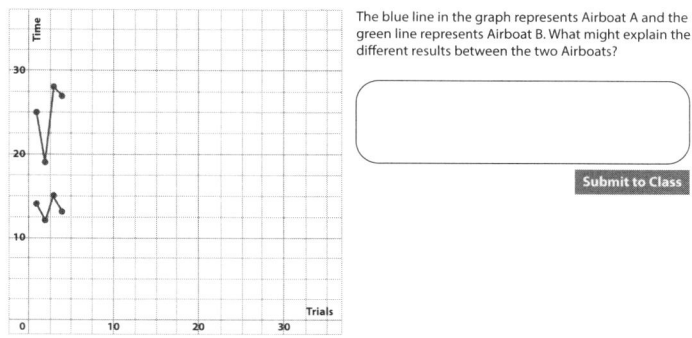

The color image for this figure is available at *www.nsta.org/eureka*.

2. In your group, tell about a time when someone was innovative, and then record that story in your science journal.

**CONTENT**

Evaluate students' developing understanding about how the data they collected informed their understanding about how to modify the design of the sail between airboat A and airboat B. You might find a rubric similar to the one in Table 6.1 (p. 172) helpful.

# 6 USING MATHEMATICS AND COMPUTATIONAL THINKING

Table 6.1

Rubric for Assessing Students for the Airboat Design Process

| Skill | Not Yet | Beginning | Developing | Secure |
|---|---|---|---|---|
| Asking Questions | Student did not ask questions. | Student asked questions that cannot be answered by collecting data. | Student asked some questions that can be answered by collecting data and some questions that cannot. | Student understands the difference between questions that can be answered by collecting data and questions that cannot, and asked questions that can be answered by collecting data. |
| Planning and Carrying Out Investigations | Student did not design or redesign his or her boat. | Student began to design or conduct an investigation to gather data. | Student designed an investigation to gather data and made some decisions about changes in variables. | Student designed an investigation to gather data and made all decisions about changes in variables. |
| Using Mathematics and Computational Thinking | Student did not use mathematical concepts or skills (e.g., measuring or estimating) to answer scientific questions. | Student used limited mathematical concepts or skills (e.g., measuring or estimating) to answer scientific questions. | Student used mathematical concepts or skills (e.g., measuring or estimating) to answer scientific questions but could not articulate the concepts or skills. | Student used mathematical concepts or skills (e.g., measuring or estimating) to answer scientific questions and could articulate the concepts or skills. |

# SCIENTISTS AND ENGINEERS ARE
# COURAGEOUS

## Learning About **Galileo Galilei**

Courageous (adj.): brave or fearless

### Lesson: *M* is for Motion
### Description

In this lesson, students explore lines and curves that are produced by the motion of their bodies.

### Objectives

Students will consider how the character trait of being courageous helped Galileo Galilei share his scientific ideas and will explore graphs in a kinesthetic activity using the Vernier Go!Motion data probe.

- Before beginning the lesson, students will describe motion.
- Students will hear the story *Starry Messenger* by Peter Sís and discuss how it relates to the character trait of being courageous.
- As a class, students will create and observe graphs of the motion of their bodies to explore how computational thinking supports scientific ideas.
- To conclude the lesson, students will compare data from trial runs and learn how Galileo used computational thinking to support his scientific ideas.

### Learning Outcomes

Students will (1) make a science notebook entry to explain what it means to be courageous and why being courageous is an important trait for scientists and engineers and (2) use mathematical thinking with the Vernier Go!Motion data probe and graphing tool.

## Connections to the *NGSS* and the Nature of Science, Grades 3–5

### Disciplinary Core Ideas

**PS2.A: FORCES AND MOTION**

- The patterns of an object's motion in various situations can be observed and measured; when that past motion exhibits a regular pattern, future motion can be predicted from it. (Boundary: Technical terms, such as magnitude, velocity, momentum, and vector quantity, are not introduced at this level, but the concept that some quantities need both size and direction to be described is developed.)

**PS4.C: INFORMATION TECHNOLOGIES AND INSTRUMENTATION**

- Digitized information can be transmitted over long distances without significant degradation. High-tech devices, such as computers or cell phones, can receive and decode information—convert it from digitized form to voice—and vice versa.

### Science and Engineering Practices

***Developing and Using Models:*** A practice of both science and engineering is to use and construct models as helpful tools for representing ideas and explanations. These tools include diagrams, drawings, physical replicas, mathematical representations, analogies, and computer simulations. Modeling in 3–5 builds on K–2 experiences and progresses to building and revising simple models and using models to represent events and design solutions.

- Develop and/or use models to describe and/or predict phenomena.

***Planning and Carrying Out Investigations:*** Scientists and engineers plan and carry out investigations in the field or laboratory, working collaboratively as well as individually. Their investigations are systematic and require clarifying what counts as data and identifying variables or parameters. Planning and carrying out investigations to answer questions or test solutions to problems in 3–5 builds on K–2 experiences and progresses to include investigations that control variables and provide evidence to support explanations or design solutions.

- Make observations and/or measurements to produce data to serve as the basis for evidence for an explanation of a phenomenon or test a design solution.

***Analyzing and Interpreting Data:*** Scientific investigations produce data that must be analyzed in order to derive meaning. Because data patterns and trends are not always obvious, scientists use a range of tools—including tabulation, graphical interpretation, visualization, and statistical analysis—to identify the significant features and patterns in the data. Scientists identify sources of error in the investigations and calculate the degree of certainty in the results. Modern technology makes the collection of large data sets much easier, providing secondary sources for analysis. Analyzing data in 3–5 builds on K–2 experiences and progresses to introducing quantitative approaches to collecting data and conducting multiple trials of qualitative observations. When possible and feasible, digital tools should be used.

- Analyze and interpret data to make sense of phenomena, using logical reasoning, mathematics, and/or computation.

*Using Mathematics and Computational Thinking:* In both science and engineering, mathematics and computation are fundamental tools for representing physical variables and their relationships. They are used for a range of tasks such as constructing simulations; statistically analyzing data; and recognizing, expressing, and applying quantitative relationships. Mathematical and computational thinking at the 3–5 level builds on K–2 experiences and progresses to extending quantitative measurements to a variety of physical properties and using computation and mathematics to analyze data and compare alternative design solutions.

- Organize simple data sets to reveal patterns that suggest relationships.

## Crosscutting Concept

*Patterns:* Observed patterns in nature guide organization and classification and prompt questions about relationships and causes underlying them.

- Patterns can be used as evidence to support an explanation.

## Nature of Science Connections
### SCIENCE IS A WAY OF KNOWING

- Science is both a body of knowledge and processes that add new knowledge.
- Science is a way of knowing that is used by many people.

### SCIENCE IS A HUMAN ENDEAVOR

- Men and women from all cultures and backgrounds choose careers as scientists and engineers.
- Creativity and imagination are important to science.

*Source:* NGSS Lead States 2013.

# 6
**USING MATHEMATICS AND COMPUTATIONAL THINKING**

## Overview

In this lesson, students learn how one scientist, Galileo Galilei, worked through many challenges to conduct and communicate his scientific investigations. We selected the study of motion in relation to mathematics and computational thinking for this lesson. It is meant to be an introduction to using data probes and explores motion as a big idea related to Galileo. Although the two scientific findings of Galileo discussed in this lesson were not controversial, our goal is for teachers to begin to discuss with students sensitive issues such as what makes scientific findings controversial. Through the featured book, students learn that men and women from all backgrounds choose careers as scientists and engineers. The character trait of being courageous references the bravery of Galileo in sharing his scientific beliefs in a culture and during a time when it was unpopular to do so. Students share ideas about the similar ways scientists and engineers solve problems.

## Materials

You will need one copy of the featured book, *Starry Messenger* by Peter Sís (ISBN 978-0374371913); one computer with Logger Lite software installed (downloadable at no cost from *www.vernier.com*); and one Vernier Go!Motion data probe. Each student will need his or her science notebook.

## Setting the Context
### Engage

Students will be learning about the discoveries of Galileo. Ask students whether they are aware of any discoveries he made. Share with students that when Galileo was a young man, he conducted many observations and experiments to study mathematics and motion. Galileo used pendulums extensively in his experiments and described the law of the pendulum. Once he understood their behavior, Galileo was able to use pendulums to measure time. Ask students when and where they have seen pendulums in real life. *Students might not think to mention a playground swing, even though this is a pendulum most of them will know about. Some students might mention pendulums on clocks. Pendulums are used in clocks because they swing at a fixed rate, which makes the clock mechanism work at a steady speed. Pendulums generally consist of a rod or a string with a weight on the end. In the 16th century, Galileo noticed a chandelier swinging in a church and began to record how long it took to complete one swing. He found that the time for one complete swing depended on the length of the pendulum but that its weight made no difference.* Tell students that today they are going to study motion and how to use mathematics to collect data about motion.

## Guided Reading

Tell students that they will learn about Galileo Galilei, a highly courageous scientist in his time, by reading *Starry Messenger*. Introduce the book by holding up the cover and asking "What images on the book cover show us what we will learn about Galileo Galilei?" Read the story aloud. The following questions may be used to guide students' attention to detail as you read. (Page numbers reference unnumbered book pages, beginning with the title page as page 1.)

1. **Page 3:** For hundreds of years, people believed that Earth was at the center of the universe. Why did people believe this? *They did not doubt it or wonder whether it was true. They just followed tradition.*

2. **Pages 8–19:** As a young boy, Galileo was very curious and always had stars on his mind. How did he figure out how to make an instrument to see things far away? *Galileo was very smart. He studied mathematics and physics and amused people with his experiments. He heard about a telescope, figured out how it worked, and made one. He was amazed by what he could see with his telescope and published his observations in a book.*

3. **Pages 20–24:** Galileo became famous. People began to celebrate the stars and celebrate Galileo. Why did the Catholic Church begin to worry about Galileo's fame? *Galileo no longer believed that Earth was at the center of the universe. His telescope observations caused him to speak out against the truths the ancient philosophers had taught.*

4. **Pages 25–27:** Galileo was ordered to stop believing what he could see with his eyes. What happened when Galileo was summoned to appear before the Pope? *Galileo was worried. He knew other people had been punished for not following tradition. Galileo was condemned to spend the rest of his life in prison. Although he never looked at the stars after that day, he still had stars on his mind. He continued to pass his ideas to others while he was in prison, and his ideas still live on.*

5. **Page 31:** Three hundred years later, Galileo was pardoned by the Catholic Church. What caused the Catholic Church to pardon Galileo, and what does it mean to "pardon" someone? *When the Catholic Church pardoned Galileo, they admitted he was not wrong; he was right all along.*

## Making Sense
### Explore

This lesson has been adapted from Vernier's Lesson 21: Elementary Science and is used with permission. The Vernier website also contains a video about using the motion probe. Before class, install the Logger Lite software on a computer and set it

# 6 USING MATHEMATICS AND COMPUTATIONAL THINKING

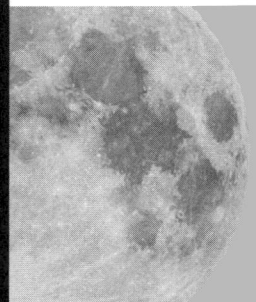

**Galileo Galilei**

up for data collection with your class. Connect the Go!Motion probe to the computer, open the door on the probe to locate the switch, and then set the switch to "Normal" (this has a picture of a person walking). Position the Go!Motion probe on a table so there is a space in front of it that is 6 ft. wide and 9 ft. long and so the probe faces where the motion it will collect will occur. Start the Logger Lite software and open the file for this activity by clicking the "Open" button, opening the "Elementary Books" folder, clicking on "Elementary Science," and opening the file "20a Go Motion." All students must be able to see the screen on the computer, so project it if possible.

To begin, ask students whether they have ever wondered how automatic doors at stores work. Ask, "How is it that the doors know just when to open?" *Students may offer a variety of answers, but as long as the word* sensor *is mentioned, they will be on the right track!* Tell students that places with automatic doors, such as stores, have a sensor near the doors that sends out invisible ultrasound waves that reflect back to the sensor when they hit an object, such as your body. These ultrasound waves always travel at the same speed. The sensor detects the reflected waves and, from how long it took those waves to return to it, determines how far away the object is. Show the Go!Motion probe (connected to a computer) to the class and tell students that it works like the sensors in store doors.

Invite students to come up one at a time to move back and forth in front of the probe so they can see how it senses how far away they are and watch the computer draw a graph of their movement in real time. To start the graphing, click on "Experiment" and then "Start Collection." A position–time graph will appear. To clear the screen, click on "Clear Data." Repeat as many times as needed to run a few trials and see what patterns students observe.

Next, click on "Predict" (the pencil icon) at the top of the Logger Lite window; this will allow you to use the stylus to draw a horizontal line. Ask students to try to re-create your line with their motion. Repeat with other lines (e.g., a vertical line and a curved line).

At the end of the lesson, draw a letter *M* and have students try to recreate it with their motion. (The program generates the prediction in one color and the actual motion in another so you can easily distinguish them; see Figure 6.5). Build up to the *M* by starting with lines or line segments first.

### Figure 6.5
### Screenshots of Predicted and Actual Motion Data to Recreate the Letter *M*

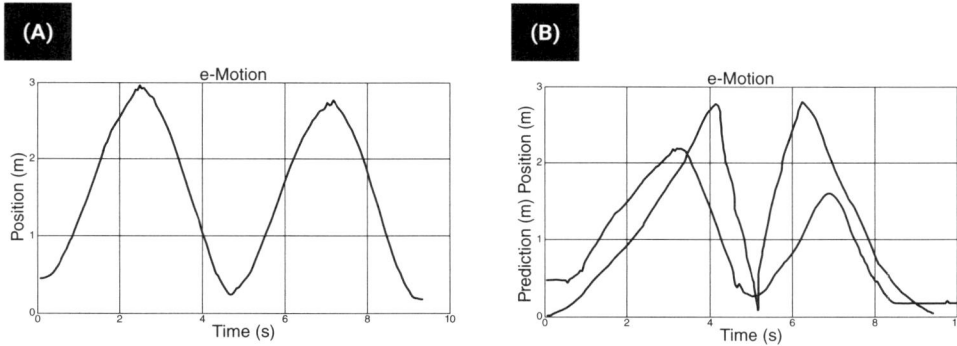

(A) The *M* drawn with the stylus for a prediction. (B) The graph displaying the predicted and the actual data.

Encourage students to write or illustrate in their science notebooks their mathematical computational thinking about motion and mathematics observations as they re-create the *M*. Figure 6.6 (p. 180) gives a sample data collection sequence.

## Explain
Encourage students to explain the relationship between the motion of their bodies and the graph generated by the computer program and to share their ideas

# 6 USING MATHEMATICS AND COMPUTATIONAL THINKING

**Figure 6.6**

**Sample Data Collection Sequence for the Go!Motion Probe**

1. Start _____ feet from the Go!Motion probe.

2. Stand still for _____ seconds.

3. Move _____ (forward or backward) for _____ seconds, moving _____ (quickly or slowly).

4. Move _____ (forward or backward) for _____ seconds, moving _____ (quickly or slowly).

5. Move _____ (forward or backward) for _____ seconds, moving _____ (quickly or slowly).

6. Move _____ (forward or backward) for _____ seconds, moving _____ (quickly or slowly).

7. Stand still for the last _____ seconds.

with others. The idea with this device is to allow students to see what they did with their bodies after the kinesthetic experience through analyzing a real-time graph of their motion.

## Extend
Extend the learning from this activity by challenging students to draw a letter *W* on the position–time graph. Ask students to predict how they need to move to re-create the *W* on the graph. Ask, "What strategies might you use?" Encourage students to think about how they might reverse the directions of the movements they made to re-create the letter *M* previously. Then, invite students to enact their strategy. Figure 6.7 shows the results of one student's effort to do this.

## Evaluate
Summative evaluation of this lesson will include assessment of students' understanding of (1) the character trait of being courageous and (2) how to think mathematically with the Go!Motion data probe and graphing tool.

### CHARACTER TRAIT
Remind students that in the book *Starry Messenger*, Galileo Galilei was courageous when he spoke of his scientific findings, even though he knew there would be consequences from the Catholic Church. Encourage students to answer the following questions:

1. Why is being courageous an important character trait for scientists and engineers to have? *Discoveries by scientists may be very far beyond what is commonly known, so these ideas may not be easily understood by nonscientists. This was true in Galileo's case. Because his work upheld the idea that Earth was not the center of the universe, Galileo had gone against the Bible and everything the ancient philosophers had taught. His work thus challenged the doctrine of the Catholic Church, and people thought they would have to choose science over religion to accept Galileo's findings.*

SCIENTISTS AND ENGINEERS ARE **COURAGEOUS**—GALILEO GALILEI

2. What other types of findings might scientists and engineers need to be courageous about?

3. Invite students to work in pairs and tell each other about a time they were courageous.

**CONTENT**

Students should have recorded their experiments in words and in an illustration (including a picture with words). Students should be able to describe what they saw in terms of time and motion (direction and distance) and relate these factors to the graphs. The rubric in Table 6.2 will help you evaluate students' illustrations and mathematical thinking in their science notebooks.

Figure 6.7

Graph of a Student's Prediction Versus Actual *W* Motion

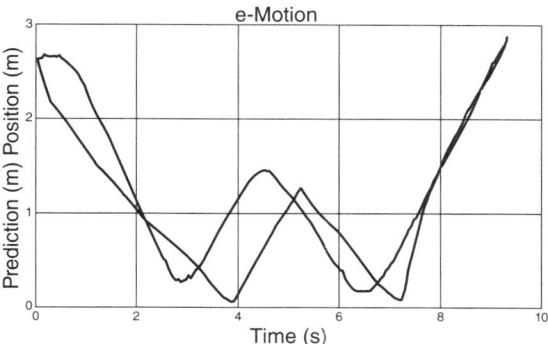

Table 6.2

Rubric for Assessing Students in the Go!Motion Data Probe Investigation

| Content or Skill | Not Yet | Beginning | Developing | Secure |
|---|---|---|---|---|
| **Drawing and Illustration** | Student has no drawing or illustration. | Student's drawing is still at the imagination level. | Student's drawing is moving from imagination to evidence-based reality. | Student's drawing is moving from imagination to evidence-based reality, and includes key words and lines or arrows. |
| **Using Mathematics and Computational Thinking** | Student did not use mathematical concepts or skills (e.g., measuring or estimating) to answer scientific questions. | Student used limited mathematical concepts or skills (e.g., measuring or estimating) to answer scientific questions. | Student used mathematical concepts or skills (e.g., measuring or estimating) to answer scientific questions but could not articulate the concepts or skills. | Student used mathematical concepts or skills (e.g., measuring or estimating) to answer scientific questions and could articulate the concepts or skills. |

# 6 USING MATHEMATICS AND COMPUTATIONAL THINKING

## SCIENTISTS AND ENGINEERS ARE
# CONFIDENT

### Learning About Jacques Cousteau

Confident (adj.): having a strong belief in your own abilities

### Lesson: How Do Submersibles Work?
**Description**

In this lesson, students will use a Vernier Go!Motion probe to chart a simulated ocean floor and build a model to demonstrate how air–water exchanges allow submarines to dive deep into oceans.

### Objectives

In this lesson, students will consider how the character trait of being confident helped Jacques Cousteau explore uncharted territory—oceans.

- Before beginning the lesson, students will learn how the invention of the Aqua Lung allowed Jacques Cousteau to explore oceans.

- Students will hear the story *Manfish: A Story of Jacques Cousteau* by Jennifer Berne and discuss how it relates to the character trait of being confident.

- As a class, students will use a Vernier Go!Motion probe to explore how scientists map the ocean floor.

- To conclude the lesson, students will listen to a TED Talk by Sylvia Earle.

### Learning Outcomes

Students will (1) make a science journal entry to explain what it means to be confident and why being confident is an important trait for scientists and engineers and (2) analyze data to chart a simulated ocean floor.

# Connections to the NGSS and the Nature of Science, Grades 3–5

## Disciplinary Core Ideas

**ESS2.A: EARTH MATERIALS AND SYSTEMS**

- Earth's major systems are the geosphere (solid and molten rock, soil, and sediments), the hydrosphere (water and ice), the atmosphere (air), and the biosphere (living things, including humans). These systems interact in multiple ways to affect Earth's surface materials and processes. <u>The ocean supports a variety of ecosystems and organisms, shapes landforms, and influences climate.</u> Winds and clouds in the atmosphere interact with the landforms to determine patterns of weather.

**ESS3.C: HUMAN IMPACTS ON EARTH SYSTEMS**

- Human activities in agriculture, industry, and everyday life have had major effects on the land, vegetation, streams, ocean, air, and even outer space. But individuals and communities are doing things to help protect Earth's resources and environments.

**PS1.A: STRUCTURE AND PROPERTIES OF MATTER**

- Measurements of a variety of properties can be used to identify materials. (Boundary: At this grade level, mass and weight are not distinguished, and no attempt is made to define the unseen particles or explain the atomic-scale mechanism of evaporation and condensation.)

**PS4.C: INFORMATION TECHNOLOGIES AND INSTRUMENTATION**

- Digitized information can be transmitted over long distances without significant degradation. High-tech devices, such as computers or cell phones, can receive and decode information—convert it from digitized form to voice—and vice versa.

## Science and Engineering Practices

***Planning and Carrying Out Investigations:*** Scientists and engineers plan and carry out investigations in the field or laboratory, working collaboratively as well as individually. Their investigations are systematic and require clarifying what counts as data and identifying variables or parameters. Planning and carrying out investigations to answer questions or test solutions to problems in 3–5 builds on K–2 experiences and progresses to include investigations that control variables and provide evidence to support explanations or design solutions.

- Make observations and/or measurements to produce data to serve as the basis for evidence for an explanation of a phenomenon or test a design solution.

# 6 USING MATHEMATICS AND COMPUTATIONAL THINKING

*Using Mathematics and Computational Thinking:* In both science and engineering, mathematics and computation are fundamental tools for representing physical variables and their relationships. They are used for a range of tasks such as constructing simulations; statistically analyzing data; and recognizing, expressing, and applying quantitative relationships. Mathematical and computational thinking at the 3–5 level builds on K–2 experiences and progresses to extending quantitative measurements to a variety of physical properties and using computation and mathematics to analyze data and compare alternative design solutions.

- Organize simple data sets to reveal patterns that suggest relationships.
- Describe, measure, estimate, and/or graph quantities such as area, volume, weight, and time to address scientific and engineering questions and problems.

*Constructing Explanations and Designing Solutions:* The products of science are explanations and the products of engineering are solutions. Constructing explanations and designing solutions in 3–5 builds on K–2 experiences and progresses to the use of evidence in constructing explanations that specify variables that describe and predict phenomena and in designing multiple solutions to design problems.

- Apply scientific ideas to solve design problems.

*Obtaining, Evaluating, and Communicating Information:* Scientists and engineers must be able to communicate clearly and persuasively the ideas and methods they generate. Critiquing and communicating ideas individually and in groups is a critical professional activity. Obtaining, evaluating, and communicating information in 3–5 builds on K–2 experiences and progresses to evaluating the merit and accuracy of ideas and methods.

- Communicate scientific and/or technical information orally and/or in written formats, including various forms of media and may include tables, diagrams, and charts.

## Crosscutting Concept

*Patterns:* Observed patterns in nature guide organization and classification and prompt questions about relationships and causes underlying them.

- Similarities and differences in patterns can be used to sort, classify, communicate and analyze simple rates of change for natural phenomena and designed products.
- Patterns of change can be used to make predictions.
- Patterns can be used as evidence to support an explanation.

## Nature of Science Connections

**SCIENTIFIC INVESTIGATIONS USE A VARIETY OF METHODS**

- Science methods are determined by questions.
- Science investigations use a variety of methods, tools, and techniques.

**SCIENCE KNOWLEDGE IS BASED ON EMPIRICAL EVIDENCE**

- Science findings are based on recognizing patterns.
- Science uses tools and technologies to make accurate measurements and observations.

**SCIENTIFIC KNOWLEDGE IS OPEN TO REVISION IN LIGHT OF NEW EVIDENCE**

- Science explanations can change based on new evidence.

**SCIENCE IS A WAY OF KNOWING**

- Science is both a body of knowledge and processes that add new knowledge.
- Science is a way of knowing that is used by many people.

**SCIENTIFIC KNOWLEDGE ASSUMES AN ORDER AND CONSISTENCY IN NATURAL SYSTEMS**

- Science assumes consistent patterns in natural systems.
- Basic laws of nature are the same everywhere in the universe.

**SCIENCE IS A HUMAN ENDEAVOR**

- Men and women from all cultures and backgrounds choose careers as scientists and engineers.
- Science affects everyday life.
- Creativity and imagination are important to science.

**SCIENCE ADDRESSES QUESTIONS ABOUT THE NATURAL AND MATERIAL WORLD**

- Science findings are limited to questions that can be answered with empirical evidence.

*Source:* NGSS Lead States 2013.

*Note:* When an activity supports only part of a standard, underlining indicates the relevant part.

# 6 USING MATHEMATICS AND COMPUTATIONAL THINKING

## Overview
In this lesson, students learn how one scientist, Jacques Cousteau, made a huge contribution to our understanding of oceans. Through the featured book, students learn about Cousteau's journey from exploring oceans by himself to later working with a team of people on his ship *Calypso*, which had onboard a submersible for exploration. Oceanographers use sound waves to investigate objects below the surface of the water. A signal is sent down and bounces back from the ocean floor. For many hundreds of years, oceans remained an unexplored area of Earth, even though these important parts of our planet cover 70% of Earth's surface. Through the featured book, students learn that men and women from all backgrounds choose careers as scientists. The character trait of being confident references Jacques Cousteau's disposition of wanting to explore oceans simply because no one before him had done so and even though he would have to invent many of the underwater apparatuses he would need. Students will share ideas about how scientists' and engineers' approaches to solving problems are similar and different.

## Materials
You will need one copy of the book *Manfish: A Story of Jacques Cousteau* by Jennifer Berne (ISBN 978-0811860635), a computer with Vernier Logger Lite software installed (free download from *www.vernier.com*), one Vernier Go!Motion data probe, a board about 3 ft. long, masking tape, and two or three empty boxes of different sizes. Each student will need his or her science notebook and safety glasses or safety goggles.

## Safety Notes
(1) Personal protective equipment should be worn during the setup, hands-on, and takedown segments of the activity. (2) Wash hands with soap and water upon completing this activity.

## Setting the Context
### Engage
Ask students whether they have ever been swimming, snorkeling, or scuba diving underwater in an ocean or a lake. They may instead know someone who has snorkeled or scuba dived or have watched movies or videos about undersea exploration. Discuss students' responses as a class. Encourage students to think about what they noticed when they were underwater or watched someone swimming underwater, such as how they got air or how they were able to see if it was dark.

SCIENTISTS AND ENGINEERS ARE **CONFIDENT**—JACQUES COUSTEAU

Ask students why they think we need to explore oceans and how scientists might study ocean life and the ocean floor.

## Guided Reading

Students will learn about the work of Jacques Cousteau and the several inventions he developed to do ocean exploration, such as the Aqua-Lung and an underwater camera. Introduce the book by holding up the cover and asking "What do you think this story is about?" Read the story aloud. The following questions may be used to guide students' attention to detail as you read. (Page numbers reference unnumbered book pages, beginning with the title page as page 1.)

1. **Pages 4–8:** From the time he was very young, Jacques Cousteau loved oceans. How did he come to experience oceans so closely as a young child? *Cousteau grew up along the Atlantic Ocean, and he wondered why rocks sank but he floated. He was fascinated by machines and saved his money to buy his own video camera. He loved making videos with his family, and he dreamed about one day being able to breathe underwater.*

2. **Pages 8–19:** Even after finishing school and joining the French Navy, Cousteau wondered what it would be like to be underwater for an extended period of time. How did wearing diving goggles for the first time affect him? *Experiencing the underwater world while wearing diving goggles changed Cousteau's life. From then on, he and his friends continued to dive, he built a waterproof case for his camera so he could film underwater, and he invented a rubber suit to stay warm in cold waters and flippers so he could kick better. Once he had invented the Aqua-Lung, he could breathe underwater, see the way fish see, and go where fish go.*

3. **Pages 20–25:** Cousteau was ready to explore the world's oceans, so he converted a Navy ship into a research vessel named *Calypso*. How did the Aqua-Lung help Cousteau explore? *Cousteau and his friends were able to dive deep underwater, where they filmed plants and animals no one had seen before. These films were shown in theaters and on television, so people the world over also got to explore the wonders of the world's oceans for the first time.*

4. **Pages 26–29:** Cousteau began to recognize that people were unintentionally polluting the world's oceans. What did he do to warn people not to dump garbage and chemicals into Earth's oceans? *Cousteau spoke to world leaders to ask them to save our oceans and our planet. He spoke to students and hoped that they would one day explore ocean worlds not yet explored.*

5. Why do you think the author titled this book *Manfish*? *Jacques Cousteau explored underwater worlds where no one else had ever been and that no one could*

# 6 USING MATHEMATICS AND COMPUTATIONAL THINKING

*have imagined. His dream was to be able to breathe underwater and swim through oceans as free as a fish. This dream inspired his invention of the Aqua-Lung, which allowed him as a man to swim underwater essentially like a fish.*

**Jacques Cousteau**

## Making Sense
### Explore

This lesson was adapted from "Experiment 12: Ocean Floor Mapping" from *Middle School Science With Vernier* and is used with permission. The Vernier website also has a video about using the data probe. Before class begins, install the Logger Lite software on a computer and set it up for data collection with your class. Connect the Go!Motion probe to the computer, open the door on the probe to locate the switch, and set the switch to "Normal" (this has a picture of a person walking). Position the Go!Motion probe on a table so that there is a space about 6 ft. wide and 9 ft. long in front of it. Ensure that the round screen on the probe is uncovered and pointing downward. Tape the probe to the yardstick so it is supported and secure

SCIENTISTS AND ENGINEERS ARE **CONFIDENT**—JACQUES COUSTEAU

(see Figure 6.8). Start the Logger Lite software and introduce students to the Ocean Floor experiment. Explain that they will be using the probe to explore three different (simulated) places on the ocean floor. Have students predict what the simulated ocean floor will look like (e.g., not all of it will be flat) and fill in a chart similar to the one in Table 6.3 to record their prediction and their data.

### Figure 6.8
### Setup for the Ocean Floor Experiment

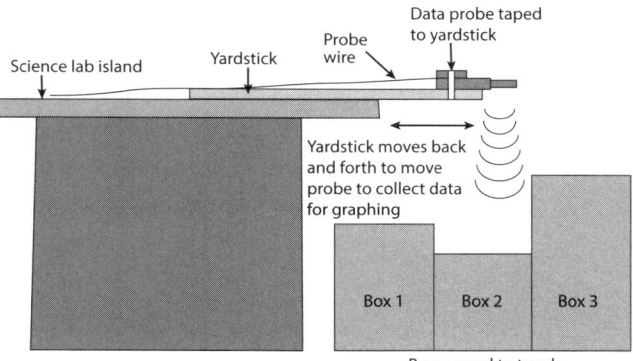

1. Prepare Ocean Floor 1 (one box) for data collection. Place one box beneath the motion probe, allowing at least 15 in. of distance between the probe and the top of the box (see Figure 6.8). Align the motion probe so it will pass over the box when it is moved outward from the table edge. (The end of island in a science lab would work well.) Open the cover on the probe and make sure the switch is set to "Normal." In the Logger Lite software, go to "Open" and open the "Middle School With Vernier" folder. Then, select the "12 Ocean Floor" experiment file. The data collection parameters are already set up for a length of 15 seconds and an ideal data collection rate. When you are ready to start collecting data, move the yardstick to position the motion probe so it

### Table 6.3
### Table for Recording Ocean Floor Activity Data

| Ocean Floor | Prediction | Actual |
|---|---|---|
| Ocean Floor 1 (One Box) | | |
| Ocean Floor 2 (Two Boxes) | | |
| Ocean Floor 3 (Three Boxes) | | |

**EUREKA!** GRADE 3–5 **SCIENCE ACTIVITIES AND STORIES**

# 6 USING MATHEMATICS AND COMPUTATIONAL THINKING

is behind the box beneath it. After the data collection starts, slowly slide the yardstick across the table so that the motion probe moves outward and goes over and beyond the box. Determine and record the distance from the probe to the floor. Identify the flat portion of the graph that represents the box, and click and drag the stylus across this region to select the data. Choose the "Statistics-Position" button from the "Analyze" menu. Record the mean (average) distance to the box in feet. Choose the "Statistics" tab from the "Analyze" menu to turn off the statistical analysis. Have students sketch and label the graph in Table 6.3.

2. Prepare Ocean Floor 2. Set up two boxes side by side, flush against each other, and at different heights. The top of the higher box must be at least 15 in. from the motion detector. Have students predict in Table 6.3 what the graph will look like, and then repeat the process in step 1 to collect the data.

3. Prepare Ocean Floor 3. Set up three boxes side by side, flush against each other, and at different heights. The top of the highest box must be at least 15 in. from the motion detector. Have students predict in Table 6.3 what the graph will look like, and then repeat the process in step 1 to collect the data.

## Explain

Discuss with students how oceanographers use sound to investigate objects below the surfaces of bodies of water. Explain that a sound wave signal is sent out and that the sound waves are reflected back when they hit the surface of a submerged object. Scientists calculate the depth of the submerged surface using the speed of sound in water and the time it takes for the signal to bounce back. This system is called sonar. Explain that the probe they used in the Ocean Floor activity works in the same way.

## Extend

On their one-to-one devices or as a class through the teacher's computer, have students visit the National Oceanic and Atmospheric Administration website, which has timely and relevant science podcasts and videos. Ask students to listen to or watch three podcasts or videos. A video of a TED Talk by Sylvia Earle is particularly interesting and relevant to this lesson (*http://oceantoday.noaa.gov/sylviaearle*) and relevant to this lesson. Ask students to discuss whether ocean exploration is necessary today and to predict what ocean exploration might look like in the future. Students should record their answers to these questions in their science notebooks or discuss their answers in small groups.

SCIENTISTS AND ENGINEERS ARE **CONFIDENT**—JACQUES COUSTEAU

## Evaluate

Summative evaluation of this lesson will include assessment of students' understanding of (1) why being confident is an important character trait for scientists and engineers and (2) how to analyze data to chart a simulated ocean floor.

**CHARACTER TRAIT**

Encourage students to answer the following questions:

1. If Jacques Cousteau had not explored unknown territory in Earth's oceans, how might our knowledge of what lives there today be different?

2. Why is being confident an important character trait for scientists and engineers in the development of new inventions? *Although others might eventually have thought to explore oceans and created tools to do so, Cousteau was confident and envisioned this before anyone else. The point here is to review Cousteau's efforts to create new inventions from the perspective of one character trait—that of being confident. Cousteau was confident that his ideas for underwater exploration would work and that his studies of oceans would reveal many new discoveries for understanding Earth.*

3. Invite students to recall a time they were confident and write about it in their science notebooks.

**CONTENT**

Evaluate students' demonstrated applications of mathematical and computational thinking during their analysis of the simulated ocean floor. The rubric shown in Table 6.4 can be used to guide your evaluation of students' thinking as demonstrated in their science notebooks.

Table 6.4

### Rubric for Assessing Student Analysis of the Ocean Floor Activity

| Skill | Not Yet | Beginning | Developing | Secure |
|---|---|---|---|---|
| Using Mathematics and Computational Thinking | Student did not use mathematical concepts or skills (e.g., measuring or estimating) to answer scientific questions. | Students did not use mathematical concepts or skills (e.g., measuring and estimating) to answer scientific questions. | Students used mathematical concepts or skills (e.g., measuring and estimating) to answer scientific questions. | Students made decisions about which mathematical concepts or skills (e.g., measuring and estimating) to use to answer a scientific question. |

## References

Berne, J. 2008. *Manfish: A story of Jacques Cousteau.* San Francisco: Chronicle Books.

Desmos. 2016. *www.desmos.com.*

Incometech.com. Graph-paper PDF generator. *http://incompetech.com/graphpaper/plain.*

NGSS Lead States. 2013. *Next Generation Science Standards: For states, by states.* Washington, DC: National Academies Press. *www.nextgenscience.org/next-generation-science-standards.*

Online-stopwatch.com. *www.online-stopwatch.com/large-stopwatch.*

Sís, P. 1996. *Starry messenger.* New York: Farrar, Straus and Giroux (BYR).

Teach Engineering. 2016. Lesson: Take off with paper airplanes. *www.teachengineering.org/lessons/view/cub_airplanes_lesson06.*

Vernier. Logger Lite software. *www.vernier.com/products/software/logger-lite/#download.*

Wallmark, L. 2015. *Ada Byron Lovelace and the thinking machine.* Berkeley, CA: Creston Books.

## Additional Resources

Ada Lovelace Day. 2015. Celebrating women in STEM. *http://findingada.com.*

Cousteau Society. 2016. *www.cousteau.org/who/calypso.*

Einstein. The all in one K–12 STEM solution. *http://einsteinworld.com/home. Website promoting handheld devices that engage elementary students in the scientific process through interactive apps and data collection devices.*

National Oceanic and Atmospheric Administration. Sylvia Earle TED conference. *http://oceantoday.noaa.gov/sylviaearle.*

# 7

# Constructing Explanations (Science) and Designing Solutions (Engineering)

The practice of constructing explanations and designing solutions is very important in both science and engineering. This chapter will focus on three engineers who designed solutions based on science explanations they developed. Their solutions—the oil cup (Elijah McCoy), the Brooklyn Bridge (John Roebling), and a windmill (William Kamkwamba)—improved the lives of many people. It is easy to see why the words *clever, persistent,* and *inventive* so aptly describe these three individuals. We expect that in helping your students identify of these traits, you will help humanize the work of scientists and engineers as you teach science.

## Recommended Science Teaching Strategy: KLEW Charts

The *Next Generation Science Standards* (*NGSS*; NGSS Lead States 2013) state that the goal of science is to construct explanations of the world in which we live and that the goal of engineering is to design solutions. In grades 3–5, students are encouraged to use evidence to construct explanations that specify variables as they describe and predict phenomena during the design of multiple solutions to a problem. Having students construct explanations of observed relationships or use evidence to construct or support an explanation are variations on designing a solution to a problem.

When we think about students applying scientific ideas to solve design problems, we often think of the egg-drop challenge. The egg drop is commonly used in science classes for students of all ages to challenge them to design something—in this case, an apparatus to catch an egg from a one-story drop. To solve this problem, student teams must integrate their understanding of the scientific principles of gravity, speed, force, and motion into their design. Providing a variety of construction materials helps to make the environment more creative for teams. Students' responses to these kinds of lessons are always positive because the practical application of the scientific knowledge tends to encourage collaboration and results in a meaningful product.

In science teaching, we sometimes focus student efforts on content-specific explanations, but an overreliance on this limits our students' opportunity to see the real-world benefit of designing solutions. Science fairs or invention conventions can provide particularly important opportunities for students to form personal connections with science and engineering practices. These practices should grow in complexity and sophistication as grade levels advance. The more opportunities students have to address real-world problems and design solutions, the more scientifically literate they will become.

# 7 CONSTRUCTING EXPLANATIONS (SCIENCE) AND DESIGNING SOLUTIONS (ENGINEERING)

Students' construction of explanations and design of solutions in grades 3–5 builds on their experiences from kindergarten through grade 2. It also progresses to using evidence to construct explanations that specify variables that describe and predict and designing multiple solutions to design problems. At the grades 3–5 level, teaching students about the role of scientific evidence becomes critical to future understanding. Likewise, asking students to provide evidence for their observations needs to be consistent and continuous.

One of the best ways we have seen to introduce and reinforce scientific evidence in the classroom is the KLEW chart (Hershberger, Zembal-Saul, and Starr 2006), a modification of a well-known reading comprehension strategy known as KWL (Ogle 1986). As part of the KWL approach to engaging with texts, students document what they know (K), what they want to know (W), and what they have learned (L). The KLEW chart asks students to consider the following questions: "What do we think we know?" (K), "What are we learning?" (L), "What is our evidence?" (E), and "What do we still wonder about?" (W). It has been adapted for science teaching as the KLEW(S) chart (Hershberger, Kur, and Haefner 2013), in which students also consider the question "What scientific principles or vocabulary help explain the phenomena?" (S). You might adjust these prompts to fit the interests of an engineer who identifies a problem and then designs a new product to solve that problem.

Hershberger, Kur, and Haefner (2013) contend that ". . . when students are engaged in developing explanations (and integrating scientific principles in their thinking, conversations, and writing) the classroom becomes a community of scientists who use evidence to support their ideas and make connections to their everyday experiences" (p. 66). We have also found this to be true. We encourage you to engage students in the development of KLEW charts during the lessons in this chapter. You might begin by making one large chart as a class (supported collaborative effort) and move toward having students develop their own charts in their science notebooks (individual, independent effort). (Think about how you will align KLEW with the 5E lesson model. For example, in the Engage phase, you might focus on the *K* in the chart, and in the Explore and Explain phases, you might focus on the *L*, *E*, and *S*. In the Extend and Evaluate phases, you could add to several sections of your KLEW chart, but you might focus on the *W*.)

# SCIENTISTS AND ENGINEERS ARE
# CLEVER

## Learning About **Elijah McCoy**

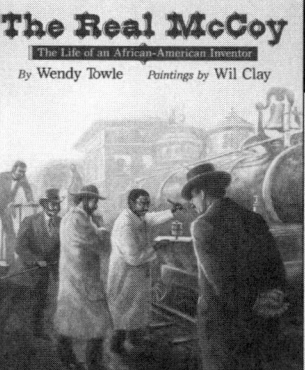

Clever (adj.): having ingenuity, resourcefulness, and a mental quickness in achieving a purpose

### Lesson: Racing Against Friction

### Description

In this lesson, students will observe friction and apply oil to their model racetrack to observe the effects of a change in friction.

### Objectives

Students will consider how the character trait of being clever helped Elijah McCoy and will engage in an experiment to observe different degrees of friction and the effects of lubrication.

- Before beginning the lesson, students will observe several different grades (roughnesses) of sandpaper.

- As a class, students will discuss where they have heard the word *friction* and describe what the word *friction* means to them.

- Students will hear the story *The Real McCoy: The Life of an African-American Inventor* by Wendy Towle and discuss how it relates to the word *clever*.

- Students will make two ramps covered with different grades of sandpaper and observe how toy cars run down these ramps.

# 7 CONSTRUCTING EXPLANATIONS (SCIENCE) AND DESIGNING SOLUTIONS (ENGINEERING)

- To conclude the lesson, students will become familiar with the saying "the real McCoy." Students will understand the meaning of the word *clever* and will brainstorm to find a solution to a friction-related problem in their own lives.

## Learning Outcomes

Students will (1) make a science notebook entry to explain what it means to be clever and why being clever is an important trait for scientists and engineers and (2) observe the effects of friction and lubrication on how toy cars travel down sandpaper-covered ramps.

## Connections to the *NGSS* and the Nature of Science, Grades 3–5
### Disciplinary Core Ideas
#### PS2.A: FORCES AND MOTION

- Each force acts on one particular object and has both strength and a direction. An object at rest typically has multiple forces acting on it, but they add to give zero net force on the object. Forces that do not sum to zero can cause changes in the object's speed or direction of motion. (Boundary: Qualitative and conceptual, but not quantitative addition of forces are used at this level.)

- The patterns of an object's motion in various situations can be observed and measured; when that past motion exhibits a regular pattern, future motion can be predicted from it. (Boundary: Technical terms, such as magnitude, velocity, momentum, and vector quantity, are not introduced at this level, but the concept that some quantities need both size and direction to be described is developed.)

#### ETS1.A: DEFINING AND DELIMITING ENGINEERING PROBLEMS

- Possible solutions to a problem are limited by available materials and resources (constraints). The success of a designed solution is determined by considering the desired features of a solution (criteria). Different proposals for solutions can be compared on the basis of how well each one meets the specified criteria for success or how well each takes the constraints into account.

#### ETS1.B: DEVELOPING POSSIBLE SOLUTIONS

- At whatever stage, communicating with peers about proposed solutions is an important part of the design process, and shared ideas can lead to improved designs.

- Testing a solution involves investigating how well it performs under a range of likely conditions.

## Science and Engineering Practices

***Asking Questions and Defining Problems:*** A practice of science is to ask and refine questions that lead to descriptions and explanations of how the natural and designed world works and which can be empirically tested. Asking questions and defining problems in grades 3–5 builds from grades K–2 experiences and progresses to specifying qualitative relationships.

- Ask questions that can be investigated and predict reasonable outcomes based on patterns such as cause and effect relationships.

***Constructing Explanations and Designing Solutions:*** The products of science are explanations and the products of engineering are solutions. Constructing explanations and designing solutions in 3–5 builds on K–2 experiences and progresses to the use of evidence in constructing explanations that specify variables that describe and predict phenomena and in designing multiple solutions to design problems.

- Construct an explanation of observed relationships (e.g., the distribution of plants in the back yard).
- Use evidence (e.g., measurements, observations, patterns) to construct or support an explanation or design a solution to a problem.
- Identify the evidence that supports particular points in an explanation.
- Apply scientific ideas to solve design problems.

## Crosscutting Concepts

***Cause and Effect:*** Events have causes, sometimes simple, sometimes multifaceted. Deciphering causal relationships, and the mechanisms by which they are mediated, is a major activity of science and engineering.

- Cause and effect relationships are routinely identified, tested, and used to explain change.

***Structure and Function:*** The way an object is shaped or structured determines many of its properties and functions.

- Different materials have different substructures, which can sometimes be observed.
- Substructures have shapes and parts that serve functions.

## Nature of Science Connections
### SCIENTIFIC INVESTIGATIONS USE A VARIETY OF METHODS

- Science methods are determined by questions.
- Science investigations use a variety of methods, tools, and techniques.

# 7 CONSTRUCTING EXPLANATIONS (SCIENCE) AND DESIGNING SOLUTIONS (ENGINEERING)

**SCIENCE KNOWLEDGE IS BASED ON EMPIRICAL EVIDENCE**

- Science findings are based on recognizing patterns.
- Science uses tools and technologies to make accurate measurements and observations.

**SCIENCE IS A WAY OF KNOWING**

- Science is both a body of knowledge and processes that add new knowledge.
- Science is a way of knowing that is used by many people.

**SCIENCE IS A HUMAN ENDEAVOR**

- Men and women from all cultures and backgrounds choose careers as scientists and engineers.
- Science affects everyday life.
- Creativity and imagination are important to science.

*Source:* NGSS Lead States 2013.

## Overview

In this lesson, students learn how one person with a clever idea invented a significant, long-lasting improvement for transportation. Elijah McCoy shared his inventions with others and challenged the way people thought about African American inventors. With this book, students learn that men and women from all backgrounds choose careers as scientists and engineers. The character trait of being clever refers to McCoy's quick thinking and creative attempts to solve problems. Students will share ideas about scientists and engineers as inventors and will discuss the patent process. In the hands-on portion of the lesson, students experience friction and experiment with lubrication.

## Materials

You will need a copy of the book *The Real McCoy: The Life of an African-American Inventor* by Wendy Towle (ISBN 978-0590435963). Each student group will need two toy cars (e.g., Matchbox or Hot Wheels brands), one ramp made from foam core board or cardboard, two aluminum pans, masking tape, two sheets of sandpaper of different grades (one smooth and one rough), two ½-cup containers of vegetable oil, and (plenty of!) paper towels. Each student will need indirectly vented chemical splash goggles.

## Safety Notes

(1) Personal protective equipment should be worn during the setup, hands-on, and takedown segments of the activity. (2) Immediately wipe up spilled oil on tables and floors. It creates a slip-and-fall hazard. (3) Use caution when working with sandpaper—it can scrape skin. (4) Wash hands with soap and water upon completing this activity.

## Setting the Context
### Engage

To engage students, ask them whether they have ever watched the television show "Shark Tank" and heard the "sharks" talk about patents. *You can find resources about patents online at Inventingpatents.com* (http://inventingpatents.com/shark-tanks-advice-regarding-filing-patents), *Van Dyke Law* (https://rayvandyke.com/2014/11/26/shark-tank-and-the-types-of-patents), *and other websites. You also might show a video clip from the television show "Shark Tank" that includes a conversation about the word* patent (www.youtube.com/watch?v=oXsPJaNMNVI). Ask students whether they have heard the word *patent* before and what they think it might mean. Then ask, "Why do you think we have patents?" and "Can you think of one item that has a patent?" If time allows, you might have them perform an internet search for items with a patent and/or look for information about the patent process. You can also use a KLEW chart for patents like the example available at *www.nsta.org/eureka* to initiate your discussion of this section of the lesson with students.

### Guided Reading

Inform students that they will be learning about friction and the work of an inventor who was especially clever by reading *The Real McCoy: The Life of an African-American Inventor*. Introduce the book by asking "What does it look like is happening on the front cover?" Read the story aloud. Encourage students to notice and think about the challenges Elijah McCoy faced as an African American inventor. The following questions may be used to guide students' attention to detail as you read. (Page numbers reference unnumbered book pages, beginning with the note from the author as page 1.)

1. **Pages 6–7:** Elijah McCoy's parents realized that he had a special talent for working with tools and machines, so they sent him to school in Scotland when he was 16 years old. Why did McCoy go to Scotland to attend school?

# 7 CONSTRUCTING EXPLANATIONS (SCIENCE) AND DESIGNING SOLUTIONS (ENGINEERING)

**Elijah McCoy**

What kinds of challenges do you imagine he faced as a young African American making that 3,000-mile journey? *In the United States, it was illegal for slaves to go to school. In Scotland, McCoy could attend school to learn to read and write but would live away from his parents. He might have struggled to find food, water, or shelter.*

2. **Pages 8–9:** McCoy returned to the United States as a master mechanic and engineer. What kinds of challenges did he face when he returned from school? *While McCoy was away at school, President Abraham Lincoln issued the Emancipation Proclamation. Now McCoy could live anywhere in the United States as a free man; however, he had a hard time finding work because many people still thought of African Americans as slaves. He could only find a job as a fireman and oilman for the Michigan Central Railroad.*

3. **Pages 16–17:** McCoy wanted to make his work as an oilman (oiling the axles, bearings, and other moving parts of the railcars) more efficient. He invented a lubricating cup that automatically dripped oil where it was needed so that

the train did not need to stop as frequently. Why did people ask for "the real McCoy"? *Once railroad owners and train engineers saw how well McCoy's cup worked, they all wanted it. Others tried to copy his invention, but their copies did not work as well. For this reason, engineers always asked for "the real McCoy."*

4. **Pages 20–21:** Soon Elijah McCoy began developing more inventions. In 1882, he and his wife, Mary McCoy, moved to an integrated neighborhood in Detroit, Michigan, where he became a highly respected mechanical consultant. What is an integrated neighborhood? *Segregated neighborhoods are neighborhoods in which all the people must be of the same race (e.g., all African American). Integrated neighborhoods are neighborhoods that allow and encourage people of all races to live together in the same area.*

5. **Pages 22–23:** Soon McCoy was patenting new inventions that would help with work around the house, such as a portable ironing board and a lawn sprinkler. As the author of the featured book explains, "Elijah was so prolific that he sometimes patented two or three new devices a year." What does it mean to be prolific? *Prolific means having abundant inventiveness or productivity. In this case, it refers to McCoy's creative, productive work as an inventor.*

6. **Pages 26–27:** By 1920, McCoy had started his own company to manufacture and sell his new graphite lubricator. A short time later, he and Mary were in a car accident from which they never recovered their health. Elijah McCoy died in a home for poor, elderly people. How did it happen that his life ended this way? *The author is not explicit here, but certainly Elijah McCoy's engineering inventions were not known to most people, as he was among the first African American engineers. The historical marker at Elijah McCoy's home site suggests that racial discrimination diminished the scale of his accomplishments.*

## Making Sense
### Explore
Organize students into groups of four or five and provide each group with a set of materials. Have students use masking tape to attach a sheet of sandpaper to each ramp using a different sandpaper grade for each. Then, have students position their ramps directly over the aluminum pans, sloped so that the oil can drip into the pans (see Figure 7.1).

### Figure 7.1
**Position of the Ramps Over the Aluminum Pans**

# 7 CONSTRUCTING EXPLANATIONS (SCIENCE) AND DESIGNING SOLUTIONS (ENGINEERING)

Figure 7.2

Engineer: _____

# RACING AGAINST FRICTION WORKSHEET

**Predictions** *Circle your prediction.*

Prediction 1: I predict the car will travel faster on the (**rougher/smoother**) sandpaper.

Prediction 2: I predict the oil will (**help/hinder**) the motion of the car.

**Observations**

Smoother Sandpaper

**Observations**

In complete sentences, describe what you saw.

1.

2.

3.

4.

5.

**Conclusion**

I learned that …

_____

_____

_____

**New Question**

I wonder what would happen if …

_____

_____

_____

Provide students with the Racing Against Friction Worksheet (see Figure 7.2). Direct students to observe the two grades of sandpaper on their ramps and note any differences. *Students may observe that one sandpaper sheet feels rougher than the other.* Then, have students complete prediction 1 on their worksheets and share their prediction with the class. Encourage discussion about how the differences in roughness might affect how their cars will move down the ramps.

Take this opportunity to talk with students about some common daily predictions. For example, when we see dark clouds in the sky, we might predict that it will rain. Or, from the cover of a book, we might anticipate what story the book tells. The point is to encourage students to think a bit about what they already know before engaging in the experiment phase.

Invite students to begin rolling their cars down each sandpaper ramp and observing what happens (Figure 7.3 [A]). Then, to extend consideration of the friction factor, tell students that next they will slowly pour oil on their ramps (see Figure 7.3 [B]) and then retest their cars. Before they begin, ask them whether they have any questions about this procedure and what they predict will happen and have them complete prediction 2 on the worksheet. You also might first demonstrate for students how to pour the oil and place their cars on the ramps so they will roll down the oiled area of the sandpaper. Remember to immediately clean up any oil spills with paper towels.

### Figure 7.3
### Testing of Cars on Sandpaper Ramps

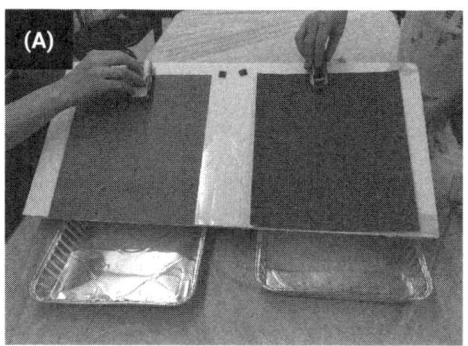

(A) Students first observe differences in how their cars perform on the two grades of dry sandpaper. (B) Students slowly pour oil on the sandpapers. They then retest the cars' performance on the oiled sandpapers.

Encourage students to discuss their observations in their groups and then with the class. Ask the following questions:

- What did you find out?

- How does this relate to Elijah McCoy's oil cup?
- At what point in the activity did you observe the effects of friction?
- When did you observe the effects of lubrication?

Ask students to write about and illustrate their observations and reasoning in the "Observation" areas of the worksheet. Remind them that their diagrams should be accurate illustrations with correct labeling of what they observed and that their written observations should include true statements that can be supported by evidence.

In the "Conclusion" section of the worksheet, have students make connections between their predictions and their observations and summarize what they learned from the process of the trials and from their observations. Evaluate the following questions:

- What did students find out? Answers might include an observation about the relationship between the oil and the sandpaper. Look for explanations that discuss different observations about different grades of sandpaper.

- How well can students connect this activity to Elijah McCoy's oil cup? Ask students to connect what they saw with what they read in the book. Look for a connection between their explanations and understandings of the text.

- Ask students "At what point in the activity did you observe the effects of friction?" Look for evidence in their answers and the fact that they could repeat their experiment and find a similar answer.

- Similarly, ask students to verbalize or illustrate in their science journals the point when they observed the effects of lubrication.

Finally, prompt students to come up with a new question and record it in the "New Question" section of the worksheet. This is an opportunity to teach students that every scientific investigation has the potential to generate a new question. Students' questions should be based on and progress from their trial results and conclusions. You might encourage students to begin their questions with phrases such as "Next time, I'd like to try ..." or "Now I wonder ..." Students' questions might relate to developing something new, such as with Elijah McCoy and his oil cup.

## Explain

Encourage students to construct an explanation for their observations. This could be done individually, in pairs or small groups, and/or as a class. It is beneficial to do all three in sequence to allow opportunities for students to modify their ideas as others share their ideas. Encourage students to summarize their observations and pose questions prompted by this investigation. Students should directly compare how the cars behaved on ramps with (1) smoother, dry sandpaper versus rougher, dry sandpaper; (2) dry sandpaper versus oiled sandpaper of the same grade (smooth or rough); and (3) smoother, oiled sandpaper versus rougher, oiled sandpaper. Ask students what they observed and what their evidence is.

Introduce a discussion about friction. *Friction is a force that holds back the sliding of an object (Physicsforkids.com 2015). Although liquids produce some resistance as objects move through them (drag), they also tend to reduce friction by smoothing out the surfaces of objects. This explains why the cars rolled more quickly and easily down the lubricated ramps and why the McCoy oil cup invention was important.* You could prompt students to experience the force of resistance by rubbing together the palms of their hands. After a minute or so of the back-and-forth rubbing, they will begin to feel heat on their palms due to the resistance caused by the skin-against-skin friction. Ask, "How does this science activity help you understand Elijah McCoy's clever solutions for trains?" *Have students review pages 14–17 of the featured book.*

## Extend

Ask the class to brainstorm to identify a problem in their lives that can be solved by engineering. Encourage them to consider problems that are related to friction (e.g., shoes that will help you stop quickly or not slip on wet sidewalks or skateboard wheels that allow you to travel on various surfaces at a preferred rate). Then, move the discussion from the large group to small groups.

Encourage students to choose one idea and record it in their science notebooks, including an illustration of the problem and the proposed solution, with labels to identify the key features. When students share their ideas, encourage conversation about the various phenomena related to the problem and the solution. Review the process of obtaining a patent, the importance of patent protection, and the types of patents. Invite students to view a clip from the television show "Shark Tank" on YouTube (*www.youtube.com/watch?v=oXsPJaNMNVI*) in which a fireman named Jeff Stroope asks one of the "sharks" to help him market his newly patented product, an easier and faster fire hose connection.

## Evaluate

Summative evaluation of this lesson will include assessment of students' understanding of (1) the character trait of being clever and (2) the effects of friction and lubrication on how toy cars travel down sandpaper ramps.

### CHARACTER TRAIT

Encourage students to answer the following questions:

1. If Elijah McCoy had not invented the oil cup, lawn sprinklers, or rubber heels, how long do you think it would have been before someone else did?

# 7 CONSTRUCTING EXPLANATIONS (SCIENCE) AND DESIGNING SOLUTIONS (ENGINEERING)

*Although others might eventually have thought of these ideas, McCoy was clever and thought of these things before anyone else did, thus affecting society.*

2. Why is being clever an important attribute for scientists and engineers? *Clever people are innovative and often think of solutions, whereas others remain stuck on a seemingly impossible problem.*

3. How was Elijah McCoy clever? *The point here is to review McCoy's oil cup and other engineering inventions through the lens of one character trait—that of being clever. McCoy solved the friction problem with the train parts when others did not even see the problem, much less think of an oil cup to keep the parts lubricated.*

4. Think about a time when you were clever and write about it in your science notebook.

**CONTENT**
Summative evaluation of this lesson might focus on students' predictions and observations recorded on the Racing Against Friction Worksheet (Figure 7.2. p. 202). The worksheet prompts students to make predictions, observations, and a conclusion and then to ask a new question.

To assess the "Predictions" section of the worksheet, note whether students made a prediction. The accuracy of the prediction is not important. Although predictions often rely on observations, they may come from students' prior experiences. Therefore, if a student makes any prediction, this indicates that he or she has put some thought into what might happen.

In the "Observation" areas of the worksheet, students were prompted to respond with a diagram (picture and words) and five written observations. For the diagrams, look for accurate illustrations and correct labeling of what they observed in the activity. As you evaluate students' written observations, look for their use of true statements, which can be supported by evidence, instead of opinions, which cannot.

In the "Conclusion" section of the worksheet, students should have summarized what they learned and made connections between their predictions and their observations. Look for indications of student learning and understanding of the scientific method (e.g., recognition that data are evidence that can lead to new understanding). Students should be able to explain the relationship between the roughness of the sandpaper and the speed at which the cars rolled down the ramp (i.e., the rougher the paper, the slower the car because of the increase in friction). They should also recognize that the oil on the sandpaper (regardless of the sandpaper grade) helped the cars to overcome the friction, as evidenced by their rolling faster down the ramps.

In the "New Question" section of the worksheet, students were prompted to come up with a new question. Look for students' questions to be explored through scientific methods. The first clue will be whether it is a question that can be answered rather than a hypothetical question. How will they go about finding their answer to the question? What steps will they need to take? What data will need to be collected? Will the data they collected answer their question or another question?

A rubric like the one in Table 7.1 may help you to assess students' completed Racing Against Friction Worksheets.

Table 7.1

## Rubric for Assessing Students' Racing Against Friction Worksheets

| Content or Skill | Not Yet | Beginning | Developing | Secure |
|---|---|---|---|---|
| **Prediction** | Student made no Prediction. | Student made one prediction but cannot verbally explain the reason for the prediction. | Made two predictions but cannot verbally explain reasons for those predictions. | Made two or more predictions and can verbally explain reasons for those predictions. |
| **Observation** | Student did not provide observations. | Student listed one observation but did not link the observation to accurate, evidenced-based statements. | Student listed two or three observations but may or may not have linked the observations to accurate, evidenced-based statements. | Student listed more than three observations and linked all observations to accurate, evidenced-based statements. |
| **Conclusion** | Student provided no answer about what he or she student learned. | Student provided an answer about what he or she learned but it does not match the reality of the activity. | Student provided an answer about what he or she learned but although the answer matches the reality of the activity, it is not complete. | Student provided a complete answer about what he or she learned that matches the reality of the activity. |
| **Asking Questions** | Student did not ask questions. | Student cannot ask new evidence-based questions from the explore phase. | Student can ask new evidence-based questions from the explore phase. | Student can ask new evidence-based questions from the explore phase. The student has an idea about how to begin to answer these questions. |

# 7

CONSTRUCTING EXPLANATIONS (SCIENCE) AND DESIGNING SOLUTIONS (ENGINEERING)

## SCIENTISTS AND ENGINEERS ARE
# PERSISTENT

Learning About **John Roebling**

Persistent (adj.): able to continue doing something in spite of obstacles or warnings

### Lesson: Exploring Suspension Bridges
#### Description

In this lesson, students create a model of a suspension bridge and make learning connections to the Brooklyn Bridge—the suspension bridge built by John Roebling and his family.

#### Objectives

In this lesson, students will consider how the character trait of being persistent helped John Roebling and his family design and build suspension bridges and how this will help them in their own efforts in creating a model suspension bridge.

- Before beginning the lesson, students will describe the types of bridges they have seen or read about.

- As a class, students will view and learn about the Brooklyn Bridge online and locate it on a map.

- Students will hear the story *The Brooklyn Bridge: The Story of the World's Most Famous Bridge and the Remarkable Family That Built It* by Elizabeth Mann and discuss how it relates to the character trait of being persistent.

- Students will make a model of a suspension bridge and observe how weight is supported through this type of bridge.

- To conclude the lesson, students will complete a bridge challenge, learn about other bridge types, and research at least two other bridge types and record the structural differences between them.

SCIENTISTS AND ENGINEERS ARE **PERSISTENT**—JOHN ROEBLING

## Learning Outcomes

Students will (1) make a science notebook entry to explain what it means to be persistent and why being persistent is an important trait for scientists and engineers and (2) construct a model of a suspension bridge and develop explanations of how suspension bridges work.

## Connections to the *NGSS* and the Nature of Science, Grades 3–5
### Disciplinary Core Ideas
**PS2.A: FORCES AND MOTION**

- Each force acts on one particular object and has both strength and a direction. An object at rest typically has multiple forces acting on it, but they add to give zero net force on the object. Forces that do not sum to zero can cause changes in the object's speed or direction of motion. (Boundary: Qualitative and conceptual, but not quantitative addition of forces are used at this level.)

**PS2.B: TYPES OF INTERACTIONS**

- Objects in contact exert forces on each other.

**ETS1.A: DEFINING AND DELIMITING ENGINEERING PROBLEMS**

- Possible solutions to a problem are limited by available materials and resources (constraints). The success of a designed solution is determined by considering the desired features of a solution (criteria). Different proposals for solutions can be compared on the basis of how well each one meets the specified criteria for success or how well each takes the constraints into account.

## Science and Engineering Practice

***Developing and Using Models:*** A practice of science is to ask and refine questions that lead to descriptions and explanations of how the natural and designed world works and which can be empirically tested. Asking questions and defining problems in grades 3–5 builds from grades K–2 experiences and progresses to specifying qualitative relationships.

- Develop and/or use models to describe and/or predict phenomena.

- Develop a diagram or simple physical prototype to convey a proposed object, tool, or process.

- Use a model to test cause and effect relationships or interactions concerning the functioning of a natural or designed system.

# 7 CONSTRUCTING EXPLANATIONS (SCIENCE) AND DESIGNING SOLUTIONS (ENGINEERING)

## Crosscutting Concept

***Structure and Function:*** The way an object is shaped or structured determines many of its properties and functions.

- Different materials have different substructures, which can sometimes be observed.
- Substructures have shapes and parts that serve functions.

## Nature of Science Connections

### SCIENCE MODELS, LAWS, MECHANISMS, AND THEORIES EXPLAIN NATURAL PHENOMENA

- Science theories are based on a body of evidence and many tests.
- Science explanations describe the mechanisms for natural events.

### SCIENCE IS A WAY OF KNOWING

- Science is both a body of knowledge and processes that add new knowledge.
- Science is a way of knowing that is used by many people.

### SCIENCE IS A HUMAN ENDEAVOR

- Men and women from all cultures and backgrounds choose careers as scientists and engineers.
- Most scientists and engineers work in teams.
- Science affects everyday life.
- Creativity and imagination are important to science.

*Source:* NGSS Lead States 2013.

*Note:* When an activity supports only part of a standard, underlining indicates the relevant part.

SCIENTISTS AND ENGINEERS ARE **PERSISTENT**—JOHN ROEBLING

## Overview

In this lesson, students learn how one family, the Roeblings, worked through many challenges to complete a bridge for Brooklyn, New York. Through the featured book, students learn that men and women from all backgrounds choose careers as scientists and engineers. The character trait of being persistent references the determination of John Roebling and his son and daughter-in-law, Washington and Emily Roebling, to solve the problems they encountered in building the Brooklyn Bridge. Students will share ideas about scientists and engineers and discuss how problems are solved. Students will explore various solutions for building bridges and learn why John Roebling decided that a suspension bridge was the best solution for his bridge project.

## Materials

You will need one copy of the book *The Brooklyn Bridge: The Story of the World's Most Famous Bridge and the Remarkable Family That Built It* by Elizabeth Mann (ISBN 978-0965049306). For each small group (or the whole class), you will need two chairs with backs that will allow a rope to be tied to them, 32 ft. of rope, a 3 ft. × 2 ft. piece of cardboard, scissors, books of various weights and sizes, and toy cars. Each student will need his or her science notebook and safety glasses or goggles.

## Safety Notes

(1) Personal protective equipment should be worn during the setup, hands-on, and takedown segments of the activity. (2) Use caution when working with sharps (scissors, and so on). They can cut or puncture skin. (3) Make sure that chairs used in building the bridge model are weighed down so as not to fall over when a load is placed on the bridge. (4) Wash hands with soap and water upon completing this activity.

## Setting the Context
### Engage

Before class begins, conduct an internet image search for different types of bridges and print out pictures of some. Ask students whether they have ever been on a bridge. If so, do they recall what type of bridge it was? Do they know there are different types of bridges? As students share stories, ask "Why do you think we have different types of bridges?" To start this section of the lesson, have the class start a KLEW chart for bridges like the example available at *www.nsta.org/eureka*. Provide student pairs with a picture of a bridge and invite them to record observations about it in their science notebooks. Discuss students' observations as a class.

# 7 CONSTRUCTING EXPLANATIONS (SCIENCE) AND DESIGNING SOLUTIONS (ENGINEERING)

## Guided Reading

Inform students that they will be learning about the work of John Roebling; his son, Washington Roebling; and his daughter-in-law, Emily Roebling, as they solved problems in designing and building the Brooklyn Bridge, which connects the New York City boroughs of Manhattan and Brooklyn. Find these two boroughs of New York on a map and tell students that they were not always connected. Introduce the book by holding up the cover and asking "What do you think this story is about?" Read the story aloud. The following questions may be used to guide students' attention to detail as you read. (Page numbers reference unnumbered book pages, beginning with the title page as page 1.)

1. **Page 5:** John Roebling was an engineer who specialized in building bridges. What experience inspired his thinking about the Brooklyn Bridge? *Roebling was riding a ferry across the East River from Manhattan to Brooklyn on a very cold day. The ferry traveled very slowly and bumped against chunks of ice along the way. He decided there should be a bridge there because, as he exclaimed, "This ferry isn't good enough."*

2. **Pages 8–11:** Most people thought it would be impossible to build a bridge across such a wide, powerful river. What were some of the challenges Roebling had to solve in his bridge design? What design problems did he expect to have to solve? *The bridge would have to be strong to withstand the wind and the river currents, high so that tall boats could pass beneath it, and long because the river was half a mile wide.*

3. **Pages 13–14:** Before beginning to build the bridge, John Roebling suffered an injury and died. His son, Washington Roebling, decided to become the chief engineer of the Brooklyn Bridge. Why do you think Washington Roebling took over building the Brooklyn Bridge? *Although Washington Roebling was not as experienced as his father, he shared his father's dream of building a bridge across the East River. He decided he had to carry out his father's dream.*

4. **Pages 16–17:** Washington Roebling was concerned about how to build strong foundations to support the bridge tower. How did he engineer a way to secure the bridge towers? *Washington Roebling engaged a shipyard to build caissons (large boxes with no floor) he could submerge in the river. The caissons allowed workers to be underwater while they drilled down into bedrock. When the drilling reached the bedrock, the caisson was filled with concrete and became the foundation for the bridge tower.*

5. **Pages 20–25:** Washington Roebling and his workers soon became aware of a condition they called caisson disease. This condition was caused by the

### SCIENTISTS AND ENGINEERS ARE **PERSISTENT**—JOHN ROEBLING

**John Roebling**

weight of the water on the outside of the caisson, which increased the air pressure inside the caisson. Today, we call this condition "the bends," and we know how to prevent and cure it. What happened when Washington Roebling was overcome with caisson disease? *Washington Roebling became permanently bedridden and never returned to the bridge. He was limited to watching the bridge work continue from his bedroom window.*

6. **Pages 25–26:** After Washington Roebling became ill, his wife Emily Roebling carried his instructions to the workmen on the bridge. What challenges do you think Emily Roebling faced in bringing the construction to completion? *Emily Roebling talked with her husband about the work, carried his instructions to the men on the bridge, and became involved in making important decisions. It was hard for her because she was not an engineer, and at that time, women did not work on construction projects.*

# 7 CONSTRUCTING EXPLANATIONS (SCIENCE) AND DESIGNING SOLUTIONS (ENGINEERING)

7. **Pages 36–41:** The cable work began when the towers were built, and this work was at dangerously high altitudes. How did the Roeblings solve the problem of finding people willing to do the cable work on the bridge? *They hired sailors who were used to working high up on the masts of tall ships. These workers also knew how to hold on in strong winds.* As engineers, John and Washington Roebling wanted to improve transportation across the East River, but they were also interested in the safety of the final structure. How did they ensure that the Brooklyn Bridge would be safe? *The main cables were made of steel, and the suspender cables attached the main cables to the steel beams on the floor of the bridge. Beams were bolted together to ensure a strong roadway floor. Washington also added extra cables called diagonal stays.* John Roebling also believed the people of New York deserved a beautiful bridge. How did he ensure that the the Brooklyn Bridge would be beautiful? *John Roebling designed a combination of bridge features that created an elegant, beautiful appearance, including high arches in the stone towers, swooping main cables, patterned suspender cables, and diagonal stays. In addition, a raised walkway gave pedestrians a breathtaking view of New York Harbor.*

## Making Sense
### Explore
Invite students to work as a team to create their bridge. You might prefer to have the class build one bridge together; if so, it will be important to discuss the process as it is happening. Assign responsibilities for specific materials to groups of students: one group for the ropes, one for the chairs, one for the books, and one for the holes in the cardboard. Show students illustrations in the featured book and ask "How do you think you can make a model suspension bridge using these materials?"

To build the model, work with students to tie two long pieces of rope to the backs of two chairs placed 2 to 9 ft. apart, as shown in Figure 7.4 (A). Pull the chairs apart so the ropes are taut. Poke holes along the two long edges of the cardboard, then thread additional rope through them, looping it over the suspension rope with each upward run, as shown in Figure 7.4 (B). When the cardboard is securely suspended on both sides, place books and other objects on it to test the strength of the bridge model (Figure 7.4 [C]). Prompt students to write three to five sentences in their science notebooks about their observations and reasoning and to make a drawing of the class's bridge labeled with words associated with how it functions (see Figure 7.5).

### Explain
Encourage students to observe how a suspension bridge works. Explain that in a suspension bridge, there is nothing beneath the road to support it. As weight pushes down on the bridge deck, it travels up the cables (or, for the model, the ropes) and is

SCIENTISTS AND ENGINEERS ARE **PERSISTENT**—JOHN ROEBLING

Figure 7.4

Stages in Building a Model of a Suspension Bridge

 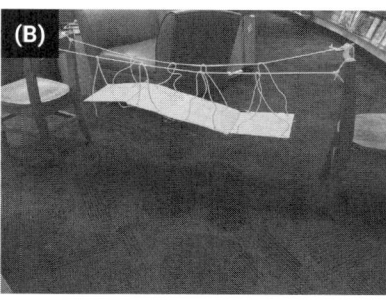 

(A) Two ropes are tied to the back of each chair and stretched taut. (B) Students poke holes in the cardboard along each long side. Then, they thread another rope through each set of holes and over the taut ropes so the cardboard bridge hangs from the suspension ropes. (C) Students place books and other objects on the cardboard to see how much weight the suspension bridge model will support.

transferred to the towers. The towers then disperse the compression directly into Earth's surface. You might refer students to HowStuffWorks.com (*science.howstuffworks.com*) and the Public Broadcasting System web page on bridges (*www.pbs.org/wgbh/buildingbig/bridge*) for more information. Finally, compare the features of the class's suspension bridge model with those of the Brooklyn Bridge.

## Extend

Set up a bridge challenge for your class. Divide the class into small groups, and provide each group with similar materials to work with, such as plastic building blocks, paper, or cardboard, and some objects for measuring strength, such as washers or pennies. Invite students to build a bridge that will support five or more of the objects. Ask students to review and compare the various designs, choices of materials, and strengths of other groups' bridges. Ask, "Why do you think John Roebling believed a suspension bridge was the best solution for the problem of connecting Brooklyn to Manhattan?" *The bridge would need to span a river about one half mile wide.*

Figure 7.5

Example of a Student's Completed Illustration

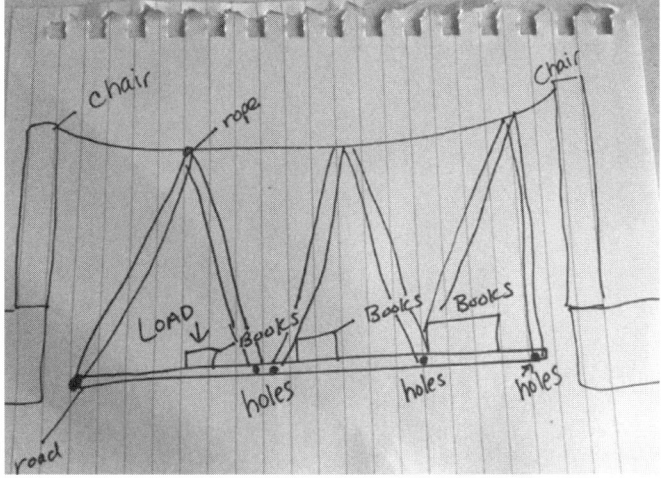

**EUREKA!** GRADE 3–5 **SCIENCE ACTIVITIES AND STORIES**

## Evaluate

Summative evaluation of this lesson will include assessment of students' understanding of (1) the character trait of being persistent and (2) how a suspension bridge is designed.

**CHARACTER TRAIT**

Encourage students to answer the following questions:

1. If Washington Roebling had not continued his father's work, how might the Brooklyn Bridge be different today?

2. Why is being persistent an important character trait for scientists and engineers? *Although others might have eventually thought to put a suspension bridge across the East River to connect Manhattan and Brooklyn, John Roebling was persistent and envisioned this engineering feat before anyone else did. The point here is to review Roebling's effort to construct the Brooklyn Bridge through the lens of one character trait—that of being persistent. Persistence helps one keep working even when the going gets tough. Washington Roebling and his wife Emily Roebling continued to organize the work on the bridge through multiple setbacks.*

**CONTENT**

In the "Explore" phase (p. 214), students were prompted to make a drawing of the class's completed bridge and to label it with words associated with how it functions (see Figure 7.5). Use a rubric such as the one in Table 7.2 to assess students' illustrations and three to five written observations about the bridge in their science notebooks. The student observations should be in sentence form.

Table 7.2

## Rubric for Assessing Students on the Suspension Bridge Model Activity

| Content or Skill | Not Yet | Beginning | Developing | Secure |
|---|---|---|---|---|
| **Drawing and Illustration** | Student did not provide a drawing. | Student drawing indicates student cannot link his or her reasoning to the evidence observed in class. | Student drawing indicates student can link his or her reasoning to the evidence observed in class, although some aspects of the drawing may be labeled incorrectly. | Student drawing indicates student can link his or her reasoning to the evidence observed in class. All aspects of the drawing are labeled correctly. |
| **Observations** | Student did not provide observations. | Student listed one observation but did not link the observation to accurate, evidenced-based statements. | Student listed two or three observations but not all observations were linked to accurate, evidenced-based statements. | Student listed more than three observations and linked all observations to accurate, evidenced-based statements. |

**CONSTRUCTING EXPLANATIONS (SCIENCE) AND DESIGNING SOLUTIONS (ENGINEERING)**

# SCIENTISTS AND ENGINEERS ARE
# INVENTIVE

## Learning About **William Kamkwamba**

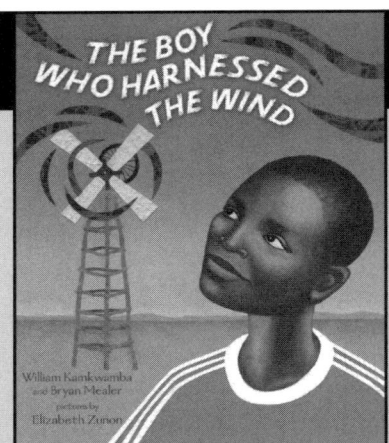

Inventive (adj.): good at thinking up new ideas or ways of doing things

### Lesson: Inventing a Solution
### Description

In this lesson, students will construct a windmill model and learn how wind is a source of energy.

### Objectives

Students will consider how the character trait of being inventive helped William Kamkwamba create a windmill to provide electricity for his village and will describe how windmills generate electricity.

- Before beginning the lesson, students will watch a short video of William Kamkwamba giving a TED Talk.
- As a class, students will build a model of a windmill.
- Students will hear the story *The Boy Who Harnessed the Wind* by William Kamkwamba and Bryan Mealer and discuss how it relates to the word *inventive*.
- In small groups, students will construct a model windmill and determine how they might produce energy.
- To conclude the lesson, students will follow Kamkwamba's inventiveness and enhance their windmill design by incorporating bioinspiration.

## Learning Outcomes

Students will (1) make a science notebook entry to explain what it means to be inventive and why being inventive is an important trait for scientists and engineers and (2) follow the engineering design cycle to build and test a windmill and construct explanations of how windmills work.

## Connections to the NGSS and the Nature of Science, Grades 3–5
### Disciplinary Core Ideas
#### ESS3.C: HUMAN IMPACTS ON EARTH SYSTEMS

- Human activities in agriculture, industry, and everyday life have had major effects on the land, vegetation, streams, ocean, air, and even outer space. But individuals and communities are doing things to help protect Earth's resources and environments.

#### PS2.A: FORCES AND MOTION

- Each force acts on one particular object and has both strength and a direction. An object at rest typically has multiple forces acting on it, but they add to give zero net force on the object. Forces that do not sum to zero can cause changes in the object's speed or direction of motion. (Boundary: Qualitative and conceptual, but not quantitative addition of forces are used at this level.)

- The patterns of an object's motion in various situations can be observed and measured; when that past motion exhibits a regular pattern, future motion can be predicted from it. (Boundary: Technical terms, such as magnitude, velocity, momentum, and vector quantity, are not introduced at this level, but the concept that some quantities need both size and direction to be described is developed.)

#### ETS1.A: DEFINING AND DELIMITING ENGINEERING PROBLEMS

- Possible solutions to a problem are limited by available materials and resources (constraints). The success of a designed solution is determined by considering the desired features of a solution (criteria). Different proposals for solutions can be compared on the basis of how well each one meets the specified criteria for success or how well each takes the constraints into account.

#### ETS1.B: DEVELOPING POSSIBLE SOLUTIONS

- Research on a problem should be carried out before beginning to design a solution. Testing a solution involves investigating how well it performs under a range of likely conditions.

- At whatever stage, communicating with peers about proposed solutions is an

# 7 CONSTRUCTING EXPLANATIONS (SCIENCE) AND DESIGNING SOLUTIONS (ENGINEERING)

important part of the design process, and shared ideas can lead to improved designs.

- Tests are often designed to identify failure points or difficulties, which suggest the elements of the design that need to be improved.
- Testing a solution involves investigating how well it performs under a range of likely conditions.

### ETS1.C: OPTIMIZING THE DESIGN SOLUTION

- Different solutions need to be tested in order to determine which of them best solves the problem, given the criteria and the constraints.

## Science and Engineering Practices

***Asking Questions and Defining Problems:*** A practice of science is to ask and refine questions that lead to descriptions and explanations of how the natural and designed world works and which can be empirically tested. Asking questions and defining problems in grades 3–5 builds from grades K–2 experiences and progresses to specifying qualitative relationships.

- Ask questions about what would happen if a variable is changed.
- Identify scientific (testable) and non-scientific (non-testable) questions.
- Ask questions that can be investigated and predict reasonable outcomes based on patterns such as cause and effect relationships.
- Use prior knowledge to describe problems that can be solved.
- Define a simple design problem that can be solved through the development of an object, tool, process, or system and includes several criteria for success and constraints on materials, time, or cost.

***Planning and Carrying Out Investigations:*** Scientists and engineers plan and carry out investigations in the field or laboratory, working collaboratively as well as individually. Their investigations are systematic and require clarifying what counts as data and identifying variables or parameters. Planning and carrying out investigations to answer questions or test solutions to problems in 3–5 builds on K–2 experiences and progresses to include investigations that control variables and provide evidence to support explanations or design solutions.

- Make observations and/or measurements to produce data to serve as the basis for evidence for an explanation of a phenomenon or test a design solution.

***Constructing Explanations and Designing Solutions:*** The products of science are explanations and the products of engineering are solutions. Constructing explanations and designing solutions in 3–5 builds on K–2 experiences and progresses to the use of evidence in constructing explanations that specify variables that describe and predict phenomena and in designing multiple solutions to design problems.

- Use evidence (e.g., measurements, observations, patterns) to construct or support an explanation or design a solution to a problem.
- Apply scientific ideas to solve design problems.

***Obtaining, Evaluating, and Communicating Information:*** Scientists and engineers must be able to communicate clearly and persuasively the ideas and methods they generate. Critiquing and communicating ideas individually and in groups is a critical professional activity. Obtaining, evaluating, and communicating information in 3–5 builds on K–2 experiences and progresses to evaluating the merit and accuracy of ideas and methods.

- Communicate scientific and/or technical information orally and/or in written formats, including various forms of media and may include tables, diagrams, and charts.

## Crosscutting Concepts

***Systems and System Models:*** A system is an organized group of related objects or components; models can be used for understanding and predicting the behavior of systems.

- A system can be described in terms of its components and their interactions.
- A system is a group of related parts that make up a whole and can carry out functions its individual parts cannot.

***Structure and Function:*** The way an object is shaped or structured determines many of its properties and functions.

- Different materials have different substructures, which can sometimes be observed.
- Substructures have shapes and parts that serve functions.

## Nature of Science Connections
### SCIENTIFIC INVESTIGATIONS USE A VARIETY OF METHODS

- Science methods are determined by questions.
- Science investigations use a variety of methods, tools, and techniques.

### SCIENCE IS A WAY OF KNOWING

- Science is both a body of knowledge and processes that add new knowledge.
- Science is a way of knowing that is used by many people.

# 7 CONSTRUCTING EXPLANATIONS (SCIENCE) AND DESIGNING SOLUTIONS (ENGINEERING)

**SCIENCE IS A HUMAN ENDEAVOR**

- Men and women from all cultures and backgrounds choose careers as scientists and engineers.
- Science affects everyday life.
- Creativity and imagination are important to science.

*Source:* NGSS Lead States 2013.

## Overview

In this lesson, students learn about one person, William Kamkwamba, who was trying to solve a problem and improve the quality of life for his entire village. Through the featured book, students learn that men and women from all backgrounds choose careers as scientists and engineers. The character trait of being inventive references William Kamkwamba's confidence and willingness to take a risk. In the process, he became a leader who inspired others to improve their quality of life. Students share ideas about how William worked like a scientist to solve his engineering problem.

## Materials

You will need a copy of the book *The Boy Who Harnessed the Wind* by William Kamkwamba and Bryan Mealer (ISBN 978-0803735118). For each student group and for the class as a whole, you will need three large paper cups, two foam cups, masking tape, cardboard scraps, a 12 in. × 12 in. piece of card stock, a bamboo skewer, and a hair dryer. Each student will need his or her science notebook and safety glasses or goggles.

## Safety Notes

(1) Personal protective equipment should be worn during the setup, hands-on, and takedown segments of the activity. (2) Use caution when working with sharps (skewer, scissors). They can cut or puncture skin. (3) Use caution when working with a hair dryer. Keep away from water to avoid electrical shock. Plug into a ground fault interrupter (GFI)–protected circuit. (4) Wash hands with soap and water upon completing this activity.

SCIENTISTS AND ENGINEERS ARE **INVENTIVE**—WILLIAM KAMKWAMBA

## Setting the Context
### Engage
To engage students, ask "Have you ever seen a windmill?" and "What do you think windmills are used for?" As a class, begin a KLEW chart for windmills like the example provided at *www.nsta.org/eureka*. If possible, conduct an internet search and share photographs or videos of windmills with the class. Invite students to record in their science notebooks five observations about the pictures of windmills. Discuss these observations as a class.

### Guided Reading
Inform students that they will be learning about the work of a person who used science and engineering to solve a problem and help his community. You might want to share the video "William and the Windmill—Documentary of William Kamkwamba" (*www.youtube.com/watch?v=HY2qcnazBFk*). Introduce the book by showing students the cover and asking "What does the front cover tell you about the story we are about to read?" Tell the students that the story takes place in a small village in Malawi, Africa. Show students a world map and ask, "Can we find Malawi on the map?" Read the story aloud. The following questions may be used to guide students' attention to detail as you read. (Page numbers reference unnumbered book pages, beginning with the title page as page 1.)

1. **Pages 3–5:** William Kamkwamba was an unusual boy. He saw that people in his community had no money for electricity. Because they had no lights, they went to bed when the Sun went down. For Kamkwamba, the darkness was best for dreaming. What things did he dream about at night? *Kamkwamba dreamed of building things and taking them apart. He had built small toy cars from radio parts and bottle cap wheels. His grandfather's tales of magic whispered to him while he slept.*

2. **Pages 6–9:** Kamkwamba's father scolded him for daydreaming while he worked with his family in their maize fields at early dawn. What was Kamkwamba thinking about while he worked in the fields? *He was distracted by a truck rumbling down the road and wondered what made the engine go. He realized that magic could not bring the needed rain. Without rain, the sun would scorch the maize fields and his family would starve.*

3. **Pages 10–11:** Soon, Kamkwamba's father told him he would need to drop out of school. Why does Kamkwamba look so sad in the picture on page 11? What is the "monster in his belly" and "lump in his throat" the authors describe there? *Kamkwamba and his family began to eat just one meal a day. They watched other hungry people pass by as they ate, and he watched the lucky students walking to school. He was hungry and sad to miss school.*

# 7 CONSTRUCTING EXPLANATIONS (SCIENCE) AND DESIGNING SOLUTIONS (ENGINEERING)

4. **Pages 12–15:** Kamkwamba sulked under the mango tree for weeks before he remembered the library down the road. How did the library help him feel better? *At the library, Kamkwamba used an English dictionary to help him read science books and learn about trucks and radios. He also learned about a machine that looked like a fan and could "produce electricity and pump water." He closed his eyes and dreamed about a windmill drawing up water from the ground for the thirsty fields and pulling electricity from the breeze and lighting up Malawi. He thought of the windmill as "a weapon to fight hunger" (p. 14).* How did visualizing the windmill help William Kamkwamba accomplish his dream? *The windmill was a reality in his mind's eye.*

5. **Pages 16–20:** For weeks, Kamkwamba worked to build his windmill. What kinds of materials did he use to make his windmill? *Kamkwamba went to the junkyard and collected a tractor fan, some pipe, some bearings, a broken bicycle, and a small generator that powered headlights on a bike. He enlisted his brother and a cousin to help him cut down blue gum trees to build the tower.*

6. **Page 21:** Once William Kamkwamba had erected his windmill, a crowd gathered to watch. Some giggled and others teased. How do you suppose that made Kamkwamba feel? *The author is not explicit here but gives no indication that these reactions deterred Kamkwamba from his dream.*

7. **Pages 22–27:** When the wind came, William Kamkwamba was able to light a small lightbulb. What did his friends and family think of him once the wind began to blow? What did Kamkwamba himself think? *A crowd gathered to congratulate him. All the doubters clapped and cheered. Still, Kamkwamba was not completely satisfied. He was ready to build a windmill that could soak the ground and help to grow food. As he reasoned, "light could not fill empty bellies" (p. 27).*

8. **Pages 30–31:** In the epilogue, you can read about other ways William Kamkwamba was inventive. Why do you think he might have kept on building and inventing solutions for his village? *Kamkwamba not only built his windmill, but he also installed a generator and eventually charged a car battery to light his family's home. He also built the "Green Machine"—a windmill-powered pump for pulling water from a small well to help his mother water her garden and grow vegetables. Now a college graduate with an engineering degree from Dartmouth*

### SCIENTISTS AND ENGINEERS ARE **INVENTIVE**—WILLIAM KAMKWAMBA

*College in the United States, Kamkwamba wants to return to Malawi to work on renewable energy.*

**William Kamkwamba**

Source: *https://commons.wikimedia.org/wiki/File:William_Kamkwamba_at_TED_in_2007.jpg*. Photo by Erik Hersman. Used under Creative Commons license CC BY 2.0.

## Making Sense
### Explore

Have students work as a class to assemble a windmill as described in the steps below. Students will then work as groups to modify that design to try to increase the speed at which the windmill vanes rotate. Using the Windmill Wheel Template (Figure 7.6, p. 226), cut out one wheel for each group and one for the initial class windmill.

1. Assemble the base of the windmill (Figure 7.7, p. 227). Then, tape the three large paper cups together, and attach that cup structure to a scrap of cardboard. Use masking tape to join the two foam cups together and then to attach that cup pair to the paper cups.

2. Make the wheel for the windmill (see Figure 7.8, p. 227). First, trace the Windmill Wheel Template onto card stock, making sure to transfer the

dotted lines from the template. Cut out the wheel and then cut along the dotted lines on the vanes and fold as shown in Figure 7.8 (B).

## Figure 7.6
### Windmill Wheel Template

Figure 7.6 is available for download in full-page size at *www.nsta.org/eureka*.

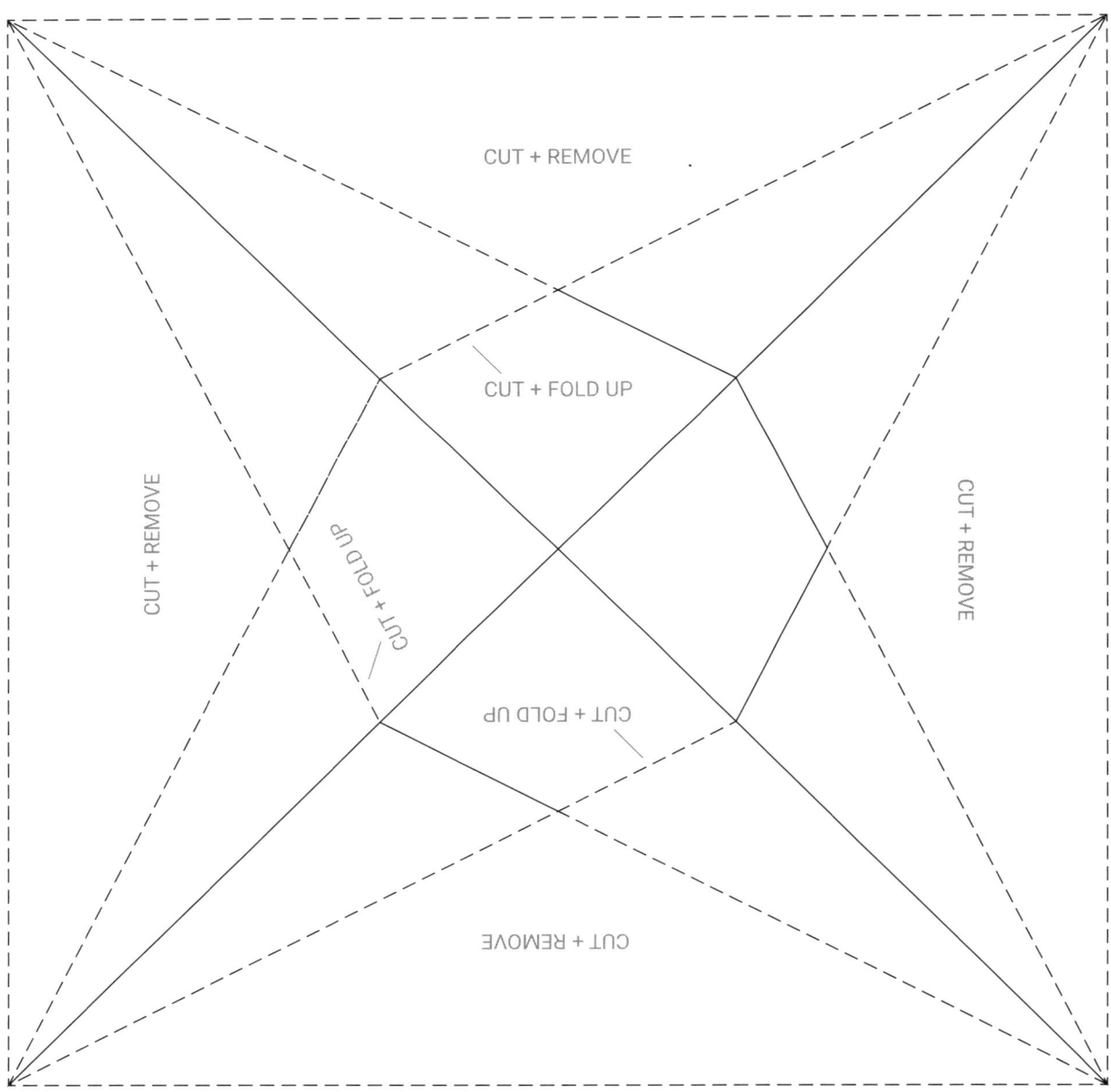

SCIENTISTS AND ENGINEERS ARE **INVENTIVE**—WILLIAM KAMKWAMBA

Figure 7.7

## Construction of the Windmill Base

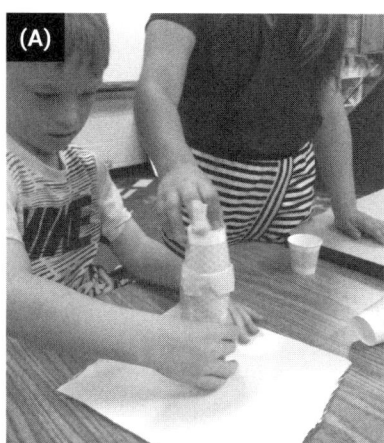 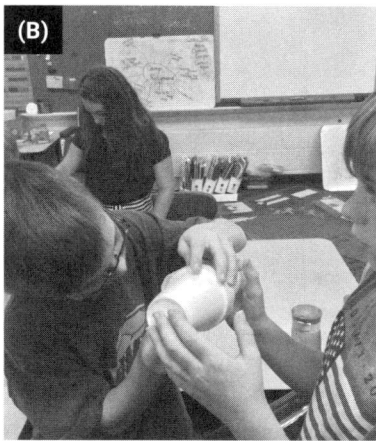 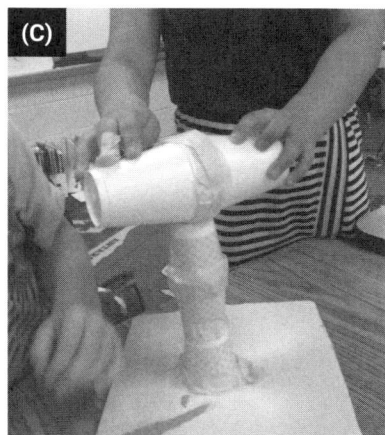

(A) First, tape the large paper cups together. (B) Next, tape the foam cups together. (C) Attach the foam cups to the paper cups, and then attach that cup structure to a cardboard base.

Figure 7.8

## Making the Windmill Wheel

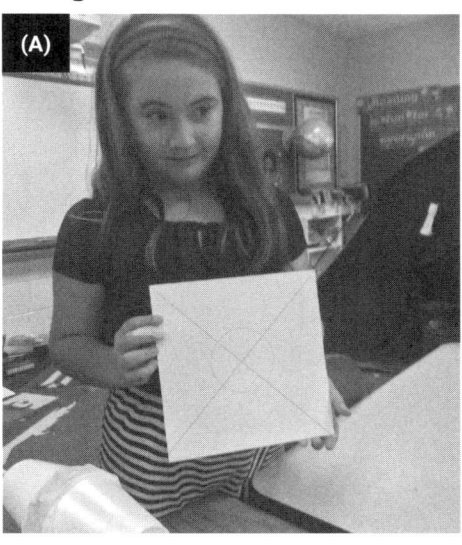 

(A) Copy the Windmill Wheel Template (Figure 7.6) onto card stock. (B) After the windmill is cut out and the dotted lines are cut, fold the parts of the vanes upward.

# 7 CONSTRUCTING EXPLANATIONS (SCIENCE) AND DESIGNING SOLUTIONS (ENGINEERING)

Figure 7.9

Attaching the Windmill Wheel to the Base

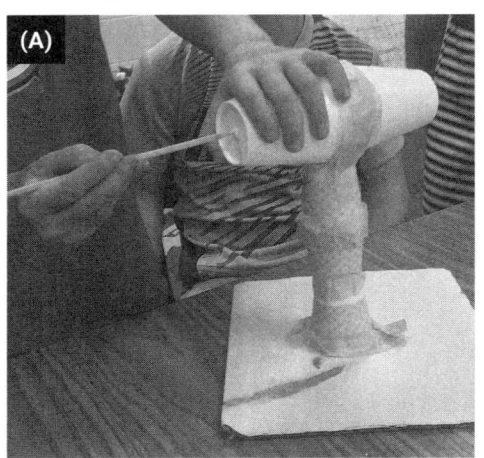

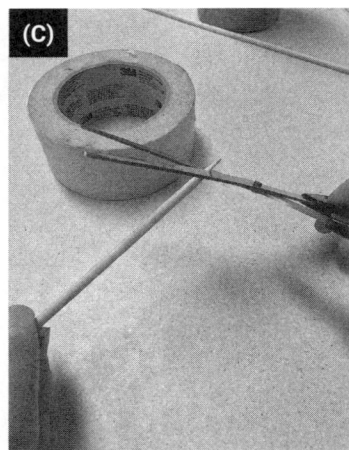

(A) Push the skewer through the bottoms of both foam cups. (B) Push the center of the windmill wheel onto the skewer. (C) Cut off the end of the skewer. This will be covered with tape.

3. Attach the windmill wheel to the windmill base (Figure 7.9) by pushing a skewer through the foam cups and then attaching the vanes to the skewer. Cut off the point of the skewer and place tape over the cut end.

4. Test the windmill by simulating wind using a hair dryer (Figure 7.10). Experiment with the position of the hair dryer to create a constant rate of rotation of the windmill vanes.

Encourage students to write about and illustrate their observations and reasoning in their science notebooks. Tell them to record the number of times the windmill wheel rotates in a given period of time, such as 30 seconds or 1 minute. We suggest coloring one vane on the windmill wheel to make counting easier. Figure 7.11 shows how one student chose to record observations.

Invite students to discuss their observations in small groups and to talk about their problems to solve as a whole class. Then, have them work in groups to build a modified design of the class windmill to try to make the windmill wheel rotate faster. Variables that students might change include the design of vanes or the base, the mass of the paper vanes, and the speed of the "wind" (air blown by the hair dryer)—and the students may think of other variables to change (even better!). In this engineering investigation, students will observe each other's designs and collect data to try to improve the windmill.

Encourage students to use their science notebooks to indicate their progress through the design cycle as they develop ideas and test attributes of their windmill designs. In our science lessons, we support a mix of prepared data collection charts and student-made data collection charts. With younger students (and usually with all students at the beginning of each school year), we like to use prepared charts that model collection methods of one variety or another. As the year progresses, we encourage students to create their own methods of recording (which can also include their own decisions about what to test or record). In this lesson, for example, students might record the number of times the vanes rotate in 30 seconds and then again in 1 minute. Once students have gathered these data, they could try exploring other variables, such as the shape or length of the vanes or shape of the base, the weight of the paper vanes, and other reasonable design features. The idea here is that students' data collection should help to inform their understanding of the function of the windmill and their ideas about improvements for a subsequent windmill design.

Figure 7.10

**Testing the Windmill**

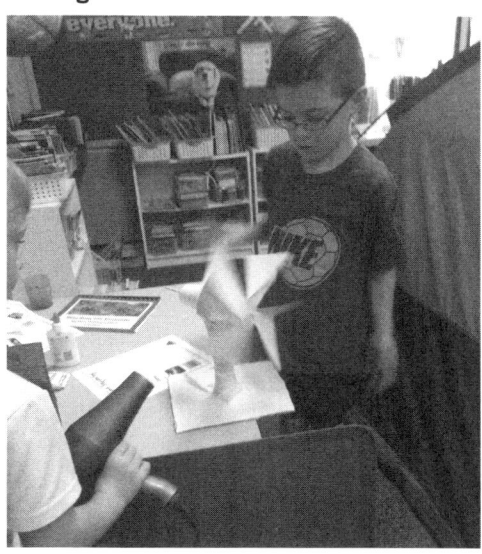

## Explain

Explain to students how windmills produce energy. You can help students visualize how windmill wheels make a shaft rotate by attaching a cup to a skewer. Windmill wheels spin when the wind blows across them. The spinning wheel, in turn, spins a shaft, which connects to a generator and makes electricity. See the website of the U.S. Department of Energy (*http://energy.gov/eere/wind/how-do-wind-turbines-work*). Instead of using electricity to make wind, as with a fan, windmills use wind to make electricity.

Figure 7.11

**Student Notebook Chart for Counting Rotations**

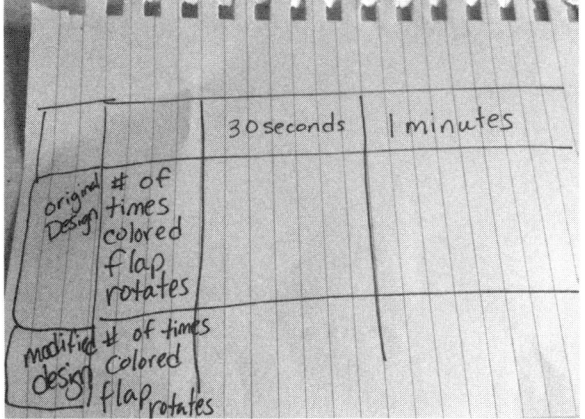

## Extend

The term *bioinspiration* means getting inspiration from biological structures or processes to stimulate research in nonbiological science and technology. The term *force-fit* means to take two or more seemingly disconnected and/or dissimilar objects and force them (or parts or attributes of them) together to create something new. Force-fitting is a tried-and-true creative thinking strategy.

# 7 CONSTRUCTING EXPLANATIONS (SCIENCE) AND DESIGNING SOLUTIONS (ENGINEERING)

To extend this activity, have students force-fit at least one animal attribute to their windmill prototype. Each student will create a redesign diagram. This is a complex, higher-level thinking activity, requiring testing and observation, questioning, creativity, and more testing! Such creative thinking exercises can inspire students to new levels of ingenuity and determination. You might simply prompt students to modify or improve the vanes on the windmill model they built. Consider reviewing the wind energy lessons developed by the Kid Wind Project (*www.kidwind.org*) or taking your students on a virtual tour through a windmill museum (e.g., see the video by Tours-TV.com [*www.youtube.com/watch?v=fgeejQpntqc*]).

## Evaluate

Summative evaluation of this lesson will include assessment of students' understanding of (1) why being inventive is an important character trait for scientists and engineers, (2) the engineering design cycle for building and testing a windmill, and (3) how windmills work.

### CHARACTER TRAIT

Encourage students to answer the following questions:

1. If William Kamkwamba had not created the windmill for his village, what might have happened?

2. Why is being inventive an important trait for scientists? *Although others might eventually have thought to build a windmill, William Kamkwamba envisioned this engineering feat before anyone else did. The point here is to review Kamkwamba's efforts to construct a windmill through the lens of the character trait of being inventive. Being inventive enabled Kamkwamba's ingenuity and determination. He cleverly thought to use discarded materials to build his windmill. His creative thinking helped him to be positive and creative and to not be limited by what other people thought. He was willing to work hard and to learn to read English to find a way to help the Malawi people to have energy for light and water.*

3. Think of a time you were inventive and write about it in your science notebook.

### CONTENT

Students' data collection and science notebook drawings and writings throughout the activity should show their understanding of how windmills work and of the engineering design cycle for building, testing, and refining the design of a windmill. The observations should include opportunities for improvement in the windmill design. These can be in words or pictures. What did they notice about the number of rotations and the designs? What part of the windmill needed the largest revision (e.g., blade design or windmill height)? Figure 7.12 shows two examples of

SCIENTISTS AND ENGINEERS ARE **INVENTIVE**—WILLIAM KAMKWAMBA

Figure 7.12

Student Windmill Drawings in Science Notebooks

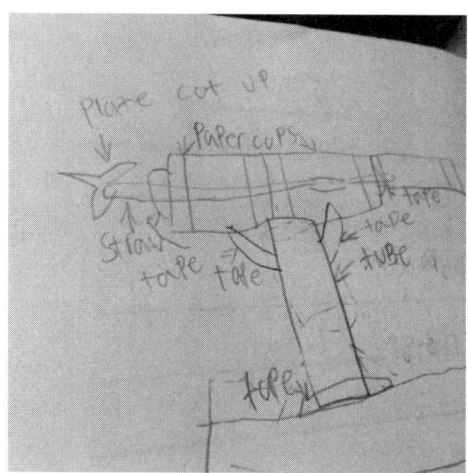 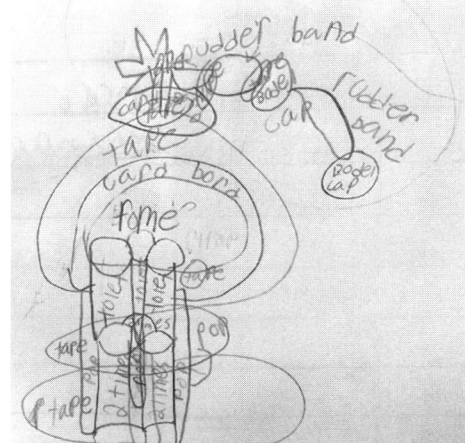

windmill diagrams that students drew in their science notebooks. Table 7.3 (p. 232) will help you assess students' ability to work in a group on the design and redesign process. To assess students' observations and illustrations about the windmill, you might find a rubric such as the one in Table 7.4 (p. 232) helpful.

# 7 CONSTRUCTING EXPLANATIONS (SCIENCE) AND DESIGNING SOLUTIONS (ENGINEERING)

Table 7.3

Rubric for Assessing Students on the Windmill Design and Redesign

| Skill | Not Yet | Beginning | Developing | Secure |
|---|---|---|---|---|
| Design and Redesign Process | Student could not create a windmill model in a group setting. | Student could create a windmill model as part of a group. | Student could create a windmill model as part of a group and test one material for the vanes. | Student could create a windmill model as part of a group and test two or more materials for the vanes. Student or group was able to redesign based on this information. |

Table 7.4

Rubric for Assessing Students on the Windmill Observations and Illustrations

| Content or Skill | Not Yet | Beginning | Developing | Secure |
|---|---|---|---|---|
| Drawing and Illustration | Student did not provide a drawing. | Student drawing indicates student cannot link his or her reasoning to the evidence observed in class. | Student drawing indicates student can link his or her reasoning to the evidence observed in class, although some aspects of the drawing may be labeled incorrectly. | Student drawing indicates student can link his or her reasoning to the evidence observed in class. All aspects of the drawing are labeled correctly. |
| Observations | Student did not provide observations. | Student listed one observation but did not link the observation to accurate, evidenced-based statements. | Student listed two or three observations but not all observations were linked to accurate, evidence-based statements. | Student listed more than three observations and linked all observations to accurate, evidenced-based statements. |

## References

Hershberger, K., C. Zembal-Saul, and M. L. Starr. 2006. Evidence helps the KWL get a KLEW. *Science and Students* 43 (5): 50–53.

Hershberger, K., J. Kur, and L. Haefner. 2013. And action! *Science and Students* 51 (3): 56–63.

Kamkwamba, W., and B. Mealer. 2012. *The boy who harnessed the wind.* New York: Dial Books.

Mann, E. 1996. *The Brooklyn Bridge: The story of the world's most famous bridge and the remarkable family that built it.* New York: Mikaya Press.

NGSS Lead States. 2013. *Next Generation Science Standards: For states, by states.* Washington, DC: National Academies Press. www.nextgenscience.org/next-generation-science-standards.

Ogle, D. M. 1986. K-W-L: A teaching model that develops active reading of expository text. *The Reading Teacher* 39 (6): 564–570.

Physicsforkids.com. 2015. Friction basics. www.physics4kids.com/files/motion_friction.html.

The LipTV. 2013. William and the windmill—documentary of William Kamkwamba. https://youtu.be/HY2qcnazBFk.

Towle, W. 1993. *The real McCoy: The life of an African-American inventor.* New York: Scholastic.

## Additional Resources

Howstuffworks.com. 2017. How bridges work. *http://science.howstuffworks.com/engineering/civil/bridge.htm*. Web page that explains how suspension bridges function.

Inventingpatents.com. 2017. Shark Tank and patents. *http://inventingpatents.com/shark-tanks-advice-regarding-filing-patents*. Blog site that explains why an inventor needs a patent to protect his or her invention.

Kid Wind Project. 2016. Teaching the world about wind. *www.kidwind.org*. Organization that provides relatively inexpensive materials to guide students' understanding of wind energy. Lesson documents and materials kits are available for purchase.

Public Broadcasting System. 2016. Building big: Bridges. *www.pbs.org/wgbh/buildingbig/bridge*. Web page that discusses bridges and provides some interesting bridge challenges.

Shark Tank. 2011. HyConn on Shark Tank. *www.youtube.com/watch?v=oXsPJaNMNVI*. Episode of "Shark Tank" television show in which a fireman who has invented a new fire hose connection approaches the "sharks" for a business partnership to help him get his product to market.

Tours-TV.com. 2014. Mid-America Windmill Museum Kendallville. *www.youtube.com/watch?v=fgeejQpntqc*. Short video showing images of historical windmills.

Van Dyke Law. 2014. Shark Tank and the types of patents. *https://rayvandyke.com/2014/11/26/shark-tank-and-the-types-of-patents*. Website that explains the difference between a utility patent and a design patent.

# 8

# Engaging in Argument From Evidence

The practice of constructing explanations and designing solutions is very important in both science and engineering. This chapter will focus on three scientists engaged in arguments from evidence during their work. How we understand an alternative way to produce energy (Nikola Tesla), the need to protect the delicate ecosystem of undersea life (Sylvia Earle), and the visual appearance of dinosaurs (Waterhouse Hawkins) can all be credited to arguing from evidence. These scientists had to compare and refine arguments based on evaluation of evidence they presented. It is easy to see how the terms *risk taker*, *fearless*, and *creative* describe the character of these three scientists and engineers.

## Recommended Science Teaching Strategy: Science Talk

The *Next Generation Science Standards* (*NGSS*; NGSS Lead States 2013) introduces argumentation as a process for reaching agreements about explanations and design solutions. In science, reasoning and argument based on evidence are essential to determining the best explanation for natural phenomenon (NGSS Lead States 2013). In engineering, reasoning and argument help to identify the best solution to a design problem.

Thus, scientific argumentation is critical to the grade 3–5 classroom for students to fully comprehend the work of scientists and engineers and how they benefit society.

"Talking science" involves learning to communicate scientific information to others while maintaining commitment to the findings and the interpretations of science (Price et al. 2011). In the classroom, this includes encouraging students to use appropriate science terms to make claims backed by evidence as they communicate with their classmates. McNeill, Katsh-Singer, and Pelletier (2015) describe the argumentation framework of claim, evidence, and reasoning (CER) in the following way: a claim answers questions or problems, which could be an explanation or model. Evidence is data that support the claim, such as observations and measurements, and reasoning explains why the evidence supports the claim using scientific ideas or principles. The CER framework will be used to describe the argumentation lessons throughout this chapter.

One of our favorite argumentation lessons is commonly called "The Checks Lab" (Randak and Loundagin 2016). This activity is designed to help students experience the true nature of science; that is, that science knowledge is built on evidence that can be observed or deduced from

# 8 ENGAGING IN ARGUMENT FROM EVIDENCE

the natural world. In this group activity, students are given an envelope that contains copies of 16 checks written by one or more fictional characters. Students do not look at any checks until the teacher gives specific instructions to remove the first four checks (all at once); this is the "claim" portion of the activity. In this way, students are focusing on the evidence in front of them and trying to piece together the story about the fictional characters. Each piece of evidence can be confusing and often creates more questions than it answers, but the pieces taken as a whole help students build hunches. The worksheets included with the checks lab activity help students sort through the information, identify misleading information, and develop tentative hypotheses through reasoning. The science talk about CER is the focus of this lesson, as students are asked to develop a scenario that accounts for the checks they have reviewed. We particularly like the way this activity demonstrates how scientific explanations are always tentative because new discoveries often present new, conflicting information.

When teaching students how some explanations get replaced by other, more acceptable explanations in both science and engineering, your role is to facilitate arguments based on evidence. Science talk helps students think through scientific explanations while communicating with others. Importantly, researchers have found that students also develop language and literacy skills when they have opportunities to use these skills in authentic situations.

# SCIENTISTS AND ENGINEERS ARE
# RISK TAKERS

## Learning About **Nikola Tesla**

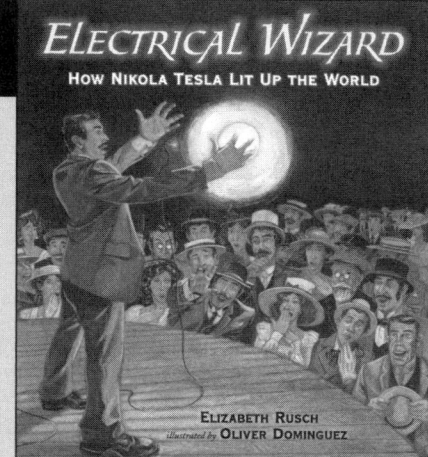

Risk taker (n.): a person inclined to take risks

### Lesson: Electric Action

**Description**

In this lesson, students observe and explore the differences between direct current (DC) and alternating current (AC) electrical systems.

### Objectives

Students will consider how the character trait of being a risk taker helped Nikola Tesla and become familiar with DC and AC electricity by building models that generate each type.

- Before beginning the lesson, students will be asked to make a lightbulb turn on using a battery and wires.

- Students will hear the story *Electrical Wizard: How Nikola Tesla Lit Up the World* by Elizabeth Rusch and discuss how it relates to the term *risk taker*.

- In small groups, students will turn on a lightbulb using AC electricity and observe how manual generators produce electricity that lights a lightbulb.

- To conclude the lesson, students will complete a Venn diagram to compare AC and DC electricity.

### Learning Outcomes

Students will (1) make a science notebook entry to explain what it means to be a risk taker and why being a risk taker is an important trait for scientists and engineers and (2) create a Venn diagram to demonstrate their scientific understanding of AC and DC electricity and their ability to use the claim, evidence, and reasoning (CER) process.

# Connections to the NGSS and the Nature of Science, Grades 3–5

## Disciplinary Core Ideas

**PS2.B: TYPES OF INTERACTIONS**

- <u>Electric, and magnetic forces between a pair of objects do not require that the objects be in contact.</u> The sizes of the forces in each situation depend on the properties of the objects and their distances apart and, for forces between two magnets, on their orientation relative to each other.

**PS3.A: DEFINITIONS OF ENERGY**

- Energy can be moved from place to place by moving objects or through sound, light, or electric currents.

**ETS1.A: DEFINING AND DELIMITING ENGINEERING PROBLEMS**

- Possible solutions to a problem are limited by available materials and resources (constraints). The success of a designed solution is determined by considering the desired features of a solution (criteria). Different proposals for solutions can be compared on the basis of how well each one meets the specified criteria for success or how well each takes the constraints into account.

## Science and Engineering Practices

***Constructing Explanations and Designing Solutions:*** The products of science are explanations and the products of engineering are solutions. Constructing explanations and designing solutions in 3–5 builds on K–2 experiences and progresses to the use of evidence in constructing explanations that specify variables that describe and predict phenomena and in designing multiple solutions to design problems.

- Use evidence (e.g., measurements, observations, patterns) to construct or support an explanation or design a solution to a problem.

- Identify the evidence that supports particular points in an explanation.

***Engaging in Argument From Evidence:*** Argumentation is the process by which explanations and solutions are reached. Engaging in argument from evidence in 3–5 builds on K–2 experiences and progresses to critiquing the scientific explanations or solutions proposed by peers by citing relevant evidence about the natural and designed world(s).

- Respectfully provide and receive critiques from peers about a proposed procedure, explanation, or model by citing relevant evidence and posing specific questions.

- Construct and/or support an argument with evidence, data, and/or a model.

## Crosscutting Concepts

*Patterns:* Observed patterns in nature guide organization and classification and prompt questions about relationships and causes underlying them.

- Patterns of change can be used to make predictions.

*Systems and System Models:* A system is an organized group of related objects or components; models can be used for understanding and predicting the behavior of systems.

- A system can be described in terms of its components and their interactions.

*Energy and Matter:* Tracking energy and matter flows, into, out of, and within systems helps one understand their system's behavior.

- Energy can be transferred in various ways and between objects.

## Nature of Science Connections
### SCIENTIFIC KNOWLEDGE IS OPEN TO REVISION IN LIGHT OF NEW EVIDENCE

- Science explanations can change based on new evidence.

### SCIENCE IS A WAY OF KNOWING

- Science is both a body of knowledge and processes that add new knowledge.
- Science is a way of knowing that is used by many people.

### SCIENCE IS A HUMAN ENDEAVOR

- Men and women from all cultures and backgrounds choose careers as scientists and engineers.
- Science affects everyday life.
- Creativity and imagination are important to science.

*Source:* NGSS Lead States 2013.

*Note:* When an activity supports only part of a standard, underlining indicates the relevant part.

# 8 ENGAGING IN ARGUMENT FROM EVIDENCE

## Overview

In this lesson, students learn how Nikola Tesla was trying to solve a problem and improved the quality of life for many people. Through the featured book, students learn that men and women from all backgrounds choose careers as scientists. The character trait of being a risk taker references Tesla's willingness to take a chance and create an alternative to the direct current. Students share ideas about how Tesla worked like a scientist to create a new way for people to think about energy. This lesson is not meant to be an introductory lesson about electricity; rather, it assumes that students will have gained some prior knowledge and experiences with currents (and circuits) in previous grades.

In Tesla's time, all the electricity in the United States was supplied by DC, the system developed by Thomas Edison. He engaged in an argument from evidence and asked questions about an alternative to DC electricity, which was AC electricity. This created a long and unpleasant battle over the kind of system that was best and has been referred to as the "war of the currents." In the end, Tesla's AC system won out and became the system we use in our homes today. Our goal in creating this lesson is to help students understand and actually see how there is more than one way to generate electricity and that magnetism and electricity are related. An electric current produces a magnetic field, and a change in a magnetic field can also produce an electric current.

## Materials

You will need one copy of the book *Electrical Wizard: How Nikola Tesla Lit Up the World* by Elizabeth Rusch (ISBN 978-0763658557). Each group of students will need a hand generator, a C-cell or D-cell battery, a flashlight bulb, a large paper clip, two electric wires with stripped ends, and a 9 in. × 12 in. piece of construction paper. (Transparent hand generators are available from science supply companies at low cost.) Each student will need his or her science notebook and safety glasses or goggles.

## Safety Notes

(1) Personal protective equipment should be worn during the setup, hands-on, and takedown segments of the activity. (2) Use caution in working with sharps (wires). They can cut or puncture skin or eyes. (3) Use caution when working with flashlight bulbs. They can get hot and burn skin. (4) Wash hands with soap and water upon completing this activity.

SCIENTISTS AND ENGINEERS ARE **RISK TAKERS**—NIKOLA TESLA

## Setting the Context
### Engage

Engage students by asking them whether they have ever wondered how electricity works. Ask them what they think is necessary for electricity. Show students a battery, a large metal paper clip, and a small lightbulb, and ask them how these materials can be used to get the lightbulb to light. Allow several students to attempt this and then demonstrate it to students. Straighten out the paper clip but then curve it at one end. Place the lightbulb on one end of the battery. Touch the straighter end of the paper clip to the lightbulb base and the curved end to the bottom of the battery. All of these items must touch simultaneously, which can be tricky and might require several hands, but when all touch, the bulb will light.

Have a class discussion about students' thoughts and observations on what is required for an electrical current. Some students might have prior knowledge and say that circuits or complete circuits are required; if so, invite them to explain what a complete circuit is and why they believe that is required. Encourage students to

**Nikola Tesla**

# 8 ENGAGING IN ARGUMENT FROM EVIDENCE

realize that although we are not always able to see how electricity works, we can form some ideas or hypotheses.

## Guided Reading

Inform students that they will learn about a scientific process called *argument from evidence* and about a person who used it to challenge what was known about electricity and develop a new way to generate electricity. Introduce the book by showing students the cover and asking "What does the front cover tell you about the story we are about to read?" Read the story aloud. Encourage students to notice and think about the risks that Nikola Tesla took as he developed his ideas about AC electricity. The following questions may be used to guide students' attention to detail as you read the story aloud. (Page numbers reference unnumbered book pages, beginning with the title page as page 1.)

1. **Pages 3–5:** Nikola Tesla was a curious child. What type of electricity did he first discover? *At age 3, Tesla was petting his cat one evening when "the fur snapped with tiny sparks." When his father told him it was electricity—like the lightning he could see during a rainstorm—Tesla thought of this as a magic trick. (The book also gives a more complete explanation of static electric sparks on page 35.)*

2. **Pages 6–7:** As a college student, Tesla had a flash of inspiration during class one day. What was it, and what was his professor's reaction? *Tesla took a risk and told his professor that his motor did not have to run on DC electricity. The professor told Tesla he was wrong and that although Tesla might do great things, he would never run motors with AC electricity. A few days later, Tesla was certain he would find a way to do it.*

3. **Page 13:** Nikola Tesla had trouble finding people who believed in a new electrical system based on AC. He sailed to America to meet Thomas Edison, a man he expected would be interested in his ideas. Why did Edison turn him away? *Edison saw Tesla as a rival, as he had already introduced DC electricity to people in America.*

4. **Pages 14–15:** Soon Tesla was "desperate for money to build his inventions." What risks did he take during this time? *Tesla invited people with money (e.g., bankers, businessmen, and other influential people, such as Mark Twain) into his laboratory for "strange demonstrations of the wonders of alternating current." He hoped that these magic shows would interest some of these people in investing in his inventive electrical machines.*

5. **Pages 16–17:** As Tesla's fame grew, Thomas Edison began a campaign to discourage people's interest in Tesla's new technology. How did Edison try to scare the public away from the concept of AC electricity? *Edison "blanketed*

*New York with pamphlets" and electrocuted animals with AC electricity to warn people of its danger. As the author says, though, "direct current is just as deadly, but no one mentioned this in the demonstrations."*

6. **Pages 20–23:** The Chicago World's Fair changed things for Tesla because his mysterious invention safely lit the entire fair. How was Tesla able to light the World's Fair? What risk did he take? *Tesla lit the fair with lamps powered by AC electricity. He took the risk of failing. Edison had made people worried that AC electricity was dangerous and might start a fire or blow up the fairgrounds.*

7. **Pages 26–29:** Tesla moved on to work out how he could use the concept of spinning wheels to turn Niagara Falls into the largest electrical project ever attempted. How did Tesla's risk pay off in this example? *When his generator was ready, Tesla sent Niagara Falls's rushing water toward the turbine—and it worked. Just one year later, more turbines and generators were built to provide electricity to houses and railways in Buffalo, New York, 22 miles away. Tesla said, "I saw my boyhood plan carried out and wondered at the unfathomable mystery of the mind."*

## Making Sense
### Explore

Invite students to work in groups and explore two ways to make lightbulbs light, one with a hand generator and wires (Figure 8.1) and the other with a battery and wires. Ask students to record their observations (in small groups) and their concerns (as a whole class) about the similarities and differences between these two ways to make electricity. To start, have students determine what their claim is—the statement or conclusion that answers the original question or problem. Encourage them to write and illustrate their observations and reasoning in their science notebooks. Next, encourage students to gather evidence—scientific data that support the claim. To support the claim, the data need to be appropriate and

### Figure 8.1
**Students Work With Hand Generators in Groups**

# 8 ENGAGING IN ARGUMENT FROM EVIDENCE

Figure 8.2

**Student Science Notebook Entry and Foldable**

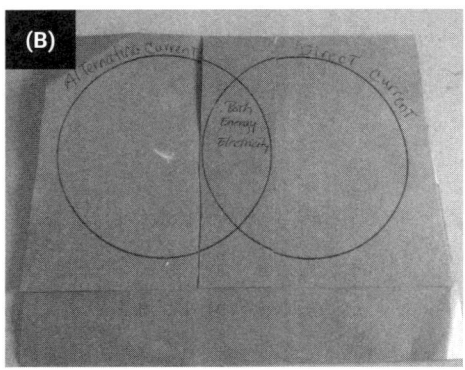

(A) Student illustration and explanation about how the hand generator works.
(B) Example of a foldable that students can create to help organize their comparison of AC and DC electricity.

sufficient. Encourage students to create a foldable Venn diagram (see Figure 8.2).

For the foldable Venn diagram, students use a "hamburger fold" (Zike 2008). They fold a piece of paper in half along the long edge, draw a Venn diagram on the top half, and then cut the Venn diagram into three unequal parts (e.g., two cuts on either side of the overlapping space in the middle). Now, students can lift these flaps to add notes and illustrations about the similarities and differences between AC and DC electricity on the bottom half of the fold. Colored copy paper works well, and students can glue this folded diagram right in their science notebooks. (If students make the fold a few inches before the middle of the paper, it will leave a band along the bottom where they can label their diagrams. See the example in Figure 8.2.)

## Explain

Ask students to explain how each system produces electricity. Ask, "Which system makes sense for powering our houses with electricity?" Students now engage in the reasoning phase of CER. Reasoning is a justification that connects the evidence to the claim. It shows why the data count as evidence by using appropriate and sufficient scientific principles. (The featured book *Electrical Wizard* has "Scientific Notes" that provide background about the differences between these two currents [pp. 34–35].) In DC electricity, the electrons move in only one direction, whereas in AC electricity, the electrons reverse direction over and over. The spinning hand cranks used in this activity spin a loop of wire between two magnets. Students should see that they can adjust from high voltage to low voltage with the hand generator but that the voltage from the battery remains constant. This observation will guide students' thinking about the efficiency of AC electricity.

## Extend

This lesson section includes two different opportunities for you and your students: the Mystery Tube and Timeline activities. In the Mystery Tube activity (modified from Bell [2008]), students engage in argument from evidence about a mystery tube in the same way Nikola Tesla engaged in an argument from evidence based on something he could not see. In the Timeline activity, the teacher helps students research the historical use of argument from evidence and how it advanced our common knowledge about electricity.

The Mystery Tube activity is relevant because it prompts students to think about solving a problem in which they cannot observe the answer and must make logical assumptions based on available data. The activity requires preconstruction of the mystery tubes (see the "Mystery Tubes" lesson on the Understanding Science Lessons website, UC Berkeley 2010) and viewing of the video "Mystery Tubes for Classroom Science Inquiry" (see Nolan 2013). Each mystery tube will require one cardboard tube (toilet paper tubes or oatmeal boxes will work, but mailing tubes are the most durable), several lengths of rope (clothesline variety), rubber bands of various sizes, and a metal washer or other metal ring. During the activity, students will (1) talk about observation versus inference and the idea that many things in science cannot be proven but instead must be inferred and (2) reveal the impact of human perspective on science.

Show students a model tube with strings looped through a ring or simply overlapping in the middle (see Figure 8.3). This model from Bell (2008) is one of the best we have found, although you can find other variations through an internet search.

Ask students to make observations (statements of knowledge based on what they see) about the mystery tube itself without touching it. Then, ask them to make observations while touching the mystery tube (e.g., pulling the strings outside the tube as they wish). Encourage them to make inferences about what they think is happening inside the tube. Depending on your students' experience with making observations and inferences, a quick reminder may be necessary

### Figure 8.3

**Arrangement of Ropes in a Mystery Tube**

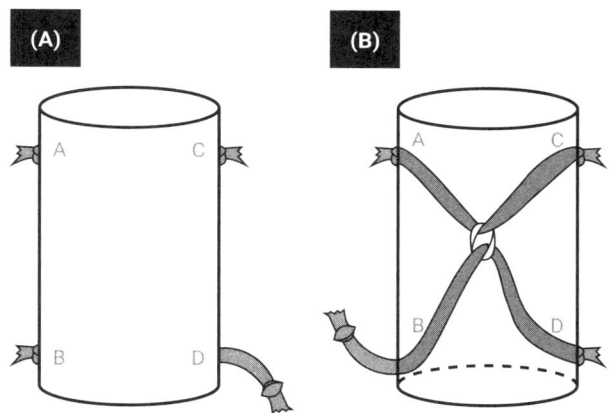

(A) Outside view. From the outside, one cannot know how the inside is organized. Rubber bands wrapped around each exposed rope end keep the ropes from pulling completely out of the tube. (B) Inside view. A metal ring connects rope A–C with rope B–D. Closing the ends of the tube will keep students from peeking inside.

*Source:* Modified from Bell 2008. Used with permission.

# 8 ENGAGING IN ARGUMENT FROM EVIDENCE

here. Observations are based on factual information; inferences are steps in the reasoning process as one moves from ideas to conclusions.

Students may find that when one string is pulled, it causes a reaction on the opposite side of the mystery tube. Allow students enough time to experiment with the tube to draw some kind of conclusion about what is happening inside the tube when the strings are pulled. Ask them to write a hypothesis (*if ..., then ...* statement) about what the ropes are doing inside the tube. We have learned that at this point in these kinds of situations, it is better to keep asking questions rather than answering students' questions. For example, every time a student or a group of students says to you, "We think this is what's happening," ask them in return, "How do you know?" "Are you sure?" "Can you replicate the action?" and "Will it happen every time the string is pulled?"

Then, if possible, give them a collection of materials (e.g., toilet paper tubes and strings) and ask them to re-create the model as well as they can. If it is not possible to provide students with these materials, ask them to create a diagram (picture with labels) showing what is happening inside the tube. Finally, ask students to show their models to the rest of the class. Students will likely create different models that work like the original or draw accurate illustrations as to the mechanics inside the tube. Help students realize that, in science, we can make models that explain what we cannot see, but we may not know for certain whether they are correct. New technologies (such as Tesla's) can dispel these unknowns. You will choose whether to allow students to see what is inside your model—before you do, just be sure they have gotten the point of the activity!

In the Timeline activity, students will construct a class timeline of some major events in the history of electricity. Divide students into five groups. Each group will research a scientist who made a discovery or improvement that affects how we use electricity today. Assign each group one of the following scientists to research (in parentheses is the discovery or improvement students are likely to discuss): the ancient Greeks (static electricity), Benjamin Franklin (key on kite string as a lightning rod), Michael Faraday (electric motor), Thomas Edison (DC electricity and the first successful lightbulb), and Nikola Tesla (AC electricity). Instruct students to research their scientist(s) and record the information they learn on a fact sheet. Fact sheets can be made using a large index card or a small poster. Each fact sheet should include the scientist's name, dates of birth and death (or, for the ancient Greeks, the time range during which they made their discoveries), and the most significant development in knowledge of or application of electricity by that scientist. Consider creating a timeline for your classroom from the ancient Greeks to present day using yarn and the fact sheets. Have each group to present their findings and place their fact sheet in the appropriate time period.

## Evaluate

Summative evaluation of this lesson will include assessment of students' understanding of (1) how being a risk taker is a beneficial character trait for scientists and engineers and (2) the difference between AC electricity and DC electricity.

### CHARACTER TRAIT

Encourage students to answer the following questions:

1. If Nikola Tesla had not invented AC electricity when he did, how long do you think it would have been until someone else made the same discovery?

2. Why is being a risk taker an important character trait for scientists to have? *Risk takers are willing to explore bold new ideas.*

3. How was Nikola Tesla a risk taker? *Students' answers should focus on how different our lives would be today if electricity had been developed 100 years earlier or 100 years later. Nikola Tesla was a risk taker and willing to find the support he needed to continue to engineer the things he could visualize, even when others did not believe in him. The point here is to review Tesla's science and engineering inventions through the lens of one character trait—that of being a risk taker. Risk takers are willing to take risks even in the face of failure or when no one else believes in their ideas. In Tesla's case, his revolutionary ideas about AC electricity transformed the world, even though Edison tried to undermine his success.*

4. If your class did the activity with the timeline in the Extend phase (p. 245), have students journal about the risks that were taken at each juncture in history of electrical advancements. If your class did not create that timeline, give students a writing prompt from the story that asks them to focus on the character trait of being a risk taker.

### CONTENT

Assess students' foldable Venn diagrams for accurate application of the CER process. If your students are just beginning to use the CER framework, you might want to focus on one strategy or simply count the number of correct statements. If you want to quantify, go through all the students' foldables and gather an accurate count to establish an appropriate starting point. For example, in some classes there could be 25 scientifically accurate observations and/or statements, but in another class it could be 5. It is important to gauge where your particular students are to establish a guideline. Once you have determined the highest and lowest number of scientifically accurate statements, you can begin to assign a point value. Remember to include in your count the content that is both inside

# 8 ENGAGING IN ARGUMENT FROM EVIDENCE

and outside the circles for AC and DC. Your evaluation table might be similar to the one shown in Table 8.1.

If you want to focus on evaluating the CER framework in the foldable Venn diagram activity, a rubric similar to the one in Table 8.2 might assist you. You can also use this rubric to evaluate students' understanding of the Mystery Tube activity.

Table 8.1

Sample Rubric for Assessing Students on the Number of Scientifically Accurate Statements

| Content | Not Yet | Beginning | Developing | Secure |
|---|---|---|---|---|
| AC and DC Foldable (Similarities and Differences) | Student did not provide scientifically accurate statements. | Student provided 1–5 scientifically accurate statements. | 6–9 scientifically accurate statements | 10 or more scientifically accurate statements |

Table 8.2

Sample Rubric for Assessing Students on the Foldable Venn Diagram or the Mystery Tube Activity

| Content | Not Yet | Beginning | Developing | Secure |
|---|---|---|---|---|
| Claim | Student did not provide a claim. | Student provided a claim but it was inaccurate. | Student provided an accurate claim but it was incomplete. | Student provided an accurate, complete claim. |
| Evidence | Student did not provide evidence. | Student provided evidence but it was inaccurate. | Student provided accurate evidence but it did not support the claim. | Student provided accurate evidence that supported the claim. |
| Reasoning | Student did not provide reasoning. | Student provided reasoning but it was inaccurate. | Student provided accurate reasoning but it did not connect the evidence to the claim. | Student provided accurate reasoning that connected the evidence to the claim. |

# SCIENTISTS AND ENGINEERS ARE FEARLESS

## Learning About Sylvia Earle

Fearless (adj.): very brave; unafraid

### Lesson: Mysterious Sawfish
**Description**

In this lesson, students will observe photographs of two sawfish nostrums (bills) and use evidence to debate whether they are from the same species (adult and baby) or different species.

### Objectives

Students will consider how the character trait of being fearless helped Sylvia Earle to explore marine plant and animal life, and will follow the claim, evidence, reasoning (CER) framework in determining whether two sawfish nostrums are from the same species.

- Before beginning the lesson, students will imagine what it would be like to live underwater for two weeks.

- Students will hear the story *Life in the Ocean: The Story of Oceanographer Sylvia Earle* by Claire A. Nivola and discuss how it relates to the character trait of being fearless.

- Students will argue whether evidence they gather from observation of the nostrums (also called bills) of two sawfish supports the fish being the same species or different species.

- To conclude the lesson, students will gain experience in making observations and forming an argument from evidence.

## Learning Outcomes

Students will (1) make a science notebook entry to explain what it means to be fearless and why being fearless is an important trait for scientists and engineers and (2) engage in student-driven discussion using the CER framework.

## Connections to the *NGSS* and the Nature of Science, Grades 3–5
### Disciplinary Core Ideas
#### LS1.A: STRUCTURE AND FUNCTION

- Plants and animals have both internal and external structures that serve various functions in growth, survival, behavior, and reproduction.

#### LS2.A: INTERDEPENDENT RELATIONSHIPS IN ECOSYSTEMS

- The food of almost any kind of animal can be traced back to plants. Organisms are related in food webs in which some animals eat plants for food and other animals eat the animals that eat plants. Some organisms, such as fungi and bacteria, break down dead organisms (both plants or plants parts and animals) and therefore operate as "decomposers." Decomposition eventually restores (recycles) some materials back to the soil. Organisms can survive only in environments in which their particular needs are met. A healthy ecosystem is one in which multiple species of different types are each able to meet their needs in a relatively stable web of life. Newly introduced species can damage the balance of an ecosystem.

#### LS3.A: INHERITANCE OF TRAITS

- Many characteristics of organisms are inherited from their parents.
- Other characteristics result from individuals' interactions with the environment, which can range from diet to learning. Many characteristics involve both inheritance and environment.

#### LS4.A: EVIDENCE OF COMMON ANCESTRY AND DIVERSITY

- Fossils provide evidence about the types of organisms that lived long ago and also about the nature of their environments.

#### LS4.D: BIODIVERSITY AND HUMANS

- Populations live in a variety of habitats, and change in those habitats affects the organisms living there.

**ESS3.C: HUMAN IMPACTS ON EARTH SYSTEMS**

- Human activities in agriculture, industry, and everyday life have had major effects on the land, vegetation, streams, ocean, air, and even outer space. But individuals and communities are doing things to help protect Earth's resources and environments.

## Science and Engineering Practices

***Constructing Explanations and Designing Solutions:*** The products of science are explanations and the products of engineering are solutions. Constructing explanations and designing solutions in 3–5 builds on K–2 experiences and progresses to the use of evidence in constructing explanations that specify variables that describe and predict phenomena and in designing multiple solutions to design problems.

- Use evidence (e.g., measurements, observations, patterns) to construct or support an explanation or design a solution to a problem.
- Identify the evidence that supports particular points in an explanation.

***Engaging in Argument From Evidence:*** Argumentation is the process by which explanations and solutions are reached. Engaging in argument from evidence in 3–5 builds on K–2 experiences and progresses to critiquing the scientific explanations or solutions proposed by peers by citing relevant evidence about the natural and designed world(s).

- Compare and refine arguments based on an evaluation of the evidence presented.
- Distinguish among facts, reasoned judgment based on research findings, and speculation in an explanation.
- Respectfully provide and receive critiques from peers about a proposed procedure, explanation or model by citing relevant evidence and posing specific questions.
- Construct and/or support an argument with evidence, data, and/or a model.

## Crosscutting Concepts

***Patterns:*** Observed patterns in nature guide organization and classification and prompt questions about relationships and causes underlying them.

- Patterns can be used as evidence to support an explanation.

***Scale, Proportion, and Quantity:*** In considering phenomena, it is critical to recognize what is relevant at different size, time, and energy scales, and to recognize proportional relationships between different quantities as scales change.

- Natural objects and/or observable phenomena exist from the very small to the immensely large or from very short to very long time periods.
- Standard units are used to measure and describe physical quantities such as weight, time, temperature, and volume.

## Nature of Science Connections

**SCIENCE KNOWLEDGE IS BASED ON EMPIRICAL EVIDENCE**

- Science findings are based on recognizing patterns.

**SCIENTIFIC KNOWLEDGE IS OPEN TO REVISION IN LIGHT OF NEW EVIDENCE**

- Science explanations can change based on new evidence.

**SCIENCE IS A WAY OF KNOWING**

- Science is both a body of knowledge and processes that add new knowledge.
- Science is a way of knowing that is used by many people.

**SCIENTIFIC KNOWLEDGE ASSUMES AN ORDER AND CONSISTENCY IN NATURAL SYSTEMS**

- Science assumes consistent patterns in natural systems.

**SCIENCE IS A HUMAN ENDEAVOR**

- Men and women from all cultures and backgrounds choose careers as scientists and engineers.
- Science affects everyday life.

**SCIENCE ADDRESSES QUESTIONS ABOUT THE NATURAL AND MATERIAL WORLD**

- Science findings are limited to questions that can be answered with empirical evidence.

*Source:* NGSS Lead States 2013.

*Note:* When an activity supports only part of a standard, underlining indicates the relevant part.

## Overview

In this lesson, students will learn how a fearless person, Sylvia Earle, became a prominent and compelling advocate for oceans. When Earle shared her knowledge and observations of oceans, it changed the way people thought about ocean life. With the featured book, students will learn that men and women from all backgrounds choose careers as scientists. The character trait of being fearless references Sylvia Earle's brave attempt to learn as much as she could about what she called "the blue heart of the planet" (see page 1 of the book). Students will share ideas about scientists working as explorers and discuss what they know about ocean life. In the activity portion, students will experience an argument-from-evidence debate.

## Materials

You will need one copy of the book *Life in the Ocean: The Story of Oceanographer Sylvia Earle* by Claire A. Nivola (ISBN 978-0374380687). Each group of students will need one set of sawfish pictures. Each student will need his or her science notebook.

## Setting the Context
### Engage

Ask students whether they have ever wondered what it would be like to dive into an ocean. Tell them that they are going to learn about a scientist who spent two weeks underwater in an ocean. Ask them to record in their science notebooks some things they might find in an ocean if they spent two weeks there. Provide reference books from the school library or access to the internet to help spur students' interest. Two possible website resources are NeoK12 Education (*www.neok12.com/Marine-Animals.htm*) and the National Geographic Society (*ocean.nationalgeographic.com/ocean/ocean-life*).

### Guided Reading

Students will be learning about life in the ocean as well as what it means to engage in argument from evidence by reading the featured book *Life in the Ocean: The Story of Oceanographer Sylvia Earle*. Introduce the book by asking "What do you observe about the person on the front cover?" and "What seems to be happening in the picture?" Read the story aloud. Encourage students to notice and think about the challenges Sylvia Earle faced as a woman working as an oceanographer. The following questions may be used to guide students' attention to detail as you read. (Page numbers reference unnumbered book pages, beginning with the first page of the actual story as page 1.)

# 8 ENGAGING IN ARGUMENT FROM EVIDENCE

1. **Pages 2–5:** From when she was very young, Sylvia Earle spent hours exploring outside. What prompted Sylvia to claim she was a biologist and botanist? *Earle's mother helped her think of her outings as "investigations" and helped Sylvia put her descriptions of what she saw in a notebook. Earle also kept collections of tadpoles, salamanders, insects, and plants in jars. All these things helped her to think of herself as a scientist, and the influence of her mother and the books she read probably helped her understand that biologists study plants and animals and botanists study plants.*

2. **Pages 6–9:** When Earle was 12 years old, her family moved to Clearwater, Florida. She left behind the orchard, creek, and woods. Now she had the Atlantic Ocean in her backyard. How did Earle's move to Florida change her life? *As her mother said, "Sylvia lost her heart to the water." Earle received a pair of swim goggles for her next birthday and began new investigations of tiny crabs, darting fish, and seahorses.*

3. **Pages 10–15:** Over her lifetime, Earle accomplished many firsts as an ocean explorer. What ocean exploration or adventure most shows that Earle was fearless? *The story describes several such events, such as joining an expedition in which she was the only woman, leading a team of divers in a deep-sea laboratory for two weeks, walking on the ocean floor in an aqua suit, and testing deep-sea submersibles. The story also relays Earle's fearless response to a whale that swam straight at her. Earle somehow knew the whales were only interested in also observing her.*

4. **Pages 14–17:** Earle always wanted to know what it would be like to live in the ocean. How did her two weeks of life in the deep-sea station (50 ft. below the water's surface) change her life forever? *Earle got to swim among the fish and coral reefs for as long as 12 hours a day. She saw the same fish each day and began to think of these ocean animals as people in a neighborhood.*

5. **Pages 26–29:** Earle became concerned about how little people know about oceans. Why did she want people to learn more about the ocean? *Earle claimed that we know more about space than we do our own planet. She believed that if we do not learn more about the oceans, we will never really care for them. The book describes some of the ocean damage that caused Sylvia*

SCIENTISTS AND ENGINEERS ARE **FEARLESS**—SYLVIA EARLE

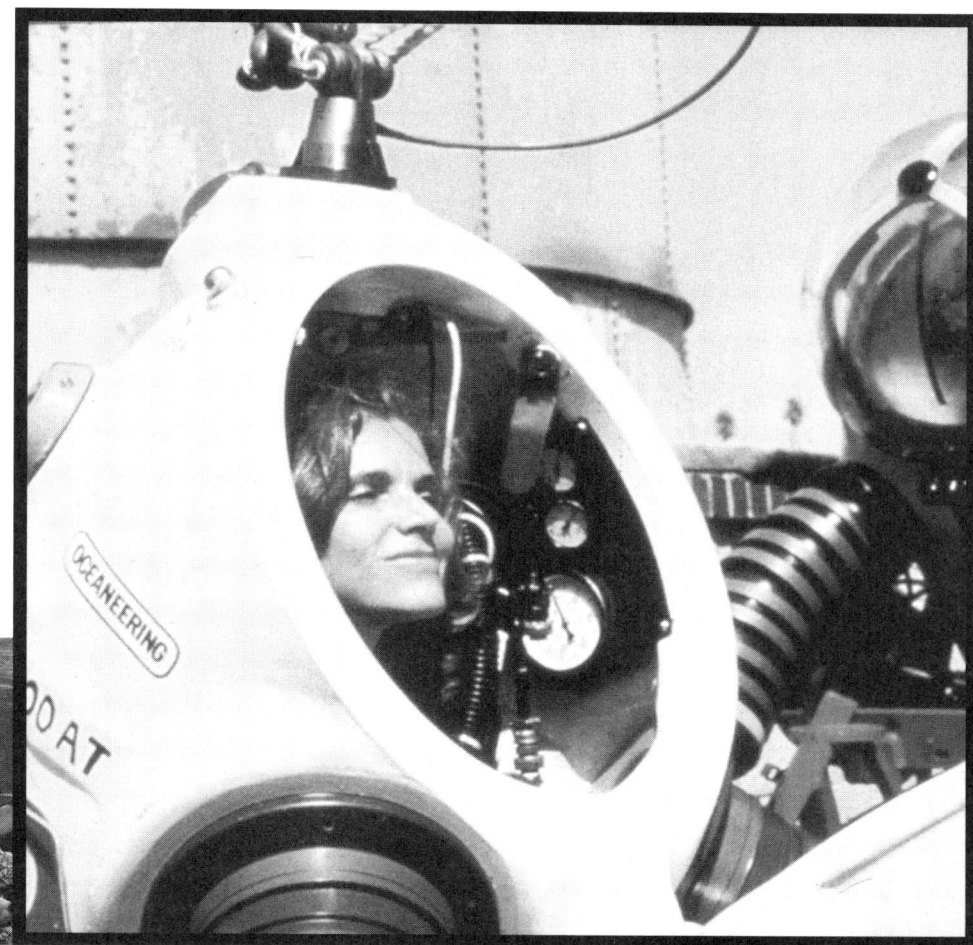

to become concerned, such as crude-oil spills, nuclear-waste dumping, and ocean drilling.

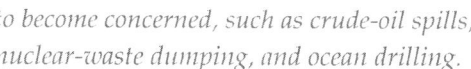

Sylvia Earle

## Making Sense
### Explore

Invite students to the carpet. You might introduce this activity as a simulation—an opportunity to fearlessly explore an endangered deep-sea creature: the sawfish. Project an image of a sawfish such as the one found at *www.nwf.org/Wildlife/Wildlife-Library/Amphibians-Reptiles-and-Fish/Sawfish.aspx*.

Share some background information on this critically endangered species. Sawfish spend most of their time on the ocean floor and have a flat body and head. The sawfish's most distinctive feature is its saw-like *nostrum* (also called its *bill*), which serves as a digging tool to unearth buried crustaceans or as a weapon with which to slash its prey. Like rays, a sawfish's mouth and nostrils are on its flat underside. Sawfish are usually light gray or brown in color. They live in salt water throughout tropical and warm temperate regions in the Atlantic and Indo-Pacific

# 8 ENGAGING IN ARGUMENT FROM EVIDENCE

Oceans. Few details of their ecology are known precisely. Sawfish tend to prefer shallow, muddy, brackish water, spending most of their time on or near the bottom of the ocean and only visiting the surface occasionally. They are nocturnal and usually sleep during the day and hunt at night for food. See the National Wildlife Federation website (*www.nwf.org*) for additional information.

Tell students that they are going to see pictures of two sawfish nostrums and that their job is to answer the following question: "Are the two nostrums, which are noticeably different in size, from the same species or different species?" *Note:* This question prompts students to develop a claim based on evidence.

Display or project the photographs of sawfish nostrums in Figures 8.4 and 8.5. As they examine the nostrums in

### Figure 8.4

**Two Sawfish Nostrums Side by Side**

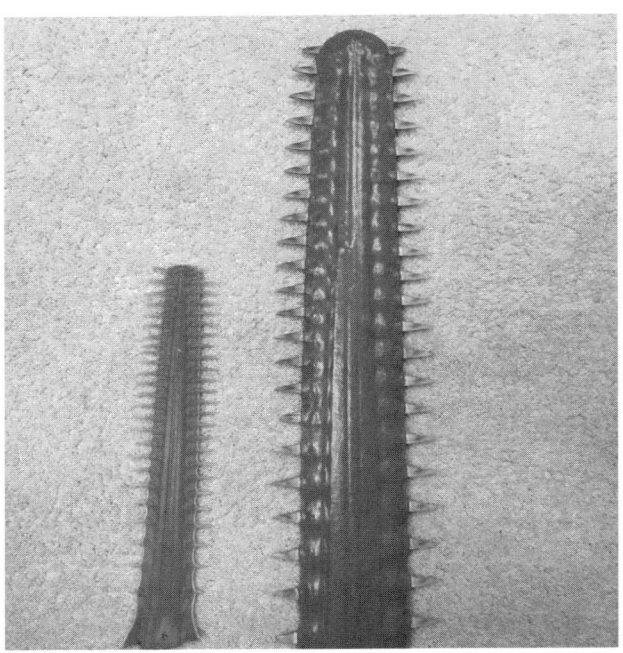

*Source:* Photo by Andrew Queler. Used with permission. Available online at *www.nsta.org/eureka*.

Figure 8.4, prompt them to notice the teeth and ask, "How are the teeth on these two nostrums alike, and how are they different?" and "Do both nostrums have the same number of teeth?" After students have counted the teeth on each nostrum, draw their attention to the shape of the tip of each nostrum. Ask, "How does the shape of the tip of the nostrum on the left compare to the tip of the nostrum on the right?"

Invite students to examine the nostrums in Figure 8.5. Ask these questions: "Is it possible that the smaller nostrum is from a baby and that the larger one is from an adult of the same species? Does it look as though a sawfish with a nostrum like the smaller one would grow up to have a nostrum like the larger one? Or do you think that the smaller one is from a different species? What evidence can help us answer these questions?"

Encourage students to summarize their observations and the evidence prompted by the initial question: "Are the two nostrums from the same species or different species?" Prompt students to use the SCUMPS acronym (size, color, use, material, parts, and shape) to draw their attention to detailed similarities and differences between the two sawfish as they form their claims (Figure 8.6).

When students have developed their claims (a statement or conclusion that answers the original question or problem), ask students who believe the nostrums might belong to an adult and a baby from the same species to stand together in one area. Then, invite students who believe the nostrums are from different species to stand together in a different area. Begin the debate by asking students to state their claim about the nostrums. Encourage students to change groups while their classmates share the evidence and observations supporting their claim if they hear something that changes their mind about their own claim. At this point, students will be focused on the evidence and data that support their claim. Encourage students to point out detailed observations of the pictures to support their claim. Keep the debate going for several rounds, encouraging students to continue weighing arguments and evidence throughout the activity. This is the reasoning phase of the lesson, in which students are called on to justify or connect evidence to their claim. Finally, encourage students to write and/or illustrate their observations and reasoning in their science notebooks.

## Explain

Guide students' consideration of the evidence as they make a decision about the two sawfish nostrums. Encourage students to listen to the arguments presented and to feel free to change their group whenever a student makes an argument that changes their mind. Encourage students to stick to factual evidence and follow the SCUMPS guide (see Figure 8.6). For example, the shape and size of the nostrums provide

### Figure 8.5

### Two Sawfish Nostrums, One on Top of the Other

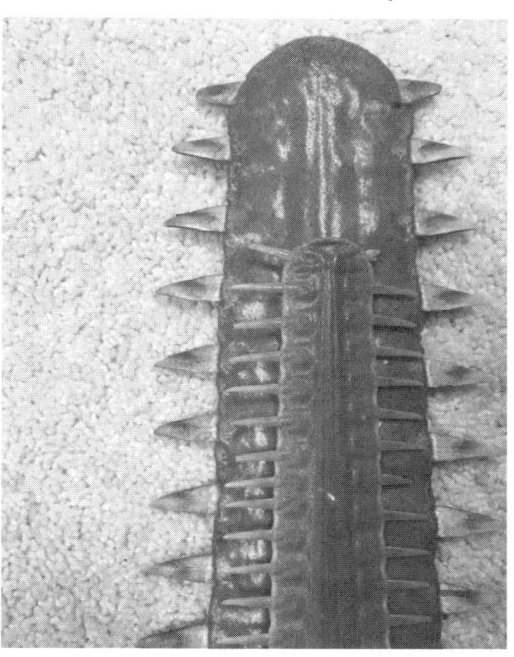

*Source:* Photo by Andrew Queler. Used with permission. Available online at *www.nsta.org/eureka*.

### Figure 8.6

### The Meaning of the Acronym SCUMPS

The SCUMPS acronym can help students make good observations while they gather data to determine whether these nostrums are from the same sawfish species.

important evidence. The two sawfish nostrums differ in their length and in the number and shape of teeth. A fair argument might be, "Hold on, I noticed that the two colors are exactly the same." Yes, this is one of the common characteristics. Another student might notice, "Yes, they are the same color, but one nostrum has rounded teeth and the other has triangular teeth." So, although students might initially assume that these are an adult and a baby of the same species, there are three important differences: tooth shape, nostrum size, and nostrum shape. Ask students to reflect on what they are learning about the importance of evidence when it comes to scientific knowledge.

The correct answer is that Figures 8.4 (p. 256) and 8.5 (p. 257) show nostrums of adult sawfish of different species. The smaller one is from *Pristis clavata,* whose common name is the *dwarf sawfish.* The larger one is from *Pristis microdon.*

## Extend

Find some other ways to explore the oceans. Your students might like to collect some books from the school library. The book *Ocean: A Visual Encyclopedia* (Woodward 2015) provides photographs and accurate facts and supports a variety of reading levels. (The pictures alone will give land-locked students a good second-hand look at ocean life.) You might have students follow along with Dr. Bob Ballard through the Nautilus Live website (*www.nautiluslive.org*) as he and the exploration corps continue their ocean explorations. You might recall that Bob Ballard is the ocean explorer who discovered the Titanic. He has figured out some amazing ways to share his explorations with students of all ages through live-streaming video.

## Evaluate

Students will (1) explain why being fearless is an important character trait for scientists and engineers and (2) engage in student-driven discussion using the CER framework.

**CHARACTER TRAIT**

Encourage students to answer the following questions:

1. If Sylvia Earle had not become an advocate of oceans when she did, how might ocean life be different today?

2. Why is being fearless an important character trait for scientists to have? *A fearless person is willing to take risks and to explore the unknown.*

3. How was Sylvia Earle fearless? *Although others might eventually have thought of these ideas, Earle was fearless and made these ocean discoveries before anyone else did. The point here is to review Earle's broad ocean awareness through the lens of the character trait of being fearless. Fearless people are willing to take risks when others remain doubtful or cautious. In Earle's case, she set out to know all she could about*

*ocean life—even by living on the ocean floor for two weeks—when others did not even wonder about life beneath the water's surface or think about the importance of caring about what damage is being done to the oceans and endangered sea life such as sawfish.*

**CONTENT**

In the activity, students were asked to summarize in their science notebooks their observations and evidence prompted by the sawfish debate. They were also encouraged to gather factual evidence and use the SCUMPS acronym as a guide while researching the similarities and differences between the two sawfish nostrums. Ask students to reflect on what they are learning about the importance of evidence when it comes to scientific knowledge. Use a rubric such as the one in Table 8.3 to evaluate students' science notebook entries as evidence of their ability to apply the CER framework.

Table 8.3

## Rubric for Assessing Student Learning From the Sawfish Activity

| Content | Not Yet | Beginning | Developing | Secure |
| --- | --- | --- | --- | --- |
| **Claim** | Student did not provide a claim. | Student provided a claim but it was inaccurate. | Student provided an accurate claim but it was incomplete. | Student provided an accurate, complete claim. |
| **Evidence** | Student did not provide evidence. | Student provided evidence but it was inaccurate. | Student provided accurate evidence but it did not support the claim. | Student provided accurate evidence that supported the claim. |
| **Reasoning** | Student did not provide reasoning. | Student provided reasoning but it was inaccurate. | Student provided accurate reasoning but it did not connect the evidence to the claim. | Student provided accurate reasoning that connected the evidence to the claim. |

# 8 ENGAGING IN ARGUMENT FROM EVIDENCE

# SCIENTISTS AND ENGINEERS ARE
# CREATIVE

### Learning About **Waterhouse Hawkins**

Creative (adj.): able to use one's imagination and easily think of new ideas

### Lesson: Building Dinosaurs

**Description**

In this lesson, students will create a three-dimensional (3-D) model of a dinosaur from a two-dimensional model using argument-from-evidence principles.

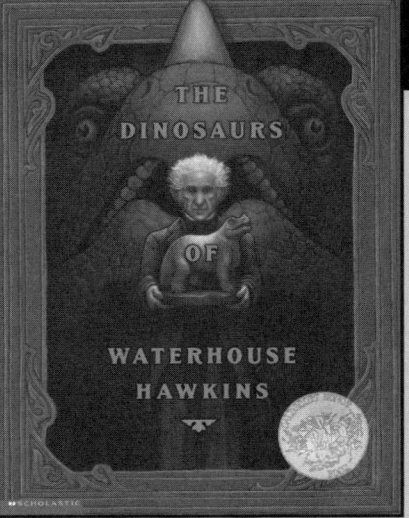

### Objectives

Students will consider how the character trait of being creative helped Waterhouse Hawkins to create life-size replicas of dinosaurs and will become familiar with using evidence to construct explanations about their own models.

- To begin the lesson, the class will discuss how we know the colors of extinct animals.
- Students will hear the story *The Dinosaurs of Waterhouse Hawkins* by Barbara Kerley and discuss how it relates to the character trait of being creative.
- Students will make a model of the skin of a dinosaur and provide evidence for its color(s), the placement of any scales, and other features.

### Learning Outcomes

Students will (1) make a science notebook entry to explain what it means to be creative and why being creative is an important trait for scientists and engineers and (2) demonstrate understanding of how scientists engage in arguing from evidence.

# Connections to the NGSS and the Nature of Science, Grades 3–5

## Disciplinary Core Ideas

**LS1.A: STRUCTURE AND FUNCTION**

- Plants and animals have both internal and external structures that serve various functions in growth, survival, behavior, and reproduction.

**LS4.A: EVIDENCE OF COMMON ANCESTRY AND DIVERSITY**

- Some kinds of plants and animals that once lived on Earth are no longer found anywhere.
- Fossils provide evidence about the types of organisms that lived long ago and also about the nature of their environments.

**LS4.C: ADAPTATION**

- For any particular environment, some kinds of organisms survive well, some survive less well, and some cannot survive at all.

## Science and Engineering Practices

***Constructing Explanations and Designing Solutions:*** The products of science are explanations and the products of engineering are solutions. Constructing explanations and designing solutions in 3–5 builds on K–2 experiences and progresses to the use of evidence in constructing explanations that specify variables that describe and predict phenomena and in designing multiple solutions to design problems.

- Use evidence (e.g., measurements, observations, patterns) to construct or support an explanation or design a solution to a problem.
- Identify the evidence that supports particular points in an explanation.

***Engaging in Argument From Evidence:*** Argumentation is the process by which explanations and solutions are reached. Engaging in argument from evidence in 3–5 builds on K–2 experiences and progresses to critiquing the scientific explanations or solutions proposed by peers by citing relevant evidence about the natural and designed world(s).

- Compare and refine arguments based on an evaluation of the evidence presented.
- Respectfully provide and receive critiques from peers about a proposed procedure, explanation, or model by citing relevant evidence and posing specific questions.
- Construct and/or support an argument with evidence, data, and/or a model.
- Use data to evaluate claims about cause and effect.

***Obtaining, Evaluating, and Communicating Information:*** Scientists and engineers must be able to communicate clearly and persuasively the ideas and methods they generate.

# 8  ENGAGING IN ARGUMENT FROM EVIDENCE

Critiquing and communicating ideas individually and in groups is a critical professional activity. Obtaining, evaluating, and communicating information in 3–5 builds on K–2 experiences and progresses to evaluating the merit and accuracy of ideas and methods.

- Obtain and combine information from books and other reliable media to explain phenomena.
- Read and comprehend grade-appropriate complex texts and/or other reliable media to summarize and obtain scientific and technical ideas and describe how they are supported by evidence.
- Communicate scientific and/or technical information orally and/or in written formats, including various forms of media and may include tables, diagrams, and charts.

## Crosscutting Concepts

***Patterns:*** Observed patterns in nature guide organization and classification and prompt questions about relationships and causes underlying them.

- Similarities and differences in patterns can be used to sort, classify, communicate and analyze simple rates of change for natural phenomena and designed products.
- Patterns of change can be used to make predictions.
- Patterns can be used as evidence to support an explanation.

***Scale, Proportion, and Quantity:*** In considering phenomena, it is critical to recognize what is relevant at different size, time, and energy scales, and to recognize proportional relationships between different quantities as scales change.

- Natural objects and/or observable phenomena exist from the very small to the immensely large or from very short to very long time periods.

***Systems and System Models:*** A system is an organized group of related objects or components; models can be used for understanding and predicting the behavior of systems.

- A system can be described in terms of its components and their interactions.
- A system is a group of related parts that make up a whole and can carry out functions its individual parts cannot.

## Nature of Science Connections
### SCIENCE KNOWLEDGE IS BASED ON EMPIRICAL EVIDENCE

- Science findings are based on recognizing patterns.
- Science uses tools and technologies to make accurate measurements and observations.

**SCIENTIFIC KNOWLEDGE IS OPEN TO REVISION IN LIGHT OF NEW EVIDENCE**

- Science explanations can change based on new evidence.

**SCIENCE MODELS, LAWS, MECHANISMS, AND THEORIES EXPLAIN NATURAL PHENOMENA**

- Science theories are based on a body of evidence and many tests.
- Science explanations describe the mechanisms for natural events.

**SCIENCE IS A WAY OF KNOWING**

- Science is both a body of knowledge and processes that add new knowledge.
- Science is a way of knowing that is used by many people.

**SCIENCE IS A HUMAN ENDEAVOR**

- Men and women from all cultures and backgrounds choose careers as scientists and engineers.
- Science affects everyday life.
- Creativity and imagination are important to science.

**SCIENCE ADDRESSES QUESTIONS ABOUT THE NATURAL AND MATERIAL WORLD**

- Science findings are limited to questions that can be answered with empirical evidence.

*Source:* NGSS Lead States 2013.

## Overview

In this lesson, students learn how one person with a creative mind, Waterhouse Hawkins, invented a way for hundreds of thousands of people to experience life-size replicas of dinosaurs. Waterhouse Hawkins shared his dinosaur creations with others and challenged the way people thought about art and science. Through the featured book, students learn that men and women from all backgrounds choose careers as scientists. The character trait of being creative references Waterhouse Hawkins's artistic attempts to solve problems. In the hands-on activity portion of this lesson, students will experience the challenge of building 3-D models.

## Materials

You will need one copy of the book *The Dinosaurs of Waterhouse Hawkins* by Barbara Kerley (ISBN 978-0439114943). Student pairs will need modeling clay and a laminated copy of the Dinosaur Replicas Handout (provided later). Each student will need his or her science notebook and safety glasses or goggles.

## Safety Notes

(1) Personal protective equipment should be worn during the setup, hands-on, and takedown segments of the activity. (2) Wipe up clay at the conclusion of the activity while it is still moist. Do not breathe in clay dust! (3) Wash hands with soap and water upon completing this activity.

## Setting the Context
### Engage

Ask students whether they have ever wondered how scientists know what color dinosaurs were, given that there were no humans in the time of the dinosaurs and therefore no photographs or pictures. Talk with students about what processes scientists might follow to make the educated guesses they do. Ask them to develop a claim (statement or conclusion) that answers this question.

### Guided Reading

Students will be learning about engaging in argument from evidence and the work of an artist who was especially creative by reading *The Dinosaurs of Waterhouse Hawkins*. Introduce the book by asking "What do you notice about the person on the front cover?" and "What does it look like is happening on the front cover?" Read the story aloud. Encourage students to notice and think about the challenges artist and scientist Waterhouse Hawkins might have faced. The following questions may

SCIENTISTS AND ENGINEERS ARE **CREATIVE**—WATERHOUSE HAWKINS

**Waterhouse Hawkins**

be used to guide students' attention to detail as you read. (Page numbers reference unnumbered book pages, beginning with the title page of the actual story as page 1.)

1. **Pages 4–7:** Hawkins had liked to draw everything in the world around him since he was a young boy. When he was a young man, what was unusual about his workshop? *He had found his true passion. He still enjoyed drawing and painting animals but had come to love sculpting models of them. Now he was building dinosaurs even though most people were not sure what dinosaurs looked like. Hawkins helped scientists fill in the gaps created by missing bone pieces by creating perfect models of dinosaurs under the watchful eye of the scientist Richard Owen.*

2. **Pages 8–9:** The time came for Hawkins to share his work with others. Who were the special visitors to Hawkins's workshop? *Queen Victoria and Prince Albert came to see the extraordinary creatures Hawkins had made. These were the first dinosaur models ever made—they wondered how he had made them.*

**EUREKA!** GRADE 3–5 **SCIENCE ACTIVITIES AND STORIES**

# 8 ENGAGING IN ARGUMENT FROM EVIDENCE

*Hawkins explained that he had looked at the found fossils (teeth, bones, and spikes) and compared them to living animals. For example, Iguanodon had teeth like an iguana's; thus, Hawkins reasoned, it must have looked like an iguana, but of a giant size indicated by the found Iguanodon bones. In another case, Megalosaurus's jawbone was like a lizard's, so Hawkins made the model look like a lizard more than 40 ft. long.*

3. **Pages 10–11:** Waterhouse Hawkins's models were correct in every detail "from scales on the nose to nails on the toes." To what did Hawkins analogize the building of his dinosaurs? In what ways are the models and their analogy alike and different? *Hawkins explained that "It is no less than building a house upon four columns." With the help of assistants, he created clay figures, erected iron skeletons, built brick foundations, and then covered the whole thing with concrete casts made from the dinosaur mold. Similarities of the analogy include the brick foundation in both, the model's iron skeleton and a house's wood frame, and the model's concrete covering and a house's siding and roof.*

4. **Pages 12–15:** It became time for Hawkins to share his dinosaur models with England's leading scientists. How did he decide to share his models with the top scientists and supporters of his day? *He hosted a New Year's Eve party inside an Iguanodon model. Dinner was served from silver platters. Guests agreed that the Iguanodon model was a "marvelous success."*

5. **Pages 20–29:** Waterhouse soon opened a show of his dinosaur models in the Crystal Palace in London, England, where crowds of people got to see dinosaurs for the first time. News of his success traveled to New York, and he traveled to America to teach others about dinosaurs. Soon Hawkins began building his dinosaurs for the new Paleozoic Museum in New York's Central Park. What disaster happened to him there? *Vandals broke into his workshop, smashed the dinosaurs into pieces, and buried them in the park. Hawkins assumed it was the work of Boss Tweed, who thought the museum was a waste of money.*

6. **Pages 30–34:** With this disaster, Hawkins lost two years of work. The author wrote, "His dinosaurs were broken and so was his spirit." How do you think Hawkins was able to carry on his work after his dinosaurs were destroyed? *Determined and dedicated, he found another way to give America her dinosaurs—by creating a series of paintings showing the development of life on Earth and his beloved dinosaurs.*

7. **Pages 36–37:** When Hawkins returned to London, 30 Iguanodon skeletons had been discovered in Belgium. How did these new fossils influence paleontologists' understanding of Iguanodon? *It now seemed clear to paleontologists that Iguanodon walked upright on its hind legs and that the spike on its*

*nose might actually be a thumb. Hawkins wondered what other surprises scientists would dig up as they continued to search for dinosaurs. This makes an important point about scientific knowledge—that it changes when new information (evidence) is found.*

8. **Pages 38–41:** Hawkins was not disappointed by these new discoveries. He was glad his models had given people their first encounter with dinosaurs. Today, people still visit the models at the Crystal Palace Park in England, but where are the American models? *The pieces of Hawkins's dinosaur models remain buried somewhere in New York's Central Park.*

## Making Sense
### Explore

Invite pairs of students to construct a 3-D model of a dinosaur using what they know about animals and animal coloring. Ask them to find scientific data (evidence) that are appropriate and sufficient to support their claim. Prompt students for evidence during the entire activity. Prompts might include questions such as "Where would your dinosaur be likely to have scales?" *Students can use their pencils to imprint scales.* "How do you know this?" and "On what animals are you basing you assumptions?" *This could be reptiles, birds, mammals, or amphibians.*

Provide each student with a laminated copy of the Dinosaur Replicas Handout (Figure 8.7, p. 268). Have students begin creating their model by placing modeling clay over their dinosaur (see Figure 8.8, p. 269), and by talking with their partners about why they think the dinosaur looked this way or that way (i.e., have them engage in argument). Encourage the use of evidence found in library and internet resources. Encourage students to find ways to explore the skin of dinosaurs, such as by looking at the skins of amphibians in library books or on websites (e.g., see San Diego Zoo Kids [2017] and Kidzone Worksheets for Children [2017] in the "Additional Resources" section [p. 272]). Have students find two or three pictures of the dinosaur species in their handout and identify the common features of its skin.

Invite students to record their observations as small groups and then again as a whole class. Ask, "What did you learn?" and "How does this relate to Waterhouse Hawkins's dinosaurs?" Encourage students to write or illustrate their claim, evidence, and reasoning about their dinosaur's skin color in their science notebooks. Then, ask students to make an entry in their science notebooks that explains how they made a decision about the covering on their dinosaur model.

### Explain

Encourage students to summarize their reasoning about the similar characteristics of birds, amphibians, and dinosaurs. Students' reasoning should be a justification

## 8 ENGAGING IN ARGUMENT FROM EVIDENCE

Figure 8.7

### Dinosaur Replicas Handout

Print each dinosaur skeleton in full-page size. Full-page versions are available for download at *www.nsta.org/eureka*.

SCIENTISTS AND ENGINEERS ARE **CREATIVE**—WATERHOUSE HAWKINS

Figure 8.8

### Students' Work in Building 3-D Dinosaur Models

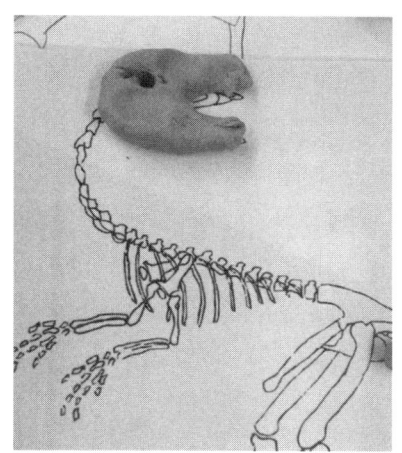 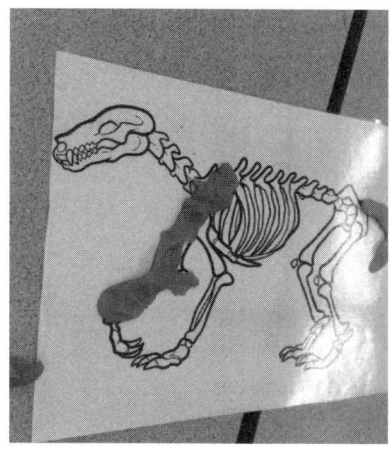 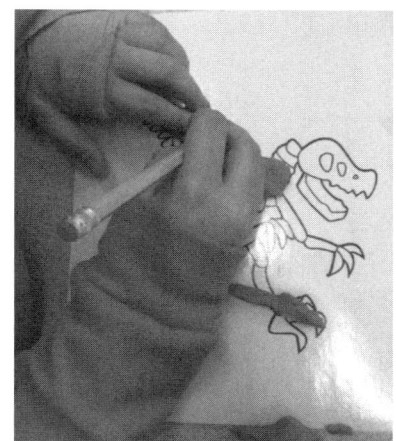

that connects their points of evidence to their claim. Reasoning uses appropriate and sufficient scientific principles to show why the data count as evidence. Introduce discussion about how scientists use what they know about birds, reptiles, and amphibians to re-create dinosaurs of long ago. For example, Highfield (2008) explains how scientists determined that the chicken is the closest living relative of the *Tyrannosaurus rex*. Scientists analyzed the collagen and soft tissue preserved in the bones of fossils of *T. rex* and another dinosaur and compared them with the collagen and soft tissue of 21 modern-day vertebrates. Those studies showed that the proteins from the *T. rex* bones were most similar to the proteins of birds. Ask "How does this science activity help you think about Waterhouse Hawkins's creative replicas for dinosaurs?" If time allows, revisit the book and find specific examples of how Hawkins's model dinosaurs reflected features of living animals.

### Extend

Introduce students to how paleontologists read fossilized footprints with the book *Big Beast Book: Dinosaurs and How They Got That Way* (Booth 1988). The book presents a paleontologist's discovery of an actual trail left by an Apatosaurus and introduces three imaginary scenes left by other dinosaurs (p. 60). Encourage students to do some research about each type of dinosaur and decipher a meaning for each set of prints. The *Big Beast Book* contains another possible extension in which students create a trackway to compare the footprints and stride of an Apatosaurus and a young *Homo sapiens* (p. 61). A third possible extension is an art and science lesson that engages students in a study of the sculpture *Rearing Horse* by Adriaen de Vries. That lesson is available from the J. Paul Getty Museum (see J. Paul Getty Museum 2017). Following observation and class discussion, students

# 8 ENGAGING IN ARGUMENT FROM EVIDENCE

draw and then sculpt an animal from life, trying to capture the animal's arrested motion.

## Evaluate

Summative evaluation of this lesson will include assessment of students' understanding of (1) why being creative is an important character trait for scientists and engineers and (2) how scientists engage in argument from evidence to determine their hypotheses of dinosaurs' skin colors.

### CHARACTER TRAIT

Encourage students to answer the following questions:

1. If Waterhouse Hawkins had not created scale models of dinosaurs, do you think someone else would have?

2. Why is being creative an important character trait for scientists and engineers to have?

3. How was Waterhouse Hawkins creative? *Although others might have eventually thought of these ideas, Hawkins was creative and thought of them before anyone else did. The point here is to review Hawkins's creative ability to visualize and build dinosaur models from his review of a few pieces of fossil teeth and bone. Creative people use their imaginations and are good at thinking of new ideas. By using his creativity, Hawkins made models from stone, wire, and clay that captured the size, shape, and spirit of ancient creatures. He helped scientists and other viewers of his models to not just see the fossil bones but from them to also visualize the development of life on Earth.*

### CONTENT

Students' models and science notebook entries should include scientific findings and reflect reasonable guesses as to the texture and coloring of dinosaur skin coverings. Use the rubric in Table 8.4 to evaluate students' use of the CER framework in their investigations.

## Table 8.4
## Rubric for Assessing Student Understanding

| Content | Not Yet | Beginning | Developing | Secure |
|---|---|---|---|---|
| Claim | Student did not provide a claim. | Student provided a claim but it was inaccurate. | Student provided an accurate claim but it was incomplete. | Student provided an accurate, complete claim. |
| Evidence | Student did not provide evidence. | Student provided evidence but it was inaccurate. | Student provided accurate evidence but it did not support the claim. | Student provided accurate evidence that supported the claim. |
| Reasoning | Student did not provide reasoning. | Student provided reasoning but it was inaccurate. | Student provided accurate reasoning but it did not connect the evidence to the claim. | Student provided accurate reasoning that connected the evidence to the claim. |

## References

Bell, R. L. 2008. *Teaching the nature of science through process skills.* New York: Pearson.

Booth, J. 1998. *The big beast book: Dinosaurs and how they got that way.* New York: Little, Brown and Company.

Highfield, R. *The Telegraph.* 2008. Chicken is T Rex's Closest Living Relative. April 24. www.telegraph.co.uk/news/science/science-news/3340709/Chicken-is-T-rexs-closes-living-relative.html.

J. Paul Getty Museum. 2017. Capturing the moment in 3-D. www.getty.edu/education/teachers/classroom_resources/curricula/sculpture/lesson01.html.

Kerley, B. 2001. *The dinosaurs of Waterhouse Hawkins.* New York: Scholastic.

McNeill, K. L., R. Katsh-Singer, and P. Pelletier. 2015. Assessing science practices—Moving your class along a continuum. *Science Scope* 39 (4): 21–28.

NGSS Lead States. 2013. *Next Generation Science Standards: For states, by states.* Washington, DC: National Academies Press. www.nextgenscience.org/next-generation-science-standards.

Nivola, C. A. 2012. *Life in the ocean: The story of oceanographer Sylvia Earle.* New York: Farrar, Straus and Giroux (BYR).

Price, J. F., D. S. Pimentel, K. McNeill, M. Barnett, and E. Strauss. 2011. Science in the 21st century: More than just the facts. *The Science Teacher* 78 (7): 36–41.

Randak, S., and J. Loundagin. 2016. The checks lab. evolution.berkeley.edu/evolibrary/teach/ensi/ensi_checks_lab.html.

Rusch, E. 2013. *Electrical wizard: How Nikola Tesla lit up the world.* Somerville, MA: Candlewick Press.

University of California Museum of Paleontology, Berkeley, and the Regents of the University of California (UC Berkeley). 2010. An understanding science lesson: Mystery tubes. undsci.berkeley.edu/lessons/mystery_tubes.html.

Zike, D. 2008. *Notebook foldables for spirals, binders, and composition books.* San Antonio, TX: Dinah-Might Adventures.

# 8 ENGAGING IN ARGUMENT FROM EVIDENCE

## Additional Resources

California State University. 2016. Ocean life for kids. *web.calstatela.edu/faculty/eviau/edit557/oceans/linda/lfish.htm. Teaches students about several types of ocean life.*

Kidzone Worksheets for Children. 2017. All about amphibians. *www.kidzone.ws/animals/amphibian1.htm. Students can view colors and skin coverings of amphibians.*

National Geographic Society. 2017. Ocean life. *ocean.nationalgeographic.com/ocean/ocean-life. Short videos and descriptions of ocean life that are written for more advanced readers but will be interesting to all.*

National Wildlife Federation. 2016. Sawfish. *www.nwf.org/Wildlife/Wildlife-Library/Amphibians-Reptiles-and-Fish/Sawfish.aspx. Source for photos and descriptions of sawfish.*

NautilusLive.com. 2016. *www.nautiluslive.org.*

NeoK12 Education. 2016. Marine animals. *www.neok12.com/Marine-Animals.htm. Provides short video clips of sea life, such as sharks, octopuses, whales, salmon, stingrays, and jellyfish.*

Nolan, K. 2013. Mystery tubes for classroom science inquiry. *www.youtube.com/watch?v=heOzqD88m18. A high school science teacher demonstrates his mystery tubes made of polyvinyl chloride (PVC) pipes.*

San Diego Zoo Kids. 2017. Amphibians. *kids.sandiegozoo.org/animals/amphibians. Close-up images of animal colors and coverings for students to study.*

Smithsonian's National Zoo and Conservation Biology Institute. 2016. Fun facts about reptiles and amphibians. *http://nationalzoo.si.edu/Animals/ReptilesAmphibians/Facts/. Helps students learn the similarities between living and extinct animals.*

Woodward, J. 2015. *Ocean: A visual encyclopedia.* New York: DK Publishing.

# 9

# Obtaining, Evaluating, and Communicating Information

The practice of obtaining, evaluating, and communicating information is germane to both science and engineering. This chapter will focus on three scientists who obtained, evaluated, and communicated information about their area of science and their scientific work toward improving society. Rachel Carson's advocacy that made people aware of the harmfulness of pesticides, Wangari Maathai's environmental leadership, and Carl Sagan's education of the public about the vastness of our galaxy improved the lives of many people. It is easy to see why the words *persuasive, passionate,* and *inquisitive* describe the character traits of these three scientists. In helping your students to identify these character traits as you teach science, you will also help to humanize scientists and engineers and the work they do.

## Recommended Science Teaching Strategy: Citizen Science

The *Next Generation Science Standards* (NGSS; NGSS Lead States 2013) expect students to be critical consumers of information—this requires not only the ability to read and understand reports in media but also to critically evaluate that information. It is important for students to be able to understand science and engineering methodologies so that they might recognize flaws in experimental design when they find things on the internet and in print as adults. For these reasons, it is important for elementary students to gather data and understand what makes an investigation valid; in the classroom, this is called the fair test. The concept of knowing what does and does not make a fair test will carry over to future science understanding and, ultimately, to science communication. One of the best ways to facilitate and reinforce the importance of data collection, evaluation, and communication is through citizen science in the classroom.

The concept behind citizen science is that one need not be a professional scientist to be able to contribute to scientific knowledge by investigating the world through obtaining, evaluating, and communicating information. By this description, each of us can be a citizen scientist. Science is no longer a subject to learn so much as it is a way to experience the world through our senses and to contribute to science. Some citizen science initiatives require more teacher planning and management, but the science learning they provide and the sense of environmental responsibility they engender in students are worth the effort.

One of the best ways to introduce students to citizen science is through programs such as Trout in the Classroom (*www.troutintheclassroom.org*), a nationwide (currently 34 states) environmental education program run by Trout Unlimited that connects students with their state's watersheds. This program involves students in raising trout (or salmon, depending on the region) from egg to fry, studying stream habitats, appreciating water resources and conservation ethics, and understanding the local ecosystems. The program is effective because students begin to see themselves as scientists and develop a great kinship with their baby trout. Many teachers proclaim the advantages of such long-term study in their classrooms and point out their amazement at their students' sense of responsibility about caring for the fish, even to the point of checking the quality of the stream habitat where they will release the fish. The website resources guide teachers and students through the project basics (e.g., equipment lists and guides on trout care and feeding); lesson plans and activity ideas (on extended topics such as ecosystems, Earth structures, habitat and environment, water chemistry, weather and climate, and genetics); suggested resource books; and potential sources of funding to help offset the cost of the required aquarium, air pump and other aquarium setup supplies, and water chiller for the classroom. Learning access in this program is optimal—the focus of study (the trout aquarium) is in the classroom and can be managed on a variable calendar.

Two other citizen science projects that are appropriate for grades 3–5 are Project FeederWatch (*www.feederwatch.org*), run by The Cornell Lab, and Project BudBurst (*www.budburst.org*), run by the Chicago Botanical Garden. Project FeederWatch runs for 21 weeks from November to April. For a modest registration fee, it provides you and your students with a project kit that includes an identification number and bird identification guides. The return commitment is to observe birds in your schoolyard for two consecutive days each week. You and your students then choose the days and times for best viewing and pick an accessible spot on the school grounds—perhaps in a playground area that has shrubs or trees or near a bird feeder outside your classroom window. Weekly tally sheets guide data collection, which will include the date, time of day, weather, precipitation, and observed species. Each week, you and your students log into the project website and enter your local data in the FeederWatch database. The data your class provides, combined with those of scientists and other citizen science participants, show the populations of bird species throughout North America, reveal weekly changes in the distributions and abundance of those populations, and help scientists create accurate bird population maps. Thus, FeederWatch data provide valuable information about bird populations that cannot be ascertained any other way.

Project Budburst is a nationwide effort to engage citizen scientists of all ages in collecting data on the dates of the first emergence of leaves, first flowers, and first ripe fruits of wildflowers and herbs, deciduous trees and shrubs, evergreen trees and shrubs, grasses, and conifers. Observational data collection is relatively straightforward and does not require special instruments. BudBurst Buddies is a free companion program available on the website that provides materials and instructions for young students to observe and report plant changes over the growing season. To participate, students pick a plant to watch and make multiple observations of that plant during the year. Following the format of the BudBurst Buddies journal, each time students make observations, they note the date and look to see whether their plant has bare twigs or branches, flowers, leaves, seeds, or fruit. Once you and your students make four observations and submit them online, you will receive an official BudBurst Buddies certificate. More importantly, students are gathering and communicating scientific data that are entered into a database and mapped to show trends in seasonal events.

These are but a few of the citizen science opportunities you might incorporate into your science teaching. There are, of course, many other opportunities to link your students' science classroom efforts to the real world of gathering and sharing science data. You might begin with the list of projects provided by the National Geographic Society (*www.nationalgeographic.org/idea/citizen-science-projects*).

**9**

OBTAINING, EVALUATING, AND COMMUNICATING INFORMATION

# SCIENTISTS AND ENGINEERS ARE
# PERSUASIVE

Learning About **Rachel Carson**

Persuasive (adj.): able to succeed in making someone do or believe something by giving the person good reasons

### Lesson: New Uses
### Description

In this lesson, students will engage in the scientific process of constructing and designing solutions as they make a video journal about lifestyle choices that can reduce an individual's environmental impact on Earth.

### Objectives

Students will consider how the characteristics of being persuasive helped Rachel Carson in speaking out about environmental issues.

- Before beginning the lesson, students will debate a contemporary environmental alternative.
- As a class, students will discuss examples of environmentally friendly alternatives.
- Students will hear the story *Rachel Carson and Her Book That Changed the World* by Laurie Lawlor and discuss how it relates to the character trait of being persuasive.
- Students will make a video journal to demonstrate their understanding of specific ways to reduce their environmental impact.
- To conclude the lesson, students will share their videos with the class.

NATIONAL SCIENCE TEACHERS ASSOCIATION

## Learning Outcomes

Students will (1) make a science notebook entry to explain what it means to be persuasive and why being persuasive is an important trait for scientists and engineers and (2) create a video journal to persuade others about lifestyle choices that can reduce an individual's environmental impact.

## Connections to the NGSS and the Nature of Science, Grades 3–5
### Disciplinary Core Ideas
#### LS2.A: INTERDEPENDENT RELATIONSHIPS IN ECOSYSTEMS

- The food of almost any kind of animal can be traced back to plants. Organisms are related in food webs in which some animals eat plants for food and other animals eat the animals that eat plants. Some organisms, such as fungi and bacteria, break down dead organisms (both plants or plants parts and animals) and therefore operate as "decomposers." Decomposition eventually restores (recycles) some materials back to the soil. Organisms can survive only in environments in which their particular needs are met. A healthy ecosystem is one in which multiple species of different types are each able to meet their needs in a relatively stable web of life. Newly introduced species can damage the balance of an ecosystem.

#### LS2.C: ECOSYSTEM DYNAMICS, FUNCTIONING, AND RESILIENCE

- When the environment changes in ways that affect a place's physical characteristics, temperature, or availability of resources, some organisms survive and reproduce, others move to new locations, yet others move into the transformed environment, and some die.

#### LS4.D: BIODIVERSITY AND HUMANS

- Populations live in a variety of habitats, and change in those habitats affects the organisms living there.

#### ESS3.C: HUMAN IMPACTS ON EARTH SYSTEMS

- Human activities in agriculture, industry, and everyday life have had major effects on the land, vegetation, streams, ocean, air, and even outer space. But individuals and communities are doing things to help protect Earth's resources and environments.

### Science and Engineering Practices

***Asking Questions and Defining Problems:*** A practice of science is to ask and refine questions that lead to descriptions and explanations of how the natural and designed world works and which can be empirically tested. Asking questions and defining problems in grades 3–5 builds from grades K–2 experiences and progresses to specifying qualitative relationships.

- Use prior knowledge to describe problems that can be solved.
- Define a simple design problem that can be solved through the development of an object, tool, process, or system and includes several criteria for success and constraints on materials, time, or cost.

***Constructing Explanations and Designing Solutions:*** The products of science are explanations and the products of engineering are solutions. Constructing explanations and designing solutions in 3–5 builds on K–2 experiences and progresses to the use of evidence in constructing explanations that specify variables that describe and predict phenomena and in designing multiple solutions to design problems.

- Use evidence (e.g., measurements, observations, patterns) to construct or support an explanation or design a solution to a problem.
- Identify the evidence that supports particular points in an explanation.

***Obtaining, Evaluating, and Communicating Information:*** Scientists and engineers must be able to communicate clearly and persuasively the ideas and methods they generate. Critiquing and communicating ideas individually and in groups is a critical professional activity. Obtaining, evaluating, and communicating information in 3–5 builds on K–2 experiences and progresses to evaluating the merit and accuracy of ideas and methods.

- Obtain and combine information from books and/or other reliable media to explain phenomena or solutions to a design problem.
- Communicate scientific and/or technical information orally and/or in written formats, including various forms of media and may include tables, diagrams, and charts.

## Crosscutting Concept

***Cause and Effect:*** Events have causes, sometimes simple, sometimes multifaceted. Deciphering causal relationships, and the mechanisms by which they are mediated, is a major activity of science and engineering.

- Cause and effect relationships are routinely identified, tested, and used to explain change.
- Events that occur together with regularity might or might not be a cause and effect relationship.

### Nature of Science Connections
**SCIENCE KNOWLEDGE IS BASED ON EMPIRICAL EVIDENCE**

- Science findings are based on recognizing patterns.

**SCIENCE IS A HUMAN ENDEAVOR**

- Men and women from all cultures and backgrounds choose careers as scientists and engineers.
- Science affects everyday life.
- Creativity and imagination are important to science.

*Source:* NGSS Lead States 2013.

## Overview

In this lesson, students will learn about one scientist, Rachel Carson, who was persuasive in her communication about the risks of insecticide application (DDT [Dichlorodiphenyltrichloroethane] in particular). Carson argued that citizens have the right to know how pesticides are being used on their private property. Through the featured book, students will learn that men and women from all backgrounds choose careers as scientists. The character trait of being persuasive references Rachel Carson's ability to convey her passion about the environment through her writing. As an advocate for the environment, Carson often argued in such a way that everyday people were able to understand scientific research. In this way, she communicated to common people what the scientific community understood about the environmental impact of DDT. In doing so, Carson acted as a citizen scientist and spawned a revolution. She believed that people would protect only what they loved, so she worked to establish a "sense of wonder" about nature.

## Materials

You will need a copy of the book *Rachel Carson and Her Book That Changed the World* by Laurie Lawlor (ISBN 978-0823423705) and a set of the Environmental Issue Cards (template provided). Each student group will need access to an electronic device (e.g., computer, smartphone, or tablet) to create a video. Each student will need his or her science notebook.

# 9 OBTAINING, EVALUATING, AND COMMUNICATING INFORMATION

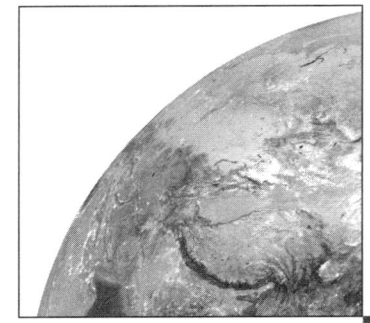

## Setting the Context

### Engage

Engage the class by asking students to share their ideas about what it means to be persuasive; that is, to make a good argument. Introduce a contemporary issue that is relevant to students (e.g., whether zoos are good or bad for wild animals or whether plastic bags should be banned). Ask students to choose a side—yes or no, for or against, good or bad, and so forth—and to think of reasons why they take this side and why they believe others should also. Talk about the two sides of the issue and help the group for each side decide what main talking points to use to try to persuade the other side to agree with them.

### Guided Reading

Inform students that they will learn about a scientist who was especially persuasive by reading *Rachel Carson and Her Book That Changed the World*. Carson was revolutionary in applying her persuasiveness to educate people about critical science issues. Introduce the book by asking "What do you notice about the person on the front cover?" and "What does it look like is happening on the front cover?" Read the story aloud. Encourage students to notice and think about the challenges Rachel Carson might have faced as a woman who was an environmental watchdog. The following questions may be used to guide students' attention to detail as you read. (Page numbers reference unnumbered book pages, beginning with the title page as page 1.)

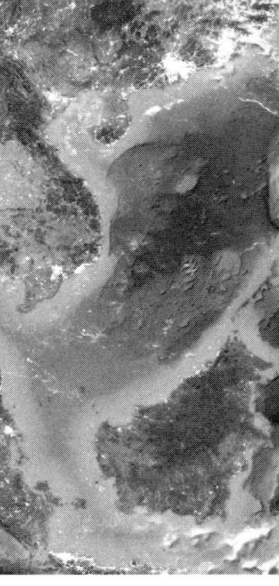

1. **Pages 3–5:** As a child, Rachel Carson was a curious and determined little girl who spent much time exploring the woods, orchards, and fields around her home. How did she decide to become a writer? *At age 11, Carson wrote a story that won a prize and was published in* St. Nicholas Magazine *for children. This recognition helped her decide to become a writer.*

2. **Pages 6–9:** Carson's mother worked hard to make it possible for Carson to attend college. How did her hometown change during her time away at college? *Carson returned home to find the woods cut down for factories and houses and the river polluted. These things left her sad and worried about the environment and her own future and may have influenced her decision to become a biologist.*

SCIENTISTS AND ENGINEERS ARE **PERSUASIVE**—RACHEL CARSON

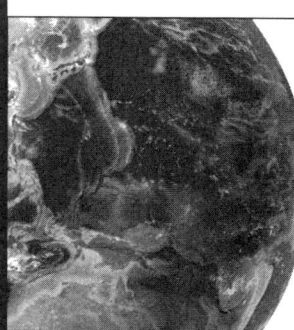

Rachel Carson

3. **Pages 10–15:** Carson enjoyed her biology studies, especially those that were at Woods Hole Marine Biological Laboratory in Massachusetts, along the Atlantic Ocean. After Carson graduated with her master's degree, why was she unable to find a job? *The unemployment rate was high then—during the Great Depression—and no one wanted to hire a woman biologist. Luckily, the chief of the U.S. Bureau of Fisheries offered her a job fixing "dull radio scripts about sea life," which turned into a full-time job as a biologist.*

4. **Pages 16–20:** Carson's first book, *Under the Sea-Wind: A Naturalist's Picture of Ocean Life*, went fairly unnoticed. She worked as a biologist for 15 years (counting fish and tracking alligators)—a job few women before her had performed. What created Carson's love of the ocean and motivated her to publish two more books, *The Sea Around Us* and *The Edge of the Sea*? *Her years of work experience certainly influenced her and, as she wrote in her journal,*

# 9 OBTAINING, EVALUATING, AND COMMUNICATING INFORMATION

Figure 9.1

Environmental Issue Cards

| | |
|---|---|
| **Plastic bags** | **Carpet cleaners** |
| **Sport utility vehicles (SUVs)** | **Household cleaning products** |
| **Personal care products** | **Disposable food containers** |
| **Electricity** | **Gasoline** |

SCIENTISTS AND ENGINEERS ARE **PERSUASIVE**—RACHEL CARSON

*"Once you are aware of the wonder and beauty of the Earth, you will want to learn about it."* Invite students to talk about what this means and how, through her books, Carson might have wanted to share her love of the oceans with all of us and her love of the Maine coast with her nephew.

5. **Pages 26–30:** In 1958, Carson began to explore the heavy use of chemicals to kill insects in parks and nature preserves. What prompted her concern about insecticides? *Carson was concerned about declining bird populations and was worried that insecticides were deadly to birds, insects, fish, and other animals—and to people, too. She wanted to let people know about the effects of these chemicals so they could fight for clean air and clean water.*

## Making Sense
### Explore

Students will learn about lifestyle options (known as *green improvements*) that have less of a negative effect on the environment. Provide some examples of alternative household items by reading excerpts from either *Heloise's Hints for a Healthy Planet* (Heloise 1990), *Design for a Livable Planet: How You Can Help Clean Up the Environment* (Naar 1990), and/or *The Green Consumer* (Makower 1993). You might share an alternative to something students are familiar with. For example, Heloise (1990) suggests warming vinegar mixed with cinnamon and cloves in the microwave to absorb odors rather than using a commercial air deodorizer that simply masks odors.

Next, divide the class into eight groups. Randomly assign each group an Environmental Issue Card (Figure 9.1) and challenge them to research and choose an Earth-friendly option for their assigned issue. After students have spent some time reviewing internet resources and books in the school library, have them use their science notebooks to create and plan a video to persuade others to choose the alternative they propose. Encourage students to address the following questions:

- What concerns guided their choice of this particular improvement?
- How will their suggestion reduce humans' impact on Earth?
- How can they convince their classmates to choose the proposed alternative?

### Explain

Ask students to explain the rationale for their green improvement as they share their videos with the class. There are many helpful resources students might access in this effort. We like *The New 50 Simple Things I Can Do to Save the Earth* (EarthWorks Group 2009b). The goal here is to encourage students to choose conscious, Earth-friendly behavior and lend their voices to helping take care of the planet.

## 9 OBTAINING, EVALUATING, AND COMMUNICATING INFORMATION

### Extend
Share the book *A River Ran Wild* (Cherry 1992). It tells the story of the Nashua River, which had become ecologically dead after years of factory and town growth along its banks. The story and detailed illustrations tell of a community of adults and students who worked to restore the river to its original, natural quality. The book inspires environmental action and protection as it describes the community benefits of a restored river.

### Evaluate
Summative evaluation of this lesson will include assessment of students' (1) understanding of Rachel Carson's character trait of being persuasive and (2) demonstrated ability to create an accurate, persuasive video journal about how they can adjust their own impact on Earth.

#### CHARACTER TRAIT
Encourage students to answer the following questions:

1. Why is being persuasive an important character trait for scientists to have?

2. How was Rachel Carson persuasive? *Being persuasive is important because knowledgeable scientists in any one particular area, such as biology and environmental science, can inform people like us how to make good decisions on questions such as how to help our environment. Rachel Carson was persuasive and well known for her ability to convince others to alter the use of pesticides. Helping students think about Rachel Carson's persuasive skills will encourage them to think about how scientists improve the lives of many.*

3. Invite students to make a record in their science notebooks that explains why being persuasive is an important trait for scientists.

#### CONTENT
Evaluate students' videos based on how well they demonstrate students' ability to understand human behaviors that limit human impact on Earth and to persuade their classmates to make positive changes in those behaviors. You could focus on the following questions when evaluating videos: Did the students come up with viable alternative solutions? Did students include factual data to build a solid argument? Were students persuasive in convincing others to modify their current behaviors? You can also use the rubric in Table 9.1.

Table 9.1

Rubric for Assessing Students' Videos

| Content or Skill | Not Yet | Beginning | Developing | Secure |
|---|---|---|---|---|
| **Video** | Student did not produce a video or a description of an environmental issue. | Student produced a video but the video and its description of the environmental issue were incomplete. | Student produced a compelling video but the video's description of the environmental issue was incomplete. | Student produced a compelling video that accurately and completely described the environmental issue. |
| **Obtaining Scientific Information** | Student did not obtain scientific information about an environmental issue. | Student obtained some scientific information (one or two facts) about an environmental issue. | Student obtained accurate scientific information (three or more facts) about an environmental issue but the presentation was not complete. | Student obtained accurate and relevant scientific information (three or more facts) about an environmental issue and organized a convincing presentation. |
| **Evaluating Scientific Information** | Student did not evaluate scientific information about an environmental issue. | Student provided limited evidence of their ability to evaluate scientific information about an environmental issue. | Student provided evidence of their ability to accurately evaluate scientific information about an environmental issue. | Student provided evidence of their ability to convincingly evaluate scientific information about an environmental issue. |
| **Communicating Scientific Information** | Student did not communicate scientific information about an environmental issue. | Student communicated incomplete scientific information about an environmental issue. | Student communicated accurate scientific information about an environmental issue. | Student organized accurate scientific information to raise concern about an environmental issue. |

# 9 OBTAINING, EVALUATING, AND COMMUNICATING INFORMATION

# SCIENTISTS AND ENGINEERS ARE
# PASSIONATE

### Learning About **Wangari Maathai**

Passionate (adj.): having or showing strong feelings

### Lesson: Arbor Day and Earth Day
**Description**

In this lesson, students will compare Arbor Day and Earth Day as celebrations of important Earth resources.

## Objectives

In this lesson, students will consider how the character trait of being passionate helped Wangari Maathai help her community and will learn about two common community celebrations (Arbor Day and Earth Day) that encourage us to protect the environment.

- Before beginning the lesson, students will conduct research to find definitions of Arbor Day and Earth Day to learn about their histories.
- As a class, students will discuss how citizen science relates to those two days.
- Students will hear the story *Seeds of Change: Wangari's Gift to the World* by Jen Cullerton Johnson and will discuss how it relates to the character trait of being passionate.
- Students will complete a Venn diagram to compare the features of Arbor Day and Earth Day.
- To conclude the lesson, students will discuss how passionate people use these two days as an opportunity to attend to the needs of the environment in their communities.

## Learning Outcomes

Students will (1) make a science notebook entry to explain what it means to be passionate and why being passionate is an important trait for scientists and engineers and (2) compare Earth Day and Arbor Day to demonstrate their understanding of how communities can do things to help protect Earth's resources and environments.

## Connections to the *NGSS* and the Nature of Science, Grades 3–5
### Disciplinary Core Ideas
**LS2.A: INTERDEPENDENT RELATIONSHIPS IN ECOSYSTEMS**

- <u>The food of almost any kind of animal can be traced back to plants. Organisms are related in food webs in which some animals eat plants for food and other animals eat the animals that eat plants.</u> Some organisms, such as fungi and bacteria, break down dead organisms (both plants or plants parts and animals) and therefore operate as "decomposers." Decomposition eventually restores (recycles) some materials back to the soil. Organisms can survive only in environments in which their particular needs are met. A healthy ecosystem is one in which multiple species of different types are each able to meet their needs in a relatively stable web of life. Newly introduced species can damage the balance of an ecosystem.

**LS2.C: ECOSYSTEM DYNAMICS, FUNCTIONING, AND RESILIENCE**

- When the environment changes in ways that affect a place's physical characteristics, temperature, or availability of resources, some organisms survive and reproduce, others move to new locations, yet others move into the transformed environment, and some die.

**LS4.C: ADAPTATION**

- For any particular environment, some kinds of organisms survive well, some survive less well, and some cannot survive at all.

**ESS3.C: HUMAN IMPACTS ON EARTH SYSTEMS**

- Human activities in agriculture, industry, and everyday life have had major effects on the land, vegetation, streams, ocean, air, and even outer space. But individuals and communities are doing things to help protect Earth's resources and environments.

### Science and Engineering Practices

***Engaging in Argument From Evidence:*** Argumentation is the process by which explanations and solutions are reached. Engaging in argument from evidence in 3–5 builds on K–2 experiences and progresses to critiquing the scientific explanations or solutions proposed by peers by citing relevant evidence about the natural and designed world(s).

- Compare and refine arguments based on an evaluation of the evidence presented.
- Respectfully provide and receive critiques from peers about a proposed procedure, explanation, or model by citing relevant evidence and posing specific questions.
- Construct and/or support an argument with evidence, data, and/or a model.

***Obtaining, Evaluating, and Communicating Information:*** Scientists and engineers must be able to communicate clearly and persuasively the ideas and methods they generate. Critiquing and communicating ideas individually and in groups is a critical professional activity. Obtaining, evaluating, and communicating information in 3–5 builds on K–2 experiences and progresses to evaluating the merit and accuracy of ideas and methods.

- Obtain and combine information from books and other reliable media to explain phenomena.
- Communicate scientific and/or technical information orally and/or in written formats, including various forms of media and may include tables, diagrams, and charts.

## Crosscutting Concepts

***Cause and Effect:*** Events have causes, sometimes simple, sometimes multifaceted. Deciphering causal relationships, and the mechanisms by which they are mediated, is a major activity of science and engineering.

- Events that occur together with regularity might or might not be a cause and effect relationship.

***Systems and System Models:*** A system is an organized group of related objects or components; models can be used for understanding and predicting the behavior of systems.

- A system can be described in terms of its components and their interactions.

## Nature of Science Connections
### SCIENCE IS A WAY OF KNOWING

- Science is both a body of knowledge and processes that add new knowledge.
- Science is a way of knowing that is used by many people.

### SCIENTIFIC KNOWLEDGE ASSUMES AN ORDER AND CONSISTENCY IN NATURAL SYSTEMS

- Science assumes consistent patterns in natural systems.

**SCIENCE IS A HUMAN ENDEAVOR**

- Men and women from all cultures and backgrounds choose careers as scientists and engineers.
- Science affects everyday life.
- Creativity and imagination are important to science.

Source: NGSS Lead States 2013.

Note: When an activity supports only part of a standard, underlining indicates the relevant part.

## Overview

In this lesson, students will learn how one passionate person, Wangari Maathai, followed her desire to plant trees to make the world a better place. Through the featured book, students learn that men and women from all backgrounds choose careers as scientists. The character trait of being passionate references Maathai's unique thinking and creative efforts as a citizen scientist.

## Materials

You will need a copy of the book *Seeds of Change: Wangari's Gift to the World* by Jen Cullerton Johnson (ISBN 978-1600603679). Student groups will need internet access. Each student will need his or her science notebook and a copy of the Venn Diagram Template.

## Setting the Context
### Engage

Inform students that they will be learning about the history of Arbor Day and Earth Day. Ask students to do research individually on the internet about Arbor Day and Earth Day; have them find to four to six facts about each. Two online sources where students can find ample information are the Arbor Day Foundation (*www.arborday.org*) and the Earth Day Network (*www.earthday.org*) websites. Have students record their research in their science notebooks. *The focus of Arbor Day is trees and what they give to the environment, so typically this day is observed by planting trees. In the United States, Arbor Day is always the last Friday in April; however, it is observed in many other*

# 9 OBTAINING, EVALUATING, AND COMMUNICATING INFORMATION

*countries, where the date of celebration varies according to climate and planting season. Earth Day is observed annually around the world on April 22. The focus of Earth Day is on awareness of environmental issues and ways to take care of Earth. These celebrations might focus on a variety of locally relevant issues, such as renewable energy, planting trees, or cleaning up areas of neighborhoods.*

## Guided Reading

Tell students that they will be learning about Wangari Maathai, a scientist who was passionate about trees, by reading *Seeds of Change: Wangari's Gift to the World*. Students will connect Maathai's efforts with modern-day Arbor Day and Earth Day practices. Introduce the book by asking, "What do you observe about the person on the front cover?" and "What seems to be happening on the front cover?" Read the story aloud. Encourage students to notice and think about the challenges Wangari Maathai faced as a woman who returned to her country with a passion for change. The following questions may be used to guide students' attention to detail as you read. (Page numbers reference unnumbered book pages, beginning with the title page as page 1.)

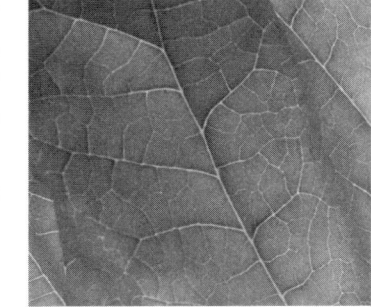

1. **Pages 1–7:** When Maathai was a young girl, her mother taught her to appreciate the mugumo tree. What things did Maathai's mother point out about this tree? *Maathai's mother helped her appreciate the smooth trunk and oval leaves. Maathai also learned to appreciate the way this tree and its figs fed their family and wild animals of the jungle. Her mother made her promise never to cut down the mugumo tree.* Why did Maathai's mother say, "Our people believe that our ancestors rest in the tree's shade?" *The Kikuyu of Kenya had depended on the mugumo tree's fruit and shade for many generations.*

2. **Pages 8–13:** As Maathai grew, she said she must go to school. Why did Maathai want to go to school? *Maathai had many chores, such as fetching water, working in the garden, and taking care of the chickens. Her brother went to school and talked to her about what he was learning. Maathai dreamed of going to school just like her brother. It was unusual for a young Kenyan girl to be educated, but Maathai's parents decided to send her to school.*

3. **Pages 14–17:** Soon Maathai continued her schooling far away, in the capital city of Kenya, Nairobi, but she was homesick. What clues in the story help you to know this was so? *Maathai was sad to go, but she was anxious to learn.*

SCIENTISTS AND ENGINEERS ARE **PASSIONATE**—WANGARI MAATHAI

**Wangari Maathai**

Source: *www.flickr.com/ photos/44222307@ N00/140284053/*. Photo by Flickr member DMOSH. Used under Creative Commons license CC BY 2.0.

*Her mother said, "Where you go, we go." Maathai dreamed of her home, her family, and the sweet figs of the mugumo tree.*

4. **Pages 18–19:** When Maathai finished college, she traveled to America to continue her studies. How did America change Maathai? *In America, Maathai discovered the spirit of possibility and freedom that she wanted to share with Kenyan women. Although there were few women professors (and fewer still who taught science), Maathai accepted a teaching job at the University of Nairobi and led the way for more women to become scientists and be treated with the same respect as male scientists.*

5. **Pages 20–21:** Maathai continued to be troubled by the changes in her country—more and more land was being sold to foreign companies that cut down the trees to clear the land for coffee plants. Why did Maathai decide she must do something? *She saw that the custom of not cutting down the*

# 9 OBTAINING, EVALUATING, AND COMMUNICATING INFORMATION

*mugumo trees had been lost. She could not bear to allow the land to be destroyed, and she worried what would happen to those who depended on the land.*

6. **Pages 22–29:** Maathai's solution was an idea as small as a seed but as tall as a tree. How did Maathai's idea about working together help to bring back the trees? *Maathai enlisted other women to help plant seedlings; after all, planting was considered women's work. She understood that trees would benefit generations to come. She traveled across the country and worked with women to plant rows and rows of trees. The women called themselves "The Green Belt Movement." As Maathai said, "We might not change the big world, but we can change the landscape of the forest."*

7. **Pages 30–33:** As green belts of trees moved across Kenya, businesspeople rose up in protest. They wondered why they should give up their land and profits for trees. How did the businesspeople try to stop Maathai and the other women? *Wealthy businesspeople paid corrupt police officers to arrest Maathai. Maathai knew that the people who put her in jail did not like the changes to the land or to the women. The government was afraid of too many advances made by the women.*

8. **Pages 34–37:** To save her country, Maathai knew she would need to go out into the world to spread her message. How did she come to be awarded the Nobel Peace Prize? *Maathai shared her message with world leaders—a message of the importance of the trees and women's rights. At home, she came to be recognized as Mama Miti (Mother of Trees) and was elected to lead Kenya to a new democracy as the Minister of the Environment. Maathai remembered her passion for the childhood lesson of the mugumo tree, and she understood that commitment to an idea brings hope for the future.*

## Making Sense
### Explore

Discuss with students how Maathai was passionate and persistent about trees as an environmental resource and how she organized a group of women to plant rows of trees that looked like bands of green across the land. Today, we observe Earth Day and Arbor Day to remind us of the importance of trees and other environmental resources.

Divide the class into table groups. Have pairs of students complete a Venn diagram to compare and contrast these celebrations using the information they researched earlier about Arbor Day and Earth Day (Figure 9.2). Ask, "How are Arbor Day and Earth Day alike and how are they different?" When students have completed their Venn diagrams, invite the student pairs to share this compare-and-contrast experience and communicate their "similar" and "different" facts to their table group.

Figure 9.2

Venn Diagram Template

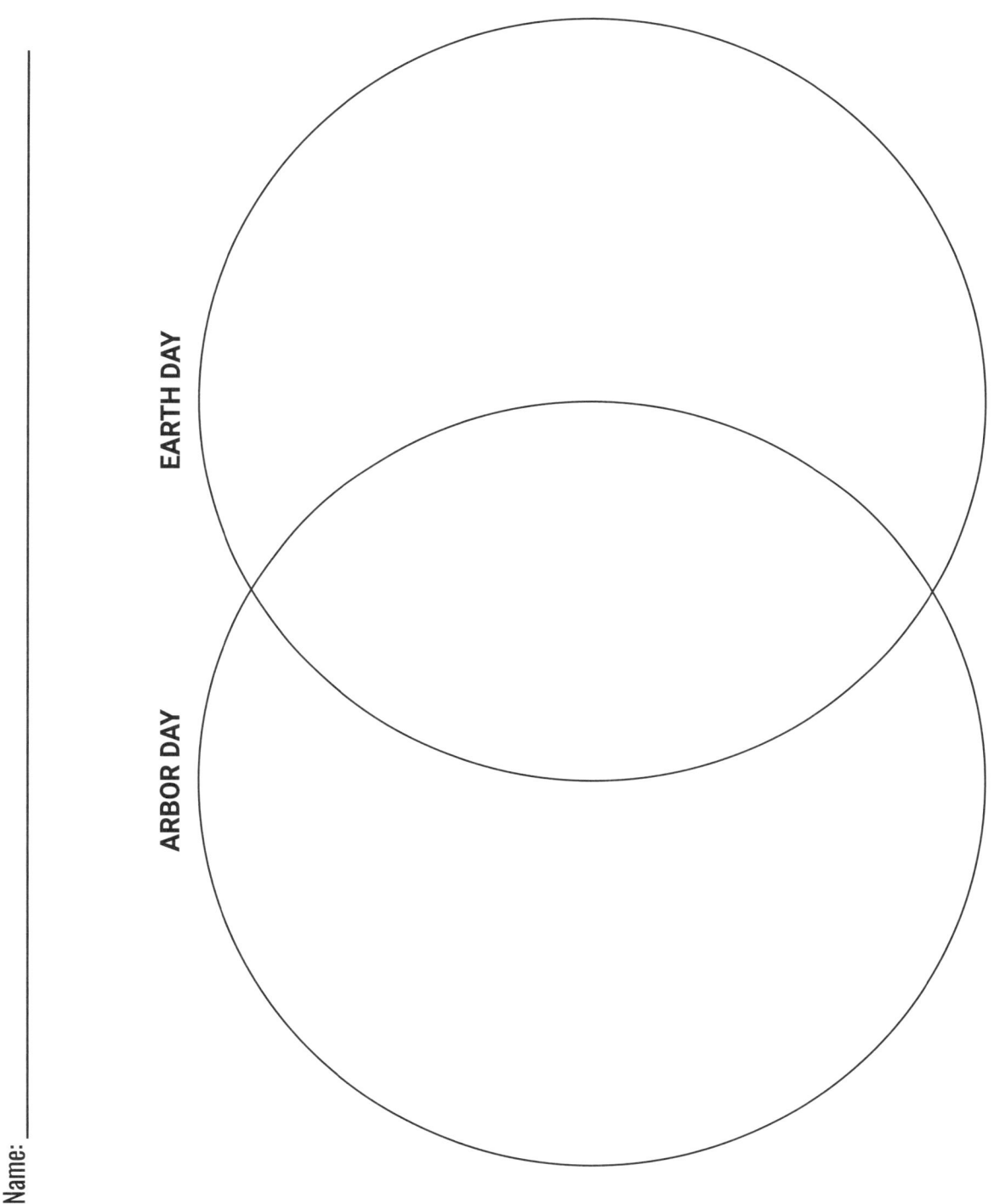

Name: _____

### Explain

Ask students to share what passion is behind each of these annual days celebrating the environment. Guide students' reviews of their Venn diagrams as they talk about the similar and different features of these events. Encourage them to recognize how these celebrations help focus people's attention on environmental needs in the community and on opportunities for citizen science.

### Extend

Choose an "act of green" (e.g., an environmental campaign such as recycling) or plan an Arbor Day or Earth Day event to promote environmental awareness at your school. Students might be interested in planting a special tree in their schoolyard such as a Survivor Tree seedling. *The Survivor Tree is the American elm that took the brunt of the bombing of the Murrah Federal Building in Oklahoma City, Oklahoma, in 1995 and survived. Each year, a local nursery collects seeds from that tree and grows Survivor Tree seedlings, which are made available for planting elsewhere. See the news story "Propagating the Survivor" from Oklahoma KFOR Channel 4 at* www.kfor.com/2013/04/22/propagating-the-survivor. You can also generate your own ideas for events; learn what others have done through sources such as the EarthWorks Group (*http://50simplekids.scarabmedia.com*), the Earth Day Network (*www.earthday.org*), and the Arbor Day Foundation (*www.arborday.org*). The idea here is to experience what it was like for Wangari Maathai to share her passion for the mugumo tree with others.

### Evaluate

Summative evaluation of this lesson will include assessment of students' understanding of (1) why being passionate is an important character trait for scientists and engineers and (2) how the purposes of and events for Earth Day and Arbor Day are similar and different.

#### CHARACTER TRAIT

Remind students that passionate people can pursue a noble cause and make a difference and that therefore being passionate is an important character trait for scientists and engineers. Ask the following question:

1. How was Wangari Maathai passionate? *Maathai believed in the importance of the mugumo tree to the future of her people. As an educated woman, she knew the trees were important to the quality of life in Kenya—for her people and for the wild animals of the jungle. She stood up to greedy businesspeople and labored hard to organize replanting of the trees cleared for coffee plantations. She worked to earn the respect of leaders and a position as the Minister of the Environment.*

**CONTENT**

Students should recognize the observance of Arbor Day and Earth Day as opportunities for citizen scientists to make a difference. You might evaluate students' Venn diagrams for accuracy. Student diagrams should list at least three differences and at least three similarities between Arbor Day and Earth Day and show an understanding that these celebrations get people actively involved in making some type of change or activity that helps the environment in their communities. You may decide to use a rubric like the one in Table 9.2 to evaluate students' Venn diagrams.

Table 9.2

Rubric for Assessing Students on the Venn Diagram Activity

| Content or Skill | Not Yet | Beginning | Developing | Secure |
| --- | --- | --- | --- | --- |
| **Venn Diagram** | Student did not create a Venn diagram. | Student created a Venn diagram containing one difference and one similarity. | Student created a Venn diagram containing two differences and two similarities. | Student created a Venn diagram containing three or more differences and three or more similarities. |
| **Obtaining Information (Four to Six Facts)** | Student did not obtain information about Earth Day and Arbor Day. | Student obtained one to three facts about Earth Day and Arbor Day. | Student obtained four to five facts about Earth Day and Arbor Day. | Student obtained six accurate and relevant facts about Earth Day and Arbor Day. |
| **Evaluating Information (Four to Six Facts)** | Student did not evaluate information about Earth Day and Arbor Day. | Student evaluated one to three facts about Earth Day and Arbor Day. | Student evaluated four to five facts about Earth Day and Arbor Day. | Student evaluated six accurate and relevant facts about Earth Day and Arbor Day. |
| **Communicating Information in Table Groups** | Students did not communicate information about Earth Day and Arbor Day. | Students communicated partial information about Earth Day and Arbor Day. | Students communicated full information about Earth Day and Arbor Day. | Student communicated full and detailed information about Earth Day and Arbor Day. |

# 9
OBTAINING, EVALUATING, AND COMMUNICATING INFORMATION

# SCIENTISTS AND ENGINEERS ARE
# INQUISITIVE

Learning About **Carl Sagan**

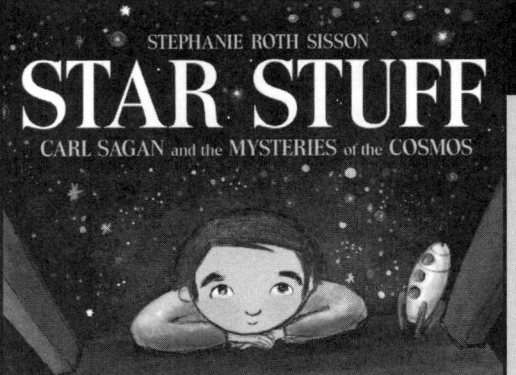

Inquisitive (adj.): having a disposition of asking many questions

### Lesson: Gravity Versus Microgravity
### Description

In this lesson, students will investigate the difference between mass and weight under Earth's gravity and compare the weight of a mass on Earth to its weight under microgravity in space.

### Objectives

Students will consider how the character trait of being inquisitive helped Carl Sagan understand the weightless effect that occurs in the microgravity environment of space.

- Before beginning the lesson, students will hypothesize how mass and weight are related.
- As a class, students will discuss how mass and weight might change in space.
- Students will hear the story *Star Stuff: Carl Sagan and the Mysteries of the Cosmos* by Stephanie Roth Sisson and discuss how it relates to the character trait of being inquisitive.
- Students will compare the mass and weight of a full juice pouch to the mass and weight of an empty juice pouch.
- To conclude the lesson, students will view a video to observe how juice pouches of the same size and design behave in the microgravity environment of space.

## Learning Outcomes

Students will (1) make a science notebook entry to explain what it means to be inquisitive and why being inquisitive is an important trait for scientists and engineers and (2) describe their new understanding of weightlessness and its significance in space exploration.

## Connections to the *NGSS* and the Nature of Science, Grades 3–5
### Disciplinary Core Ideas
#### ESS1.A: THE UNIVERSE AND ITS STARS

- The sun is a star that appears larger and brighter than other stars because it is closer. Stars range greatly in their distance from Earth.

#### PS2.B: TYPES OF INTERACTIONS

- The gravitational force of Earth acting on an object near Earth's surface pulls that object toward the planet's center.

## Science and Engineering Practices

***Planning and Carrying Out Investigations:*** Scientists and engineers plan and carry out investigations in the field or laboratory, working collaboratively as well as individually. Their investigations are systematic and require clarifying what counts as data and identifying variables or parameters. Planning and carrying out investigations to answer questions or test solutions to problems in 3–5 builds on K–2 experiences and progresses to include investigations that control variables and provide evidence to support explanations or design solutions.

- Plan and conduct an investigation collaboratively to produce data to serve as the basis for evidence, using fair tests in which variables are controlled and the number of trials considered.

- Make observations and/or measurements to produce data to serve as the basis for evidence for an explanation of a phenomenon or test a design solution.

***Analyzing and Interpreting Data:*** Scientific investigations produce data that must be analyzed in order to derive meaning. Because data patterns and trends are not always obvious, scientists use a range of tools—including tabulation, graphical interpretation, visualization, and statistical analysis—to identify the significant features and patterns in the data. Scientists identify sources of error in the investigations and calculate the degree of certainty in the results. Modern technology makes the collection of large data sets much easier, providing secondary sources for analysis. Analyzing data in 3–5 builds on K–2 experiences and progresses to introducing quantitative approaches to collecting data and conducting multiple trials of qualitative observations. When possible and feasible, digital tools should be used.

# 9 OBTAINING, EVALUATING, AND COMMUNICATING INFORMATION

- Represent data in tables and/or various graphical displays (bar graphs, pictographs, and/or pie charts) to reveal patterns that indicate relationships.
- Analyze and interpret data to make sense of phenomena, using logical reasoning, mathematics, and/or computation.

**Constructing Explanations and Designing Solutions:** The products of science are explanations and the products of engineering are solutions. Constructing explanations and designing solutions in 3–5 builds on K–2 experiences and progresses to the use of evidence in constructing explanations that specify variables that describe and predict phenomena and in designing multiple solutions to design problems.

- Construct an explanation of observed relationships (e.g., the distribution of plants in the back yard).
- Use evidence (e.g., measurements, observations, patterns) to construct or support an explanation or design a solution to a problem.
- Identify the evidence that supports particular points in an explanation.

**Engaging in Argument From Evidence:** Argumentation is the process by which explanations and solutions are reached. Engaging in argument from evidence in 3–5 builds on K–2 experiences and progresses to critiquing the scientific explanations or solutions proposed by peers by citing relevant evidence about the natural and designed world(s).

- Compare and refine arguments based on an evaluation of the evidence presented.
- Distinguish among facts, reasoned judgment based on research findings, and speculation in an explanation.
- Respectfully provide and receive critiques from peers about a proposed procedure, explanation or model.by citing relevant evidence and posing specific questions.
- Construct and/or support an argument with evidence, data, and/or a model.
- Use data to evaluate claims about cause and effect.
- Make a claim about the merit of a solution to a problem by citing relevant evidence about how it meets the criteria and constraints of the problem.

**Obtaining, Evaluating, and Communicating Information:** Scientists and engineers must be able to communicate clearly and persuasively the ideas and methods they generate. Critiquing and communicating ideas individually and in groups is a critical professional activity. Obtaining, evaluating, and communicating information in 3–5 builds on K–2 experiences and progresses to evaluating the merit and accuracy of ideas and methods.

- Obtain and combine information from books and/or other reliable media to explain phenomena or solutions to a design problem.
- Communicate scientific and/or technical information orally and/or in written formats, including various forms of media and may include tables, diagrams, and charts.

## Crosscutting Concept

***Cause and Effect:*** Events have causes, sometimes simple, sometimes multifaceted. Deciphering causal relationships, and the mechanisms by which they are mediated, is a major activity of science and engineering.

- Cause and effect relationships are routinely identified, tested, and used to explain change.

## Nature of Science Connections

### SCIENCE KNOWLEDGE IS BASED ON EMPIRICAL EVIDENCE

- Science uses tools and technologies to make accurate measurements and observations.

### SCIENCE IS A WAY OF KNOWING

- Science is both a body of knowledge and processes that add new knowledge.

### SCIENTIFIC KNOWLEDGE ASSUMES AN ORDER AND CONSISTENCY IN NATURAL SYSTEMS

- Science assumes consistent patterns in natural systems.
- Basic laws of nature are the same everywhere in the universe.

### SCIENCE IS A HUMAN ENDEAVOR

- Men and women from all cultures and backgrounds choose careers as scientists and engineers.
- Science affects everyday life.

*Source:* NGSS Lead States 2013.

## Overview

In this lesson, students learn how one inquisitive person, Carl Sagan, furthered our knowledge about the solar system. Sagan was not afraid to ask questions about galaxies beyond our own and challenged space exploration with his questions. Through the featured book, students learn that men and women from all backgrounds choose careers as scientists. The character trait of being inquisitive refers to Sagan's unique thinking and creative attempts to ask questions and think beyond our solar system. In the activity, teams of two students will each measure the force that gravity exerts on objects of different mass by suspending them on elastic strings made from cut rubber bands and measuring the distance the band stretches. Students compare their results to those of a similar experiment done on the International Space Station (ISS) and discuss their conclusions.

## Materials

You will need a copy of the book *Star Stuff: Carl Sagan and the Mysteries of the Cosmos* by Stephanie Roth Sisson (ISBN 978-1596439603). Student pairs will need two nonlatex rubber bands (size 19), two plastic juice pouches (one emptied and one full; Capri Sun brand works well), a beam balance or digital scale, a pair of scissors, a ruler, adhesive tape (any kind), 50 pennies, and the Gravity Versus Microgravity Data Sheet (provided later). The class will need access to the "Mass vs. Weight: Stretching Mass" lesson video by the National Aeronautics and Space Administration (NASA; see NASA 2014). Each student will need his or her science notebook and safety glasses or goggles.

## Safety Notes

(1) Personal protective equipment should be worn during the setup, hands-on, and takedown segments of the activity. (2) Use caution in working with sharps (scissors). They can cut or puncture skin or eyes. (3) Remember not to drink any juice used in the lab activity. (4) Wash hands with soap and water upon completing this activity.

SCIENTISTS AND ENGINEERS ARE **INQUISITIVE**—CARL SAGAN

## Setting the Context
### Engage

**Carl Sagan**

Tell students they will be learning about gravity (on Earth) and microgravity (in space) and the effect each has on mass and weight. Ask students whether they have ever thought about going into space and how space might affect their actions and body. Students may have an idea of what we call weightlessness. This lesson will help them further understand that although astronauts and objects they have seen floating in space seem weightless, they still have mass. On Earth and in space, measures of mass (how much matter an object has) remain constant, but measures of weight (how strongly gravity pulls on that matter) change in relation to differences in the gravitational force. Mass and matter play critical roles in the activities and experiments performed by the astronauts on the ISS. Ask students to think about life in space. Ask, "What daily routines might be difficult to perform in space?" An example might be brushing teeth. Share the NASA video about how the ISS works (*www.youtube.com/watch?v=SGP6Y0Pnhe4*; NASA 2015b)

**EUREKA!** GRADE 3–5 **SCIENCE ACTIVITIES AND STORIES**

# 9 OBTAINING, EVALUATING, AND COMMUNICATING INFORMATION

to help students learn more about the novel challenges of daily life in microgravity and seeming weightlessness. Astronaut Sunita (Suni) Williams's demonstrations of weightlessness throughout the tour are particularly appropriate for students in grades 3–5.

## Guided Reading

Inform students that through reading the book *Star Stuff: Carl Sagan and the Mysteries of the Cosmos*, they will learn about what it might be like for humans to travel into space and about the scientist Carl Sagan, who was particularly inquisitive about space. Introduce the book by asking "What do you notice about the person on the front cover?" and "What seems to be happening on the front cover?" Read the story aloud. Encourage students to notice and think about the challenges Carl Sagan might have faced as a forward-thinker in science. The following questions may be used to guide students' attention to detail as you read. (Page numbers reference unnumbered book pages, beginning with the title page as page 1.)

1. **Pages 1–9:** When Carl Sagan was a small boy, he was curious about everything. What did Sagan enjoy about the 1939 World's Fair? *It was like nothing he had seen before. He saw a mechanical man and a time capsule with messages to the future.*

2. **Pages 10–15:** Sagan wondered about the stars. What happened when Sagan found a book about the stars? *Sagan read the book about stars, and his heart beat faster with every page he turned. He read about the Sun and other stars that have planets circling them, too. He wanted to travel to the stars.*

3. **Pages 16–23:** Sagan read stories about life on other planets, and he longed to know what planets were really like. What did he do to learn more? *He was so curious that he continued to go to school to study life and space and finally attended college to become Dr. Carl Sagan. He worked with other scientists to investigate planets that are close to us. He was so excited about what he had learned that he decided to go on television.*

4. **Pages 24–31:** Sagan began to produce television shows to teach other people about space. What idea did he have about communicating to someone out there in space? *Sagan began to think that there might be other life in space because Earth and every thing on it are made of "star stuff." He recorded a disk of information about Earth with music and pictures for the NASA Voyager spacecrafts to carry a friendly greeting into space. Even now, the Voyager spacecrafts continue to journey through interstellar space.*

## Making Sense
### Explore

In this activity, students will gather data about two juice pouches to learn how the force of gravity on Earth is different from the force of gravity in space. We have modified the NASA "Mass vs. Weight: Stretching Mass" lesson (*www.youtube.com/watch?v=E_aRkuLFEeE*; NASA 2014) and data collection to make it appropriate for grades 3–5.

To prepare for the class, cut the rubber bands in half to make elastic strings. Tie a knot at each end of the elastic strings to make it easier to securely tape them onto the juice pouches (one end) and for students to hold them in their hands (other end). For each student pair, inflate the emptied juice pouch with air by inserting a straw and blowing into the pouch. Remove the straw and cover the hole with a piece of tape.

In class, before beginning the activity, lead a class discussion about gravity and microgravity. Then, provide pairs of students with an air-filled juice pouch and a juice-filled one and a copy of the Gravity Versus Microgravity Data Sheet (Figure 9.3, p. 304). Next, have each student pair use a beam balance or digital scale to measure the mass of each pouch and record the measurements on their data sheet.

Have them tape one end of an elastic string to the top of the air-filled drink pouch. Repeat for the liquid-filled pouch. They should affix the elastic string to the same spot on each pouch.

Have the first student in each pair suspend their air-filled drink pouch above the floor by holding its elastic string against a wall, pressing just below the knot on the unattached end of the elastic string. Next, have the other student in each pair suspend the liquid-filled pouch in the same way (see Figure 9.4, p. 305), and then measure how much each drink pouch has stretched the elastic string. Ensure that for the measurements students use the same start and end points to start and end the measurements for each pouch (e.g., for each, measure from where the elastic string contacts the wall to the top of the drink pouch). Check to be sure that team procedures are consistent. Remind students to record their measurements on their data sheets.

When students have completed their data sheets, have them view the NASA "Mass vs. Weight: Stretching Mass" video. Then, direct students to write on their data sheets and in their science notebooks their conclusions about this comparison of the effects that Earth's gravity and microgravity in space have on weight.

### Explain

In this lesson, students will develop some understanding of the concept of microgravity—or weightlessness in space—in terms of the difference in weight of a mass measured under Earth's gravity versus under microgravity in space. As the teacher, you will want to guide students in their observations about the

# 9
**OBTAINING, EVALUATING, AND COMMUNICATING INFORMATION**

Figure 9.3
Gravity Versus Microgravity Data Sheet

Name: _____

# GRAVITY versus MICROGRAVITY

## Hanging Juice Pouch Data

Mass/size _____  Weight _____.

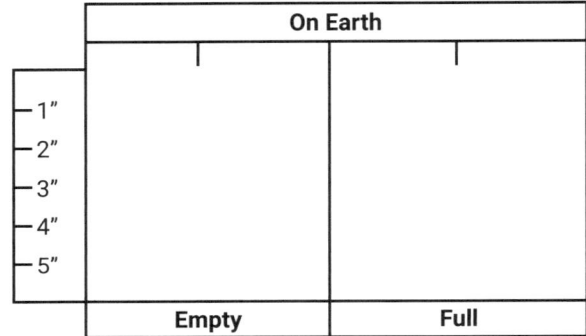
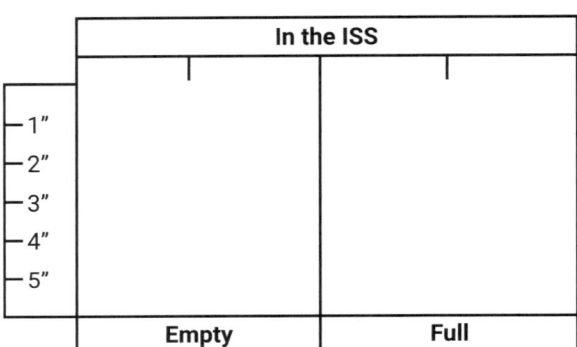

## Conclusions

1. How did the mass or weight change when in the ISS?

2. How does microgravity affect astronauts' daily routines?

NATIONAL SCIENCE TEACHERS ASSOCIATION

SCIENTISTS AND ENGINEERS ARE **INQUISITIVE**—CARL SAGAN

drink pouches. Ask, "What were the variables?" Students might initially identify the presence and absence of juice as the variable between the pouches they test on Earth. The ISS video will help students realize that the force of gravity is another variable (because the amount of gravity differs between Earth and microgravity in space). In the ISS video, they will see that in microgravity, neither juice pouch places any stress (or pull) on the elastic string and that mass (or physical size) does not change.

### Figure 9.4

**Comparing the Stretch of the Elastic String for Air-Filled and Liquid-Filled Pouches**

### Extend

Think about applying for a NASA-provided opportunity for groups of school students to interact with astronauts onboard the ISS through a live question and answer session. See the information on this in the Johnson Space Center "In-Flight Education Downlinks" (see NASA 2016). Another possible extension activity would be to organize students into expert groups to learn more about how astronauts manage microgravity challenges (e.g., floating juice pouches) when they eat, sleep, and exercise in space. Videos and narrative details are available on the internet from NASA (*www.nasa.gov/audience/foreducators/stem-on-station/ditl_eating*; NASA 2015a).

### Evaluate

Summative evaluation of this lesson will include assessment of students' (1) understanding of why being inquisitive is an important trait for scientists and engineers and (2) data gathering, data analysis, and new understanding of astronauts' management of weightlessness in microgravity during the Gravity Versus Microgravity activity.

# 9 OBTAINING, EVALUATING, AND COMMUNICATING INFORMATION

**CHARACTER TRAIT**

To be inquisitive is to ask many questions. Ask students "What questions can you ask during this activity?" Focus students on the questions they asked, and note that by asking questions, they are being inquisitive like scientists. One of the greatest disservices we can do in the science classroom is to provide step-by-step instructions, as is done in some high school laboratory manuals. Students need to experience through their own explicit curiosity why being inquisitive is an important character trait for scientists and engineers. Ask students to think about how Carl Sagan was inquisitive. Ask, "What discoveries did Carl's Sagan's inquisitiveness lead to?" and "How did one person's curiosities affect people's interest in space and space travel?"

**CONTENT**

Encourage students to review their Gravity Versus Microgravity Data Sheets. Discuss the differences between mass and weight as measured on Earth and in the ISS. Discuss the question "What is being measured by the stretch of the elastic string?" Review students' data sheets and then ask, "What do we now know about weightlessness and its effect on space exploration?" Astronauts need to manage life in a microgravity environment. Large masses might not weigh much, but they do take up storage space. Because everything does not weigh much due to the much weaker gravitational pull, everything on the space shuttle must be strapped down—including sleeping astronauts. You might use a rubric such as the one in Table 9.3 to assist you in your evaluation.

Table 9.3

Rubric for Assessing Students on the Gravity Versus Microgravity Activity

| Content or Skill | Not Yet | Beginning | Developing | Secure |
|---|---|---|---|---|
| **Obtaining Information: Juice Pouch Data** | Student did not obtain data about juice bag. | Student obtained data about the juice bag but all data were incomplete and not accurate. | Student obtained data about the juice bag but some data were incomplete or inaccurate. | Student obtained data about the juice bag and all data were complete and accurate. |
| **Evaluating Information: Understanding of Mass and Weight Change in the ISS** | Student did not interpret the data to form a conclusion. | Student interpreted data but did not form a conclusion because the interpretation was incomplete. | Student interpreted the data completely and formed a conclusion, but did not conclude that neither mass nor weight changed in the ISS. | Student interpreted the data completely and concluded that gravity changed but mass and weight did not change in the ISS. |
| **Communicating Information: Effect of Microgravity** | Student did not write a response to describe the effect of microgravity in the ISS. | Student wrote a response to describe the effect of microgravity in the ISS but the response was not clear. | Student wrote a clear response to describe the effect of microgravity in the ISS but did not provide examples of this effect in the response. | Student wrote a clear response to describe the effect of microgravity in the ISS and provided examples of this effect in the response. |

# 9 OBTAINING, EVALUATING, AND COMMUNICATING INFORMATION

## References

Cherry, L. 1992. *A river ran wild: An environmental history*. New York: Harcourt Brace Jovanovich.

The Cornell Lab and Bird Studies Canada. 2016. Project FeederWatch. *http://feederwatch.org/about/project-overview*.

Heloise. 1990. *Hints for a healthy planet*. New York: Perigee Books.

Johnson, J. C. 2010. *Seeds of change: Wangari's gift to the world*. New York: Lee and Low Books.

KFOR.com News Channel. 2013. Propagating the survivor. *www.kfor.com/2013/04/22/propagating-the-survivor*.

Lawlor, L. 2012. *Rachel Carson and her book that changed the world*. New York: Holiday House.

Makower, J. 1993. *The green consumer*. New York: Penguin Books.

Naar, J. 1990. *Design for a livable planet: How you can help clean up the environment*. New York: HarperCollins.

National Aeronautics and Space Administration (NASA). 2014. Mass vs. weight: Stretching mass. *www.youtube.com/watch?v=E_aRkuLFEeE*.

National Aeronautics and Space Administration (NASA). 2015a. For educators: Eating in space. *www.nasa.gov/audience/foreducators/stem-on-station/ditl_eating*.

National Aeronautics and Space Administration (NASA). 2015b. How it works: The International Space Station. *www.youtube.com/watch?v=SGP6Y0Pnhe4*.

National Aeronautics and Space Administration (NASA). 2016. Johnson Space Center. In-flight education downlinks. *www.nasa.gov/offices/education/centers/johnson/downlinks*.

NGSS Lead States. 2013. *Next Generation Science Standards: For states, by states*. Washington, DC: National Academies Press. *www.nextgenscience.org/next-generation-science-standards*.

Sisson, S. R. 2014. *Star stuff: Carl Sagan and the mysteries of the cosmos*. New York: Roaring Brook Press.

## Additional Resources

Carson, R. 1941. *Under the sea-wind: A naturalist's picture of ocean life*. New York: Simon and Schuster.

Carson, R. 1951. *The sea around us*. New York: Oxford University Press.

Carson, R. 1955. *The edge of the sea*. New York: Houghton Mifflin.

EarthWorks Group. 2009a. Kids can save the Earth. *http://50simplekids.scarabmedia.com*. *Website with a kid-friendly assortment of news, games, and eco-tips.*

EarthWorks Group. 2009b. *The new 50 simple things I can do to save the Earth*. Kansas City, MO: Andrews McMeel Publishing.

National Geographic. 2016. Citizen science projects. *www.nationalgeographic.org/idea/citizen-science-projects*. *Website listing multiple citizen science efforts.*

# 10

# Beyond *Eureka!*
## Teaching How Scientists and Engineers Work

In this final chapter, we suggest three fiction books that highlight the nature of science (and science and engineering practices) especially well and propose guidelines and suggestions to help you create your own lessons in the *Eureka!* format. First, we discuss the three books—*Papa's Mechanical Fish* by Candace Fleming, *What Do You Do With an Idea?* by Kobi Yamada, and *Rosie Revere, Engineer* by Andrea Beaty—that, although they lack a science focus, have storylines that exemplify the practices of scientists and engineers. Then, we suggest guidelines for sharing biographical trade books (such as those featured in Chapters 2 through 9) with your students. And finally, we outline ways to develop and plan your own *Eureka!*-style lessons to combine character traits with core disciplinary concepts defined in the *Next Generation Science Standards* (*NGSS*; NGSS Lead States 2013).

As we canvassed selected biographies of scientists to include in this book, we discovered fiction books that, although they didn't quite fit with our goal of introducing the life and work of successful scientists and engineers, did model the thinking skills of scientists and engineers. We expect that these books will help you to encourage your students' science and engineering practices by helping them to ask questions, solve problems, and design solutions.

In the first book, *Papa's Mechanical Fish*, the main character, Papa, asks the ever-important question, "Have you ever wondered...," throughout the story. This story encourages students to understand a scientist's sense of wonder and countless questions. We provide an accompanying design challenge lesson to provide a starting point for linking Papa's processes to the work of scientists and engineers. *Papa's Mechanical Fish* highlights the iterative process used by scienctists and engineers—the repetition of a process, with improved efficiency each time.

In the second book, *What Do You Do With an Idea?*, a young boy describes the experience of developing an idea and not being able to think of anything else. His idea has a life of its own. This book is important because all science and engineering work starts with a burning idea. The book encourages students to welcome and nurture the unique (a creative thinking skill we do not always teach directly). This lesson's activity focuses on the processes of idea generation and development in science and engineering design.

In the third book, *Rosie Revere, Engineer*, the protagonist Rosie Revere describes her enthusiastic journey to become a great engineer, during which she also learns the value of failure. This book is important to share with young students because they often believe that scientists and engineers get it right the first time they try to create something new. Concept mapping strategies can help you and your students work through the creative processes of inventive science and engineering. The concept mapping strategy in the engineering design process used in this lesson's activity can help you and your students work through the creative processes of inventive science and engineering.

## Recommended Science Teaching Strategy: Concept Mapping

We enjoy concept mapping and use it as much as possible. As with any other process, the more opportunities students get to illustrate their thinking of concepts, the better they become at it. Concept mapping can be done with a whole group, small groups, or individual students. Making concept maps with large sheets of chart paper and sticky notes provides students with the opportunity to practice relating the meanings of various science concepts. Students construct actual maps of concepts through laying out how particular science concepts are related. This is particularly beneficial when students are negotiating the meanings of science concepts they already know while exploring how new science concepts are connected to them. This process can be used to assess the relationship between students' understanding of a concept or concepts and the language they use to describe these concepts. We really like concept mapping because students significantly increase their vocabulary as they construct their maps.

Donna particularly enjoys the flexibility provided by concept mapping. She groups students in a way that promotes equitable participation within the groups. There is also flexibility in the topics that can be explored through concept mapping. The concept maps given in this chapter represent the design cycle instead of the understanding of science concepts—to map the concepts of the design, students need to understand them. If you have previously done concept mapping with your students, the concept mapping of the design processes of scientists and engineers exemplified in this chapter will build on these experiences. (If you have never done concept mapping before, you can find directions in "Appendix E" (p. 351) that can help you introduce concept mapping to your classroom.)

# SCIENTISTS AND ENGINEERS USE MODIFICATION

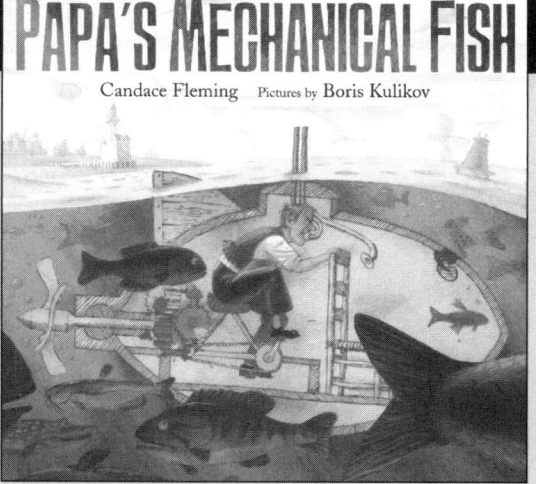

## Lesson: Food Delivery Design Challenge

### Description

Students will design a boat using specified materials to carry cookies (pennies). This is a float-and-sink challenge with a design element.

### Objectives

In this lesson, students will explore floating and sinking and engineering design.

- As a class, students will make cost and materials choices and design boats that will carry cookies (pennies).
- Students will hear the story *Papa's Mechanical Fish* by Candace Fleming and will discuss the design process that Papa uses.
- Students will make blueprints for a boat and then build their boats while keeping costs within a specified budget.
- To conclude the lesson, students will test their boats to find the number of pennies it can hold before sinking.

### Learning Outcomes

Students will (1) design a boat and (2) build a boat based on their design to address the challenge presented.

# Connections to the *NGSS* and the Nature of Science, Grades 3–5

## Disciplinary Core Ideas

**PS1.A: STRUCTURE AND PROPERTIES OF MATTER**

- <u>Measurements of a variety of properties can be used to identify materials.</u> (Boundary: At this grade level, mass and weight are not distinguished, and no attempt is made to define the unseen particles or explain the atomic-scale mechanism of evaporation and condensation.)

**ETS1.A: DEFINING AND DELIMITING ENGINEERING PROBLEMS**

- Possible solutions to a problem are limited by available materials and resources (constraints). The success of a designed solution is determined by considering the desired features of a solution (criteria). Different proposals for solutions can be compared on the basis of how well each one meets the specified criteria for success or how well each takes the constraints into account.

**ETS1.B: DEVELOPING POSSIBLE SOLUTIONS**

- Tests are often designed to identify failure points or difficulties, which suggest the elements of the design that need to be improved.
- Testing a solution involves investigating how well it performs under a range of likely conditions.

**ETS1.C: OPTIMIZING THE DESIGN SOLUTION**

- Different solutions need to be tested in order to determine which of them best solves the problem, given the criteria and the constraints.

## Science and Engineering Practices

***Asking Questions and Defining Problems:*** A practice of science is to ask and refine questions that lead to descriptions and explanations of how the natural and designed world works and which can be empirically tested. Asking questions and defining problems in grades 3–5 builds from grades K–2 experiences and progresses to specifying qualitative relationships.

- Identify scientific (testable) and non-scientific (non-testable) questions.
- Use prior knowledge to describe problems that can be solved.
- Define a simple design problem that can be solved through the development of an object, tool, process, or system and includes several criteria for success and constraints on materials, time, or cost.

SCIENTISTS AND ENGINEERS USE **MODIFICATION**

***Planning and Carrying Out Investigations:*** Scientists and engineers plan and carry out investigations in the field or laboratory, working collaboratively as well as individually. Their investigations are systematic and require clarifying what counts as data and identifying variables or parameters. Planning and carrying out investigations to answer questions or test solutions to problems in 3–5 builds on K–2 experiences and progresses to include investigations that control variables and provide evidence to support explanations or design solutions.

- Plan and conduct an investigation collaboratively to produce data to serve as the basis for evidence, using fair tests in which variables are controlled and the number of trials considered.
- Make observations and/or measurements to produce data to serve as the basis for evidence for an explanation of a phenomenon or test a design solution.
- Make predictions about what would happen if a variable changes.
- Test two different models of the same proposed object, tool, or process to determine which better meets criteria for success.

***Analyzing and Interpreting Data:*** Scientific investigations produce data that must be analyzed in order to derive meaning. Because data patterns and trends are not always obvious, scientists use a range of tools—including tabulation, graphical interpretation, visualization, and statistical analysis—to identify the significant features and patterns in the data. Scientists identify sources of error in the investigations and calculate the degree of certainty in the results. Modern technology makes the collection of large data sets much easier, providing secondary sources for analysis. Analyzing data in 3–5 builds on K–2 experiences and progresses to introducing quantitative approaches to collecting data and conducting multiple trials of qualitative observations. When possible and feasible, digital tools should be used.

- Analyze and interpret data to make sense of phenomena, using logical reasoning, mathematics, and/or computation.
- Compare and contrast data collected by different groups in order to discuss similarities and differences in their findings.
- Use data to evaluate and refine design solutions.

***Using Mathematics and Computational Thinking:*** In both science and engineering, mathematics and computation are fundamental tools for representing physical variables and their relationships. They are used for a range of tasks such as constructing simulations; statistically analyzing data; and recognizing, expressing, and applying quantitative relationships. Mathematical and computational thinking at the 3–5 level builds on K–2 experiences and progresses to extending quantitative measurements to a variety of physical properties and using computation and mathematics to analyze data and compare alternative design solutions.

- Organize simple data sets to reveal patterns that suggest relationships.

***Constructing Explanations and Designing Solutions:*** The products of science are explanations and the products of engineering are solutions. Constructing explanations and designing solutions in 3–5 builds on K–2 experiences and progresses to the use of evidence in constructing explanations that specify variables that describe and predict phenomena and in designing multiple solutions to design problems.

- Use evidence (e.g., measurements, observations, patterns) to construct or support an explanation or design a solution to a problem.
- Identify the evidence that supports particular points in an explanation.
- Generate and compare multiple solutions to a problem based on how well they meet the criteria and constraints of the design solution.

## Crosscutting Concepts

***Cause and Effect:*** Events have causes, sometimes simple, sometimes multifaceted. Deciphering causal relationships, and the mechanisms by which they are mediated, is a major activity of science and engineering.

- Cause and effect relationships are routinely identified, tested, and used to explain change.
- Events that occur together with regularity might or might not be a cause and effect relationship.

***Structure and Function:*** The way an object is shaped or structured determines many of its properties and functions.

- Different materials have different substructures, which can sometimes be observed.
- Substructures have shapes and parts that serve functions.

## Nature of Science Connections
### SCIENCE KNOWLEDGE IS BASED ON EMPIRICAL EVIDENCE

- Science findings are based on recognizing patterns.

### SCIENTIFIC KNOWLEDGE IS OPEN TO REVISION IN LIGHT OF NEW EVIDENCE

- Science explanations can change based on new evidence.

### SCIENCE IS A HUMAN ENDEAVOR

- Men and women from all cultures and backgrounds choose careers as scientists and engineers.
- Creativity and imagination are important to science.

*Source:* NGSS Lead States 2013.

*Note:* When an activity supports only part of a standard, underlining indicates the relevant part.

SCIENTISTS AND ENGINEERS USE **MODIFICATION**

## Overview

*Papa's Mechanical Fish,* a historical fiction book, is based on the inventive work of Lodner Phillips (whom the character Papa represents). Papa is an inventor who has not yet made anything that works perfectly. He is captivated by simple questions such as, "Have you ever wondered what it's like to be a fish?" This question sends him off to his workshop to modify his mechanical fish invention. Eventually, and after many trials, Papa creates a submarine that can take his family for a trip to the bottom of Lake Michigan. This story models the nature of engineers' work in that many trials are sometimes needed to solve problems in a design.

## Materials

You will need a copy of the book *Papa's Mechanical Fish* by Candace Fleming (ISBN 978-0374399085) and a float tank for the boat tests. Student groups will need craft sticks, aluminum foil, pennies, plastic drinking straws, paper, glue, and masking tape. Each student will need his or her science notebook and safety glasses or goggles. We recommend placing large towels under the float tanks to soak up water spills.

## Safety Notes

(1) Personal protective equipment should be worn during the setup, hands-on, and takedown segments of the activity. (2) Use caution in working with sharps (craft sticks, scissors). They can cut or puncture skin or eyes. (3) Immediately wipe up spilled water—it creates a slip-and-fall hazard. (4) Wash hands with soap and water upon completing this activity.

## Setting the Context
### Engage

Invite students to think about how boats are designed by either showing them pictures of different kinds of boats or asking them questions such as "What boat design is best?" Ask them to sketch a boat design based on their ideas about boats. Have them write down key ideas in boat design such as the shape of the hull, whether the bottom is flat or rounded, and so forth. If you show pictures of boats, have students write down three to five key ideas about boat design that they infer from those pictures. Those ideas may be useful as they design their own boats in this lesson.

### Guided Reading

Tell students that they will learn about floating and sinking and about engineering design by reading *Papa's Mechanical Fish.* Introduce the book by asking "What do you notice about the person on the front cover?" and "What does it look like is happening on the front cover?" Read the story aloud. Encourage students to notice and think about the challenges that the main character Papa faces as an inventor. The following questions may be used to guide students' attention to detail as you read. (Page numbers reference unnumbered book pages, beginning with the title page as page 1.)

1. **Pages 8–15:** One day, Papa decided he had had enough thinking, so he took his family fishing. No sooner did the family begin to fish than Virena asks her Papa about fish. Why do you think Papa gets distracted by his daughter's questions? *Papa is convinced he will invent something that works perfectly one day; as he says, "All I need is a fantastic idea." Virena's question about what it must be like to be a fish inspired Papa's ideas about building a mechanical fish that would "dive like a salmon" and "glide like a trout."*

2. **Pages 15–29:** Papa's first three mechanical fish were Whitefish, Whitefish II, and Whitefish III. Why do you think Papa kept improving his design? How did the design change in the second, third, and fourth versions? *Whitefish had a tube sticking out of the top so Papa could breathe underwater and a pole so he could push himself along the bottom—and it almost worked. When his son, Cyril, asked what it is like to be a fish, Papa began to think about how fish move through the water—with their tails and fins! So, he made Whitefish II big enough to hold two people and added a wooden fin on the top and a propeller in the back to help it move through the water as Papa peddled—and again, it almost worked. Then, Cyril helped Papa think about how fish stay dry with their special scales. So, Papa made Whitefish III big enough to hold three people and gave it a steering wheel, replaced the pedals with levers, and covered it in waterproof copper—and again, it almost worked. But this time Papa could not see out of it! That spawned a fourth design. Papa was inspired by each attempt, learned from his tests, and modified each generation of the mechanical fish.*

3. **Pages 30–33:** The design of Whitefish IV was very different from that of the earlier mechanical fish. What things did Papa deem necessary then that were not included in his first sketches? *Whitefish IV could hold seven people and had an air cooling system, an air compression system, an air purifying system, velvet carpet, and comfortable chairs. Steam ran the engine, a battery ran the headlights, and 12 portholes allowed passengers to look out underwater.*

4. **Pages 12–35:** Papa's new ideas about how fish swim through water, how fish stay dry in the water, and how fish know where they are going helped him to think of ways to improve his first invention. Why do you think he thought so much about what fish could do? *Papa's thinking about how fish lived in the water helped him think about the tasks that a mechanical fish would also need to perform.*

SCIENTISTS AND ENGINEERS USE **MODIFICATION**

## Making Sense

### Explore

In the featured book, the main character, Papa, learns how to create a working submarine by refining the designs of three different failed models. The story shows that inventions are not designed overnight or the first time someone has an idea. Inventions require planning, testing, and refining designs. We like how this story models the process of working on an idea until it succeeds!

This lesson introduces the Food Delivery Boat Challenge, in which students must design a boat to carry food (pennies) from the United States to families in underdeveloped countries. The boat carrying the food will travel thousands of miles across the Atlantic Ocean. To save money, time, and effort, the boat must ship as much food per trip as possible. To accomplish that, students must design the largest boat possible and then build a model of it using the available materials and staying within a specified budget.

Ahead of class, set up the student tables with the float tank filled with water and the boat-building materials: craft sticks, aluminum foil, pennies, plastic drinking straws, paper, glue, and masking tape. Be sure each student wears the safety glasses or goggles.

To begin this activity, ask students to list what engineers do in the design process and what questions Papa asked to help him improve his invention (see Figure 10.1). Discuss how Papa's questions helped him to improve his invention.

### Figure 10.1

**Examples of Preliminary Thinking to Guide Students in Their Sketches**

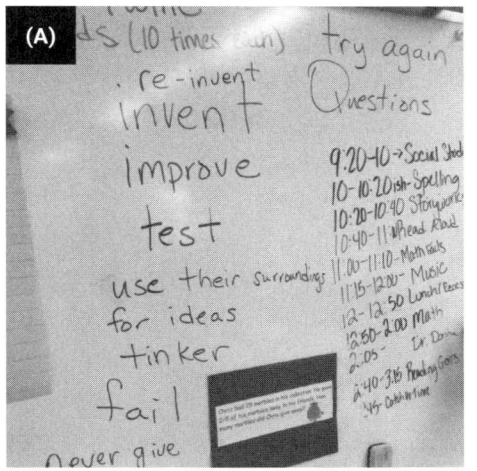 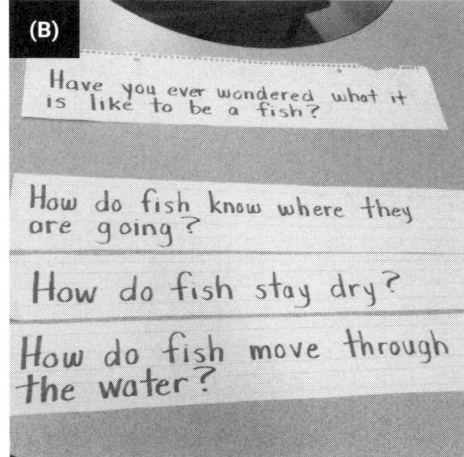

(A) The class created a word wall to record responses to the question "What do engineers do in the design process?" (B) The class highlighted the questions that prompted Papa's design changes, starting with the first "Have you ever wondered …" question. Papa used these questions to illustrate his thinking about how he applied his knowledge about fish to his invention, the submarine.

### Table 10.1
#### Sample Chart of Building Material Costs

| Item | Price |
| --- | --- |
| Lumber (craft sticks) | $40 each |
| Sheet metal (aluminum foil) | $22/sheet |
| Welding materials (glue) | $30 rental fee |
| Reinforcements (plastic straws) | $25 each |
| Cable/rope (masking tape) | $10/in. |
| Paper | $20/sheet |

Explain to students that they are to work in groups to construct a model boat using any or all of the following materials: craft sticks, aluminum foil, all-purpose glue, masking tape, plastic straws, and paper. Tell them that they will be able to test their designs in the float tank before they decide on their final design and that each group can spend up to $500 to build their boat. Provide the cost of each material (see, e.g., Table 10.1). Then, invite students to sketch a boat design. Encourage them to think about how they will use the design process and information from the story as they create their sketches. Remind students that the purpose of the Food Delivery Boat Challenge is to create a boat that will support the most pennies—that is, that it will deliver the most food to families in need. As you coach each group, encourage students to think about critical questions, such as the following:

- Which parts of the design will be important for this goal?
- How will weight be best supported?
- What might be the most economical way to build this design?

When students have completed their initial sketches, encourage them to build and test their design in the float tank to see how many pennies it can hold. Remind them how Papa modified his design after each test, and ask them whether they can make any changes to improve their boat. Ask students to write about and/or illustrate their observations and reasoning in their science notebooks (see Figure 10.2).

### Figure 10.2
#### Chart Showing How Students Planned a Boat Design Using the Budget

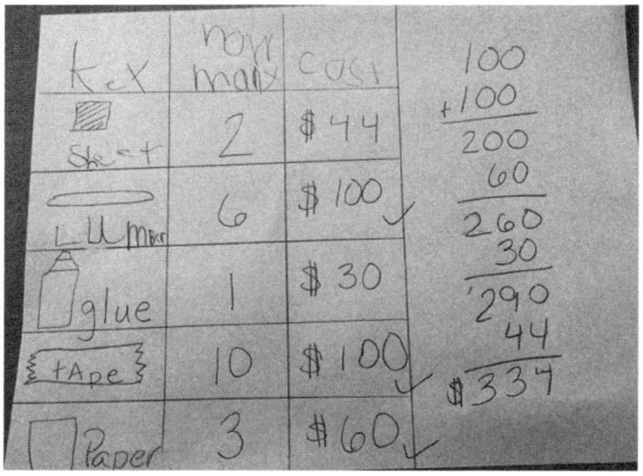

SCIENTISTS AND ENGINEERS USE **MODIFICATION**

## Explain

As a class, compare the boat designs of all the student groups. Create a chart to record students' predictions of which boat will support the most pennies. Then, test the boats, recording the number of pennies supported by each design. Create a graph to compare the number of pennies each boat held.

Guide the class in a compare-and-contrast discussion about the successes of the boats. Ask, "What patterns do you see?" "What key features led to successful designs?" and "What important things did you learn from your first attempt?" *There can be wide variance in the students' success in this challenge (see Figure 10.3). Encourage students to note successful features and what "almost worked" in the conversation in the same way Papa thought about his designs during his trial-and-error invention process. Even boats that hold just a few pennies will have taught some important lessons!*

### Figure 10.3

**Two Student Boat Designs Using Materials Available Within the Budget**

## Extend

As a class, have students list everything they can think of that scientists and engineers do in the design process. In groups, have students identify the steps of the design process they experienced by concept mapping the design process using the terms the class identified as a group. Ask, "How was this similar to or different from what Papa did in the story?" Find out other ways to explore design challenges. Encourage students to summarize their observations and any questions that were prompted by this investigation. Invite them to answer the following questions: "Which boat design held the most pennies? How did the boat designs vary in terms of cost? Which materials were used most often by students, and why? What boat design was 'the best,' and why do you think so? What modification will you make to your next boat design? What building materials were the most valuable, and why?" *Students are likely to suggest that foil is the most valuable material. When the foil is in the shape of a boat, it displaces a volume of water equal to the weight of the pennies. The surface tension of the water also helps to keep the boat afloat, so the greater the surface area* of the boat and the more waterproof its sides (thus keeping the water out as the boat lowers in the water), the more pennies it can hold.

Invite students to think about the character traits of scientists and engineers that they have learned about thus far. Ask, "Which character trait describes Papa, and why?" (See Appendix D, Glossary of Character Traits, p. 350.) Encourage visuals as part of the science notebook entries, such as a sketch, a photograph, or a chart (see Figure 10.4).

### Evaluate

Use a rubric such as the one in Table 10.2 to help you evaluate students' ability to design and build a boat that addresses the challenge presented.

Figure 10.4

### Student's Visual Representation of the Design Process Discussed in *Papa's Mechanical Fish*

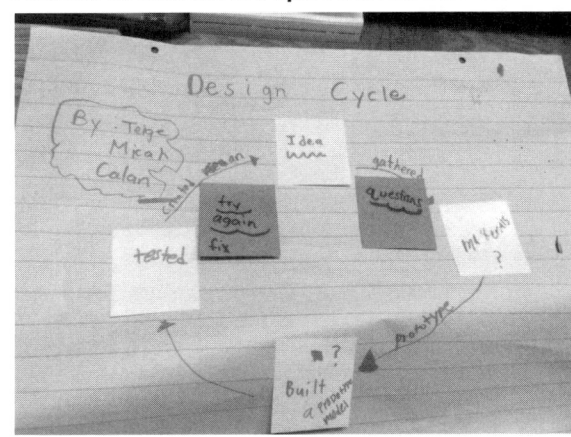

Table 10.2

### Rubric for Assessing Students on the Food Delivery Challenge Activity

| Content or Skill | Not Yet | Beginning | Developing | Secure |
| --- | --- | --- | --- | --- |
| Design and Test Process | Team did not create a boat for the challenge. | Team created a boat for the challenge but did not test its ability to carry pennies. | Team created a boat for the challenge and tested its ability to carry pennies. | Team created a boat for the challenge, tested its ability to carry pennies, and redesigned the boat based on the results. |
| Challenge Requirements | Team did not work within the challenge requirements. | Team worked within some of the challenge requirements. | Team worked within most the challenge requirements. | Team worked within all of the challenge requirements. |
| Team Cooperation | Team did not cooperate or complete task. | Team showed little or no cooperation in completing task. | Team showed some cooperation in completing task. | Team showed full cooperation in completing task. |
| Design Connections | Team members did not establish a connection between the boat's design and the benefit to society (more food delivered). | Some team members established a connection between the boat's design and the benefit to society (more food delivered). | Most team members established a connection between the boat's design and the benefit to society (more food delivered). | All team members established a connection between the boat's design and the benefit to society (more food delivered). |

# SCIENTISTS AND ENGINEERS USE
# IDEA DEVELOPMENT

## Lesson: What Do You Do With an Idea?
### Description

Students will learn about brainstorming and the design process.

### Objectives

In this lesson, students will recognize how the design process helps people turn ideas into inventions.

- As a group, students will identify an idea they would like to take through the design process and then brainstorm what it would take to make that idea a reality.

- Students will hear the story *What Do You Do With an Idea?* by Kobi Yamada and discuss what happens to ideas when they are used and when they are not.

- Students will follow the design process to create a visual representation of their idea.

- To conclude the lesson, students will share ideas and discuss the similarities and differences in their experiences of the design process.

### Learning Outcomes

Students will be able to (1) brainstorm an idea as a group and (2) define the stages of the design process for the development of that idea.

## Connections to the *NGSS* and the Nature of Science, Grades 3–5
### Disciplinary Core Idea
#### ETS1.A: DEFINING AND DELIMITING ENGINEERING PROBLEMS

- Possible solutions to a problem are limited by available materials and resources (constraints). The success of a designed solution is determined by considering the desired features of a solution (criteria). Different proposals for solutions can be compared on the basis of how well each one meets the specified criteria for success or how well each takes the constraints into account.

## Science and Engineering Practice

***Asking Questions and Defining Problems:*** A practice of science is to ask and refine questions that lead to descriptions and explanations of how the natural and designed world works and which can be empirically tested. Asking questions and defining problems in grades 3–5 builds from grades K–2 experiences and progresses to specifying qualitative relationships.

- Define a simple design problem that can be solved through the development of an object, tool, process, or system and includes several criteria for success and constraints on materials, time, or cost.

## Crosscutting Concept

***Systems and System Models:*** A system is an organized group of related objects or components; models can be used for understanding and predicting the behavior of systems.

- A system can be described in terms of its components and their interactions.
- A system is a group of related parts that make up a whole and can carry out functions its individual parts cannot.

## Nature of Science Connections
### SCIENCE IS A WAY OF KNOWING

- Science is both a body of knowledge and processes that add new knowledge.

### SCIENCE IS A HUMAN ENDEAVOR

- Men and women from all cultures and backgrounds choose careers as scientists and engineers.
- Science affects everyday life.
- Creativity and imagination are important to science.

*Source:* NGSS Lead States 2013.

SCIENTISTS AND ENGINEERS USE **IDEA DEVELOPMENT**

## Overview

The featured book, *What Do You Do With an Idea?*, tells the story of a child who comes up with a brilliant idea and learns how to bring it into the world. As the child's confidence grows, so does the idea. This story is for anyone who has ever had an idea that seemed a little too big, too odd, or too difficult. It relates to the work of scientists and engineers because their work requires new ideas. This is an encouraging story about managing new ideas and giving them time to grow.

## Materials

You will need a copy of the book *What Do You Do With an Idea?* by Kobi Yamada (ISBN 978-1938298073). Student groups will need sticky notes, chart paper, and markers.

## Setting the Context
### Engage

Ask students whether they have ever generated a list of their own ideas about how to solve problems or make the world a better place. Remind students that we sometimes have ideas that we think nobody else would care about. Invite a few students to share stories about ideas they might have had or inventive thinking they may have experienced when they were playing (with building blocks, for example).

### Guided Reading

The following questions may be used to guide students' attention to detail as you read. (Page numbers reference unnumbered book pages, beginning with the title page as page 1.)

1. **Pages 1–9:** In the story, a child discovered an idea, and over time, the idea seemed to belong to him more and more. The child was afraid to talk to other people about his idea. Why might we, like the child, be reluctant to share our ideas with other people? *At first, our ideas might even seem silly to us, too! After all, an idea is a new thought.*

2. **Pages 10–19:** The magical idea grew and wanted lots of attention, but when the child was willing to share it with others, he found that they thought it was silly or a waste of time. Why was the child discouraged by other people's reaction to his idea? *Over time, the child had become comfortable with his idea. His friends' reactions caused him to doubt whether his idea had any merit at all.*

3. **Pages 20–27:** Soon the child became protective of his idea and realized that no one else understood his idea quite like he did. The child spent more time

playing and working with his idea, and it grew even bigger. *How can an idea grow when we spend more time with it?* Pondering an idea helps us to clarify our thinking and modify the idea, which can make the idea better.

4. **Pages 26–35:** Eventually, the child could not imagine life without his idea. His idea was no longer just part of him; it was everywhere. *How did this child's idea change the world?* The child let himself have the idea and nurtured it and then one day realized he had developed it into a magical idea that he could use to make the world a better place.

5. *How does this story relate to the work of scientists and engineers?* Scientists and engineers are people who enjoy having innovative ideas and working with them until they make new discoveries or build new products that improve the quality of life.

## Making Sense

### Explore

Have students work in groups of four or five. Invite the student groups to list new ideas on sticky notes. When all groups have had a chance to list several ideas, ask each group to decide which idea they want to develop. Have them place that idea in the middle of a piece of chart paper, as shown in Figure 10.5 (A). Then, prompt students to work through the engineering design cycle to map out the steps they must

### Figure 10.5

### Examples of Students' Ideas and Brainstorming Ways to Bring Them to Life

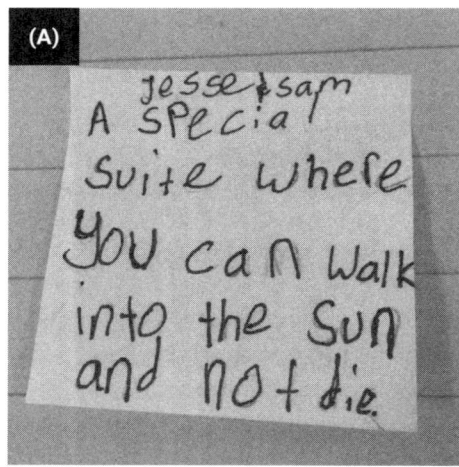
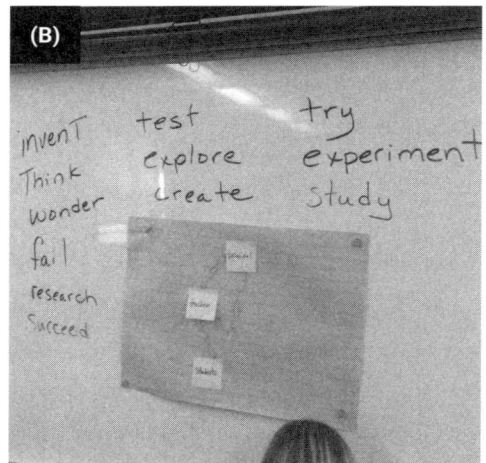

Student groups collect their ideas, choose one to develop, and then brainstorm to create a visual representation of how to bring the idea to life. (A) A sticky note containing the idea selected by the group. (B) A list of words students associated with the design process that engineers and scientists follow.

follow to bring their idea to life. *See www.teachengineering.org for information about the engineering design cycle.* Let students brainstorm possibilities as freely as possible. Encourage them to write and illustrate their observations and reasoning in their science notebooks. If students are having trouble, you might help by generating a list of things scientists and engineers do in the design process (see Figure 10.5 [B]). Students can then use these words as they explain the design process.

### Explain

Encourage students to summarize their thoughts about what steps are needed to accomplish their idea (Figure 10.6). It is important for you to acknowledge each one of these ideas as actual possibilities and let the students' imaginations run away with them. The purpose of this lesson is for students to connect with free-flowing thinking and believe that anything is possible.

### Extend

You can extend the learning in this lesson by finding other ways to explore students' ideas. For example, encourage visuals as part of the science notebook entries (e.g., sketches, photographs, or charts). Also, designate a bulletin board or a box for collecting ideas from students. Consider organizing an "invention convention" in your classroom. An invention convention is a bit like a science fair, except that in invention conventions, students are challenged to create a new product that solves a problem in their lives. Education Place is an excellent online resource to help with organizing invention conventions (*www.eduplace.com/science/invention/overview.html*; see the "Additional Resources" section, p. 338).

### Evaluate

Ask students to think about how they used the techniques used by the child in the book (e.g., playing with the idea, working with the idea, and listening to the idea). Encourage students to develop their ideas as much as possible. Evaluate students' ideas for completeness (not accuracy) by asking the following questions:

- Will the idea be tested and refined?

### Figure 10.6

**Students Mapping Out How to Accomplish Their Ideas**

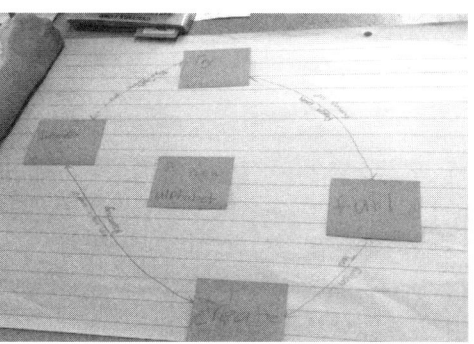

- How well planned is the idea?
- Does the idea seem plausible?

Invite the students to think about the character traits they have learned about. Ask, "Which character traits describe the child in this story, and why?" (See Appendix D, p. 350).

It can be difficult to assess brainstorming activities; a rubric such as the one in Table 10.3 may be used to assess students' progress as a group in the brainstorming process. Table 10.3 also could be used to assess students during the design process for the development of an idea.

Table 10.3

### Rubric for Assessing Student Brainstorming Activity

| Content or Skill | Not Yet | Beginning | Developing | Secure |
| --- | --- | --- | --- | --- |
| Brainstorm an Idea as a Group | There was no cooperation among group members. | There was little or no cooperation among group members. | There was some cooperation among group members. | There was full cooperation among group members. |
| Design and Test Process | No team members could define the stages of the design process for the development of an idea. | Some team members could define the stages of the design process for the development of an idea. | Most team members could define the stages of the design process for the development of an idea. | All team members could define the stages of the design process for the development of an idea. |

# SCIENTISTS AND ENGINEERS USE
# DESIGN PROCESS

## Lesson: Rosie Revere, Engineer
### Description

Students will create a concept map of the design process after learning about the challenges that book character Rosie Revere faced as a designer.

### Objectives

In this lesson, students will become familiar with the design process and how it is used in the story.

- Students will work in groups to re-create the design process in the story.

- Students will hear the story *Rosie Revere, Engineer* by Andrea Beaty and discuss what parts of the design process Revere used.

- Students will create a concept map of the design process.

- To conclude the lesson, students will share their concept maps with other groups and identify similarities and differences among them.

### Learning Outcome

Students will become familiar with the phases of the design cycle.

# Connections to the NGSS and the Nature of Science, Grades 3–5

## Disciplinary Core Ideas

### ETS1.A: DEFINING AND DELIMITING ENGINEERING PROBLEMS

- Possible solutions to a problem are limited by available materials and resources (constraints). The success of a designed solution is determined by considering the desired features of a solution (criteria). Different proposals for solutions can be compared on the basis of how well each one meets the specified criteria for success or how well each takes the constraints into account.

### ETS1.B: DEVELOPING POSSIBLE SOLUTIONS

- Research on a problem should be carried out before beginning to design a solution. Testing a solution involves investigating how well it performs under a range of likely conditions.

- At whatever stage, communicating with peers about proposed solutions is an important part of the design process, and shared ideas can lead to improved designs.

- Tests are often designed to identify failure points or difficulties, which suggest the elements of the design that need to be improved.

### ETS1.C: OPTIMIZING THE DESIGN SOLUTION

- Different solutions need to be tested in order to determine which of them best solves the problem, given the criteria and the constraints.

## Science and Engineering Practice

***Asking Questions and Defining Problems:*** A practice of science is to ask and refine questions that lead to descriptions and explanations of how the natural and designed world works and which can be empirically tested. Asking questions and defining problems in grades 3–5 builds from grades K–2 experiences and progresses to specifying qualitative relationships.

- Use prior knowledge to describe problems that can be solved.

- Define a simple design problem that can be solved through the development of an object, tool, process, or system and includes several criteria for success and constraints on materials, time, or cost.

### Crosscutting Concept

***Systems and System Models:*** A system is an organized group of related objects or components; models can be used for understanding and predicting the behavior of systems.

- A system can be described in terms of its components and their interactions.
- A system is a group of related parts that make up a whole and can carry out functions its individual parts cannot.

### Nature of Science Connection
**SCIENCE IS A HUMAN ENDEAVOR**

- Men and women from all cultures and backgrounds choose careers as scientists and engineers.
- Science affects everyday life.
- Creativity and imagination are important to science.

*Source:* NGSS Lead States 2013.

## Overview

In this lesson, students will learn about the life of a fictional character, Rosie Revere, who dreamed of being an engineer. Through the featured book, students learn that men and women from all different backgrounds choose careers as scientists and engineers. Students will share ideas about scientists and engineers and discuss the engineering design process (EDP) in the story. Students will create a concept map of their own EDP and will share their concept maps with other groups and identify similarities and differences among them.

## Materials

You will need a copy of the book *Rosie Revere, Engineer* by Andrea Beaty (ISBN 978-1419708459). Student groups will need sticky notes, chart paper, and markers. Each student will need his or her science notebook.

## Setting the Context
### Engage

Tell students that they will be listening to the story of Rosie Revere, a little girl who wants to be an engineer. Revere becomes discouraged when she creates a contraption for her aunt and fears it is a failure. However, her aunt assures her that she could only fail if she did not try at all. Ask students "Have you ever tried to create something before?" "What kinds of things would you like to create?" and "What does the process of design look like?" When the discussion is complete, invite students to create a list of words that describe what scientists and engineers do when they create something new (see Figure 10.7).

## Guided Reading

The following questions may be used to guide students' attention to detail as you read. (Page numbers reference unnumbered book pages, beginning with the title page as page 1.)

### Figure 10.7

**Example of a Student List of Words Describing the Work of Scientists and Engineers Creating Something New**

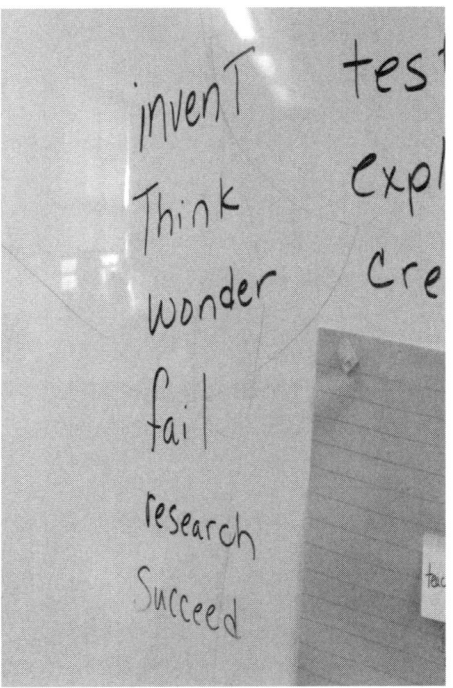

1. **Pages 1–7:** Rosie Revere was a shy girl at school, but she was a different girl in her attic. Why was Revere so shy while she was at school?
   *Revere dreamed of becoming an engineer. She collected trash treasures when no one was looking and worked in her hideaway in the attic. She built gizmos and gadgets, and hid them under her bed. She kept her dreams to herself.*

2. **Pages 8–13:** Revere liked to invent things for other people. Why was she discouraged when she built a hat for the zookeeper to keep snakes off his head?
   *The zookeeper laughed at the hat made of a fan and cheddar-cheese spray even though he told her he loved it. Revere was embarrassed, perplexed, and dismayed. She hid the cheese hat and resolved to keep her dreams to herself.*

3. **Pages 14–19:** Revere's great-great-aunt Rose was a true dynamo who loved adventure. What happened when her beloved Aunt Rose exclaimed, "The only thrill left on my list is to fly!"? *Revere could not sleep, as she wondered how she might build a gizmo so her aunt could fly by morning. Revere had an idea and worked all day to build a helio-cheese-copter. She was ready to see what a ridiculous flop it was going to be.*

4. **Pages 18–20:** Revere's helio-cheese-copter was made of things such as Hula-Hoops, skateboards, a fan, a broom, cheddar-cheese spray, and a baby-doll head. Why do you think she built her gizmos and gadgets out of materials like these? *Revere was a creative thinker and engineered things out of available materials.*

5. **Pages 20–23:** Revere's helio-cheese-copter sputtered and floated a moment and then crashed to the ground. How did Revere respond to this crash experience? *Revere was newly discouraged about her engineering skills, and she exclaimed, "And never will I be a great engineer."*

6. **Pages 24–27:** Aunt Rose exclaimed, "You did it! Hooray! It's the perfect first try!" What surprised Revere about her aunt's response? *Revere was baffled and perplexed because the helio-cheese-copter crashed. Her aunt convinced her that "the first flop was a raging success."*

7. **Pages 28–31:** Now Revere could smile ear to ear and dream the dreams of a bold engineer. How did her aunt help to change her shy behavior? *With the helio-cheese-copter flop, Revere learned that "the only true failure can come if you quit." Now she confidently built "gizmos and gadgets and doohickeys" with her second-grade classmates.*

### Figure 10.8

**Sample Concept Maps Based on the Design Process in *Rosie Revere, Engineer***

# 10 BEYOND *EUREKA!*

## Making Sense

### Explore
Invite students in groups of four or five to explain the design process that Revere used in the story using a concept map (see Figure 10.8). Encourage students to write and/or illustrate their observations and reasoning in their science notebooks.

### Explain
Invite students to think about how the story influenced their thinking about the design process. Encourage them to summarize their observations and any questions prompted by the concept mapping activity. Introduce a discussion about how the students described the design process. See the Teach Engineering website (*www.teachengineering.org*) for information about the EDP. Ask, "What did all the groups mention?" and "What feature of each group's poster was different?" If time allows, revisit the featured book to find specific examples.

### Extend
Find other ways to explore the design process. Encourage students to include visuals as part of their science notebook entries in the Explore phase (p. 331), such as sketches, photographs, and charts. You might invite students to think about how to improve the design of their classroom. Ask, "What works?" and "What are we missing?" Encourage students to try out new ideas that would improve the learning atmosphere and student productivity. Ask students, "How will you measure your success?"

### Evaluate
Evaluate students' concept maps in terms of whether they show complete ideas about the design process. Some questions might include the following:

- Does the student's concept map resemble how Rosie Revere created her invention in the story?

- How many parts of the EDP are listed?

- Did the student include a planning, building, and testing phase in the design process?

Invite the students to think about the character traits they have learned about thus far (see Appendix D [p. 350]). Ask, "Which character trait best describes Rosie Revere, and why?" A rubric such as the one in Table 10.4 may be used to assess students' progress as a group in the concept mapping and brainstorming process. Table 10.4 also could be used to assess students during the design process for the development of an idea.

Table 10.4

## Rubric for Assessing Students on the Concept Map of the Engineering Design Process

| Content or Skill | Not Yet | Beginning | Developing | Secure |
|---|---|---|---|---|
| **Concept Map and Idea as a Group** | There was no cooperation among group members. | There was little cooperation among group members. | There was a moderate amount of cooperation among group members. | There was full cooperation among group members. |
| **Design and Test Process** | No team members could define the stages of the design process as it relates to the story. | Some team members could define the stages of the design process as it relates to the story. | Most team members could define the stages of the design process as it relates to the story. | All team members could define the stages of the design process as it relates to the story. |

# LESSON GUIDELINES

## Guidelines for Selecting Biographical Trade Books for Your Classroom

To help assess whether a trade book is appropriate for use in your classroom (with respect to its science and engineering content and literature elements), consider using the "Science Trade Book Evaluation Rubric" devised by Atkinson, Matusevich, and Huber (2009). This rubric has two main sections: science and engineering content and literacy criteria. The literacy criteria include plot development, imagination, continuity (for fiction books), and whether the book contains sufficient information that is organized in appropriate text structures (for nonfiction books). The rubric also includes writing style, the suitability of the book's illustrations and graphics for the related text, and the presentation of positive ethical and cultural values (including gender and racial representations). For science and engineering content criteria, the rubric covers whether the science and engineering content is substantial, is accurate, is current, has a "human face" (is personalized), and is intellectually and developmentally appropriate for the targeted audience; however, the rubric does not specifically address the representation of scientists and engineers, particularly within the context of "science is a human endeavor." Unfortunately, we have not found a rubric to guide assessment of whether a trade book accurately represents the scientist(s) or engineer(s); however, there are lists of high-quality books to use as a resource, such as awardees of the Outstanding Science Book from the National Science Teachers Association (NSTA), the Caldecott Medal for best picture book, the Newberry Medal for best children's literature, and the Orbis Pictus Award from the National Council of Teachers of English (NCTE). To further assist you, below we provide some guidance for intentionally selecting trade books about scientists and engineers that do not reinforce negative stereotypes of them.

We propose a protocol to select excellent science and engineering trade books that focus on science as a human endeavor that includes the following six considerations (in no specific order):

1. The trade book must have a focus on science or engineering or on a scientist or engineer, regardless of the gender or ethnicity of the person(s) included within its pages. The storytelling aspect of the book is more likely to reflect science as a human endeavor than as a presentation of sets of facts. As an example, in *Rachel Carson and Her Book That Changed the World* (2012), author Laurie Lawlor focused on one scientist, Rachel Carson, and how reports linking robin deaths to pesticides led Carson to write a story in which the songbirds of the world had disappeared. This led to Carson's seminal book, *Silent Spring* (1962), and her explanation of how every strand within the web of life is connected to another and how the collapse of one endangers all the others.

2. The trade book must contain accurate information based on two considerations: (a) the

# LESSON GUIDELINES

accuracy of the science information (Rice and Snipes 1997) and (b) the attributes of the process(es) of science and engineering as delineated by the *Next Generation Science Standards* (*NGSS*; NGSS Lead States 2013). An example of a trade book that has the requisite science accuracy is *Manfish: A Story of Jacques Cousteau* by Jennifer Berne (2008). It describes how Cousteau made inventories of the sea flora and fauna in his books and documentaries and how that inventory information changed over decades of study.

3. The trade book must demonstrate a non-stereotypical representation of a scientist or engineer; it should include images of both male and female scientists and engineers while remaining historically appropriate. Jeanette Winter's portrayal of Jane Goodall in *The Watcher: Jane Goodall's Life With the Chimps* (2011) was both historically accurate and nonstereotypical. A young woman working outside without a lab coat represents the opposite of the stereotypical perception that scientists are white, middle-aged men in lab coats.

4. The trade book should illustrate the roles of the people who are engaging in the scientific enterprise. A good example is Jacqueline Briggs Martin's *Snowflake Bentley* (1998), which tells about a farmer who became interested in photographing snowflakes, persisting over many years until he was able to publish a book about snowflakes when he was 66 years old. Even then, Bentley continued his work with snowflakes.

5. The illustrations in the trade book should be aesthetically pleasing and encourage students to enjoy the book again and again. All of the books we have presented herein exemplify this. Such trade books stand out because they are very different from the typical informational texts currently found in the science sections of bookstores. Informational texts are read solely for information; however, we encourage choosing trade books that can be read for enjoyment.

6. The trade book must have age-appropriate content, and the portrayal of the practice of science and engineering must be consistent with students' learning level and experience of science and engineering practices. Being both age-appropriate and developmentally appropriate for its intended audience enables its readers to cognitively connect with what it presents. *Gregor Mendel: The Friar Who Grew Peas* by Cheryl Bardoe (2006) is an example of a book that meets these criteria. Bardoe writes of how Mendel paired different species of plants to see what traits the resulting offspring would have; he then counted how many of the offspring showed traits from their parents to see whether a mathematical pattern would emerge.

We expect that your choices about the science trade books you introduce to your students will affect your students' understanding about where scientists and engineers work and what they do. Therefore, we suggest that you gather the science and engineering trade books you use in your teaching and review them as follows:

- Assess the science and engineering content for accuracy and for developmental appropriateness to ensure that it clearly matches your students' interests, reading abilities, and capacities to grasp the science and engineering concepts presented.

- Assess the literary qualities, including the quality of the narrative, style of writing, and cultural appropriateness.

- Determine how well the main characters show the personal side of science and engineering (i.e., determine how well the books represent science as a human endeavor).

- Consider the quality of the illustrations that help tell the story as to whether they support the age and developmental level of your students. Consider the brightness of the colors and whether photographs or other types of illustrations are understandable and appropriate.

## Planning *Eureka!* Lessons on Your Own

Here are six simple steps you can use to create your own *Eureka!*-style lessons. These are, in fact, the same procedures we followed to create the 27 lessons in this book.

1. Determine an appropriate trade book. Here, we encourage you to follow the aforementioned guidelines.

2. Read the book and determine a character trait that best describes the scientist or engineer who is the central figure. You might choose a trait we have selected for the scientists and engineers in this book (see Appendix D, p. 350); however, do not feel limited to these because, of course, there are many possible character traits that can support positive outcomes for scientists and engineers.

3. Find a way to connect the story with science and engineering teaching standards (such as the disciplinary core ideas of the *NGSS*). Focusing on this content will help you to introduce the storyline as a real-world connection to a concept you are required to teach.

4. Design your objectives and assessment. Here, you can be especially attuned to the content and achievement expectations specifically delineated by your school district.

5. Develop guided reading questions. We found that storyline questions (linked to page numbers) helped us to remember the story events. Higher-level thinking questions came to us as we read the stories aloud and could be tailored to other current classroom focuses.

6. Test it out! We expect you will learn as you go—just as we did!

# LESSON GUIDELINES

## References

Atkinson, T., M. Matusevich, and L. Huber. 2009. Making science trade book choices for elementary classrooms. *The Reading Teacher* 62 (6): 484–497.

Bardoe, C. 2006. *Gregor Mendel: The friar who grew peas.* New York: Abrams.

Beaty, A. 2013. *Rosie Revere, engineer.* New York: Harry N. Abrams.

Berne, J. 2008. *Manfish: The story of Jacques Cousteau.* San Francisco: Chronicle Books.

Carson, R. 1962. *Silent spring.* Boston: Houghton Mifflin.

Fleming, C. 2013. *Papa's mechanical fish.* New York: Farrar, Straus and Giroux (BYR).

Lawlor, L. 2012. *Rachel Carson and her book that changed the world.* New York: Holiday House.

Martin, J. B. 1998. *Snowflake Bentley.* Boston: HMH Books for Young Readers.

NGSS Lead States. 2013. *Next Generation Science Standards: For states, by states.* Washington, DC: National Academies Press. *www.nextgenscience.org/next-generation-science-standards.*

Rice, D. C., and C. Snipes. 1997. Children's tradebooks: Do they affect the development of science concepts? Paper presented at the annual meeting of the National Association for Research in Science Teaching, St. Louis, MO.

Winter, J. 2011. *The watcher: Jane Goodall's life with the chimps.* New York: Schwartz and Wade Books.

Yamada, Kobi. 2014. *What do you do with an idea?* Seattle: Compendium.

## Additional Resources

Education Place. Houghton Mifflin. Invention convention. *www.eduplace.com/science/invention/overview.html.* *Website with information links to resources to help you guide students' invention processes, including finding ideas; research and planning for the invention or process; and development, testing, and marketing of the invention. Resources include recommended books, copy masters, and examples of student inventions.*

TeachEngineering.org. *www.teachengineering.org.*

# Appendix A

Overview of Featured Books

| Chapter | Scientist or Engineer | Book Title | Author(s) | ISBN | Character Trait | Lexile Measure |
|---|---|---|---|---|---|---|
| 2 | Philo Farnsworth | The Boy Who Invented TV: The Story of Philo Farnsworth | Kathleen Krull | 978-0375845611 | Thinker | 860L |
| 2 | Thomas Edison | Young Thomas Edison | Michael Dooling | 978-0823418688 | Inspired | 830L |
| 2 | George Washington Carver | A Picture Book of George Washington Carver | David A. Adler | 978-0823416332 | Diligent | AD830L |
| 3 | Annie Jump Cannon | Annie Jump Cannon, Astronomer | Carole Gerber | 978-1589809116 | Imaginative | 780L |
| 3 | George Washington Ferris Jr. | Mr. Ferris and His Wheel | Kathryn Gibbs Davis | 978-0547959221 | Visionary | 900L |
| 3 | Gregor Mendel | Gregor Mendel: The Friar Who Grew Peas | Cheryl Bardoe | 978-0810954755 | Patient | AD1030L |
| 4 | Jane Goodall | The Watcher: Jane Goodall's Life With the Chimps | Jeanette Winter | 978-0375867743 | Observant | AD820L |
| 4 | Charles Darwin | Darwin: With Glimpses Into His Private Journal and Letters | Alice B. McGinty | 978-0618995318 | Puzzler | 1060L |
| 4 | Barnum Brown | Barnum's Bones: How Barnum Brown Discovered the Most Famous Dinosaur in the World | Tracey Fern | 978-0374305161 | Intuitive | 1010L |
| 5 | Wilson Bentley | Snowflake Bentley | Jacqueline Briggs Martin | 978-0395861622 | Dedicated | AD830L |
| 5 | Luke Howard | The Man Who Named the Clouds | Julie Hannah and Joan Holub | 978-0807549742 | Dreamer | AD910L |

**APPENDIX A**

Overview of Featured Books *(continued)*

| Chapter | Scientist or Engineer | Book Title | Author(s) | ISBN | Character Trait | Lexile Measure |
|---|---|---|---|---|---|---|
| 5 | John James Audubon | The Boy Who Drew Birds: A Story of John James Audubon | Jacqueline Davies | 978-0618243433 | Curious | AD790L |
| 6 | Ada Byron Lovelace | Ada Byron Lovelace and the Thinking Machine | Laurie Wallmark | 978-1939547200 | Innovative | None |
| 6 | Galileo Galilei | Starry Messenger | Peter Sís | 978-0374371913 | Courageous | 830L |
| 6 | Jacques Cousteau | Manfish: A Story of Jacques Cousteau | Jennifer Berne | 978-0811860635 | Confident | AD800L |
| 7 | Elijah McCoy | The Real McCoy: The Life of an African-American Inventor | Wendy Towle | 978-0590435963 | Clever | None |
| 7 | John Roebling | The Brooklyn Bridge: The Story of the World's Most Famous Bridge and the Remarkable Family That Built It | Elizabeth Mann | 978-0965049306 | Persistent | 820L |
| 7 | William Kamkwamba | The Boy Who Harnessed the Wind | William Kamkwamba and Bryan Mealer | 978-0803735118 | Inventive | 910L |
| 8 | Nikola Tesla | Electrical Wizard: How Nikola Tesla Lit Up the World | Elizabeth Rusch | 978-0763658557 | Risk Taker | 840L |
| 8 | Sylvia Earle | Life in the Ocean: The Story of Oceanographer Sylvia Earle | Claire A. Nivola | 978-0374380687 | Fearless | NC1170L |
| 8 | Waterhouse Hawkins | The Dinosaurs of Waterhouse Hawkins | Barbara Kerley | 978-0439114943 | Creative | AD550L |

Overview of Featured Books *(continued)*

| Chapter | Scientist or Engineer | Book Title | Author(s) | ISBN | Character Trait | Lexile Measure |
|---|---|---|---|---|---|---|
| 9 | Rachel Carson | Rachel Carson and Her Book That Changed the World | Laurie Lawlor | 978-0823423705 | Persuasive | 890L |
| 9 | Wangari Maathai | Seeds of Change: Wangari's Gift to the World | Jen Cullerton Johnson | 978-1600603679 | Passionate | 820L |
| 9 | Carl Sagan | Star Stuff: Carl Sagan and the Mysteries of the Cosmos | Stephanie Roth Sisson | 978-1596439603 | Inquisitive | AD760L |
| 10 | — | Papa's Mechanical Fish | Candace Fleming | 978-0374399085 | Work Method: Modification | AD480L |
| 10 | — | What Do You Do With an Idea? | Kobi Yamada | 978-1938298073 | Work Method: Idea Development | AD340L |
| 10 | — | Rosie Revere, Engineer | Andrea Beaty | 978-1419708459 | Work Method: Design Process | AD860L |

# Appendix B

## Timeline of Featured Scientists and Engineers

Philo Farnsworth (1906–1971)
Rachel Carson (1907–1964)
Jacques Cousteau (1910–1997)
Carl Sagan (1934–1996)
Jane Goodall (1934–)
Sylvia Earle (1935–)
Wangari Maathai (1940–2011)
William Kamkwamba (1987–)

Luke Howard (1772–1864)
John James Audubon (1785–1851)

John Roebling (1806–1869)
Waterhouse Hawkins (1807–1894)
Charles Darwin (1809–1882)
Ada Byron Lovelace (1815–1852)
Gregor Mendel (1822–1884)
Elijah McCoy (1844–1929)
Thomas Edison (1847–1931)
Nikola Tesla (1856–1943)
George Washington Ferris Jr. (1859–1896)
George Washington Carver (1860s–1943)
Annie Jump Cannon (1863–1941)
Wilson Bentley (1865–1931)
Barnum Brown (1873–1963)

Galileo Galilei (1564–1642)

# Appendix C

## Lesson Connections to the *NGSS* and the Nature of Science, Grades 3–5*

| Disciplinary Core Ideas† | 2 Philo Farnsworth | 2 Thomas Edison | 2 George Washington Carver | 3 Annie Jump Cannon | 3 George Washington Ferris Jr. | 3 Gregor Mendel | 4 Jane Goodall | 4 Charles Darwin | 4 Barnum Brown | 5 Charles Bentley | 5 Luke Howard | 5 John James Audubon | 6 Ada Byron Lovelace | 6 Galileo Galilei | 6 Jacques Cousteau | 7 Elijah McCoy | 7 John Roebling | 7 William Kamkwamba | 8 Nikola Tesla | 8 Sylvia Earle | 8 Waterhouse Hawkins | 9 Rachel Carson | 9 Wangari Maathai | 9 Carl Sagan | 10 Papa's Mechanical Fish | 10 What Do You Do With an Idea? | 10 Rosie Revere, Engineer |
|---|---|---|---|---|---|---|---|---|---|---|---|---|---|---|---|---|---|---|---|---|---|---|---|---|---|---|---|
| PS1.A: Structure of Matter | | | | | | | | | | • | | | | | • | | | | | | | | | | • | | |
| PS1.B: Chemical Reactions | | | | | | | | | | | | | | | | | | | | | | | | | | | |
| PS2.A: Forces and Motion | | | | | | | | | | | | | • | • | | • | • | | • | | | | | | | | |
| PS2.B: Types of Interactions | | | | | | | | | | | | | | | | | • | | • | | | | | | | | |
| PS3.A: Definition of Energy | | • | | | | | | | | | | | | | | | | | | | | | | • | | | |
| PS3.B: Conservation of energy and energy transfer | | • | | • | | | | | | | | | | | | | | | | | | | | | | | |
| PS4.A: Wave properties | | • | | | | | | | | | | | | | | | | | | | | | | | | | |
| PS4.B: Electromagnetic radiation | | | | • | | | | | | | | | | | | | | | | | | | | | | | |

*Refer to individual lessons for expanded *NGSS* and Nature of Science information.

†PS = physical science, LS = life science, ESS = Earth and space science, ETS = engineering, technology and the application of science.

# APPENDIX C

## Lesson Connections to the *NGSS* and the Nature of Science, Grades 3–5* (continued)

| Lesson | PS4.C: Information technologies and instrumentation | LS1.A: Structure and function | LS2.A: Interdependent relationships in ecosystems | LS2.C: Ecosystem dynamics, functioning, and resilience | LS3.A: Inheritance of traits | LS3.B: Variation of traits | LS4.A: Evidence of common ancestry and diversity |
|---|---|---|---|---|---|---|---|
| 2 Philo Farnsworth | | | | | | | |
| 2 Thomas Edison | | | | | | | |
| 2 George Washington Carver | | • | | | | | |
| 3 Annie Jump Cannon | | | | | | | |
| 3 George Washington Ferris Jr. | | | | | | | |
| 3 Gregor Mendel | | • | | | • | • | |
| 4 Jane Goodall | | | | | | | |
| 4 Charles Darwin | | | | | | • | |
| 4 Barnum Brown | | | • | | | | • |
| 5 Charles Bentley | | | • | | | | |
| 5 Luke Howard | | | | | | | |
| 5 John James Audubon | | | | | • | | |
| 6 Ada Byron Lovelace | | | | | | | |
| 6 Galileo Galilei | • | | | | | | |
| 6 Jacques Cousteau | • | | | | | | |
| 7 Elijah McCoy | | | | | | | |
| 7 John Roebling | | | | | | | |
| 7 William Kamkwamba | | | | | | | |
| 8 Nikola Tesla | | | | | | | |
| 8 Sylvia Earle | | • | • | | • | | • |
| 8 Waterhouse Hawkins | | • | | | | | • |
| 9 Rachel Carson | | | • | • | | | |
| 9 Wangari Maathai | | | • | • | | | |
| 9 Carl Sagan | | | | | | | |
| 10 Papa's Mechanical Fish | | | | | | | |
| 10 What Do You Do With an Idea? | | | | | | | |
| 10 Rosie Revere, Engineer | | | | | | | |

*Refer to individual lessons for expanded *NGSS* and Nature of Science information.

†PS = physical science, LS = life science, ESS = Earth and space science, ETS = engineering, technology and the application of science.

## Lesson Connections to the *NGSS* and the Nature of Science, Grades 3–5* (continued)

| | 2 Philo Farnsworth | 2 Thomas Edison | 2 George Washington Carver | 3 Annie Jump Cannon | 3 George Washington Ferris Jr. | 3 Gregor Mendel | 4 Jane Goodall | 4 Charles Darwin | 4 Barnum Brown | 5 Charles Bentley | 5 Luke Howard | 5 John James Audubon | 6 Ada Byron Lovelace | 6 Galileo Galilei | 6 Jacques Cousteau | 7 Elijah McCoy | 7 John Roebling | 7 William Kamkwamba | 8 Nikola Tesla | 8 Sylvia Earle | 8 Waterhouse Hawkins | 9 Rachel Carson | 9 Wangari Maathai | 9 Carl Sagan | 10 Papa's Mechanical Fish | 10 What Do You Do With an Idea? | 10 Rosie Revere, Engineer |
|---|---|---|---|---|---|---|---|---|---|---|---|---|---|---|---|---|---|---|---|---|---|---|---|---|---|---|---|
| LS4.B: Natural selection | | | | | | | | • | | | | | | | | | | | | | | | | | | | |
| LS4.C: Adaptation | | | | | | | | | | | | • | | | | | | | | | • | | • | | | | |
| LS4.D: Biodiversity and humans | | | | | | | | | | | | | | | | | | | | • | | • | | | | | |
| ESS1.A: The universe and its stars | | | | • | | | | | | | | | | | | | | | | | | | | • | | | |
| ESS2.A: Earth's materials and systems | | | | | | | | | | • | • | | | | | | | | | | | | | | | | |
| ESS2.C: The roles of water in Earth's surface processes | | | | | | | | | | • | • | | | | | | | | | | | | | | | | |
| ESS3.C: Human impacts on Earth systems | | | | | | | | | | | | | | | | | | | | • | | • | • | | | | |
| ETS1.A: Defining and delimiting engineering problems | • | | | | • | | | | | | | | • | | | • | • | | • | | | | | | • | • | • |

*Refer to individual lessons for expanded *NGSS* and Nature of Science information.

†PS = physical science, LS = life science, ESS = Earth and space science, ETS = engineering, technology and the application of science.

## Lesson Connections to the *NGSS* and the Nature of Science, Grades 3–5* (continued)

| | 2 Philo Farnsworth | 2 Thomas Edison | 2 George Washington Carver | 3 Annie Jump Cannon | 3 George Washington Ferris Jr. | 3 Gregor Mendel | 4 Jane Goodall | 4 Charles Darwin | 4 Barnum Brown | 5 Charles Bentley | 5 Luke Howard | 5 John James Audubon | 6 Ada Byron Lovelace | 6 Galileo Galilei | 6 Jacques Cousteau | 7 Elijah McCoy | 7 John Roebling | 7 William Kamkwamba | 8 Nikola Tesla | 8 Sylvia Earle | 8 Waterhouse Hawkins | 9 Rachel Carson | 9 Wangari Maathai | 9 Carl Sagan | 10 Papa's Mechanical Fish | 10 What Do You Do With an Idea? | 10 Rosie Revere, Engineer |
|---|---|---|---|---|---|---|---|---|---|---|---|---|---|---|---|---|---|---|---|---|---|---|---|---|---|---|---|
| ETS1.B: Developing possible solutions | • | | | | • | | | | | | | | • | | • | • | | | | | | | | | • | | • |
| ETS1.C: Optimizing the design solution | | | | | | | | | | | | | | | • | | | | | | | | | | • | | • |
| **Science and Engineering Practices** | | | | | | | | | | | | | | | | | | | | | | | | | | | |
| Asking questions and defining problems | | • | • | • | • | • | • | • | • | • | • | • | • | | • | | | • | | | | • | | | • | • | • |
| Developing and using models | | | • | • | • | • | | | | | | • | | • | | | | | | | | | | | | | |
| Planning and carrying out investigations | | | | | | | • | • | • | • | • | • | | | | | • | | | | | | | • | | | |
| Analyzing and interpreting data | | | | | | | | | • | • | • | • | | • | | | | | | | | | | • | • | | |

*Refer to individual lessons for expanded *NGSS* and Nature of Science information.

†PS = physical science, LS = life science, ESS = Earth and space science, ETS = engineering, technology and the application of science.

APPENDIX C

## Lesson Connections to the NGSS and the Nature of Science, Grades 3–5* (continued)

| Lesson | Using mathematics and computational thinking | Constructing explanations and designing solutions | Engaging in argument from evidence | Obtaining, evaluating, and communicating information | **Crosscutting Concepts** | Patterns | Cause and effect | Scale, proportion, and quantity | Systems and system models |
|---|---|---|---|---|---|---|---|---|---|
| 2 Philo Farnsworth | | • | | | | • | | | |
| 2 Thomas Edison | | | | | | | • | | |
| 2 George Washington Carver | | | | | | | | | |
| 3 Annie Jump Cannon | | | | | | | | | |
| 3 George Washington Ferris Jr. | | | | | | • | | • | |
| 3 Gregor Mendel | | | | | | • | • | | |
| 4 Jane Goodall | | | | | | • | | | |
| 4 Charles Darwin | | | | | | • | | | |
| 4 Barnum Brown | | | | | | • | • | | |
| 5 Charles Bentley | | • | | | | • | | • | • |
| 5 Luke Howard | | | | | | • | | • | • |
| 5 John James Audubon | • | • | • | • | | • | • | • | • |
| 6 Ada Byron Lovelace | • | • | | | | | • | | |
| 6 Galileo Galilei | • | | | | | • | | | |
| 6 Jacques Cousteau | • | • | | • | | • | | | |
| 7 Elijah McCoy | | • | | | | | • | | |
| 7 John Roebling | | | | | | | | | |
| 7 William Kamkwamba | | • | | • | | | | | • |
| 8 Nikola Tesla | | • | • | | | • | | | • |
| 8 Sylvia Earle | | • | • | | | • | | | |
| 8 Waterhouse Hawkins | | • | • | • | | • | | • | • |
| 9 Rachel Carson | | • | | | | | • | | |
| 9 Wangari Maathai | | | • | • | | | • | | • |
| 9 Carl Sagan | | • | • | • | | | • | | |
| 10 Papa's Mechanical Fish | • | • | | | | | • | | • |
| 10 What Do You Do With an Idea? | | | | | | | | | • |
| 10 Rosie Revere, Engineer | | | | | | | | | • |

*Refer to individual lessons for expanded NGSS and Nature of Science information.

†PS = physical science, LS = life science, ESS = Earth and space science, ETS = engineering, technology and the application of science.

## APPENDIX C

### Lesson Connections to the NGSS and the Nature of Science, Grades 3–5* (continued)

| | Energy and matter | Structure and function | Stability and change | **Nature of Science** | Scientific investigations use a variety of methods. | Scientific knowledge is based on empirical evidence. | Scientific knowledge is open to revision in light of new evidence. |
|---|---|---|---|---|---|---|---|
| 2 Philo Farnsworth | | | | | • | • | |
| 2 Thomas Edison | • | | | | • | | |
| 2 George Washington Carver | | • | | | | | |
| 3 Annie Jump Cannon | | | | | • | • | |
| 3 George Washington Ferris Jr. | | | | | • | • | |
| 3 Gregor Mendel | | | | | • | • | |
| 4 Jane Goodall | | • | | | • | | |
| 4 Charles Darwin | | | | | • | • | |
| 4 Barnum Brown | | • | | | • | • | • |
| 5 Charles Bentley | | • | | | • | • | |
| 5 Luke Howard | | | | | • | • | • |
| 5 John James Audubon | • | • | • | | • | • | • |
| 6 Ada Byron Lovelace | | | | | • | • | |
| 6 Galileo Galilei | | | | | | | |
| 6 Jacques Cousteau | | | | | • | • | |
| 7 Elijah McCoy | | • | | | • | • | |
| 7 John Roebling | | • | | | | | |
| 7 William Kamkwamba | | • | | | • | | |
| 8 Nikola Tesla | • | | | | | | • |
| 8 Sylvia Earle | | | | | | • | • |
| 8 Waterhouse Hawkins | | | | | | • | • |
| 9 Rachel Carson | | | | | | • | |
| 9 Wangari Maathai | | | | | | | |
| 9 Carl Sagan | | | | | | • | |
| 10 Papa's Mechanical Fish | | • | | | | • | • |
| 10 What Do You With an Idea? | | | | | | | |
| 10 Rosie Revere, Engineer | | | | | | | |

*Refer to individual lessons for expanded NGSS and Nature of Science information.

†PS = physical science, LS = life science, ESS = Earth and space science, ETS = engineering, technology and the application of science.

## Lesson Connections to the *NGSS* and the Nature of Science, Grades 3–5* (continued)

| | 2 Philo Farnsworth | 2 Thomas Edison | 2 George Washington Carver | 3 Annie Jump Cannon | 3 George Washington Ferris Jr. | 3 Gregor Mendel | 4 Jane Goodall | 4 Charles Darwin | 4 Barnum Brown | 5 Charles Bentley | 5 Luke Howard | 5 John James Audubon | 6 Ada Byron Lovelace | 6 Galileo Galilei | 6 Jacques Cousteau | 7 Elijah McCoy | 7 John Roebling | 7 William Kamkwamba | 8 Nikola Tesla | 8 Sylvia Earle | 8 Waterhouse Hawkins | 9 Rachel Carson | 9 Wangari Maathai | 9 Carl Sagan | 10 Papa's Mechanical Fish | 10 What Do You Do With an Idea? | 10 Rosie Revere, Engineer |
|---|---|---|---|---|---|---|---|---|---|---|---|---|---|---|---|---|---|---|---|---|---|---|---|---|---|---|---|
| Scientific models, laws, mechanisms, and theories explain natural phenomena. | | | • | | | | | • | | | • | • | | | | | • | | | | • | | | | | | |
| Science is a way of knowing. | | • | • | • | • | • | • | • | • | • | • | • | • | • | • | • | • | • | • | • | • | | • | • | | • | |
| Scientific knowledge assumes an order and consistency in natural systems. | | | | | | • | | • | | • | • | • | • | | • | | | | | • | | | • | • | | | |
| Science is a human endeavor. | • | • | • | • | • | • | • | • | • | • | • | • | • | • | • | • | • | • | • | • | • | • | • | • | • | • | • |
| Science addresses questions about the natural and material world. | • | | | • | | | • | | • | | | • | | | • | | | | | | • | | | | | | |

*Refer to individual lessons for expanded NGSS and Nature of Science information.

†PS = physical science, LS = life science, ESS = Earth and space science, ETS = engineering, technology and the application of science.

# Appendix D

## Glossary of Character Traits

**clever** (adj.): having ingenuity, resourcefulness, and a mental quickness in achieving a purpose

**confident** (adj.): having a strong belief in your own abilities

**courageous** (adj.): brave or fearless

**creative** (adj.): able to use one's imagination and easily think of new ideas

**curious** (adj.): eager to learn or know; inquisitive

**dedicated** (adj.): devoted to an idea or purpose and willing to give a great deal of time and energy to it

**diligent** (adj.): applying a constant effort to accomplish something; attentive and persistent in doing something

**dreamer** (n.): a person whose ideas and projects are regarded as impractical or not based in reality

**fearless** (adj.): very brave; unafraid

**imaginative** (adj.): creative or having the ability to think of unique ideas

**innovative** (adj.): introducing or using new ideas or methods or having new ideas about how something can be done

**inquisitive** (adj.): having a disposition of asking many questions

**inspired** (adj.): very good or clever; having a particular cause or influence

**intuitive** (adj.): having the ability to know or understand things without any proof or evidence

**inventive** (adj.): good at thinking up new ideas or ways of doing things

**observant** (adj.): good at noticing things

**passionate** (adj.): having or showing strong feelings

**patient** (adj.): able to quietly and steadily wait or work toward something

**persistent** (adj.): able to continue doing something in spite of obstacles or warnings

**persuasive** (adj.): able to succeed in making someone do or believe something by giving the person good reasons

**puzzler** (n.): a person who is occupied or amused by solving puzzles

**risk taker** (n.): a person inclined to take risks

**thinker** (n.): a person who reflects on or ponders

**visionary** (adj.): having or marked by foresight and imagination

# Appendix E

# Recommended Science Teaching Strategies

As you may already know, this book is fundamentally organized around the eight science and engineering practices of the *Next Generation Science Standards* (*NGSS*; NGSS Lead States 2013). Each of Chapters 2–9 supports one of the practices through featured biographical stories of scientists and engineers whose work style and achievements reflect that practice. We identified biographical picture books to help us define a key desirable character trait or disposition of each scientist or engineer and then organized a learning-cycle lesson focused on teaching the nature of science and grade 3–5 *NGSS* disciplinary core ideas, science and engineering practices, and crosscutting concepts. With this appendix, we further explain one additional feature we have included; that is, in each chapter we also included science classroom perspectives as a glimpse into real science classroom teaching. We expect that our personal "tried and true" experiences in teaching science will help to inspire others.

## Chapter 1
### Introduction: What We Did in This Book and Why

**THIS BOOK'S STRATEGY: UNDERSTANDING AND DEVELOPING STUDENTS' PERCEPTIONS OF SCIENTISTS AND ENGINEERS AS WE TEACH SCIENCE**

*Who Would Use This Strategy.* All teachers, whether of science or not, regardless of grade level.

*What the Strategy Is.* If you initiate the "Draw-a-Scientist Test" strategy at the beginning of the year or at least in the first semester, then these drawings can help you to continue a long-term dialogue about what scientists look like, where they work, and what kinds of work they do throughout the year.

Ask students to draw a scientist on a piece of paper or perhaps in their science notebooks. Ask them to be sure they include what the scientist looks like, where the scientist is working, and what the scientist is doing. It is also important for students to include a caption showing what the scientist might be saying. We usually draw a speech bubble on the board to show students what we want them to do, and we ask students not to draw stick figures if possible. These three areas of focus will facilitate your discussion once students have completed their pictures. Be sure students work independently, as it is important for students to draw and record their own thoughts about scientists.

*Why It Is Effective.* The process of asking students to draw pictures of scientists brings the opportunity for discussion about perceptions and impressions of scientists. Students may not even be aware of the perceptions they have about scientists until given explicit and implicit instruction. We know that students' ideas about who can be a scientist or engineer and the work a scientist or engineer does can change—and will likely be affected by their experiences with these biographies and related science activities. These lessons

## APPENDIX E

are uniquely developed to help students know and think about the actual work of scientists and engineers.

Figures E.1 and E.2 show examples of students' work arising from this teaching strategy.

***What It Looks Like in the Classroom.*** Ask students to clear their desks and then hand out a piece of drawing paper to everyone. Be sure they have crayons, colored pencils, and/or other art tools. It is very important that these drawings be in color. This should not be a timed activity, so students can have as much time as they need. Drawings can take as long as 30 minutes. You could walk around the room to ensure students are on task. There should not be any talking during the activity. It is extremely important that students draw their own ideas. When students finish, they should raise their hands. Review each drawing to ensure they have included a caption and clear notation about what the scientist is doing and where the scientist is working. If they have not, remind them to do so.

## Chapter 2
### Asking Questions and Defining Problems
**RECOMMENDED SCIENCE TEACHING STRATEGY: DESIGNATING MAKERSPACES**

***Who Would Use This Strategy.*** This strategy can be used by any teacher at any grade level. Students respond well to opportunities to design or create something to meet a challenge.

***What the Strategy Is.*** Pose a challenge and have students invent something new or design something to solve a problem and then ask them to improve their design in some way.

***Why It Is Effective.*** Students are naturally drawn to activities like this, as there are lots of opportunities

### Figure E.1
**Example of a Bulletin Board Created to Help Extrapolate Students' Beliefs About Scientists Through Drawings**

in the design process for expression, creativity, and exploration. (Some students actually flourish in activities such as this; these students in particular need some latitude to be able to show you how well they understand the lesson at hand.) Creative, productive thinking skills generally help to improve students' confidence with any problem solving skills. The design process, especially the test and improve phases, enables students to develop personal confidence as they overcome challenges to complete a personally meaningful product or solution. The process also helps students think beyond "one right answer" modes of operating.

Figure E.2

Close-Up Photographs of the Bulletin Board Reveal Students' Understanding of What Scientists Look Like, Where They Work, and What They Do

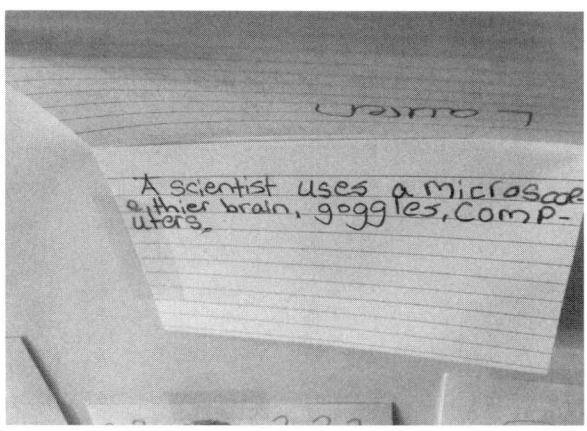
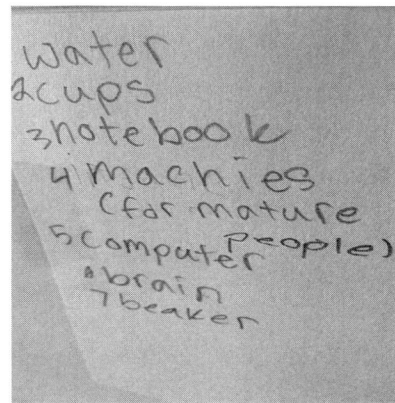

Figures E.3 and E.4 (p. 354) show examples of students' work arising from this teaching strategy.

*What It Looks Like in the Classroom.* Often, these types of challenges begin with a common theme for all students in the classroom to complete. For example, students will be asked to design a (product) that does (something specific). Once students have created an invention or a design, ask them to improve it by either changing the materials it was made from or asking them to meet another need. A classroom makerspace focuses more on students creating and building rather than the traditional regurgitating and memorizing of concepts. The maker movement encourages students to engage in science by doing what engineers actually do: "tinker" with objects and ideas until they build something unique. For these purposes, the physical organization of the classroom space positively affects students' learning. Some makerspaces opt to use a stations-based approach, wherein each student or team can visit different stations to fuse together different media and modes of creativity. For example, some challenges might focus on the

## APPENDIX E

### Figure E.3
Examples of Questions That Help Students Think About and Improve Their Designs

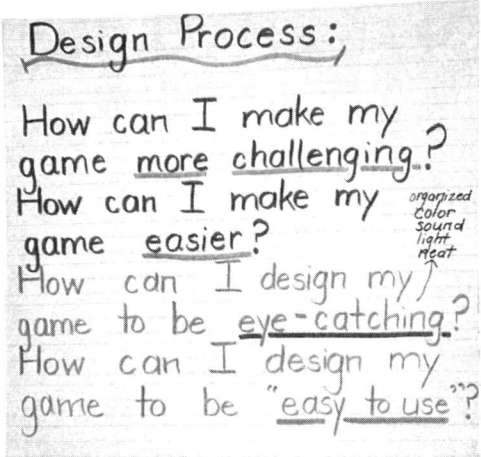

### Figure E.4
Examples of Design Process Charts Created in the Classroom

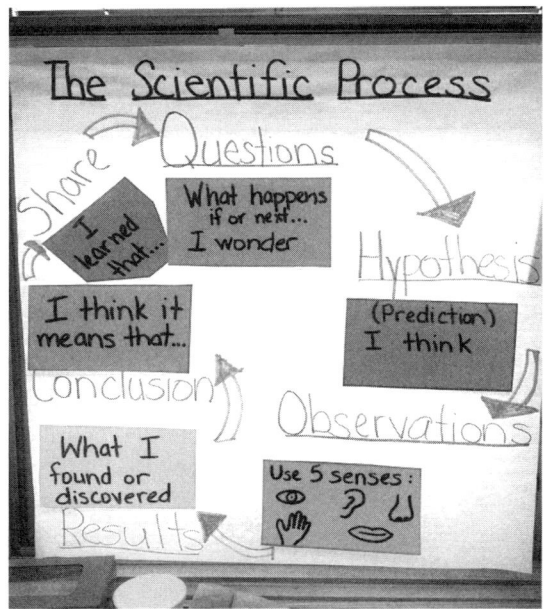

mathematics and engineering spaces and direct students to incorporate two or three different areas of the makerspace: In the end, it's *how* they incorporate them that matters. Also, it's important to mention that although makerspaces can vary, the definition of "materials" is amorphous; anything a child sees as a potential material becomes a material. This anything-is-a-material approach encourages two things: (1) teachers letting go of controlling supplies and (2) increasing students' creativity and ingenuity in the making process.

## Chapter 3
### Developing and Using Models
**RECOMMENDED SCIENCE TEACHING STRATEGY: GRAPHIC ORGANIZERS AS MODELS**

*Who Would Use This Strategy.* Any teacher could use foldables for any subject anytime they want to organize information for students or want students to organize information themselves. Visit the website Dinah.com (*www.dinah.com*) for information on books and workshops.

*What the Strategy Is.* Foldables are interactive, three-dimensional graphic organizers that can help students organize, remember, review, and learn many new kinds of information. Foldables encourage students to practice visual and spatial thinking and to use their creativity. Students cut and fold three-dimensional graphic organizers to assist them with learning new information or assessing understanding of knowledge. As models, foldables reinforce important thinking skills and communication skills and can serve as a reference for students.

*Why It Is Effective.* Foldables help increase student interest in the lesson and make new information easy to recall or organize.

*What It Looks Like in the Classroom.* Foldables can take hundreds of shapes and sizes to accomplish learning goals. The teacher usually assists students early on and over time, students gradually become able to make independent decisions about which type of graphic organizer to use when.

Figure E.5 shows an example of students' work arising from this teaching strategy.

### Figure E.5
### Foldable Showing the Phases of the Moon

## Chapter 4
### Planning and Carrying Out Investigations
**RECOMMENDED SCIENCE TEACHING STRATEGY: EFFECTIVE QUESTIONING**

*Who Would Use This Strategy.* Teachers at any grade level might incorporate this strategy to measure what students know and understand. Page Keeley has written a number of books for science teachers in elementary, middle, and high schools; see the website Uncovering Student Ideas (*www.uncoveringstudentideas.org*). We suggest that

## APPENDIX E

you look at these resources before designing your own, as they already exist.

*What the Strategy Is.* Getting students to discuss their scientific thinking is just as important as it is to get them to learn scientific concepts. Formative assessment can be used to foster productive science discussions that reflect how scientists actually think and go about their investigations. Formative assessment is one of the most effective strategies for improving the opportunity to learn for all students as described by Page Keeley (2008). Probes can help to expose ideas that are strongly held by students and resistant to change. In this way, formative assessment tools help students become aware of their own thinking.

*Why It Is Effective.* In the example of the floating orange described in Chapter 4, students are challenged to define the term *floating*. Students become actively involved in planning out investigations and understanding what a fair test means. This type of lesson is effective because the teacher depends on students' prior knowledge to guide the lesson and is assessing for understanding throughout. It's also effective because students are expressing themselves verbally and providing evidence of their understanding.

*What It Looks Like in the Classroom.* Students are presented with a question or situation and asked to predict what will happen based on their own scientific thinking.

Figure E.6 shows the floating orange challenge that exemplifies this teaching strategy.

### Figure E.6

**Testing Predictions During the Floating Orange Challenge**

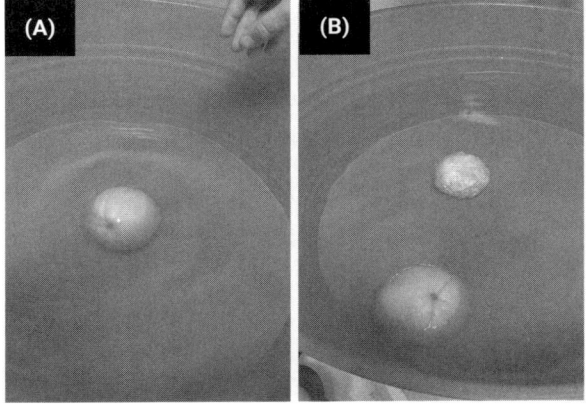

(A) The unpeeled orange floats. (B) A floating, unpeeled orange and a peeled, submerged orange. Air pockets in the peel help to keep the orange afloat, functioning much like a life jacket.

## Chapter 5
### Analyzing and Interpreting Data
**RECOMMENDED SCIENCE TEACHING STRATEGY: INTEGRATION OF SCIENCE AND MATHEMATICS**

*Who Would Use This Strategy.* Any teacher could use this strategy at any grade level.

*What the Strategy Is.* The integration of mathematics and science is, in essence, using a combination of these two core subjects to link learning with real-world situations. Science encompasses the art of questioning, investigating, hypothesizing, discovering, and communicating. Mathematics is a language that provides clarity, objectivity, and understanding. In this approach, mathematics becomes more meaningful and more useful, as it is applied to a particular context in which students are already learning. In addition, the extent to which science is studied and understood increases because of the inclusion of mathematics. In our experience, the quality of learning improves and includes an increased ability to retain the learning because material becomes meaningful and relevant to students' lives.

*Why It Is Effective.* Integrated lessons actively involve and motivate students as they investigate real-world situations. This authentic learning environment can seamlessly connect the two content areas to align more with real-world applications. Julie became acutely aware of this phenomenon when she was working with a wildlife biologist on the development of integrated curricula related to the scientist's research on pintail ducks. When asked to help design some activities that specifically included mathematics, the scientist exclaimed, "I didn't realize how much math I actually do!" Integrated classroom instruction that is so seamlessly connected gives purpose to students' learning and helps them to maintain high levels of interest as well as confidence in their mathematics skills and science abilities. In sum, science provides concrete examples of abstract mathematical ideas that can improve learning of mathematics concepts (Thomas, Cooper, and Haukos 2004). Mathematics enables students to achieve a deeper understanding of science concepts through opportunities to quantify and explain science relationships, illustrate mathematics concepts, and provide relevancy and motivation for learning mathematics (Thomas, Cooper, and Ponticell 1999).

*What It Looks Like in the Classroom.* In the science classroom, integrated activities simultaneously involve students in scientific observations and data collection to enable mathematical thinking and reasoning that helps students understand the science they are learning. In the mathematics classroom, integrated activities give meaning and purpose to the mathematics skills and processes students are learning.

# Chapter 6
## Using Mathematics and Computational Thinking
**RECOMMENDED SCIENCE TEACHING STRATEGY: PROBEWARE AND DIGITAL MEDIA**

*Who Would Use This Strategy.* Any teacher in any grade who has the financial resources to purchase equipment (probes) and software can use this strategy.

*What the Strategy Is.* This method involves using data probes to teach mathematics and computational thinking and use technology simultaneously. The Go!Motion probe by Vernier is used to collect the position, velocity, and acceleration data of moving objects, whereas Vernier's Go!Temp probe is used to collect data on temperature (see the Vernier website at *www.vernier.com*). Each of these data probes is available in class sets of eight. Both probes connect directly to a computer USB (universal serial bus) port, making it fast and easy to set up experiments and start collecting a wide range of real-time motion and temperature data. Although there are several companies that offer data probes, Vernier also offers the companion graphing and analysis software Logger Pro as well as videos for teachers to use as a resource while introducing this new pedagogical approach. Students are able to write their investigations using Logger Pro and export the data to word-processing or spreadsheet software.

*Why It Is Effective.* A review by Seth Guiñals-Kupperman in the "NSTA Recommends Technology" section of the journal *Science Scope* (2013) claims that Logger Pro is intuitive, straightforward, and inexpensive. Guiñals-Kupperman also claims that Logger Pro allows students and teachers to make very straightforward analysis of the collected data. Research has found that inquiry-based instructional science units employing computers and probeware to support students' investigations in grades 3–8 resulted in significant learning gains by students. In these cases, there were significant differences in science learning in favor of students who used the probes (Zucker et al. 2008). Metcalf and Tinker (2004) found that teachers were able to successfully conduct investigations in their classrooms and that student learning was enhanced through the use of the probes and handhelds. Specifically, students experienced the physical correlation between phenomenon and modeling, which helped them to develop understanding and to confront misconceptions.

*What It Looks Like in the Classroom.* Students work in teams or individually to collect real-world data in real time and create graphs that demonstrate mathematical understanding.

## Chapter 7
### Constructing Explanations (Science) and Designing Solutions (Engineering)
**RECOMMENDED SCIENCE TEACHING STRATEGY: KLEW CHARTS**

*Who Would Use This Strategy.* Any teacher at any grade level could use this strategy, which is typically used to introduce a new unit or topic.

*What the Strategy Is.* This strategy usually takes the form of a chart and is based on the K (knowledge) W (want to know) L (what have we learned) chart for reading comprehension (Ogle 1986). However, to modify it for use in science teaching situations, this strategy has been expanded to include an E (evidence) and an S (scientific principles). Unlike the traditional KWL chart, which is typically completed left to right, the KLEW chart does not require the columns to be completed from left to right; rather, the columns are to be completed in whatever way the students experience science. Thus, KLEW charts complement the science processes as students complete and revisit columns while constructing their overall experience.

*Why It Is Effective.* We have found it effective to use a KLEW chart at the beginning of a unit while trying to assess students' prior knowledge; when used in this way, the K column represents what we think we know. This allows for initial thinking to be recorded prior to investigation and explanation building, whether or not it is scientifically accurate. We have found it useful to use this aspect of the chart as a vehicle for reflecting on learning over time as students develop deeper understanding of science. It is also helpful to have a tangible product to which you can refer students during instruction. The addition of the E for evidence was a key modification to the KWL (Hershberger, Zembal-Saul, and Starr 2006) chart. Now when we ask students, "What is your evidence?" they are beginning to act and think like scientists. It is possible to create a KLEW chart with any content, and the charts are easily adapted to any lesson. We find them to be most helpful in identifying students' misconceptions and in finding ways to address these in a positive and productive way during class.

*What It Looks Like in the Classroom.* A chart that can be referred to before and during a unit is displayed.

Figure E.7 shows an example of students' work arising from this teaching strategy.

Figure E.7

Sample KLEW Chart to Organize Students' Learning About Rocks—From Engagement to the Evaluation Phase of the Lesson

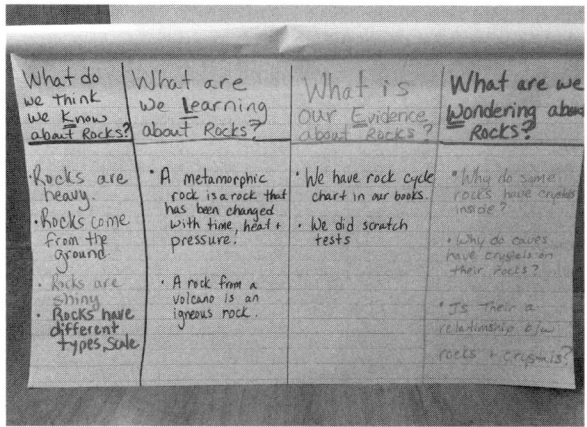

## Chapter 8
### Engaging in Argument From Evidence
**RECOMMENDED SCIENCE TEACHING STRATEGY: SCIENCE TALK**

*Who Would Use This Strategy.* Any teacher could use this strategy at any grade level.

*What the Strategy Is.* This strategy involves encouraging students to use appropriate science terms to make claims backed by evidence as they communicate with their classmates. McNeill, Katsh-Singer, and Pelletier (2015) describe the argumentation framework of claim, evidence, and reasoning (CER) in the following way: A *claim* answers questions or problems, which could be an explanation or model. *Evidence* is data that support the claim, such as observations and measurements, and *reasoning* explains why the evidence supports the claim using scientific ideas or principles.

*Why It Is Effective.* By focusing on the language in and during scientific investigations, the teacher is modeling the process of developing scientific knowledge. Students then come to know and understand the scientific process through their own deliberation and thought and language patterns.

*What It Looks Like in the Classroom.* Science talk in the classroom is something that develops over time. Students increasingly learn to document their claims with specific evidence and reasoning. You might organize an explanation map as you begin to plan an instructional unit to help you negotiate the content terrain while you teach the unit, and so be able to keep a coherent content storyline at the forefront (Zembal-Saul 2009). The more opportunities for exploration and the more freedom to express and explore relevant questions, the more science talk students will use.

## Chapter 9
### Obtaining, Evaluating, and Communicating Information
**RECOMMENDED SCIENCE TEACHING STRATEGY: CITIZEN SCIENCE**

*Who Would Use This Strategy.* Any teacher could use this strategy at any grade level.

*What the Strategy Is.* The notion of citizen science is based on the fact that all people who study the world also live in it. All men, women, and students who explore the world with their senses can be citizen scientists; there is no need to be a professional scientist to investigate the world. Citizen science is the study of the world by the people who live in it (Burns 2012). Citizen science might involve professional people (with laboratories and sophisticated science equipment), but it necessarily involves nonprofessional scientists of

## APPENDIX E

all ages and walks of life to use their senses and smarts to understand the world around them.

*Why It Is Effective.* Students begin to see themselves as scientists. Students are invested; it is exploration for the sake of exploration instead of an investigation or assignment. Citizen science activities get students involved in local community efforts to do things such as gather population data or recover wildlife habitat.

*What It Looks Like in the Classroom.* Students are involved and invested in locally relevant science research efforts. Often, students and their teachers are working alongside a local scientist, as in the case of a recent study of pintail ducks in which elementary students shadowed a wildlife biologist's study of a spring migration (Cooper, Thomas, and Motley 2011). A number of national and international citizen science initiatives have become popular in the elementary classroom. One example is the Trout in the Classroom program (*www.troutintheclassroom.org*) in which students raise trout from fry, engage in a stream habitat study, and release their trout in a nearby watershed. Other popular national citizen science opportunities include Project Budburst (*www.budburst.org*), Project FeederWatch (*http://feederwatch.org/about/project-overview*), and Monarch Watch (*www.monarchwatch.org*).

## Chapter 10
### Beyond *Eureka!*
### Teaching How Scientists and Engineers Work
**RECOMMENDED SCIENCE TEACHING STRATEGY: CONCEPT MAPPING**

*Who Would Use This Strategy.* Teachers in grades 3–5 can use concept maps as either a formative assessment before starting a unit or module or after instruction as an assessment.

*What the Strategy Is.* Concept mapping provides an opportunity for students to practice constructing relational meaning among concepts. Students construct actual maps of concepts.

*Why It Is Effective.* Students negotiate the meanings of science concepts and explore the connections among new science concepts. This process can be used to assess the relationship between students' understanding of a concept or concepts and the language associated with these terms. It can be done with a whole group, small groups, or individual students. One of the reasons we really like this strategy is that students significantly increase their vocabulary as they construct concept maps.

*What It Looks Like in the Classroom.* Donna usually introduces concept mapping by beginning with three concepts students know well: principal, teacher, and students. She then asks them to describe the relationships among the concepts. Donna asks whether these three terms are all of equal status, suggesting a hierarchy. Notice in Figure E.8 how the student decided that the principal was best represented as above the others. Donna then moves on by asking students to make a sentence to connect the two words and then links them accordingly. Students can then begin to make concept maps involving science concepts based on this understanding.

Figures E.8 and E.9 show examples of students' work arising from this teaching strategy.

Figure E.8

**Example of a Student's Introductory Concept Map Constructed With the Teacher's Help**

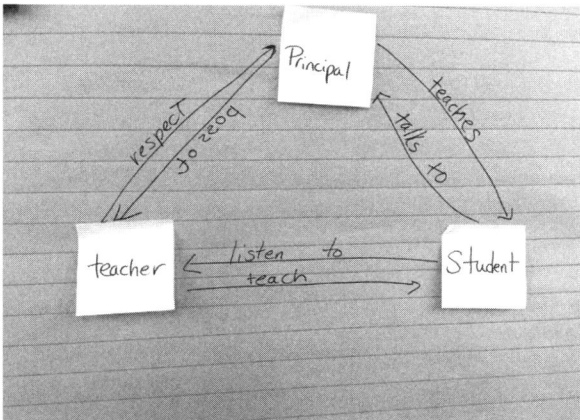

This concept map illustrates one way to help students begin mapping. In this teaching model, students were asked to map a concept they knew well. To begin, we labeled three sticky notes and asked students to describe how the labels were related. We did this as a class; students identified the concepts and the teacher drew and labeled the arrows as the students' discussion evolved. The arrows connect and link words to form sentences and reinforce the relationships.

Figure E.9

**Example of a Concept Map That Follows the Model in Figure E.8**

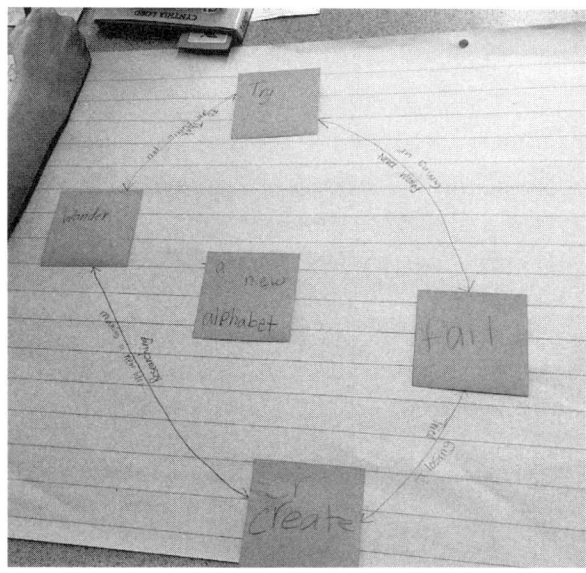

This student's concept map illustrates his or her thinking about how to design a new alphabet.

## References

Burns, L. G. 2012. *Citizen scientist: Be part of a scientific discovery from your own backyard.* New York: Henry Holt.

Cooper, S., J. Thomas, and T. Motley. 2011. No duck left behind: Children's data analysis supports scientists' theory of declining duck populations. *Science and Children* 48 (5): 45–49.

Guiñals-Kupperman, S. 2013. Vernier Logger Pro and Go!Motion sensor: NSTA recommends technology. *Science Scope* 41 (7): 98.

Hershberger, K., C. Zembal-Saul, and M. L. Starr. 2006. Evidence helps the KWL get a KLEW. 2006. NSTA Webnews Digest. *www.nsta.org/publications/news/story.aspx?id=51519*.

Keeley, P. 2008. *Science formative assessment.* Thousand Oaks, CA: Corwin Press.

McNeill, K. L., R. Katsh-Singer, and P. Pelletier. 2015. Assessing science practices—Moving your class along a continuum. *Science Scope* 39 (4): 21–28.

Metcalf, S. J., and R. F. Tinker. 2004. Probeware and handhelds in elementary and middle school science. *Journal of Science Education and Technology* 13 (1): 43–49.

NGSS Lead States. 2013. *Next Generation Science Standards: For states, by states.* Washington, DC: National Academies Press. *www.nextgenscience.org/next-generation-science-standards*.

Ogle, D. M. 1986. K-W-L: A teaching model that develops active reading of expository text. *The Reading Teacher* 39 (6): 564–570.

## APPENDIX E

Thomas, J., S. Cooper, and D. Haukos. 2004. Skateboards or wildlife? Kids decide. *Science and Children* 41 (7): 20–24.

Thomas, J. A., S. D. Cooper, and J. A. Ponticell. 1999. Doing math the science way: Staff development for integrated teaching and learning. In *Effective models for teacher education: Teacher education yearbook VIII,* ed. J. McIntyre and D. Byrd. Thousand Oaks, CA: Corwin Press.

Zembal-Saul, C. 2009. Learning to teach elementary school science as argument. *Science Education* 93 (4): 687–719.

Zucker, A. A., R. Tinker, C. Staudt, A. Mansfield, and S. Metcalf. 2008. Learning science in grades 3–8 using probeware and computers: Findings from the TEEMSS II project. *Journal of Science Education and Technology* 17: 42–48.

## Additional Resources

The Cornell Lab and Bird Studies Canada. 2016. Project FeederWatch. *http://feederwatch.org/about/project-overview*.

Dinah.com. 2017. *www.dinah.com. Website that includes Dinah Zike's strategies for maximizing project-making possibilities, in and out of the classroom. The site has links for professional development opportunities, resource books, and online tutorials. In "Notebooking Central" under "Products," you can find three-dimensional, interactive graphic organizers that have been converted to notebooking formats for recording student observations and questions.*

Monarch Watch. *www.monarchwatch.org. Website with lesson ideas and guidance about research projects, butterfly gardening, milkweed seeds, and more.*

Project Budburst. 2017. *www.budburst.org. Website with background information for citizen science projects in a schoolyard and suggestions about how to manage them.*

Trout in the Classroom. 2006. *www.troutintheclassroom.org. Website introducing the Trout in the Classroom program and providing links to teacher resources and state-sponsored websites across the United States.*

Uncovering student ideas. *www.uncoveringstudentideas.org. Website by Page Keeley that gives an overview of the various formative assessment books authored by her and various coauthors.*

Vernier. *www.vernier.com.*

# Index

Page numbers printed in **bold** type indicate tables, figures, or illustrations.

## A

*Ada Byron Lovelace and the Thinking Machine* (Wallmark), 159, 163–166, **340**
Ada Lovelace Day website, 170
age-appropriate content, trade book selection, 336
Airboat Race lesson, 159–172
    description and overview, 159, 163
    learning outcomes, 159
    making sense, 166–171, **172**
        evaluate, 170–171, **172**
        explain, 168, 170
        explore, 166–168, **167**, **169**
        extend, 170, **171**
    materials, 163
    *NGSS* and Nature of Science connections, 160–162
    objectives, 159
    safety notes, 163
    setting the context, 163–166
        engage, 163
        guided reading, 163–166
analyzing and interpreting data
    about, 119
    integration of science and mathematics, 119–120, 356–357
    *See also* Sandhill Crane Migration lesson; Sizing Up Snowflakes lesson; Water Cycle in a Bag lesson
*Annie Jump Cannon, Astronomer* (Gerber), 49, 52, 54–56, **339**
Aqua Lung, 182, 187–188
Arbor Day and Earth Day lesson, 286–295
    description and overview, 286, 289
    learning outcomes, 287
    making sense, 292–295
        evaluate, 294–295, **295**
        explain, 294
        explore, 292, **293**
        extend, 294
    materials, 289
    *NGSS* and Nature of Science connections, 287–289
    objectives, 286
    setting the context, 289–292
        engage, 289–290
        guided reading, 290–292
argument from evidence. *See* engaging in argument from evidence
asking questions and defining problems
    about, 9
    designating makerspaces, 9–10, 352–353, **354**, 355
    *See also* Edison's Three Questions lesson; How Are Fruits and Vegetables Different? lesson; Thinking and Tinkering lesson
assessment rubrics
    Airboat Race lesson, **172**
    Arbor Day and Earth Day lesson, **295**
    Building Dinosaurs lesson, **271**
    Chirping Crickets lesson, **92**
    Digging Up Dinosaurs lesson, **117**
    Edison's Three Questions lesson, **34**
    Electric Action lesson, **248**
    Exploring Suspension Bridges lesson, **217**
    Food Delivery Design Challenge, **320**
    Gravity Versus Microgravity lesson, **307**
    How Are Fruits and Vegetable Different? lesson, **45**
    How Do Submersibles Work? lesson, **191**
    Inventing a Solution lesson, **232**
    *M is for Motion* lesson, **181**
    Mysterious Sawfish lesson, **259**
    New Uses lesson, **285**
    Pass It Along lesson, **78**
    Puzzling Potatoes lesson, **103**
    Racing Against Friction lesson, **207**
    Rosie Revere, Engineer lesson, **333**
    Round and Round We Go! lesson, **68**

# INDEX

Sandhill Crane Migration lesson, **155**
Sizing Up Snowflakes lesson, **130**
Starlight—Light From the Sun lesson, **59**
Thinking and Tinkering lesson, **21**
Water Cycle in a Bag lesson, **140**
What Do You Do With an Idea? lesson, **326**
Audubon, John James, 141, 145, 146–148, **147**, 152, 153–154, 342
See also Sandhill Crane Migration lesson

## B

Babbage, Charles, 164–166
Ballard, Bob, 258
*Barnum's Bones* (Fern), 104, 108–110, **339**
Bentley, Wilson, 121, 124, 125–126, *127*, 128–129, 342
See also Sizing Up Snowflakes lesson
*Big Beast Book* (Booth), 269
bioinspiration, 229
bird banding, 145–146
book overview
5E learning-cycle format, 5
chapters and lessons structure, 2, 7–8
character traits of featured scientists, 3
children's views of scientists, 6–7, **7**
*Eureka!* title, 1–2
NGSS connections, 2–3
recommended science teaching strategies, 3–4
safety considerations, 5–6
*The Boy Who Drew Birds* (Davies), 141, 145, 146–148, **340**
*The Boy Who Harnessed the Wind* (Kamkwamba and Mealer), 218, 222, 223–225, **340**
*The Boy Who Invented TV* (Krull), 11, 13, **339**
brainstorming. *See* What Do You Do With an Idea? lesson
bridges. *See* Exploring Suspension Bridges lesson
*The Brooklyn Bridge* (Mann), 208, 211, 212–214, **212**, **340**
Brown, Barnum, 104, 107, 108–110, **109**, 116, 342
See also Digging Up Dinosaurs lesson
Building Dinosaurs lesson, 260–272
description and overview, 260, 264
learning outcomes, 260
making sense, 267–270, **271**
evaluate, 270, **271**
explain, 267, 269
explore, 267, **268**, **269**
extend, 269–270
materials, 264
*NGSS* and Nature of Science connections, 261–263
objectives, 260

safety notes, 264
setting the context, 264–267
engage, 264
guided reading, 264–267

## C

*Calypso* (research vessel), 186, 187
Cannon, Annie Jump, 49, 52, 54–56, **55**, 58, 342
See also Starlight—Light From the Sun lesson
Carson, Rachel, 276, 279, 280–281, **281**, 283, 284, 342
See also New Uses lesson
Carver, George Washington, 35, 37, 38–39, **40**, 44, 342
See also How Are Fruits and Vegetable Different? lesson
CER (claim, evidence, and reasoning), 235–236, 237, 247–248, 249, 250, 258, 259, 270, 359
character traits
clever (Racing Against Friction lesson), 195, 196, 198, 199, 205–206
confident (How Do Submersibles Work? lesson), 182, 186, 191
courageous (*M is for Motion* lesson), 173, 176, 177, 180–181
creative (Building Dinosaurs lesson), 260, 264, 269, 270
curiosity (Sandhill Crane Migration lesson), 141, 142, 145, 146, 153–154
dedication (Sizing Up Snowflakes lesson), 121, 122, 124, 125–126, 128, 129
diligence (How Are Fruits and Vegetables Different? lesson), 35, 44
dreamer (Water Cycle in a Bag lesson), 131, 132, 135, 139–140
fearless (Mysterious Sawfish lesson), 249, 250, 253, 254, 258
glossary of, 350
imaginative (Starlight—Light From the Sun lesson), 49, 50, 52, 58
innovative (Airboat Race lesson), 159, 163, 170–171
inquisitive (Gravity Versus Microgravity lesson), 296, 297, 300, 302, 305–306
inspired (Edison's Three Questions lesson), 22–23, 33–34
intuitive (Digging Up Dinosaurs lesson), 104, 105, 108, 115, 116
inventive (Inventing a Solution lesson), 218, 219, 222, 224, 230
observant (Chirping Crickets lesson), 83, 85, 90, 91
passionate (Arbor Day and Earth Day lesson), 286, 287, 289, 290, 292, 294
patience (Pass It Along lesson), 69, 71, 72, 77–78

# INDEX

persistent (Exploring Suspension Bridges lesson), 208, 209, 211, 216
persuasive (New Uses lesson), 276, 277, 279, 280, 284
puzzler (Puzzling Potatoes lesson), 93–94, 96, 102
risk taker (Electric Action lesson), 237, 240, 243, 247
thinker (Thinking and Tinkering lesson), 11, 13, 19–20
visionary (Round and Round We Go! lesson), 60, 63, 67
*Chemistry Matters* (AIMS Education Foundation), 120
*Chirping Crickets* (Berger), 90
Chirping Crickets lesson, 83–92
    description and overview, 83, 84
    learning outcomes, 83
    making sense, 88–91, **92**
        evaluate, 90–91, **91**, **92**
        explain, 89
        explore, 88, **89**, 90
        extend, 90
    materials, 86, **86**
    *NGSS* and Nature of Science connections, 84–85
    objectives, 83
    safety notes, 86
    setting the context, 86–88
        engage, 86
        guided reading, 86–88
citizen science, 273–275, 359–360
clever (character trait), 195, 196, 198, 199, 205–206
clouds. *See* Water Cycle in a Bag lesson
concept mapping, 310, 327, 329, **331**, 332, **333**, 360, **361**
confident (character trait), 182, 186, 191
constructing explanations (science) and designing solutions (engineering)
    about, 193
    KLEW charts, 193–194, 199, 211, 223, 358, **359**. *See also* Exploring Suspension Bridges lesson; Inventing a Solution lesson; Racing Against Friction lesson
    content
content
    Airboat Race lesson, 171, **172**
    Arbor Day and Earth Day lesson295, **295**
    Building Dinosaurs lesson, 270, **271**
    Chirping Crickets lesson, 91, **92**
    Edison's Three Questions lesson, 34, **34**
    Electric Action lesson, 247–248, **248**
    Exploring Suspension Bridges lesson, 216, **217**
    Gravity Versus Microgravity lesson, 306, **307**
    How Are Fruits and Vegetables Different? lesson, 44, **45**
    Inventing a Solution lesson, 230–231, **231**, 232
    *M* is for Motion lesson, 181, **181**
    Mysterious Sawfish lesson, 259, **259**
    New Uses lesson, 284, **285**
    Pass It Along lesson, 78, **78**
    Puzzling Potatoes lesson, 102, **103**
    Racing Against Friction lesson, 206–207, **207**
    Round and Round We Go! lesson, 68, **68**
    Sandhill Crane Migration lesson, 154, **155**
    Sizing Up Snowflakes lesson, 130, **130**
    Starlight—Light From the Sun lesson, 58, **59**
    Thinking and Tinkering lesson, 20, **20**, 21
    Water Cycle in a Bag lesson, 140, **140**
courageous (character trait), 173, 176, 177, 180–181
Cousteau, Jacques, 182, 186, 187–188, **188**, 191, 342
    *See also* How Do Submersibles Work? lesson
Creating Snowflakes activity, 125, 128
creative (character trait), 260, 264, 269, 270
*Crime Scene Investigations* (Walker and Wood), 77
crosscutting concepts
    Airboat Race lesson, 162
    Arbor Day and Earth Day lesson, 288
    Building Dinosaurs lesson, 262
    Chirping Crickets lesson, 84
    Digging Up Dinosaurs lesson, 106
    Edison's Three Questions lesson, 24
    Electric Action lesson, 239
    Exploring Suspension Bridges lesson, 210
    Gravity Versus Microgravity lesson, 299
    How Are Fruits and Vegetables Different? lesson, 36
    How Do Submersibles Work? lesson, 184
    Inventing a Solution lesson, 221
    *M* is for Motion lesson, 175
    Mysterious Sawfish lesson, 251
    New Uses lesson, 278
    Pass It Along lesson, 70
    Puzzling Potatoes lesson, 95
    Racing Against Friction lesson, 197
    Rosie Revere, Engineer lesson, 329
    Round and Round We Go! lesson, 62
    Sandhill Crane Migration lesson, 143
    Sizing Up Snowflakes lesson, 123
    Starlight—Light From the Sun lesson, 51
    summary table, **347–348**
    Thinking and Tinkering lesson, 12
    Water Cycle in a Bag lesson, 133
    What Do You Do With an Idea? lesson, 322
curiosity (character trait), 141, 142, 145, 146, 153–154

# INDEX

## D

Darwin, Charles, 93, 96, 98–99, **98**, 100–101, 102, 342
    See also Puzzling Potatoes lesson
*Darwin* (McGinty), 93, 96, 98–99, **339**
DDT insecticide, 279
dedication (character trait), 121, 122, 124, 125–126, 128, 129
design
    engineering design process, 17–18, **17**
    See also Food Delivery Design Challenge; Rosie Revere, Engineer lesson; What Do You Do With an Idea? lesson
designating makerspaces, 9–10, 352–353, **354**, 355
*Design for a Livable Planet* (Naar), 283
Desmos graphing tool, 157–158, 170, **171**
developing and using models
    about, 47
    Ferris wheel model, 65–66, **66**, 68
    graphic organizers as models, 47–48, 355, **355**
    stacked-paper model of the universe, 53, **53**
    See also Building Dinosaurs lesson; Pass It Along lesson; Round and Round We Go! lesson; Starlight—Light From the Sun lesson
Digging Up Dinosaurs lesson, 104–117
    description and overview, 104, 108
    learning outcomes, 105
    making sense, 110–116, **117**
        evaluate, 115–116, **117**
        explain, 114–115
        explore, 110, **111–112**, 113, **114**
        extend, 115
    materials, 108
    *NGSS* and Nature of Science connections, 105–107
    objectives, 104
    setting the context, 108–110
        engage, 108
        guided reading, 108–110
diligence (character trait), 35, 44
dinosaurs. See Building Dinosaurs lesson; Digging Up Dinosaurs lesson
*The Dinosaurs of Waterhouse Hawkins* (Kerley), 260, 264–267, **340**
disciplinary core ideas
    Airboat Race lesson, 160
    Arbor Day and Earth Day lesson, 287
    Building Dinosaurs lesson, 261
    Chirping Crickets lesson, 84
    Digging Up Dinosaurs lesson, 106
    Edison's Three Questions lesson, 23
    Electric Action lesson, 238

    Exploring Suspension Bridges lesson, 209
    Food Delivery Design Challenge, 312
    Gravity Versus Microgravity lesson, 297
    How Are Fruits and Vegetables Different? lesson, 36
    How Do Submersibles Work? lesson, 183
    Inventing a Solution lesson, 219–220
    *M is for Motion* lesson, 174
    Mysterious Sawfish lesson, 250–251
    New Uses lesson, 277
    Pass It Along lesson, 70
    Puzzling Potatoes lesson, 94
    Racing Against Friction lesson, 196
    Rosie Revere, Engineer lesson, 328
    Round and Round We Go! lesson, 61
    Sandhill Crane Migration lesson, 142
    Sizing Up Snowflakes lesson, 122
    Starlight—Light From the Sun lesson, 50
    summary table, **343–346**
    Thinking and Tinkering lesson, 12
    Water Cycle in a Bag lesson, 132
    What Do You Do With an Idea? lesson, 321–322
dreamer (character trait), 131, 132, 135, 139–140

## E

Earle, Sylvia, 182, 190, 249, 253–254, **255**, 258–259, 342
    See also Mysterious Sawfish lesson
Earth Day. See Arbor Day and Earth Day lesson
*The Edge of the Sea* (Carson), 281
edible plant parts diagram, **39**, 40, 42
Edison's Three Questions lesson, 22–34
    description and overview, 22, 25
    learning outcomes, 23
    making sense, 29–34
        evaluate, 33–34, **34**
        explain, 29, **30**, 32, **32**
        explore, 29, **30**, **31**
        extend, 32–33
    materials, 25–26
    *NGSS* and Nature of Science connections, 23–24
    objectives, 22
    safety notes, 25
    setting the context, 26–28
        engage, 26–27, **27**
        guided reading, 27–28
Edison, Thomas, 22, 25, *25*, 27–28, 33, 242, 342
    See also Edison's Three Questions lesson
effective questioning, 81–82, 355–356, **356**
egg-drop challenge, 193

Electric Action lesson, 237–248
    description and overview, 237, 240
    learning outcomes, 237
    making sense, 243–248
        evaluate, 247–248, **248**
        explain, 244
        explore, 243–244, **243**, **244**
        extend, 245–246, **245**
    materials, 240
    *NGSS* and Nature of Science connections, 237–239
    objectives, 237
    safety notes, 240
    setting the context, 241–243
        engage, 241–242
        guided reading, 242–243
*Electrical Wizard* (Rusch), 237, 240, 242–243, 244, **340**
energy phase demonstration, 26–27, **27**
engaging in argument from evidence
    about, 235
    science talk, 235–236, 359
    *See also* Building Dinosaurs lesson; Electric Action lesson; Mysterious Sawfish lesson
engineering design process (EDP)
    process chart, 17–18, **17**
    *See also* Food Delivery Design Challenge; Rosie Revere, Engineer lesson; What Do You Do With an idea? lesson
environment. *See* Arbor Day and Earth Day lesson; Gravity Versus Microgravity lesson; New Uses lesson
evidence. *See* engaging in argument from evidence
explicit questioning, 9
Exploring Suspension Bridges lesson, 208–217
    description and overview, 208, 211
    learning outcomes, 209
    making sense, 214–216, **217**
        evaluate, 216, **217**
        explain, 214–215
        explore, 214, **215**
        extend, 215
    materials, 211
    *NGSS* and Nature of Science connections, 209–210
    objectives, 208
    safety notes, 211
    setting the context, 211–214
        engage, 211
        guided reading, 212–214

## F

Farnsworth, Philo, 11, 13, 15–17, **15**, 19–20, 342
    *See also* Thinking and Tinkering lesson
fearless (character trait), 249, 250, 253, 254, 258
Ferris, Jr., George Washington, 60, 63–65, **65**, 67, 342
    *See also* Round and Round We Go! lesson
Food Delivery Design Challenge, 311–320
    description and overview, 311, 315
    learning outcomes, 311
    making sense, 317–320
        evaluate, 320, **320**
        explain, 319, **319**
        explore, 317–318, **317**, **318**
        extend, 319–320, **320**
    materials, 315
    *NGSS* and Nature of Science connections, 312–314
    objectives, 311
    safety notes, 315
    setting the context, 315–316
        engage, 315
        guided reading, 315–316
force-fitting, 229–230
Ford, Henry, 33
fossils. *See* Digging Up Dinosaurs lesson
friction. *See* Racing Against Friction lesson

## G

Galilei, Galileo, 173, 176–177, **178**, 180, 342
    *See also* M is for Motion lesson
Genetic Science Learning Center website, 72
genetic traits, 77
Goodall, Jane, 83, 85, 86–88, *87*, 90, 91, 342
    *See also* Chirping Crickets lesson
graphic organizers as models, 47–48, 355, **355**
Gravity Versus Microgravity lesson, 296–308
    description and overview, 296, 300
    learning outcomes, 297
    making sense, 303–306, **307**
        evaluate, 305–306, **307**
        explain, 303, 305
        explore, 303, **304**, **305**
        extend, 305
    materials, 300
    *NGSS* and Nature of Science connections, 297–299
    objectives, 296
    safety notes, 300
    setting the context, 301–302
        engage, 301–302

# INDEX

guided reading, 302
*The Green Consumer* (Makower), 283
green improvements, 283
*Gregor Mendel* (Bardoe), 69, 72–74, 336, **339**
guided reading
    Airboat Race lesson, 163–166
    Arbor Day and Earth Day lesson, 290–292
    Building Dinosaurs lesson, 264–267
    Chirping Crickets lesson, 86–88
    Digging Up Dinosaurs lesson, 108–110
    Edison's Three Questions lesson, 27–28
    Electric Action lesson, 242–243
    Exploring Suspension Bridges lesson, 212–214
    Food Delivery Design Challenge, 315–316
    Gravity Versus Microgravity lesson, 302
    How Are Fruits and Vegetables Different? lesson, 38–39
    How Do Submersibles Work? lesson, 187–188
    Inventing a Solution lesson, 223–225
    *M is for Motion* lesson, 177
    Mysterious Sawfish lesson, 253–255
    New Uses lesson, 280–281, 283
    Pass It Along lesson, 72–74
    Puzzling Potatoes lesson, 98–99
    Racing Against Friction lesson, 199–201
    Rosie Revere, Engineer lesson, 330–331
    Round and Round We Go! lesson, 64–65
    Sandhill Crane Migration lesson, 146–148
    Sizing Up Snowflakes lesson, 125–126
    Starlight—Light From the Sun lesson, 54–56
    Thinking and Tinkering lesson, 15–17
    Water Cycle in a Bag lesson, 135–136
    What Do You Do With an Idea? lesson, 323–324

## H

Harlen, Wynne, 10
*Have You Seen Mary?* (Kurrus), 152
Hawkins, Waterhouse, 260, 264–267, **265**, 270, 342
    *See also* Building Dinosaurs lesson
*Heloise's Hints for a Healthy Planet* (Heloise), 283
Howard, Luke, 131, 135, 136, **137**, 140, 342
    *See also* Water Cycle in a Bag lesson
How Are Fruits and Vegetables Different? lesson, 35–46
    description and overview, 35, 37
    learning outcomes, 36
    making sense, 40–46
        evaluate, 44, **45**
        explain, 42–43, **43**
        explore, **39**, 40–42, **41**, **42**
        extend, 43
    materials, 37
    *NGSS* and Nature of Science connections, 36–37
    objectives, 35
    safety notes, 37
    setting the context, 38–39
        engage, 38
        guided reading, 38–39
*How the Dinosaur Got to the Museum* (Hartland), 115
*How Do Birds Find Their Way?* (Gans), 148
How Do Submersibles Work? lesson, 182–192
    description and overview, 182, 186
    learning outcomes, 182
    making sense, 188–191
        evaluate, 191, **191**
        explain, 190
        explore, 188–190, **189**
        extend, 190
    materials, 186
    *NGSS* and Nature of Science connections, 183–185
    objectives, 182
    safety notes, 186
    setting the context, 186–188
        engage, 186–187
        guided reading, 187–188

## I

illustrations, trade book selection, 336, 337
imaginative (character trait), 49, 50, 52, 58
implicit questioning, 9
"In-Flight Education Downlinks," 305
information. *See* obtaining, evaluating, and communicating information
inheritance. *See* Pass It Along lesson
innovative (character trait), 159, 163, 170–171
inquisitive (character trait), 296, 297, 300, 302, 305–306
inspired (character trait), 22–23, 33–34
integration of science and mathematics, 119–120, 356–357
intuitive (character trait), 104, 105, 108, 115, 116
Inventing a Solution lesson, 218–233
    description and overview, 218, 222
    learning outcomes, 219
    making sense, 225–231, **232**
        evaluate, 230–231, **230**, **231**
        explain, 229
        explore, 225–226, **226**, **227**, 228–229, **228**, **229**
        extend, 229–230
    materials, 222

# INDEX

NGSS and Nature of Science connections, 219–222
objectives, 218
safety notes, 222
setting the context, 223–225
    engage, 223
    guided reading, 223–225
inventive (character trait), 218, 219, 222, 224, 230
*The Inventor's Secret* (Slade), 22, 33
*It Looked Like Spilt Milk* (Shaw), 139

## J

Jericho Historical Society, 129

## K

Kamkwamba, William, 218, 222, 223–225, **225**, 230, 342
    See also Inventing a Solution lesson
Kid Wind Project, 230
KLEW charts, 193–194, 199, 211, 223, 358, **359**

## L

lesson guidelines
    planning your own lessons, 337
    trade book selection, 335–337
*Life in the Ocean* (Nivola), 249, 253–254, **340**
light beam experiment, 29, 32, **32**
lima bean plant embryo, 42–43, **43**
Lovelace, Ada Byron, 159, 163–166, **165**, 170, 342
    See also Airboat Race lesson

## M

Maathai, Wangari, 286, 289, 290–292, **291**, 294, 342
    See also Arbor Day and Earth Day lesson
makerspaces, designating makerspaces, 9–10
*Manfish* (Berne), 182, 186, 187–188, 336, **340**
*The Man Who Named the Clouds* (Hannah and Holub), 131, 135–136, **339**
"Mass vs. Weight: Stretching Mass" lesson, 303, **304**, 305, **305**
mathematics. See using mathematics and computational thinking
McCoy, Elijah, 195, 196, 198, 199–201, **200**, 204–206, 342
    See also Racing Against Friction lesson
McCoy, Mary, 201
Mendel, Gregor, 69, 72–74, **74**, 342
    See also Pass It Along lesson
Merlin Bird ID app, 152
migration. See Sandhill Crane Migration lesson
*M is for Motion* lesson, 173–181

description and overview, 173, 176
learning outcomes, 173
making sense, 177–181
    evaluate, 180–181, **181**
    explain, 179–180
    explore, 177–179, **179**, **180**
    extend, 180, **181**
materials, 176
NGSS and Nature of Science connections, 174–175
objectives, 173
setting the context, 176–177
    engage, 176
    guided reading, 177
*Mistakes That Worked* (Jones), 18
models. See developing and using models
*Mr. Ferris and His Wheel* (Davis), 60, 63, 64–65, **339**
*My Place in Space* (Hirst and Hirst), 53
Mysterious Sawfish lesson, 249–259
    description and overview, 249, 253
    learning outcomes, 250
    making sense, 255–259
        evaluate, 258–259, **259**
        explain, **256**, 257–258, **257**
        explore, 255–257, **256**, **257**
        extend, 258
    materials, 253
    NGSS and Nature of Science connections, 250–252
    objectives, 249
    setting the context, 253–255
        engage, 253
        guided reading, 253–255
Mystery Tube activity, 245–246, **245**

## N

NASA (National Aeronautics and Space Administration), 300, 301, 303, 305
Nashua River, 284
National Council of Teachers of English (NCTE), 335
National Science Teachers Association (NSTA), 335
*Nation of Makers* website, 10
Nature of Science connections
    Airboat Race lesson, 162
    Arbor Day and Earth Day lesson, 288–289
    Building Dinosaurs lesson, 262–263
    Chirping Crickets lesson, 85
    Digging Up Dinosaurs lesson, 107
    Edison's Three Questions lesson, 24
    Electric Action lesson, 239

# INDEX

Exploring Suspension Bridges lesson, 210
Food Delivery Design Challenge, 314
Gravity Versus Microgravity lesson, 299
How Are Fruits and Vegetables Different? lesson, 37
How Do Submersibles Work? lesson, 185
Inventing a Solution lesson, 221–222
*M is for Motion* lesson, 175
Mysterious Sawfish lesson, 252
New Uses lesson, 279
Pass It Along lesson, 71
Puzzling Potatoes lesson, 95–96
Racing Against Friction lesson, 197–198
Rosie Revere, Engineer lesson, 329
Round and Round We Go! lesson, 62
Sandhill Crane Migration lesson, 144
Sizing Up Snowflakes lesson, 123–124
Starlight—Light From the Sun lesson, 51–52
summary table, **348–349**
Thinking and Tinkering lesson, 13
Water Cycle in a Bag lesson, 134
What Do You Do With an Idea? lesson, 322
*The New 50 Simple Things I Can Do to Save the Earth* (Earthworks Group), 283
New Uses lesson, 276–285
    description and overview, 276, 279
    learning outcomes, 277
    making sense, **282**, 283–284, **285**
        evaluate, 284, **285**
        explain, 283
        explore, **282**, 283
        extend, 284
    materials, 279
    *NGSS* and Nature of Science connections, 277–279
    objectives, 276
    setting the context, 280–283
        engage, 280
        guided reading, 280–281, 283
*NGSS (Next Generation Science Standards)* connections
    Airboat Race lesson, 160–162
    analyzing and interpreting data, 119
    Arbor Day and Earth Day lesson, 287–288
    asking questions and defining problems, 9
    book overview, 2–3
    Building Dinosaurs lesson, 261–262
    Chirping Crickets lesson, 84
    constructing explanations (science) and designing solutions (engineering), 193
    developing and using models, 47

Digging Up Dinosaurs lesson, 105–106
Edison's Three Questions lesson, 23–24
Electric Action lesson, 238–239
engaging in argument from evidence, 235
Exploring Suspension Bridges lesson, 209–210
Food Delivery Design Challenge, 312–314
Gravity Versus Microgravity lesson, 297–299
How Are Fruits and Vegetables Different? lesson, 36–37
How Do Submersibles Work? lesson, 183–184
Inventing a Solution lesson, 219–221
*M is for Motion* lesson, 174–175
Mysterious Sawfish lesson, 250–251
New Uses lesson, 277–278
obtaining, evaluating, and communicating information, 273
planning and carrying out investigations, 81
Puzzling Potatoes lesson, 94–95
Racing Against Friction lesson, 196–197
Rosie Revere, Engineer lesson, 328–329
Sandhill Crane Migration lesson, 142–143
Sizing Up Snowflakes lesson, 122–123
Starlight—Light From the Sun lesson, 50–51
summary table, **343–348**
teaching how scientists and engineers work, 309
Thinking and Tinkering lesson, 12
trade book selection, 336
using mathematics and computational thinking, 157–158
Water Cycle in a Bag lesson, 132–133
What Do You Do With an Idea? lesson, 321–322
NOAA website, 190
nostrums. *See* Mysterious Sawfish lesson

## O

observant (character trait), 83, 85, 90, 91
Observing Snow Crystals activity, 124, 126–127
obtaining, evaluating, and communicating information
    about, 273
    citizen science, 273–275, 359–360
    *See also* Arbor Day and Earth Day lesson; Gravity Versus Microgravity lesson; New Uses lesson
Ocean Floor Mapping activity, 188–190, **189**
*Ocean* (Woodward), 258
*On the Wing* (Lerner), 148

## P

paleontologists, 108
*Papa's Mechanical Fish* (Fleming), 309, 311, 315–316, **341**
passionate (character trait), 286, 287, 289, 290, 292, 294

# INDEX

Pass It Along lesson, 69–79
    description and overview, 69, 72
    learning outcomes, 69
    making sense, 75–79
        evaluate, 77–78, **79**
        explain, 76
        explore, 75, **76**
        extend, 76
    materials, 72
    *NGSS* and Nature of Science connections, 70–71
    objectives, 69
    safety notes, 72
    setting the context, 72–74
        engage, 72
        guided reading, 72–74
patent, 199
patience (character trait), 69, 71, 72, 77–78
pendulums. *See M is for Motion lesson*
persistent (character trait), 208, 209, 211, 216
persuasive (character trait), 276, 277, 279, 280, 284
*A Picture Book of George Washington Carver*, 35, **35**, 37, 38–39, **339**
planning and carrying out investigations
    about, 81
    effective questioning, 81–82, 355–356, **356**
    *See also* Chirping Crickets lesson; Digging Up Dinosaurs lesson; Puzzling Potatoes lesson
Platte River, 150, **150**, 152
Preserving Snow Crystals activity, 125, 127–128
probeware and digital media, 157–158, 177–180, **179**, **180**, 182, 188–190, **189**, 357–358
problems. *See* asking questions and defining problems
Project Budburst, 274–275
Project FeederWatch, 274
puzzler (character trait), 93–94, 96, 102
Puzzling Potatoes lesson, 93–103
    description and overview, 93, 96
    learning outcomes, 94
    making sense, 100–102, **103**
        evaluate, 102, **103**
        explain, 101
        explore, 100, **100**
        extend, 101
    materials, 96
    *NGSS* and Nature of Science connections, 94–96
    objectives, 93
    safety notes, 96–97
    setting the context, 97–99
        engage, 97, **97**
        guided reading, 98–99

## Q

questions. *See* asking questions and defining problems

## R

*Rachel Carson and Her Book That Changed the World* (Lawlor), 276, 279, 280–281, 283, 335, **341**
Racing Against Friction lesson, 195–207
    description and overview, 195, 198
    learning outcomes, 196
    making sense, 201–207
        evaluate, 205–207, **207**
        explain, 204–205
        explore, 201, **201**, **202**, 203–204, **203**
        extend, 205
    materials, 198–199
    *NGSS* and Nature of Science connections, 196–198
    objectives, 195–196
    safety notes, 199
    setting the context, 199–201
        engage, 199
        guided reading, 199–201
rainbows, 56
*The Real McCoy* (Towle), 195, 198, 199–201, **340**
*Rearing Horse* (sculpture), 269–270
refraction of light, 29, 32, **32**
ringing (bird banding), 145–146
risk taker (character trait), 237, 240, 243, 247
*A River Ran Wild* (Cherry), 284
Roebling, Emily, 211, 212, 213, 216
Roebling, John, 208, 211, 212–214, **213**, 215, 216, **342**
    *See also* Exploring Suspension Bridges lesson
Roebling, Washington, 211, 212–214, 216
*Rosie Revere, Engineer* (Beaty), 309–310, 327, 329, 330–331, **341**
Rosie Revere, Engineer lesson, 327–333
    description and overview, 327, 330
    learning outcomes, 327
    making sense, **331**, 332, **333**
        evaluate, 332, **333**
        explain, 332
        explore, **331**, 332
        extend, 332
    materials, 329

# INDEX

    *NGSS* and Nature of Science connections, 328–329
    objectives, 327
    setting the context, 329–331
        engage, 329–330, **330**
        guided reading, 330–331
Round and Round We Go! lesson, 60–68
    description and overview, 60, 63
    learning outcomes, 60
    making sense, 65–68
        evaluate, 67–68, **68**
        explain, 67
        explore, 65–66, **66**
        extend, 67
    materials, 63
    *NGSS* and Nature of Science connections, 61–62
    objectives, 60
    safety notes, 63
    setting the context, 63–65
        engage, 63–64
        guided reading, 64–65
Rowe Sanctuary website, 148, 150

## S

Sagan, Carl, 296, 300, **301**, 302, 306, 342
    *See also* Gravity Versus Microgravity lesson
Sandhill Crane Migration lesson, 141–156
    description and overview, 141, 145
    learning outcomes, 142
    making sense, 148–154, **155**
        evaluate, 153–154, **155**
        explain, 149–153, **149**, **150**, **151**
        explore, 148
        extend, 153, **153**
    materials, 145
    *NGSS* and Nature of Science connections, 142–144
    objectives, 141
    safety notes, 145
    setting the context, 145–148
        engage, 145–146
        guided reading, 146–148
science
    citizen science, 273–275
    as human endeavor, xii
    science process skills, x–xii
    science talk, 235–236, 359
    science teaching and science literature, ix–x, xv
    *See also* Nature of Science connections; science and engineering practices; science notebooks; science teaching strategies; teaching how scientists and engineers work
science and engineering practices
    Airboat Race lesson, 160–161
    Arbor Day and Earth Day lesson, 287–288
    Building Dinosaurs lesson, 261–262
    Chirping Crickets lesson, 84
    Digging Up Dinosaurs lesson, 105–106
    Edison's Three Questions lesson, 23
    Electric Action lesson, 238
    Exploring Suspension Bridges lesson, 209
    Food Delivery Design Challenge, 312–314
    Gravity Versus Microgravity lesson, 297–298
    How Are Fruits and Vegetables Different? lesson, 36
    How Do Submersibles Work? lesson, 183–184
    Inventing a Solution lesson, 220–221
    *M is for Motion* lesson, 174–175
    Mysterious Sawfish lesson, 251
    New Uses lesson, 277–278
    Pass It Along lesson, 70
    Puzzling Potatoes lesson, 94
    Racing Against Friction lesson, 197
    Rosie Revere, Engineer lesson, 328
    Round and Round We Go! lesson, 61
    Sandhill Crane Migration lesson, 142–143
    Sizing Up Snowflakes lesson, 122–123
    Starlight—Light From the Sun lesson, 50–51
    summary table, **346–347**
    Thinking and Tinkering lesson, 12
    Water Cycle in a Bag lesson, 132–133
    *What Do You Do With an Idea?* lesson, 322
science notebooks
    Airboat Race lesson, 159
    Chirping Crickets lesson, 88, **88**, 90, 91
    Digging Up Dinosaurs lesson, 114
    Edison's Three Questions lesson, 28, **28**
    Food Delivery Design Challenge, 318, **318**, 320, **320**
    How Are Fruits and Vegetables Different? lesson, **45**
    Inventing a Solution lesson, 219, 223, 228–229, **229**, 230–231, **231**
    *M is for Motion* lesson, 173, 179, 181
    Mysterious Sawfish lesson, 250, 259
    Pass It Along lesson, 72
    Puzzling Potatoes lesson, 94, 100, **100**
    Racing Against Friction lesson, 196, 204
    Rosie Revere, Engineer lesson, 332
    Sizing Up Snowflakes lesson, 128, 129–130
    Starlight—Light From the Sun lesson, 58, **59**

# INDEX

Water Cycle in a Bag lesson, 138
science teaching strategies
    about, 3–4, 351–352, **352**, **353**
    citizen science, 273–275, 359–360
    concept mapping, 310, 327, 329, **331**, 332, **333**, 360, **361**
    designating makerspaces, 9–10, 352–353, **354**, 355
    effective questioning, 81–82, 355–356, **356**
    graphic organizers as models, 47–48, 355, **355**
    integration of science and mathematics, 119–120, 356–357
    KLEW charts, 193–194, 199, 211, 223, 358, **359**
    probeware and digital media, 157–158, 177–180, **179**, **180**, 182, 188–190, **189**, 357–358
    science talk, 235–236, 359
"Science Trade Book Evaluation Rubric," 335
scientists
    children's views of, 6–7, **7**
    illustrations of, xii–xv
SCUMPS (size, color, use, material, parts, and shape), 256, 257–258, **257**
*The Sea Around Us* (Carson), 281
*Seeds of Change* (Johnson), 286, 289, 290–292, **341**
self-assessment, Thinking and Tinkering lesson, **20**
*Seven Blind Mice* (Young), 115
"Shark Tank" (television show), 199, 205
*Silent Spring* (Carson), xiv, 335
Sizing Up Snowflakes lesson, 121–130
    description and overview, 121, 124
    learning outcomes, 122
    making sense, 126–130, **130**
        evaluate, 129–130, **130**
        explain, 128
        explore, 126–128
        extend, 129
    materials, 124–125
    *NGSS* and Nature of Science connections, 122–124
    objectives, 121
    safety notes, 125
    setting the context, 125–126
        engage, 125
        guided reading, 125–126
Snowcrystals website, 125
*Snowflake Bentley* (Martin), 121, 124, 125–126, 336, **339**
Snowflake Bentley website, 129
soda bottle bird feeder, 153, **153**
stacked-paper model of the universe, 53, **53**
star classification, 55–56
Starlight—Light From the Sun lesson, 49–59
    description and overview, 49, 52
    learning outcomes, 50
    making sense, 56–59
        evaluate, 58, **59**
        explain, 57
        explore, 56–57
        extend, 57–58, **58**
    materials, 52
    *NGSS* and Nature of Science connections, 50–52
    objectives, 49
    safety notes, 52
    setting the context, 53–56
        engage, 53, **53**
        guided reading, 54–56
*Starry Messenger* ($S_i s$), 173, 176, 177, 180, **340**
*Star Stuff* (Sisson), 296, 300, 302, **341**
STEAM education model, and maker thinking, 10
*Steven Caney's Invention Book* (Caney), 18
*The Story of Snow* (Cassino and Nelson), 129
student-created cloud formations, 139, **139**
student evaluation. *See* content
student inventions, 18–19, **19**
sunlight, 56–57
Survivor Tree, 294
suspension bridges. *See* Exploring Suspension Bridges lesson
symmetry. *See* Sizing Up Snowflakes lesson

## T

teaching how scientists and engineers work
    about, 309–310
    concept mapping, 310, 327, 329, **331**, 332, **333**, 360, **361**
    *See also* Food Delivery Design Challenge; Rosie Revere, Engineer lesson; What Do You Do With an Idea? lesson
Tesla, Nikola, 237, 240, **241**, 242–243, 247, 342
    *See also* Electric Action lesson
thinker (character trait), 11, 13, 19–20
Thinking and Tinkering lesson, 11–21
    description and overview, 11, 13
    learning outcomes, 11
    making sense, 17–21
        assessment rubric, **21**
        evaluate, 19–20, **19**
        explain, 18
        explore, 17–18, **17**
        extend, 18–19
        self-assessment, **20**

# INDEX

    materials, 13–14
    *NGSS* and Nature of Science connections, 12–13
    objectives, 11
    safety notes, 14
    setting the context, 14–17
        engage, 14–15
        guided reading, 15–17
Trout in the Classroom program, 273–274

## U

*Under the Sea-Wind* (Carson), 281
using mathematics and computational thinking
    about, 157
    probeware and digital media, 157–158, 177–180, **179**, **180**, 182, 188–190, **189**, 357–358
    *See also* Airboat Race lesson; How Do Submersibles Work? lesson; *M* is for Motion lesson

## V

Venn diagrams, 244, **244**, 286, 289, 292, **293**, 294, 295
visionary (character trait), 60, 63, 67

## W

*The Watcher* (Winter), 83, 86–88, 336, **339**
Water Cycle in a Bag lesson, 131–140
    description and overview, 131, 135
    learning outcomes, 132
    making sense, 136–140, **140**
        evaluate, 139–140, **140**
        explain, 138
        explore, 136–138, **138**
        extend, 138–139, **139**
    materials, 135
    *NGSS* and Nature of Science connections, 132–134
    objectives, 131
    safety notes, 135
    setting the context, 135–136
        engage, 135
        guided reading, 135–136
weather. *See* Water Cycle in a Bag lesson
What Do You Do With an Idea? lesson, 321–326
    description and overview, 321, 323
    learning outcomes, 321
    making sense, 324–326
        evaluate, 325–326, **326**
        explain, 325, **325**
        explore, 324–325, **324**
        extend, 325
    materials, 323
    *NGSS* and Nature of Science connections, 321–322
    objectives, 321
    setting the context, 323–324
        engage, 323
        guided reading, 323–324
*What Do You Do With an Idea?* (Yamada), 309, 321, 323–324, **341**
Williams, Sunita, 302
windmills. *See* Inventing a Solution lesson
World's Fair in Chicago, 63–64

## Y

*Young Birder's Guide to Birds of North America* (Thompson), 152
*Young Thomas Edison* (Dooling), 22, 25, 27–28, **339**